RACIAL PREFERENCE
AND
RACIAL JUSTICE

RUSSELL NIELI is currently doing research at Princeton University, as well as lecturing in Princeton's Department of Politics. He received his master's degree and Ph.D. from Princeton University and has taught at the College of New Rochelle, Valparaiso University, and Rider College. His published works include articles in the *Journal of the History of Ideas*, the *Review of Politics*, the *Southern Review*, and *Modern Age*. He is also the author of the book *Wittgenstein: From Mysticism to Ordinary Language*, which was published in 1987 by the State University of New York Press.

RACIAL PREFERENCE AND RACIAL JUSTICE

The New
Affirmative Action Controversy

Edited by
Russell Nieli

ETHICS AND PUBLIC POLICY CENTER

The **ETHICS AND PUBLIC POLICY CENTER,** established in 1976, conducts a
program of research, writing, publications, and conferences to encourage debate
on domestic and foreign policy issues among religious, educational, academic,
business, political, and other leaders. A nonpartisan effort, the Center is supported
by contributions (which are tax deductible) from foundations, corporations, and
individuals. The authors alone are responsible for the views expressed in Center
publications.

Library of Congress Cataloging-in-Publication Data

Racial Preference & Racial Justice : controversy /
edited by Russell Nieli.
p.   cm.
Includes bibliographical references and index.
1. Affirmative action programs—Law and legislation—
United States.   2. Discrimination in employment—Law
and legislation—United States.   3. Affirmative action
programs—United States.   4. Discrimination in
employment—United States.   I. Nieli, Russell, 1948- .
KF3464.R33   1990   344.73'01133—dc20
[347.3041133]   90–44656 CIP

ISBN 0–89633–147–4

Distributed by arrangement with:
National Book Network
4720 Boston Way
Lanham, MD 20706

All Ethics and Public Policy Center books are produced on acid-free paper. The
paper used in this publication meets the minimum requirements of American
National Standard for Information Sciences—Permanence of Paper for Printed
Library Materials, ANSI Z39.48–1984.   ∞™

Ethics and Public Policy Center
1030 Fifteenth Street N.W.
Washington, D.C. 20005
(202) 682–1200

Contents

Preface   ix
  The Editor

PART ONE: GENERAL ASSESSMENTS

1. Racial Quotas   3
   Nathan Glazer

2. Fair Shakers and Social Engineers   29
   Morris B. Abram

3. Persuasion and Distrust   45
   Randall Kennedy

4. Ethnic Tribalism and Human Personhood   61
   Russell Nieli

5. Why I Believe in Affirmative Action   105
   Paul R. Spickard

6. Affirmative Action: A Liberal Program?   111
   Lee Nisbet

7. Affirmative Action Under Attack   117
   Robert F. Drinan

8. The Underhandedness of Affirmative Action   127
   Harvey C. Mansfield, Jr.

9. Why We Need Race Consciousness   141
   Charles Krauthammer

PART TWO: CONSTITUTIONAL ISSUES

10. Preferential Admissions and the Equal Protection Clause   151
    William O. Douglas

11. For Bakke   159
    Stanley Mosk

12. Against Bakke   167
    Richard B. Sobol

13. Are Quotas Unfair?   175
    Ronald Dworkin

14. Remedying Past Discrimination   **191**
    William J. Brennan, Jr.

15. Race as a 'Plus' Factor   **199**
    Lewis F. Powell, Jr.

16. The Disease as a Cure   **209**
    Antonin Scalia

17. Minority Set-Asides   **223**
    Warren E. Burger

18. Minority Set-Asides Are Unconstitutional   **229**
    Potter Stewart

19. Set-Asides Violate the Equal Protection Clause   **237**
    Sandra Day O'Connor

20. A Giant Step Backward on Set-Asides   **245**
    Thurgood Marshall

21. Race-Based Preference Violates the Fourteenth Amendment   **257**
    Lewis F. Powell, Jr.

22. Minority Teachers Serve an Important Purpose   **263**
    John Paul Stevens III

23. The Supreme Court and Civil Rights   **269**
    Robert H. Bork

PART THREE: THE CIVIL RIGHTS ACT OF 1964

24. Racial Preference in the Factory   **279**
    Carl Cohen

25. The Civil Rights Act Permits Voluntary Affirmative Action   **313**
    William J. Brennan, Jr.

26. Title VII Not Intended to Lock-In Minorities   **323**
    Harry A. Blackmun

27. Justice Debased   **329**
    Carl Cohen

28. Consent Decrees Cannot Bind Nonconsenting Parties   **353**
    William H. Rehnquist

29. Leave Consent Decrees Alone   **359**
    John Paul Stevens III

PART FOUR: THE IMPACT ON BLACKS

30. Rumors of Inferiority   **367**
    Jeff Howard and *Ray Hammond*

31. Jews and Negroes   **383**
    Ernest van den Haag

32. Affirmative Racism   **393**
    Charles Murray

33. Admitting Success   **409**
    Derek Bok

34. Are Quotas Good for Blacks?   **415**
    Thomas Sowell

35. Affirmative Action that Hurts Blacks   **429**
    William Raspberry

36. Beyond Civil Rights   **435**
    Glenn C. Loury

PART FIVE: ASIANS AT THE HEAD OF THE CLASS

37. The Asian Difference   **455**
    John H. Bunzel and *Jeffrey K. D Au*

Notes   **475**

Appendixes

   A. The Impact of Affirmative Action on Employment   **493**
      Jonathan Leonard

   B. Closing the Gap   **499**
      James P. Smith and *Finis K. Welch*

   C. The Gallup Survey   **511**

   D. Amendments Five and Fourteen   **515**

   E. Section 701 of the 1964 Civil Rights Act   **517**

   F. Executive Order 11246 (1965), Executive Order 11375 (1967),
      Revised Order 4: Required Contents of Affirmative Action Programs
      (1971)   **521**

   G. Kaiser/United Steelworkers Collective Bargaining Agreement (1974)
      525

Index   **527**

Preface

IN THE LATE 1960s, a major shift occurred in American thinking about the desirability of the then-current policy of government-enforced racial and ethnic neutrality in the areas of hiring, promotion, and university admissions. Largely as a result of the widespread urban rioting that occurred during this period, and the subsequent impact of the Kerner Commission report analyzing the causes of these disturbances, many prominent members of the federal bureaucracy and federal courts, backed by powerful allies in prestigious universities and law schools, in significant segments of the news media, in the national civil rights organizations, and in the national organizations of some of the mainline churches, came to believe that the depth of racial and ethnic problems in America necessitated a radical revision in the ideal of color-blind justice, that had provided the rallying cry for much of the post-World War II civil rights movement. Convinced that the members of certain historically disadvantaged racial and ethnic groups, particularly blacks, Hispanics, Asians, and American Indians, could not, left to their own devices, enter into the mainstream of American life within any acceptable length of time, many came to believe that a compensatory boost was needed that would help make up for some of the harmful effects of past discrimination and deprivation.

What resulted from this shift in opinion was the policy that came to be known as "affirmative action." The exact meaning of this term proved to be highly fluid and often elusive. It would eventually come to be associated with a variety of governmental policies and private initiatives that sought to extend various kinds of preferential consideration to members of racial and ethnic groups officially designated by government agencies as disadvantaged minorities. Affirmative action programs have included special admissions programs to colleges, universities, and professional schools; systems of hiring and promotion in

ix

employment based upon proportional representation of racial and ethnic groups within a given workforce or upon numerical goals or quotas; and the allocation of a portion of government contracts to businesses owned by members of minority groups. From the outset, affirmative action programs were highly controversial. National surveys indicated widespread public disapproval of the idea of race- and ethnicity-based preference in both employment and education.

The present volume, *Racial Preference and Racial Justice,* is intended to acquaint the reader with the most salient features of the "affirmative action" controversy, insofar, as it deals with the issue of preferential treatment based upon race and ethnicity. (The related issue of preferential treatment based upon gender is not addressed in any systematic way in the articles that follow). The volume is composed of more than three dozen articles and judicial opinions, addressing all of the more important aspects of the affirmative action debate. Part I is intended as a general overview of the topic, and consists of nine articles each of which has been selected on the basis of its forcefulness, cogency, and particular point of view. In some cases, both in Part I and elsewhere, the original text has been condensed in order to remove material not central to the discussion here. Many footnotes, including most purely reference footnotes, have been deleted.

Parts II and III of the volume address the most important legal issues in the debate. Part II takes up the question of the compatibility of a policy of racial and ethnic preference with the Equal Protection Clause of the Fourteenth Amendment, and Part III its compatibility with Title VII of the 1964 Civil Rights Act. Considerable attention is paid to the important cases of *Regents of the University of California* v. *Bakke* and *United Steelworkers of America* v. *Weber,* since these two cases have been among the most significant and most widely discussed in the field and have generated some of the best scholarly commentary. Attention is also focussed on minority business set-asides, which are viewed in light of *Fullilove* v. *Klutznick* and *Richmond* v. *Croson.* Other court cases that are dealt with concern ethnicity-based layoffs (*Wygant* v. *Jackson Board of Education*) and the use of race-conscious consent decrees to settle employment discrimination disputes (*Martin* v. *Wilks*). To keep in line with the article format of the volume, each judicial opinion and legal brief has been given a title to help identify its general perspective and contents.

Part IV of the volume takes up the specific impact that preferential policies have had upon black Americans. The articles in this section address related topics, including both the economic and psychological effects that preferential treatment is likely to have upon its intended beneficiaries.

The final section, is an article dealing with the impact of race- and ethnicity-based admissions policies on high-achieving Asian students, specifically upon those who have sought admission to certain of America's elite colleges and universities.

Preferential treatment based on ethnicity and race has been one of the most controversial and most divisive domestic issues in America for the past decade-and-a-half; and although the Rehnquist Supreme Court, following the addition of Anthony Kennedy, seems to have attained a five-vote majority intent on restricting the use of various affirmative action-type programs, the controversy will no doubt be with us for many years to come. The present volume is intended to offer the reader the opportunity to become acquainted with the issue of racial and ethnic preference in its moral, philosophical, psychological, historical, sociological, economic, and legal complexity. The articles and judicial opinions reproduced here are among the most important that have appeared on this topic over the past twenty years.

I would like to offer my special thanks to the Ethics and Public Policy Center. Robert Royal initially suggested the idea of the volume to me and provided ongoing support for the project; Raymond English made suggestions and kind remarks concerning an early outline of the volume; and Gretchen Baudhuin provided indispensible editorial assistance. My thanks are also owed to Professor Jennifer Hochschild of the Woodrow Wilson School at Princeton, and to my brother, Father Bruce Nieli, C.P., both of whom read very carefully my own article, and offered a number of sincere and valuable comments. Finally, I must also thank Professors Robby George and Walter Murphy of the Princeton Politics Department for suggesting to me the article by Antonin Scalia.

Princeton, New Jersey   Russell Nieli
June 30, 1989

PART ONE

General Assessments

1. *Racial Quotas*

By NATHAN GLAZER

Focus   Racially based employment policy, whether in the form of fixed "quotas" or more flexible "goals," first became the official policy of the U.S. government in the early 1970s. Nathan Glazer explains how America moved from an official policy of color blindness in employment, as represented, for instance, by the Civil Rights Act of 1964, to a policy of what he calls "affirmative discrimination," where hiring and promotion decisions are made on the basis of ethnic group representation. The shift in policy, he suggests, can be seen in the two differing meanings of the term "affirmative action." Originally, says Glazer, affirmative action denoted what was essentially an outreach program designed to encourage employers to make employment opportunities known to a wider audience. By the early 1970s, however, the term had come to be associated with race-conscious hiring and promotion policies based on statistical goals and quotas. At this point, says Glazer, "many involved in the fight against discrimination began to realize that something quite radical had happened." He describes in some detail how the latter type of affirmative action policy is actually carried out in practice by the federal courts and federal executive agencies. Glazer also discusses some of the more important arguments that have been made to defend "affirmative discrimination," though he finds each of

them in some way flawed. Nevertheless, despite
what he sees as weak arguments for the policy,
overwhelming public disapproval, and opposition
from the Nixon, Ford, and later Reagan administrations, affirmative action policy, Glazer believes, is not likely to be abandoned, at least not
by means of the legislative process. Opponents of
affirmative action, he explains, though numerous,
are not well organized and are simply no match
for the powerful Washington civil rights lobby—a
lobby that Glazer maintains owes its strength to
its access to a sympathetic mass media, and to
the widespread perception that it stands on the
moral high ground. If affirmative action policy is
ever reversed, Glazer believes, it will come about
only because of court decisions, not because of
any action by the president or Congress.

Nathan Glazer is a professor of education and
sociology at Harvard University. His published
works include *Ethnic Dilemmas, Affirmative Discrimination: Ethnic Inequality and Public Policy,*
and *Beyond the Melting Pot* (co-authored with
Daniel P. Moynihan).

I N THE LATE 1960s and early 1970s the United States entered a new phase in the long fight against racial and ethnic discrimination. It is difficult to find the proper term to characterize the new phase, because so many terms have had their meanings distorted or become slogans. One might say that we shifted from being color-blind to becoming color-conscious. Thus, the Civil Rights Act of 1964, the Voting Rights Act of 1965, the Immigration Act of 1965, the Fair Housing Act of 1968 referred to no specific groups as victims of discrimination and beneficiaries of nondiscrimination. These pieces of legislation, following the liberal orientation of the period, were color-blind: discrimination against *anyone* on grounds of race, color, religion, or national origin was banned. The Voting Rights Act of 1965 even found a color-blind formula to overcome southern resistance to blacks registering and voting: in any jurisdiction where those registering or voting fell to less than 50 per cent of those eligible on the basis of age and citizenship, its stringent provisions came into effect.

The first indications of color consciousness raised little opposition. Thus, one of the first acts of the Equal Employment Opportunity Commission (EEOC), created by the Civil Rights Act of 1964, was to require employers to report the numbers of Negroes, Orientals, Spanish Americans, and American Indians employed in different job categories on an EEO-1 form. This degree of color consciousness required only that employers be aware of the racial-ethnic affiliations of those who applied for jobs, took tests, were hired, or were promoted. Even this raised certain difficulties, for during the color-blind phase of the fight against discrimination the keeping of racial-ethnic records was forbidden in many jurisdictions. (Similarly, as we moved into the color-conscious phase of school desegregation in the 1960s,

The Development of Quotas

The justification for affirmative action is that abandoning discriminatory practices is not enough to achieve justice for groups that have faced discrimination, for the effect of past discrimination will continue. This idea of affirmative action as necessary to correct past discrimination can be traced to labor relations law. When the National Labor Relations Board finds that an employer has been discriminating against union members or those trying to organize a union, he may be required not only to stop discriminating but to restore the persons discriminated against to the situation they would have held in the absence of that discrimination.

This idea was incorporated into the great Civil Rights Act of 1964. This act banned discrimination in voting, places of public accommodation, public facilities, federal programs, federally supported public education, and employment; and it created the Equal Employment Opportunity Commission to enforce the ban on discrimination in employment "because of such individual's race, color, religion, sex or national origin." The words "affirmative action" occur in one place in the act, Section 706 (g): "If the court finds that the respondent has intentionally engaged in or is intentionally engaging in an unlawful practice charged in the complaint, the court may enjoin the respondent from engaging in such unlawful employment practice, and order such *affirmative action* (emphasis added) as may be appropriate, which may include, but is not limited to, reinstatement or hiring of employees, with or without back pay, or any other equitable relief as the court deems appropriate." That is a modest kernel from which a general requirement of quota hiring by race or color may sprout, but it has. When courts find discrimination, they may, and do, order quotas; one black must be hired for each white until a certain ratio is reached, or whatever. After the Civil Rights Act was amended in 1972 to expand the powers of the EEOC to include public employers, many police and fire departments were placed under the requirement to hire by racial and ethnic category.

Was this what Congress intended when it wrote into the Civil

Rights Act the provision for "affirmative action"? Certainly it intended that blacks or others who had suffered discrimination and as a result had not been given jobs or not been promoted should be given the jobs and promotions of which they had been unjustly and illegally deprived. It intended that members of minority groups should no longer face discrimination. Similarly, courts may require that a union activist be rehired or promoted; but they do not require that henceforth one union member be hired for every person not in the union until members reach such and such a proportion of the work force. But this is what judges who institute quotas under the authority of the affirmative action provision of the Civil Rights Act do, and this is one basis of statistical goals.

As yet only a small fraction of hiring in the United States takes place under a quota, under the authority given by the Civil Rights Act. And, it will be argued, this quota hiring is imposed only because of a finding of discrimination. It has to be pointed out that under the regulations of the Equal Employment Opportunity Commission, however, a good deal in ordinary employment practices that ordinary people—and the Congress of the United States—might not consider discriminatory will be found to be discriminatory by the EEOC and the courts, and thus will trigger employment by racial and ethnic quota. There are two chief routes to finding discrimination that seem questionable (we would all accept another route, not in question here—that is, direct evidence of discrimination).

First, it may be found that an employer has not hired members of certain groups in proportion to their presence in the population or labor force or specific categories of certain occupations. This alone is often used as a demonstration of discrimination. But it may also have to be combined with other acts of discrimination that are charged, for recent Supreme Court decisions suggest statistical disparities alone may not be acceptable as evidence of discrimination.

Second, it may be shown that the tests for employment used by employers are discriminatory. The guidelines that the EEOC issued to determine when a test is discriminatory have been upheld by the Supreme Court in the important *Griggs* v. *Duke*

Power case of 1971. These guidelines tell employers that any test "which adversely affects hiring, promotion, transfer or any other employment or membership opportunity of classes protected by Title VII constitutes discrimination unless: (a) the test has been validated and evidences a high degree of utility as hereinafter described; and (b) the person giving or acting upon the results of the particular test can demonstrate alternative suitable hiring, transfer or promotion procedures are unavailable for his use." Or, as the Supreme Court said in *Griggs:* "The Act proscribes not only overt discrimination but also practices that are fair in form, but discriminatory in practice. The touchstone is business necessity. If an employment practice which operates to exclude Negroes cannot be shown to be related to job performance, the practice is prohibited."

The EEOC, supported by the courts, had established very stringent requirements for the use of employment or promotion tests that could pass muster as nondiscriminatory in order to pressure employers into abandoning tests and using racial and ethnic quotas in their employment practices. There is considerable evidence that this is just what the effect of the EEOC guidelines on testing has been. For example, one personnel expert is quoted as saying:

I had first assumed that the validation studies talked about in the EEOC Guidelines on Employee Selection Procedures would be required for all our employee selection standards and practices. Suddenly I noticed this was not the case. It was only those tests and procedures that had an *adverse impact* on the employment opportunities of protected groups that need to be validated.

If we dropped all discriminatory standards and changed all our procedures so that approximately the same proportion of all groups were proceeding through each step of our staffing procedures, there would be no adverse impact on any protected group, and we would not be required to conduct any validation studies at all. We would not be discriminating against any protected group, so the guidelines would never be triggered.

Another is quoted as follows:

You can avoid violating Title VII and also avoid rocking the boat until you have enough hard data at hand to prove or disprove the actual relevance of various selection factors to the prediction of job performance for all groups. You do it by *temporarily equalizing* the impact of each factor being considered on each group in the applicant population while you study it.

For example, our company had been using a particular test to select employees for one job. Approximately 25 per cent of the white males in the applicant population had been passing the test by scoring above a certain score. Now we just make sure that the top 25 per cent of the applicants from each of the groups protected by Title VII also pass that test. We don't worry about what score becomes the cutoff for the various groups; we stick with the percentage passing from each group.

Both these mechanisms for demonstrating discrimination and thus, on the basis of this demonstration, requiring quota employment are specifically forbidden by the Civil Rights Act under which the EEOC operates. Section 703(j) asserts, "Nothing contained in this title shall be interpreted to require any employer . . . to grant preferential treatment to any individual or to any group because of the race, color, religion, sex, or national origin of such individual or group on account of an imbalance which may exist with respect to the total number or percentage of persons of any race, color, religion, sex, or national origin of such individual or group." And Section 703(h) asserts, "nor shall it be unlawful employment practice for an employer to give and to act upon the results of any professionally developed ability test provided that such test, its administration or action upon the results is not designed, intended, or used to discriminate because of race, color, religion, sex, or national origin."

A second source of the new requirement to hire and promote on the basis of race and ethnic group is in practice the more important. It is the "affirmative action" requirements imposed on government contractors by an executive order issued by the president. The executive—the president—has the authority to determine the conditions under which the federal government will do business. When the federal government decides with whom it will or will not do business it exercises an awesome power: every big company, just about every university and college and hospital, and many nonprofit organizations are government contractors. And the federal government requires that the contractor not only refrain from discrimination by race, creed, color, or national origin, but, further, "take affirmative action to ensure that applicants are employed, and that employees are treated during employment, without regard to their race, creed, color, or national origin. Such action shall include, but not be limited to the following: employment, upgrading, demotion, or transfer; recruitment or recruitment advertising; layoff or termination; rates of pay or other forms of compensation; and selection for training, including apprenticeship." This is the language of Executive Order 11246, issued in 1965 by Lyndon B. Johnson. This order, the fount for affirmative action, did not give rise to any argument for affirmative discrimination: it used the language and the proposals of what was generally understood as equal opportunity. The passage I have quoted from the executive order may be obscure, but it is clear that it did not suggest that specific numbers of given groups would have to be hired or promoted.

It was under this order that the "Philadelphia Plan" requiring building contractors to hire certain numbers of minorities was instituted. The building trades had long been considered most impervious to programs to overcome discrimination. This plan was upheld by the courts in *Contractors Association of Eastern Pa.* v. *Secretary of Labor,* (3rd Cir. 1971). But the extension of affirmative action into the controversial area of "goals and timetables," specific numbers that employers must try to hire or promote, derives from guidelines issued by the Department of Labor in 1971 to implement the executive order, though the approach was prefigured in guidelines of 1970.

Effects of the Quota System

The overall program of affirmative action operates under the Office of Federal Contract Compliance Programs in the Depart-

ment of Labor, but the specific authority to review the employment and promotion practices of contractors and to negotiate
and approve affirmative action plans is delegated to sixteen
federal departments and agencies each of which supervises the
affirmative action efforts of contractors in its area. Thus, the
Department of Defense has a director of contractor employment
compliance with an authorized staff of 565, the largest of the
sixteen compliance staffs. Thousands upon thousands of people
are engaged, in the federal bureaucracy and by the thousands of
contractors they supervise, in the work of affirmative action.

To what effect? Critics of affirmative action are to be found
on two wings. On the one side are the watchdogs of affirmative
action, civil rights agencies, civil rights advocates, minority and
women's groups, committees of Congress. These groups are
convinced that affirmative action is a great thrashing about and
accumulation of paper signifying nothing. Thus, according to
the criticism of the Subcommittee on Equal Opportunities of the
House Committee on Education and Labor, since 1965 only
eleven companies have been debarred from federal contracts,
only one of which was large—Blue Bell, Inc., with 19,000
employees. In an article arguing for preferences for minorities
in employment, two law school professors assert that affirmative
action plans "have been largely ineffective." Marilyn Gittell
argues that affirmative action has had no effect in higher education. These critics of affirmative action defend its *objectives,*
usually deny that programs call for *quotas* (since the programs
themselves only demand *goals,* and government agencies make
a great deal of the distinction), but nevertheless insist that
desirable as these programs are consistent as they are with the
Constitution and the Civil Rights Act of 1964, they are not
effective because they are not forcefully carried out.

The other group of critics charge that it is imposing on
government contractors the obligation to discriminate on
grounds of race, color, and national origin; that it is all too
effective in leading employers to consider in their hiring and
promotion and firing the race, color, and national origin of
employees, actual or potential; that it offends the Constitution's

demand for the "equal protection of the laws" and the Civil
Rights Act's ban on discrimination in employment. And more
than that, they say, by directly contradicting the hope of a
society that operates without discrimination, it opens up other
great social dangers.The chief critic of affirmative action in
academic employment has been Sidney Hook. I have criticized
strong affirmative action in employment generally and there has
been considerable though surprisingly muted criticism from
business.

At least as I see it, those who argue that affirmative action has
achieved nothing for minorities, that it has been effectively
countered by the actions of employers and universities, are in
error. One reason they can advance these arguments is that so
much of their experience and concrete evidence are drawn from
higher education, a world with a number of distinctive features.

First, the criteria for academic appointments, vague as they
may appear to academics, are specific and remarkably widely
accepted. Thus, it is generally accepted that the Ph.D. and
evidence of research are needed for initial appointments, and
that further research resulting in books or articles is required
for permanent appointments. If there are few people with such
qualifications among some minority, a good deal of affirmative
action may produce little in the way of appointments.

Second, appointments in universities, as compared to business and governmental institutions, are largely initiated by col-
legial peer groups, whatever the formal processes after their
recommendations to higher authority. As a result, any appointment involves a wide participation. Departments are aware they
must operate under some kind of affirmative action constraints.
But since the process of appointment is not in fact under the full
authority of administrators (as in business and government employment), the affirmative action plan that administrators agree
to can be resisted by the departments that appoint on the basis
of other criteria—academic, the supporters of this independence
assert; old cronyism, its attackers insist.

Thus, the academic environment maximizes the opportunity
for polarized views on the effectiveness of affirmative action.
Because everyone is involved in the appointment process, every-

one knows of the pressure from central administrators to give preference to minority candidates; but since everyone is involved, the qualifications are relatively firm, and the number of qualified persons from some minority groups is few, the administrative pressure may not lead to a rapid increase in minority faculty members. So one side can claim that affirmative action is a fraud; the other, that great pressure is being exerted by government officials and administrators to subvert academic standards.

The general result of affirmative action, however, is quite a different matter. It is not true that there have been no or minimal effects of affirmative action programs. Admittedly, any fact has multiple causes, and to demonstrate the effects of programs is not easy or unambiguous. Ideally, we would want to compare the employment and earnings at various occupational levels of minority and nonminority. We would want to compare those employers with government contracts and requiring affirmative action plans with those who had no contracts and did not have such plans (though even employers without government contracts might be subject to affirmative action plans because of state and local government contracts). In order to test the significance of statistical goals and timetables, we would want to compare the period between 1964 and 1970 or 1971, when employers were subject to Title VII of the Civil Rights Act and to the "soft" requirements—advertising, recruiting, and the like—with the subsequent period, when employers with government contracts were subject to the "hard" affirmative action emphasizing statistical goals, and when, in the wake of the *Griggs* decision, the pressure became stronger to hire by quota in order to avoid charges of and findings of discrimination. No analysis of employment and earnings data fully meets these tests, but various studies throw light on the matter.

1969: Before and After

One of the best to my mind is that of Richard Freeman, who analyzes black progress in earnings and occupational position overall in the economy. While his data do not distinguish between employers subject and not subject to affirmative action, they do permit a comparison before and after 1969. Was black progress in earnings relative to white during the 1960s maintained during the weakened labor market in the early 1970s? He concludes that it was: "the gains in relative income of the late 1960s did not erode in the early 1970s, despite the weakened labor market . . . More important, perhaps, the figures show only slight, if any, lessening in the income increase. Of particular interest is the large increase in the ratio of black to white median usual weekly earnings from 1969 to 1974, which suggests that black wage rates went up substantially through 1974." If economic progress in a period of tightened labor markets and antidiscrimination legislation without statistical goals was sustained during a period of weakened labor markets and enforcement of statistical goals, these statistical goals presumably had some effect.

Another analysis, by Andrew Brimmer, does compare firms that report to EEOC (more than 100 employees, and one can assume that many are government contractors) with those that do not. Comparing employment in 1966 and 1974, he finds:

Black employment in EEOC-reporting firms rose much faster than employment in the economy as a whole. For instance, blacks accounted for 23 per cent of the growth in jobs in EEOC-reporting firms, as compared with 15 per cent in the total. Within the white-collar category, however, only clerical workers and sales workers recorded relatively larger gains on EEOC-reported payrolls (43 per cent as compared with 21 per cent and 12 per cent as compared with 9 per cent, respectively). In the case of professional and technical workers, EEOC figures show blacks getting 11 per cent of the increase in jobs, as compared with 14 per cent for black professionals and technicians in the economy at large. The lag was especially noticeable among managers and officials. In the country as a whole, blacks accounted for 11 per cent of the expansion; their share in EEOC reports was only 7 per cent. In contrast, blacks got a much larger share of the new craft and service jobs in EEOC-reporting firms—for example, 27 per cent of craft jobs, as compared with 15 per cent for all firms; and 26 per cent of service jobs, as compared with 11 per cent for all employers combined.

On the basis of these figures, I conclude that the companies reporting under the EEOC requirements are opening jobs to blacks at a rate much faster than is true for all employers in the country as a whole. At the same time, however, it appears that the expansion is much slower in the upper reaches of the occupational scale than it is among job categories at the lower end. Thus, the task of occupational upgrading for blacks remains considerable.

From this comparison of firms reporting to the EEOC with the economy as a whole, it would be a mistake to conclude that blacks are not making substantial progress in professional and managerial employment. This progress, however, has been largely in government employment. According to a study of college graduates by Richard Freeman, half of black males and 72 per cent of black females work for government at all levels, compared with 27 per cent and 56 per cent of white males and females. The demand for black college graduates has been so great that black males may expect to earn 9 per cent more than white males with a degree. These general findings of black progress continuing through the first half of the 1970s are also supported by the analysis of Reynolds Farley.

Other studies report on different parts of the problem, but seemingly none contradicts the general conclusion that substantial progress took place in the relative earnings and employment and occupational position of the largest minority, blacks, that this progress has continued in the 1970s, and this progress has apparently been greater among firms reporting to the EEOC than others. Stronger evidence is the experience of employers themselves. As against universities, where one may argue whether the statistical goals of affirmative action plans are "goals" or "quotas," large employers make no bones about the matter (though for legal reasons some may gag at the word): large hierarchical organizations have quotas imposed either by consent decrees or by affirmative action plans.

The largest private corporate employer in the United States (AT&T), the steel industry, and many other employers, public and private, operate under court orders setting quotas for the employment of minorities. These are not set on the basis of formal findings of discrimination as such. Rather, charges of discrimination by the EEOC or Department of Justice have convinced the employers they would very likely be found guilty of discrimination if they were to contest them, and their liabilities for back pay would then be severe; undoubtedly, one reason they accept consent decrees is because the costs would be greater if they contested the charge in court. In consent decrees the corporation is assigned what are formally "goals" rather than "quotas," but with a judge reviewing progress reports it is a distinction without a difference.

"Mandatory Achievement of Goals"

But consent decrees cover only a small part of employment in the United States, with a much larger part covered by the affirmative action programs, which in theory also set goals rather than quotas. If we look closely at how these goals are actually met in industry, it is again very hard to see any significant difference. One well-known affirmative action program is Sears's "Mandatory Achievement of Goals" (MAG). As the country's largest retail employer, Sears has 376,000 employees. "The basic policy," the program asserts, "will be at the minimum to fill one out of every two openings with a minority man or woman of whatever races are present in your trading/hiring area." An account in the newsletter *World of Work Report* describes how MAG works:

Unit managers must maintain the *existing* representation of minorities and women in filling job replacements. More important to bring about change, 50 per cent of *all job openings* are to be filled by members of underrepresented groups. The manager has a *choice* from which underrepresented groups he can select. In categories of *nontraditional* jobs, where qualified or qualifiable candidates from underrepresented groups are in short supply, ratios of 20 per cent are applied.

A local manager can exercise a *bypass,* or deviation from these ratios, only by demonstrating a good-faith effort first to hire from any of the underused groups, or where a clearly more qualified candidate is found. In MAG's three years of operation, hundreds of bypasses have been permitted, but the total is still tiny in comparison with the 150,000 or more people Sears hires for full-time or permanent part-time work in a single year under MAG requirements.

The importance of the flexibility allowed by the bypass and by the manager's choice among underrepresented groups is, according to Ray J. Graham, MAG's creator and Sears's director of equal opportunity. that "MAG avoids the charge of being an illegal quota by its flexibility and by the inclusion of a 'safety valve' if qualifiable candidates can't be found. Sears feels that generally they can be found.

Under a charge of discrimination by the EEOC since August 1973, Sears is still trying to avoid litigation by continuing to negotiate with the EEOC. This may explain why Sears is a leader in affirmative action. But General Motors, Ford, and General Electric are laboring under the same charge; and other big corporations follow their cases closely and adapt their practices to avoid what can be expensive and damaging findings of discrimination. The practices of large companies that have in effect turned goals into quotas are not unique to Sears and other major companies facing EEOC charges. From discussions with personnel officers I get the impression that these practices are general.

Arguments for Affirmative Discrimination

Unfortunately much of the discussion of these issues is clouded by evasion and lies (understandably: the government agencies are arguably engaged in breaking the law, as are the employers that adopt group-preference hiring), so that one must engage in a kind of detective work to establish that these practices are indeed widespread. But if one has established that government agencies have increasingly imposed on employers practices that in effect require them to take account of the color and national origin of prospective and present employees in hiring and promotion, the question arises: Is this a good or a bad policy? The claim that it is a good policy rests on a number of arguments, all of which can be effectively countered.

1. *Certain groups fall below the average in income and oc-*
cupation, and they will not reach the average positions unless
employers are forced to give them preference.

It is common sociological knowledge that some minority
groups, even in the face of discrimination, have improved their
circumstances and indeed achieved more than the average income and occupational status. The groups—now called "the
affected classes"—that government agencies have stipulated as
particularly protected by antidiscrimination law have also, if
variably, made progress. Thus, blacks were making considerable
progress in the 1960s, before the introduction of statistical
requirements. Indeed, good research shows that discrimination
against young blacks of equivalent education and family background was a thing of the past by the end of the 1960s.[1] The two
chief groups of Asian Americans—Chinese and Japanese—were
not behind other Americans in income and occupational status,
having made great progress. Hispanic Americans were a diverse
group: Spanish Americans had never considered themselves a
disadvantaged minority; Cubans had made substantial progress
and had no need of affirmative action; Mexican Americans had
also been making substantial progress; and while Puerto Ricans
were the worst off of groups of Hispanic heritage, it was not at
all clear that discrimination was the root of the matter. American
Indians were indeed poorly off.

The response to this argument, then, is that some groups were
no longer disadvantaged and others were making progress, so
that the argument that statistical goals were required is grossly
overextended in relation to all the affected classes.

2. *Equity demands that each group show the same average*
performance as any other group or the average of all groups.

The objective of average income and occupation for each
group is not dictated by equity. Income and occupation are
based largely on education. Length of education and achievement in education vary greatly among groups, and for different
reasons. Income and occupational prestige also depend in large
measure on unknown factors; Christopher Jencks has suggested
luck, Daniel P. Moynihan proposed pluck, and there are other
candidates. While one might want to eliminate the effect of luck

on income and occupation (though lottery-ticket buyers would probably object), it is hardly likely it would be to the good of society to eliminate pluck. Groups vary by amount of education, quality of education, geographical distribution, occupational experience, distribution by age, and many other factors that properly affect income. To eliminate all these as elements from the overall score of a group would result in an even more peculiar and inefficient economy than we have. Further, some groups— even those bearing the badge of discrimination—have achieved more than equality. Does equity require that their income and occupations be cut down?

3. *The avoidance of resentment, rebellion, and perhaps revolution by deprived groups also requires that government ensure average income and occupational distribution for each group.*

Undoubtedly a permanently depressed group might become resentful, rebellious, riotous, criminal. Any multiethnic democracy demands equal treatment among groups. But the alternative to statistical goals, as I have argued in the answer to point 1 above, was not stagnation; no one could say that blacks, the largest minority group, were stagnating in 1970. They were making rapid progress. There were two serious problems: the large proportion of female-headed families, whose members could not be effective in the labor force, and a very high unemployment rate among youth. Inevitably, affirmative action aided most those with education and qualifications. Just what assistance it has been to the two great depressed classes among blacks is questionable. Perhaps it has been of some help, but programs separate from and in addition to simple statistical requirements for employment are needed to deal with the economic and social problems of female-headed families and unemployed black youth.

4. *Discrimination is the cause of this failure to achieve an average position in income and occupation, and discrimination is illegal.*

Discrimination is an abomination. To label it *the* cause of the economic differences between groups, even when it is extensive and pervasive, is a gross oversimplification. See the comments in answer to point 2 above.

5. *The practices that require preferential employment and promotion are in any case temporary and will come to an end when the disadvantaged have achieved equality.*

It is very hard to see how these programs will be temporary. Groups do not give up advantages they have once gained. Nor do government agencies give up the power of oversight once seized. When all affirmative action goals are fulfilled, it will still be necessary to maintain the pattern of hiring and promotion by ethnic group, because only so can one ensure that the delicate statistical balance achieved will be maintained.

Arguments Against Quotas

The opponents of statistical goals make their own arguments against them. First, they argue that this approach must arouse resentment among those not included among the "affected classes." What is gained in calming intergroup relations by increasing the economic welfare of one group is lost by the increased tensions created, in the workplace and society generally, by this very preference. Second, it encourages other groups to demand the same protection of statistical goals. Many ethnic and racial groups not included in the initial list of "affected classes" can point to discrimination in their background. "White" is an amalgam that covers Protestant, Catholic, Jew, English, Scottish, Irish, German, Italian, Polish, Lebanese, and a hundred other stocks, most of which have had some experience of discrimination. Immigrants from India have recently been demanding inclusion among "Asian Americans" (they had been considered "majority white," and not an "affected class" under affirmative action), and there have also been scattered protests from those of Italian and Polish origin. Third, it puts the government in the business of determining who belongs to which racial and ethnic group, in order to decide who should get affirmative and who reverse discrimination. This is a position that government had abandoned by 1964, because the Constitution does not permit discrimination on grounds of race and ethnic origin. And, finally, it offends against what many have believed to be the main thrust of liberalism in America, the primacy of individual rights. The outrage an American feels when he (or she) is deprived of a job or a promotion because of his race or ethnic background is no less when that person is white than when he (or she) is black, or yellow, or brown.

A full consideration of the past and the present has been necessary to assess any future development. Let us outline the forces on both sides of the issue. If one begins with popular opinion, one will discover uniformly enormous opposition to affirmative or reverse discrimination. A 1977 Gallup poll reported that 83 per cent of a national sample opposed these policies, only 10 per cent favored them. The question set was: "Some people say that to make up for past discrimination women and members of minority groups should be given preferential treatment in getting jobs and places in college. Others say that ability, as determined by test scores, should be the main consideration. Which point of view comes closest to how you feel on this matter?" The major significant differences were by race—64 per cent of nonwhites opposed such policies, only 27 per cent favored them.

Interesting as these findings are, they are of hardly any weight in the actual development of policies. At the governmental level, the judiciary, the Congress, and the executive departments play the key roles, in roughly that order. The judiciary has shaped the present policies; it is also capable of reversing them.

Action by Congress is much less likely, for it would depend on the kinds of influences that are brought to bear on its members. Any new bill to clarify the meaning of the act of 1964 as amended in 1972, more specifically to rule out preference in employment, would be fiercely challenged by the civil rights organizations, a powerful lobby in Washington. Whether they (or any other lobby) really represent their supposed constituency hardly matters; as we have seen, on this issue they may not. But they do not depend on their constituents for votes or money. These organizations, supported by foundations and in some cases government grants, find it unncessary to consult the views of those whose interests they assert they are defending. The great majority of the people who oppose such policies, on the other hand, are not organized to make their opposition effective. Business groups are critical but their position is likely to be dismissed as mere self-interest. Unions have opposed statistical goals, but those who might speak up before Congress would either be dismissed as themselves having practiced discrimination or be inhibited by their long-time alliances with civil rights groups.

Thus, as is so often the case with legislation, those who influence Congress are those who are most concerned regardless of popular opinion, which is unorganized. The principal strength of the civil rights groups consists not of money to support campaigns, not even so much of threats to organize voters against uncooperative congressmen. It consists of two chief elements. The first is access to the national media: if civil rights groups send out releases to the *Washington Post*, the *New York Times*, major TV networks, *Time* and *Newsweek*, AP and UPI, denouncing new legislation as a weakening of laws against discrimination, this is the way the story will be reported; and most congressmen would not like to see themselves allegedly supporting discrimination. Second, the civil rights groups claim to hold the higher moral ground. An opponent must have a very clear sense of his case before he is willing to argue against such a claim. Who is willing to be for discrimination, against progress for blacks and Puerto Ricans? The fact that the policies of those who claim to be more decent are discriminatory and only doubtfully assist the deprived is not clearly known to the congressmen, and they hesitate to take on organized forces that can smear them in the mass media.

The weakest element in the entire political picture is the executive branch. The EEOC is of course an independent agency, not subject to presidential control except through the appointment power; but the civil rights lobby can ensure that no president, whatever his views on reverse discrimination, would appoint to the EEOC someone who opposed strong affirmative action. The Office of Contract Compliance Programs, with its various affiliated offices in the other executive departments, directly administers policies of affirmative discrimination on the basis of implementing guidelines written under the pressure of civil rights groups, guidelines that the courts have upheld. They cannot be influenced easily in the way they implement these policies by higher executive authority—that is, the president and the cabinet officers—as was demonstrated during the presidencies of Nixon and Ford. Particularly in the latter administration, when the secretary of labor, the attorney general, and the secretary of HEW were all considered to be sympathetic to the position that reverse discrimination should be limited, it became manifest that the president and the executive branch, whatever their views, were powerless before the civil rights lobby and its two chief sources of power. And the effective control of how the mass media handle stories dealing with discrimination and the lobby's moral advantage have as yet barely been challenged.*

I have given great weight in the development and maintenance of reverse discrimination policies to the civil rights bodies. These are now much more numerous than the NAACP and the NAACP Legal Defense and Educational Fund, though these play a leading role. For example, one can consider as part of the civil rights lobby—and a very important part, because it is remarkably well funded—the U.S. Commission on Civil Rights, an independent government agency. That the civil rights lobby now favors discrimination is a difficult point to put across; few will attack it on this ground, and of those who do, few will be given wide publicity. The civil rights lobby monitors legislation and federal regulations more effectively than any group opposing affirmative discrimination. Most significantly, it uses class action suits both to establish as law the principles of reverse discrimination and, by legal intervention, to require government agencies to carry out the law as it interprets it.

This analysis of forces suggests that it is unlikely that policies of affirmative discrimination will be abandoned. One could not count on Congress or the executive branch. But the courts, to repeat, are erratic. They are controlled by the Supreme Court, where a 5-to-4 decision may reverse a complex set of policies

---

*The Carter administration and its officials had no desire to change these policies, which indeed they strengthened. The Reagan administration by contrast was critical of quotas during the campaign. Nevertheless, twenty-four months after Reagan took office, the structure of federal regulations and court decisions enforcing statistical goals and quotas stood intact, though the Justice Department had begun to intervene against quotas in selected cases.—N.G., 1983.

being implemented by many thousands spending many hundreds of millions. No one can be sure this will not happen. The Supreme Court is a mysterious body, and many kinds of influences play on it. The kinds and quality of briefs it receives may affect it. Under the Ford administration, for a moment, it seemed possible that the Justice Department might support modification of the rulings that support reverse discrimination.

But there are two other sources of briefs opposing reverse discrimination that may influence the Court. One—we should not put too much weight on this, perhaps—is business groups, who are caught between minorities claiming back pay and preferential treatment and individuals from the majority who can also effectively sue for back pay and jobs. It is hardly possible for business to be happy about a situation, such as the one AT&T faced, in which it had to give both back pay to the minorities and women it promotes and damages for discrimination to majority males with greater seniority and better qualifications. And yet a court case required it to do just that. In *McAleer* v. *AT&T* (1976), a District of Columbia court required the company to pay damages to McAleer, but said the consent decree was also valid and therefore he should not get his promotion.

More significant, to my mind, is the break in the civil rights coalition. The Jewish groups, in particular—the Anti-Defamation League of B'nai B'rith, the American Jewish Committee, the American Jewish Congress—are not happy with reverse discrimination. When it is applied in a situation to which Jews are particulary sensitive (admission to medical school, say), they take a strong and uniform position. All supported Allan Bakke in his suit alleging that he was not admitted to the medical school of the University of California at Davis because a number of places were held specifically for minority groups. How far they would go to intervene in employment cases is another matter. But legal commentators seem to agree that decisions in an educational case, such as *Bakke,* may have influence on what is legal and constitutional also in employment. If there is any halt or reversal in the development of practices of affirmative discrimination, then it will have to be because of court decisions;

and if these decisions begin to change, it will be in large measure
because dominant opinion on civil rights is no longer uniform,
and is split on whether preferential employment on the basis of
race and ethnic group is a proper response to discrimination and
disadvantage.

2. Fair Shakers and Social Engineers

By MORRIS B. ABRAM

Focus
The shift in government policy from color blindness to color consciousness was to produce by the mid-1970s an irreparable split in the older civil rights coalition—the coalition that had previously worked so successfully for passage of the 1964 Civil Rights Act and the 1965 Voting Rights Act. In the following article, Morris B. Abram, who first came to public attention in the late 1940s as a civil rights advocate in the Deep South, describes the philosophical change that took place in the early 1970s as a shift from the "fair-shake" principle of equal opportunity for individuals to the social engineer's concept of proportional representation of ethnic groups. Fair shakers, says Abram, believe that "removing all barriers to the exercise of civil and political rights and to an individual's ability to participate in the free market system is the best possible way to promote justice." The social engineer, on the other hand, rejects the liberal notion of equality of rights for individuals, and substitutes instead a principle of "color-coded group rights" that would guarantee to the members of certain ethnic groups a certain fixed share of social, economic, and political power. The social engineer's approach, Abram charges, is not only inconsistent with the American civil rights tradition, but violates "the basic

principles that hold together our heterogeneous society and secure our civil peace." "Societies that depart from color-blind, neutral, decision-making," he says, "do so at their peril." In practice, Abram charges, the policy of affirmative action has become little more than a crude spoils system among competing racial and ethnic groups. Abram counsels a return to the older fair-shake principle and contends that racial justice is best served by a "vigilant concern with equal opportunity, procedural regularity, and fair treatment of the individual." For an opposing view read Randall Kennedy's essay (selection 3).

Morris B. Abram is a former president of Brandeis University, and has served on the U.S. Commission on Civil Rights, the U.N. Commission on Human Rights, and the U.N. Subcommission on the Prevention of Discrimination and Protection of Minorities.

THE CIVIL RIGHTS movement has turned away from its original principled campaign for equal justice under law to engage in an open contest for social and economic benefits conferred on the basis of race or other classifications previously thought to be invidious. This essay, written from my perspective as an early participant in the civil rights cause, explains my view that this departure, however desirable to some in the short run, violates the basic principles that hold together our heterogeneous society and secure our civil peace. The civil rights movement, by my lights, should turn its attention back to first principles—the zealous regard for equal opportunity and the promotion of color-blind law and social policy—and away from color-conscious remedies that abandon principle and lead us further from a society free of the bane of racial discrimination.

Between the mid-1940s and the mid-1960s, the civil rights movement grew into a broad coalition united by moral principle and a shared vision of an American society without racial discrimination but with equal opportunity for all. The overarching political goal of this movement was equality—an equality to be reached by the elimination of discriminatory barriers that denied the individual the opportunity to exercise his franchise effectively, to compete for housing and employment, and to use public accommodations. Government, civil rights advocates agreed, was responsible for ensuring that each individual had access to all spheres of public activity—social, economic, and political—regardless of race, sex, or ethnic origin. Because this original vision of the civil rights movement was concerned with equality of *opportunity* and a fair shake for individuals, I will label its advocates "fair shakers."

The fair shakers were soon challenged, however, by a radically different vision of civil rights. During the late 1960s, the civil rights community began to splinter and, certainly by the mid-1970s, much of its leadership had become preoccupied with equality of *results*.[1] Those who focused on this type of equality attributed socioeconomic or political inequalities between minorities and whites, men and women, the disabled and the unimpaired, to discrimination—past and present. Absent discrimination, these result-oriented leaders claimed, all groups would be represented in the institutions and occupations of society roughly in proportion to their representation in the population. These leaders continue to believe that the only way to measure equality is in terms of such representation, and that it is the government's role to bring about proportional representation in short order. Because this new vision of the civil rights movement requires the attainment of predetermined ends, rather than the abolition of barriers to fair participation, I will call its adherents "social engineers."

My early experience in the civil rights movement now leads me to oppose the social engineers. I joined the civil rights coalition in the late 1940s, first as a citizen and then as a lawyer challenging the Georgia county unit electoral system. That system assigned electoral votes to counties disproportionately, so that in the statewide Democratic primaries—equivalent to general elections—individual votes counted less in more populated counties. Thus, the fewer than 1,900 residents of rural Echols County enjoyed two votes, while the 550,000 residents of Atlanta's Fulton County exercised only six. Proponents of this system—the social engineers of that day—justified the departure from an equal franchise on the ground that Echols County voters needed and deserved ninety-six times the franchise power of Fulton County voters because the rural voters had neither the benefits of Atlanta's good schools, libraries, health services, and communications systems, nor the massed power of the city's voting blocks.

In fact, the Georgia electoral system was the vehicle through which the racist status quo maintained its power. The social engineers were fully aware that blacks in rural areas were too intimidated to vote. By weighing the virtually all-white rural vote more heavily than the mixed white/black city vote, these segregationists contrived to ensure the election of representatives who favored their views. Ultimately, Georgia liberals, supporting a one-man, one-vote approach on fair-shake grounds, successfully overturned this system.

Early in my career, I thus learned to view with suspicion the demand that the historical disadvantage of certain groups be remedied in accordance with a substantive notion of justice—a notion entailing departure from equality before the law. The role of government in securing racial justice, I came to believe, is best limited to vigilant concern with equal opportunity, procedural regularity, and fair treatment of the individual. I have not departed from my original fair-shake view, but continue to believe that it is in keeping with our legal and political traditions; that the social engineers' advocacy of result-oriented and color-coded group rights is inconsistent with these traditions and violative of other democratic ideals and principles; and, that adherence to the fair-shake model is most likely to promote true racial equality and enlightened debate over our conceptions of social justice.

Fair-Shake Principles

The fair-shake principle is part of a long and respected American legal tradition. It was the force underlying the antislavery amendments to the Constitution, the series of laws passed in the wake of the Civil War that afforded protection of contract and property rights, and the guarantees of equality of opportunity in voting, employment, use of public accommodations, and housing in the mid-1960s. It was in accord with fair-shake principles that Congress enacted the Voting Rights Act of 1965 to stymie the effort of states such as Georgia to devalue the minority franchise—a form of racial preference for whites.

Although the fair-shake principle shaped our civil rights laws, it has, from an early date, been challenged by various forms of social engineering. In 1871, for instance, a black friend wrote to former slave Frederick Douglass, then the most prominent black leader in the country, arguing that blacks deserved government appointments based on their numbers. Douglas replied that "equality of numbers has nothing to do with equality of attainments.'' In a stunning rebuke to the concept of proportional representation on the basis of race, Douglass wrote:

> The mulattoes, on a solid census basis, ought to have so many offices, the blacks so many, and the whites so many, the Germans so many, the Irish so many, and other classes and nationalities should have offices according to their respective numbers. . . . Upon your statistical principle, the colored people of the United States ought, therefore, not only to hold one-eighth of all the offices in the country, but they should own one-eighth of all the property, and pay one-eighth of all the taxes of the country. Equal in numbers, they should, of course, be equal in everything else. They should constitute one-eighth of the poets, statesmen, scholars, authors, and philosophers of the country.

Because groups—black, white, Hispanic, male, and female—do not necessarily have the same distribution of, among other characteristics, skills, interest, motivation, and age, a fair-shake system may not produce proportional representation across occupations and professions, and certainly not at any given time. This uneven distribution, however, is not necessarily the result of discrimination.[2] Thomas Sowell has shown through comparative studies of ethnic group performance that discrimination alone cannot explain these ethnic groups' varying levels of achievement. Groups such as the Japanese, Chinese, and West Indian blacks have fared very well in American society despite racial bias against these groups.

Moreover, although it is true that concern for qualifications has sometimes masked a purposeful intent to exclude individuals on the basis of race or other invidious criteria, the mere fact that some meritocratic devices have the result of excluding proportionally higher numbers of minorities does not in itself demonstrate that minorities are not getting a fair shake. And the fair-shake principle, unlike the norm of proportional representation, is perfectly consistent with our meritocratic view of the relevant differences between individuals—a view through which our society rewards the individual for attainment and avoids patronage and spoils systems.

Presumed Discrimination

Yet many of those who opposed the use of social engineering to perpetuate segregation now depart from the fair-shake model and actively advocate social engineering to achieve proportional representation. They now insist on a presumption that unequal results are due to intentional discrimination.[3] For them, the franchise is not a right to participate equally in the electoral process but a right to the election of a "fair share" of minority representatives. Although no civil rights leader has dared to suggest weighted ballots for blacks, it is now part of civil rights gospel that blacks must not only vote but that we must draw district lines to ensure that blacks are elected. To my mind, these "piece-of-the-action" concerns depart from the civil rights movement's earlier advocacy of fair participation and return us to the spoils system that the early movement worked so hard to displace.[4]

But today's social engineers, dissatisfied with the results of the fair-shake model, invoke a new conception of justice. In their view, justice is less an individual's claim to equality before the law—an idea at the heart of our liberal tradition—than a particular distribution of social, economic, and political power among groups. This new conception of justice necessarily repudiates the ideal of the rule of law—a law that "would treat people equally, but . . . not seek to make them equal." And to achieve this newly announced goal of group justice, the social engineers proclaim that it is necessary to abandon color blindness.

Judge Damon Keith of the Court of Appeals for the Sixth Circuit has made just such a claim. "[W]e cannot have *representativeness* in America today if we are in any sense of the word *color-blind*," he writes, and "we cannot have *justice* in this country without a strong measure of *representativeness*." A civil rights attorney, commenting on the dismal results achieved by certain minorities on a 1980 federal civil service examination, equates representativeness with justice in a similar fashion. "[S]uppose that 100 whites and 100 blacks applied for fifty jobs. If there were no adverse impact in the examining procedure used to select for these jobs," he suggests, "one would expect to see twenty-five blacks and twenty-five whites hired."

These social engineers call their plan for allocating social goods by race "affirmative action." But the term as they use it departs radically from the original intent of affirmative action—to give minorities a fair shake. Executive Order 11246,[5] for example, far from calling the merit system into question, attempted only to eliminate the institutional and informational barriers that stand in the way of the minority individual's ability to compete *equally* with others for jobs and promotions.[6] Vice President Hubert H. Humphrey, who chaired the committee that drafted that order, was a committed fair shaker whose own Equal Employment Opportunity bill of 1964 prescribed affirmative action and at the same time insisted on color-blind equal opportunity.

I believe that the social engineers' result-oriented conception of racial justice is both destructive of true racial equality and potentially harmful to society. Although the social engineers concede that their color-conscious and group-based approach may produce some injustice, they argue that extreme measures are at least temporarily necessary to eliminate discrimination. In my view, however, even the laudable goal of ending racial discrimination cannot justify the adoption of means incompatible with other ends of justice.

Serious Long-Term Costs

Government constantly requires adjustments between ends and means. Crime, for instance, is a problem we desperately need to curb; but not at the expense of due process. We cannot afford to change the character of our society simply in order to achieve desired results more quickly. And, as the following discussion demonstrates, the departure from color-blind decisionmaking in law and social policy entails a number of serious long-term costs.

The social engineers' approach to affirmative action is without support in our Constitution and civil rights laws. These revisionists would have us read the Equal Protection Clause of the Constitution and the racially neutral language of civil rights legislation so as to grant preferences for groups that they designate as "subjugated." They advance this argument in the face of the plain English of the text and a legislative history that contradicts their contentions. As Justice Douglas has observed:

> The Equal Protection Clause commands the elimination of racial barriers, not their creation in order to satisfy our theory as to how society ought to be organized. . . . So far as race is concerned, *any* state-sponsored preference to one race over another . . . is in my view "invidious" and violative of the Equal Protection Clause.

And Professor Alexander Bickel agreed:

> The lesson of the great decisions of the Supreme Court and the lesson of contemporary history have been the same for at least a generation: discrimination on the basis of race is illegal, immoral, unconstitutional, inherently wrong, and destructive of democratic society. . . . Having found support in the Constitution for equality, [proponents of racial preferences] now claim support for inequality under the same Constitution.

Without doing violence to the principles of equality before the law and neutral decisionmaking, we simply cannot interpret our laws to support both color blindness for some citizens and color consciousness for others.

One possible, more practical, consequence of this social engineering is the decline of occupational and professional standards. For example, in 1981, the federal civil service exam for over 100 entry-level positions was suspended, because minorities were not passing it in sufficient proportions. In order to make the minority passing rate sufficient on the written examination for foreign service officers "relatively similar" to that for nonminorities, the Foreign Service Officers Examination Board simply adds 500 minority "near-passers" to the pool of candidates who actually passed and declares the whole group—"near-passers" and passers alike—qualified to go on to the next stage. Similarly, Department of Labor Revised Order No. 4, providing that "[n]either minority nor female employees should be required to possess higher qualifications than those of the lowest qualified incumbent,'' creates pressure on government contractors to hire candidates who are not the best available. The social engineers thus defy the existing distribution of skills and abilities—whether naturally present or socially developed—in order to achieve their objective.

A Quota System

Indeed, the social engineers' vision of affirmative action is, for all intents and purposes, a quota system. Though they usually repudiate the idea of "quotas" and insist on characterizing their preferred remedies as "goals and timetables," the effects of numerous enforcement actions and lawsuits brought by government agencies and civil rights groups belie the social engineers' characterization. These actions have effectively transformed goals into quotas by putting the burden on the employer to rebut the presumption of discrimination if the employer fails to meet its minority hiring goals. Failure to meet the goals—even if established soley by reference to population proportionality—raises a presumption of discrimination that the hapless employer can only overturn after great effort, expense, and public embarrassment.

Moreover, even beyond the practical effects of legal presumptions, there is ultimately little theoretical difference between the goals and timetables the social engineers favor, and the quotas they purport to eschew. For to what end are these goals and timetables established if not to be achieved? And what is their basis unless it be that justice requires the allocation of social goods according to race?

Several civil rights policymakers have noted with dismay that, despite their good intentions, affirmative action has degenerated into a spoils system among competing racial and ethnic groups. Thus, Laurence Silberman, President Nixon's under secretary of labor and the legal strategist who transformed the government's contract-compliance affirmative action approach from color-blind to color-conscious, today acknowledges that under Department of Labor Revised Order No. 4, a statistical imbalance is legally tantamount to a finding of discrimination, even without proof of intent.[7] Silberman concedes that the adoption of numerical standards "led ineluctably to the very quotas, guaranteeing equal results, that we initially wished to avoid." And Senator Daniel Patrick Moynihan has wondered in amazement:

> Who in the executive branch fifteen years ago would have dreamed the day would come when the federal courts would require a census in which all employees and judicial officers be classified by "race/national origin groups" including the sub-group "Arabic" and "Hebrew"? This was just the sort of thing we assumed we were working against.[8]

The social engineers' approach also fails to confront the problem of *who decides* what groups are sufficiently disadvantaged to deserve special treatment. They offer no mechanism for neutral decisionmaking on this critical issue. America is a highly pluralistic and heterogeneous society that has had to expand continuously in order to accommodate different elements; many discrete groups have suffered discrimination here. Consequently, a major problem with addressing discrimination through race-conscious laws is the balancing of historical experiences. How and by whom shall the varying grievances of different groups be weighed and judged in order to decide what varying levels of compensation society should pay?

A Crude Struggle for Status

In the absence of any neutral decisionmaking mechanisms, the attempt to end discrimination through color-conscious remedies must inevitably degenerate into a crude political struggle between groups seeking favored status. Once we have abandoned the principles of fair procedure, equal opportunity, and individual rights in favor of the advancement of a particular group, we have opened wide the door to future abuses of all kinds. Bayard Rustin recently commented upon the charge of discriminatory results that blacks and Hispanics leveled at the New York City police sergeant's exam, an exam members of these groups had helped to devise:[9]

This approach [of setting aside test scores simply because of disproportionate impact] says to blacks and Hispanics that you don't necessarily have to qualify to be included. Furthermore, if you have enough political pressure in New York City to get away with that, then what's going to happen twenty years from now in California when it is predominantly Hispanic? And then the Hispanics will say "we're very sorry but not enough Hispanics passed the test" so blacks and whites who passed have to go in another line now and wait to get called. Or what's going to happen when women, who far outnumber men in our society, begin to play this game.

Hubert H. Humphrey, one of the pioneers of color-blind affirmative action, sounded a similar cautionary note:

[O]ur standard of judgement in the last analysis is not some group's power . . . but an *equal* opportunity for *persons*.

Do you want a society that is nothing but an endless power struggle among organized groups? Do you want a society where there is no place for the independent individual? I don't.

What the social engineers fail to perceive is that societies that depart from color-blind, neutral decisionmaking do so at their peril. The history of societies that have adopted this approach in order to reach substantive social goals more quickly has been a history not of liberation but of crippling oppression. As Professor Bickel warned, "[t]he history of the racial quota is a history of subjugation, not beneficence. . . . A quota is a divider of society, a creator of castes, and it is all the worse for its racial base, especially in a society desperately striving for an equality that will make race irrelevant."

Further, the social engineers invite us to view people as statistics; they submerge personality, effort, and character under the blanket concerns of race, sex, and ethnicity. In an already divided society, this approach results in a new set of classifications: those who got where they are by merit; those who were leveraged into position by race or gender preferences; those who do not owe their position to such engineering but are viewed as the recipients of preferences by others (and themselves) and are thus stigmatized;[10] and finally those who originally earned their position without any favoritism but were displaced solely because of race, gender, or ethnicity. In such a divided system, no one really wins.

Indeed, the social engineers' approach exacerbates divisions within society by implicitly assuming that white males—even the millions who have never finished high school—are the undeserving beneficiaries of special privileges at the expense of all others.[11] This simplistic division of our complex society into white males and their victims was the hallmark of the U.S. Commission on Civil Rights when it was dominated by the social engineers. In a 1980 report on affirmative action, the commission described its view of the American system as one that "now routinely bestows privileges, favors and advantages on white males and imposes disadvantages and penalties on minorities and women." In this view, the civil rights laws are a weapon for wringing from white males the fruits of their exploitation and redistributing these fruits to all other sectors of society. Such an approach is doomed to widen and perpetuate the social divisions it purports to remedy.

Perhaps the most ironic weakness of the social engineers' redistributive approach is that it fails to help those particular members of disadvantaged groups who are most in need of assistance. Blanket orders that blindly benefit groups defined by race, sex, or ethnicity—especially when many members of such groups are prospering nicely—are an extremely crude and costly solution for social problems. While civil rights lobbyists frequently bolster their charge of continuing discrimination by pointing to the existence of the black underclass, many of their proposals can hardly have the effect of helping the millions of ghetto teenagers who lack the most basic entry-level skills. Indeed, in a recent interview, Harvard sociologist Nathan Glazer indicated that, in his opinion, group-based affirmative action has done "just about nothing" to aid the progress of black Americans.

Toward the Future

The civil rights movement has scored resounding victories and worked remarkable changes in American society through its commitment to principles of equal opportunity, fair treatment of the individual, and color blindness. As Bayard Rustin remarked in a recent interview, the period between 1954 and 1968

> was, perhaps, the most revolutionary period of any country in the world with regard to the achievement of justice for any minority group. In fact, in most of the world during that period, conditions worsened for many minorities. Racism was increasing in England. In the newly independent African countries, tribal hostilities were increasing. Ours was a most unique situation.

The movement, to continue its record of success in uniting the American people behind the moral and legal principles at the heart of our democratic and liberal traditions, should redirect its energies toward eliminating racial discrimination and toward ensuring that *all* Americans, without regard to race, sex, or ethnicity, are fairly equipped to compete for individual advancement in every arena.

We have the tools to achieve these goals. We have, for example, strict laws against intentional discrimination. The courts have broad remedial powers to eliminate such discrimination, including the authority to jail recalcitrant violators of the civil rights laws for contempt-of-court orders. The civil rights movement should press for the use of the courts' powers in a manner consistent with the fair shake principle.[12]

Similarly, despite the mixed record of recent years, we as a society are capable of devising creative social and economic initiatives to aid the truly needy. We can target job training and remedial education programs to all individuals who need them, without regard to race, sex, or ethnicity. In this way we can address past inequities without abandoning the fair-shake principle, and we can avoid perpetuating social divisions.

Although the mechanisms for change in our political system are far from perfect, this system has proven itself capable of correcting abuses and injustices with a minimum of violence and without curtailing freedom. The civil rights movement triumphed in this system because it united men and women in a just and principled cause and appealed to conservatives and liberals alike. It was, after all, a Republican president who appointed many of the judges who broke the back of white supremacy in the South. This broad-based support finally created an atmosphere in which all Americans (some more willingly than others, or course) acknowledged the inevitable justice of equality of opportunity.

Unfortunately, a different set of attitudes prevails among many of today's civil rights activists. A large segment of the civil rights lobby has turned from the struggle for equality in civil and political rights to the advocacy of redistribution of economic and social rights. And it has made support for the redistribution of these rights a precondition for being part of the movement; anyone who does not support this redistribution is labeled a racist, a bigot, or even a klansman. Some leaders have tried to read many of the original participants, including myself, out of the civil rights movement. More significantly, they are losing the support of the moderate Americans, both black and white, who sustained the movement from the outset.

This struggle has unfortunately repeated itself within the United States Commission on Civil Rights. The two members of the commission remaining as holdovers from its social engineering heyday, Mary Frances Berry and Blandina Cardenas Ramirez, have gone so far as to assert that "[c]ivil rights laws were not passed to give civil rights protection to *all* Americans, as the majority of this commission seems to believe." Their legal analysis is patently false. But Commissioners Berry and Ramirez are right about one thing—the present majority of the commission, subscribing to the fair-shake principle, *does* believe that the civil rights laws and the equal protection clause apply to all Americans. Indeed, the commission has not retreated from its historic commitment to civil rights objectives, as its critics claim; rather, the commission has returned to the principles of color blindness (including a system of color-blind affirmative action), nondiscrimination, and equality of opportunity—the principles that stand behind our civil rights laws.

The fair shakers maintain that there is a crucial difference between civil and political rights on the one hand and social and economic rights on the other. The American system guarantees civil political rights—but it does not guarantee those social and economic rights described in the U.N. Universal Declaration of Human Rights.[13] Guaranteed social and economic rights not only may sharply conflict with civil and political rights, as is the case in many Socialist societies, but may also fail to produce high standards of living. Despite its inevitable inequities, the free-market system—also a traditional element of American society—has provided most of our citizens with living standards that are among the highest in the world. As fair shakers see it, removing all barriers to the exercise of civil and political rights and to an individual's ability to participate in the free-market system is the best possible way to promote justice. In any case, eliminating discrimination and providing a safety net for the truly needy constitute the limits of what the *law* in the American system can do, *if that system is to remain free*.

My participation in the civil rights struggle has shaped my deepest moral and political beliefs. Because the cause of civil rights has meant so much to me, I now feel compelled to register my strong dissent, unpopular though it may be, from what I see as the current direction of the movement. The mantle has now passed to those who believe in enforced equality of results, guaranteed social and economic rights for particular groups, and redistribution of income and jobs. Certainly we can debate ideas such as these in our free society. I ask only that the social engineers be open and candid about their vision for America, and desist from camouflaging their redistributive goals behind the label of "civil rights." Civil rights belong to all Americans; they are too important to be captured by a set of special interest groups.

3. *Persuasion and Distrust*

By RANDALL KENNEDY

Focus
Randall Kennedy sees affirmative action as an important means of overcoming entrenched racial hierarchy in America. It has, he argues, "strikingly benefited blacks as a group and the nation as a whole," and for this reason should be retained. Affirmative action, says Kennedy, has enabled blacks to move into elite universities and into the professions, and has helped to break down debilitating racial stereotypes. While acknowledging that a policy of racial preference may inadvertently stigmatize its intended beneficiaries by suggesting that they are incapable of competing on an equal basis with others, such negative stigmatization, Kennedy believes, must be weighed against all the positive effects that accrue from having larger numbers of blacks participating in the most important institutions of American society. Affirmative action is defended by Kennedy against many common arguments, including the argument that it violates the principle of merit selection. Nonmeritocratic features pervade American society, Kennedy charges, but even if one accepts on principle the idea of merit selection, merit, he suggests, may legitimately be considered in terms of society's greatest needs, and what American society currently needs most is the elevation of blacks to higher positions. As far as the constitutional argument against affirmative action is concerned, Kennedy rejects the color-

blind theory of the Equal Protection Clause. Like Ronald Dworkin (selection 13) and William Brennan (selection 14), he says that white people who are materially disadvantaged by affirmative action policies have no constitutional claim because the damage done to them is an incidental consequence of society meeting a compelling need. The policy, he says, "does not derive from a scheme animated by racial prejudice." Kennedy also rejects the argument of those who claim that affirmative action is a betrayal of the ideals of the civil rights movement. While acknowledging that affirmative action is inconsistent with many statements made by earlier civil rights advocates, such statements, Kennedy speculates, may have been made for tactical reasons, and in any event, the older civil rights leaders, he believes, should not be seen as founding fathers whose views are binding on posterity for all times. Racial equality is not a static concept, but a "living idealization" whose meaning changes with changing historical circumstances. Kennedy concludes with reflections on Ronald Reagan and his administration, and suggests that much of the opposition to affirmative action is motivated by white-supremacist thinking and by a covert desire to maintain a system of racial subordination in America.

Randall Kennedy is an assistant professor of law at Harvard Law School.

THE CONTROVERSY OVER affirmative action[1] constitutes the most salient current battlefront in the ongoing conflict over the status of the Negro in American life. No domestic struggle has been more protracted or more riddled with ironic complication. One frequently noted irony is that the affirmative action controversy has contributed significantly to splintering the coalition principally responsible for the civil rights revolution. That coalition was comprised of a broad array of groups—liberal Democrats, moderate Republicans, the national organizations of the black and Jewish communities, organized labor and others—that succeeded in invalidating de jure segregation and passing far-reaching legislation in support of the rights of blacks, including the Civil Rights Act of 1964 and the Voting Rights Act of 1965.

For over a decade this coalition has been riven by bitter disagreement over the means by which American society should attempt to overcome its racist past. Opponents of affirmative action maintain that commitment to a nonracist social environment requires strict color blindness in decisionmaking as both a strategy and a goal. In their view, "one gets beyond racism by getting beyond it now: by a complete, resolute, and credible commitment *never* to tolerate in one's own life—or in the life or practices of one's government—the differential treatment of other human beings by race" (William Van Alstyne). Proponents of affirmative action insist that only *malign* racial distinctions should be prohibited; they favor *benign* distinctions that favor blacks. Their view is that "[i]n order to get beyond racism, we must first take race into account" and that "in order to treat some persons equally, we must treat them differently" (Justice Blackmun).

I conclude that affirmative action should generally be retained as a tool of public policy because, on balance, it is useful in overcoming entrenched racial hierarchy. In addition I argue that division within the civil rights coalition is not the *only* conflict permeating the affirmative action controversy. Also involved is a much older conflict involving sectors of our society that have never authentically repudiated the "old-style religion" of white supremacy. The most important of these sectors is the Reagan administration. I contend that a tenacious and covert resistance to further erosion of racial hierarchy explains much of the Reagan administration's racial policy, especially its attacks on affirmative action.

I focus on both overt and covert discourse, because the affirmative action debate cannot be understood without acknowledging simultaneously the force of the openly stated arguments for and against preferential treatment and the submerged intuitions that disguise themselves with these arguments. To disregard either of these features of the debate is to ignore an essential aspect of the controversy. To appreciate both is to recognize the frustrating complexity of our racial situation.

The Case for Affirmative Action

Affirmative action has strikingly benefited blacks as a group and the nation as a whole. It has enabled blacks to attain occupational and educational advancement in numbers and at a pace that would otherwise have been impossible.[2] These breakthroughs engender self-perpetuating benefits: the accumulation of valuable experience, the expansion of a professional class able to pass its material advantages and elevated aspirations to subsequent generations, the eradication of debilitating stereotypes, and the inclusion of black participants in the making of consequential decisions affecting black interests. Without affirmative action, continued access for black applicants to college and professional education would be drastically narrowed. To insist, for example, upon the total exclusion of racial factors in admission decisions, especially at elite institutions, would mean classes of college, professional, and graduate students that are virtually devoid of Negro representation.

Furthermore, the benefits of affirmative action redound not

only to blacks but to the nation as a whole. For example, the virtual absence of black police even in overwhelmingly black areas helped spark the ghetto rebellions of the 1960s. The integration of police forces through strong affirmative action measures has often led to better relations between minority communities and the police, a result that improves public safety for all. Positive externalities have accompanied affirmative action programs in other contexts as well,[3] most importantly by teaching whites that blacks, too, are capable of handling responsibility, dispensing knowledge, and applying valued skills.

The Claim That Affirmative Action Harms Blacks

In the face of arguments in favor of affirmative action, opponents of the policy frequently reply that it actually harms its ostensible beneficiaries. Various interrelated claims undergird the argument that affirmative action is detrimental to the Negro. The most weighty claim is that preferential treatment exacerbates racial resentments, entrenches racial divisiveness, and thereby undermines the consensus necessary for effective reform. The problem with this view is that intense white resentment has accompanied every effort to undo racial subordination no matter how careful the attempt to anticipate and mollify the reaction. The Supreme Court, for example, tried mightily to preempt white resistance to school desegregation by directing that it be implemented with "all deliberate speed." This attempt, however, to defuse white resistance may well have caused the opposite effect and, in any event, doomed from the outset the constitutional rights of a generation of black school children. Given the apparent inevitability of white resistance and the uncertain efficacy of containment, proponents of racial justice should be wary of allowing fear of white backlash to limit the range of reforms pursued. This admonition is particularly appropriate with respect to affirmative action insofar as it creates vital opportunities the value of which likely outweigh their cost in social friction. A second part of the argument that affirmative action hurts blacks is the claim that it stigmatizes them by implying that they simply cannot compete on an equal basis with whites. Moreover, the pall cast by preferential treatment is feared to be pervasive, hovering over blacks who have attained positions without the aid of affirmative action as well as over those who have been accorded preferential treatment. I do not doubt that affirmative action causes some stigmatizing effect. It is unrealistic to think, however, that affirmative action causes most white disparagement of the abilities of blacks.[4] Such disparagement, buttressed for decades by the rigid exclusion of blacks from educational and employment opportunities, is precisely what engendered the explosive crisis to which affirmative action is a response. Although it is widely assumed that "qualified" blacks are now in great demand, with virtually unlimited possibilities for recognition, blacks continue to encounter prejudice that ignores or minimizes their talent.[5] In the end, the uncertain extent to which affirmative action diminishes the accomplishments of blacks must be balanced against the stigmatization that occurs when blacks are virtually absent from important institutions in the society. The presence of blacks across the broad spectrum of institutional settings upsets conventional stereotypes about the place of the Negro and acculturates the public to the idea that blacks can and must participate in all areas of our national life. This positive result of affirmative action outweighs any stigma that the policy causes.[6]

A third part of the argument against affirmative action is the claim that it saps the internal morale of blacks. It renders them vulnerable to a dispiriting anxiety that they have not truly earned whatever positions or honors they have attained.[7] Moreover, it causes some blacks to lower their own expectations of themselves. Having grown accustomed to the extra boost provided by preferential treatment, some blacks simply do not try as hard as they otherwise would. There is considerable power to this claim; unaided accomplishment does give rise to a special pride felt by both the individual achiever and her community. But the suggestion that affirmative action plays a major role in undermining the internal morale of the black community is erroneous.

Although I am unaware of any systematic evidence on the self-image of beneficiaries of affirmative action, my own strong impression is that black beneficiaries do not see their attainments as tainted or undeserved—and for good reason.[8] First, they correctly view affirmative action as rather modest compensation for the long period of racial subordination suffered by blacks as a group. Thus they do not feel that they have been merely *given* a preference; rather, they see affirmative discrimination as a form of social justice. Second, and more importantly, many black beneficiaries of affirmative action view claims of meritocracy with skepticism. They recognize that in many instances the objection that affirmative action represents a deviation from meritocratic standards is little more than disappointed nostalgia for a golden age that never really existed. Overt exclusion of blacks from public and private institutions of education and employment was one massive affront to meritocratic pretensions. Moreover, a long-standing and pervasive feature of our society is the importance of a wide range of nonobjective, nonmeritocratic factors influencing the distribution of opportunity. The significance of personal associations and informal networks is what gives durability and resonance to the adage, "It's not *what* you know, it's *who* you know." As Professor Wasserstrom wryly observes, "Would anyone claim that Henry Ford II [was] head of the Ford Motor Company because he [was] the most qualified person for the job?"

Finally, and most importantly, many beneficiaries of affirmative action recognize the thoroughly political—which is to say contestable—nature of "merit"; they realize that it is a malleable concept, determined not by immanent, preexisting standards but rather by the perceived needs of society. Inasmuch as the elevation of blacks addresses pressing social needs, they rightly insist that considering a black's race as part of the bundle of traits that constitute "merit" is entirely appropriate.

A final and related objection to affirmative action is that it frequently aids those blacks who need it least and who can least plausibly claim to suffer the vestiges of past discrimination—the offspring of black middle-class parents seeking preferential treatment in admission to elite universities and black entrepreneurs seeking guaranteed set-asides for minority contractors on projects supported by the federal government. This objection too is unpersuasive. First, it ignores the large extent to which affirmative action has pried open opportunities for blue-collar black workers. Second, it assumes that affirmative action should be provided only to the most deprived strata of the black community or to those who can best document their victimization. In many circumstances, however, affirmative action has developed from the premise that special aid should be given to strategically important sectors of the black community—for example, those with the threshold ability to integrate the professions. Third, although affirmative action has primarily benefitted the black middle class, that is no reason to condemn preferential treatment. All that fact indicates is the necessity for additional social intervention to address unmet needs in those sectors of the black community left untouched by affirmative action. One thing that proponents of affirmative action have neglected to emphasize strongly enough is that affirmative discrimination is but part—indeed a rather small part—of the needed response to the appalling crisis besetting black communities. What is so remarkable—and ominous—about the affirmative action debate is that so modest a reform calls forth such powerful resistance.

Does Affirmative Action Violate the Constitution?

The constitutional argument against affirmative action proceeds as follows: *All* governmental distinctions based on race are presumed to be illegal and can escape that presumption only by meeting the exacting requirements of "strict scrutiny." Because the typical affirmative action program cannot meet these requirements, most such programs are unconstitutional. Behind this theory lies a conviction that has attained its most passionate and oft-quoted articulation in Alexander Bickel's statement:

> The lesson of the great decisions of the Supreme Court and the lesson of contemporary history have been the same for at least a generation: discrimination on the basis of race is illegal, immoral, unconstitutional, inherently wrong, and destructive of democratic society. Now this is to be unlearned and we are told that this is not a matter of fundamental principle but only a matter of whose ox is gored.

Among the attractions of this theory are its symmetry and simplicity. It commands that the government be color-blind in its treatment of persons, that it accord benefits and burdens to black and white individuals according to precisely the *same* criteria—no matter whose ox is gored. According to its proponents, this theory dispenses with manipulable sociological investigations and provides a clear *rule* that compels consistent judicial application.

In response, I would first note that the color-blind theory of the Constitution is precisely that—a "theory," one of any number of competing theories that seek to interpret the Fourteenth Amendment's delphic proscription of state action that denies any person "the equal protection of the laws." Implicitly recognizing that neither a theory of original intent nor a theory of textual construction provides suitable guidance, Professor Bickel suggests that a proper resolution of the affirmative action dispute can be derived from "the great decisions of the Supreme Court." Certainly what Bickel had in mind were *Brown* v. *Board of Education* and its immediate progeny, the cases that established the foundation of our postsegregation Constitution. To opponents of affirmative action, the lesson of these cases is that, except in the narrowest, most exigent circumstances, race can play no legitimate role in governmental decisionmaking.

This view, however, is too abstract and ahistorical. In the forties, fifties, and early sixties, against the backdrop of laws that used racial distinctions to exclude Negroes from opportunities available to white citizens, it seemed that racial subjugation could be overcome by mandating the application of race-blind law.[9] In retrospect, however, it appears that the concept of race blindness was simply a proxy for the fundamental demand that racial subjugation be eradicated. This demand, which matured over time in the face of myriad sorts of opposition, focused upon the *condition* of racial subjugation; its target was not only procedures that overtly excluded Negroes on the basis of race, but also the self-perpetuating dynamics of subordination that had survived the demise of American apartheid. The opponents of affirmative action have stripped the historical context from the demand for race-blind law. They have fashioned this demand into a new totem and insist on deference to it no matter what its effects upon the very group the Fourteenth Amendment was created to protect. *Brown* and its progeny do not stand for the abstract principle that governmental distinctions based on race are unconstitutional. Rather, those great cases, forged by the gritty particularities of the struggle against white racism, stand for the proposition that the Constitution prohibits any arrangements imposing racial subjugation—whether such arrangements are ostensibly race-neutral or even ostensibly race-blind.

This interpretation, which articulates a principle of antisubjugation rather than antidiscrimination, typically encounters two closely related objections. The first objection is the claim that the constitutional injury done to a white whose chances for obtaining some scarce opportunity are diminished because of race-based allocation schemes is legally indistinguishable from that suffered by a black victim of racial exclusion. Second, others argue that affirmative discrimination based on racial distinctions cannot be satisfactorily differentiated from racial subjugation absent controversial sociological judgments that are inappropriate to the judicial role.

As to the first objection, the injury suffered by white "victims" of affirmative action does not properly give rise to a constitutional claim, because the damage does not derive from a scheme animated by racial prejudice. Whites with certain credentials may be excluded from particular opportunities they would receive if they were black. But this diminished opportunity is simply an incidental consequence of addressing a compelling societal need: undoing the subjugation of the Negro. Whites who would be admitted to professional schools in the absence of affirmative action policies are not excluded merely because of prejudice, as were countless numbers of Negroes until fairly recently. Rather, whites are excluded "because of a rational calculation about the socially most beneficial use of limited resources for [professional] education" (Ronald Dworkin).

As to the second objection, I concede that distinctions between affirmative and malign discrimination cannot be made in the absence of controversial sociological judgments. I reject the proposition, however, that drawing these distinctions is inappropriate to the judicial role. Such a proposition rests upon the

assumption that there exists a judicial method wholly independent of sociological judgment. That assumption is false; to some
extent, whether explicitly or implicitly, *every* judicial decision
rests upon certain premises regarding the irreducibly controversial nature of social reality. The question, therefore, is not
whether a court will make sociological judgments, but the content of the sociological judgments it must inevitably make.

Prior to *Brown,* the Supreme Court's validation of segregation
statutes rested upon the premise that they did not unequally
burden the Negro. A perceived difficulty in invalidating segregation statutes was that, as written, such laws were race-neutral;
they excluded white children from Negro schools just as they
excluded Negro children from white schools. The Court finally
recognized in *Brown* that racial subjugation constituted the
social meaning of segregation laws. To determine that social
meaning, the Court had to look past form into substance and
judge the legitimacy of segregation laws given their intended and
actual effects. Just as the "neutrality" of the segregation laws
obfuscated racial subjugation, so too may the formal neutrality
of race-blind policies also obfuscate the perpetuation of racial
subjugation. That issue can only be explored by an inquiry into
the context of the race-blind policy at issue, an inquiry that
necessarily entails judicial sociology.

The Need For Analysis of Motives

There remains a disturbing lacuna in the scholarly de-
bate.Whether racism is partly responsible for the growing opposition to affirmative action is a question that is virtually absent
from many of the leading articles on the subject. These articles
typically portray the conflict over affirmative action as occurring
in the context of an overriding commitment to racial fairness
and equality shared by *all* the important participants in the
debate. For example, a recent article by Professors Richard
Fallon and Paul Weiler depicts the conflict in terms of "contending models of racial justice"—a depiction suggesting that, despite its bitterness, the affirmative action debate is at least
bounded by common abhorrence of explicit racial hierarchy.
This portrait, however, of conflict-within-consensus is all too

genial. It conjures up the absurd image of Benjamin Hooks and William Bradford Reynolds embracing one another as ideological brethren, differing on the discrete issue of affirmative action but united on the fundamentals of racial fairness.[10] It obscures the emotions that color the affirmative action debate and underestimates the alienation that separates antagonists. It ignores those who believe that much of the campaign against affirmative action is merely the latest in a long series of white reactions against efforts to elevate the status of the Negro in American society. These observers perceive critics of affirmative action not merely as *opponents* but as *enemies*. They perceive ostensibly nonracist objections to affirmative action as rationalizations of white supremacy. They fear that the campaign against affirmative action is simply the opening wedge of a broader effort to recapture territory "lost" in the civil rights revolution of the 1960s.[11] And it is precisely this apprehension that explains the bitterness and desperation with which they wage the affirmative action struggle—emotions that are simply inexplicable in terms of the picture of race relations portrayed by conventional analyses.[12]

The conventional portrait also implicitly excludes from consideration those whose opposition to affirmative action stems from racism. It concedes the presence of prejudice "out there" in the workday world of ordinary citizens. But it assumes that "in here"—in the realm of scholarly discourse and the creation of public policy—prejudice plays no role. In other words, conventional scholarship leaves largely unexamined the possibility that the campaigns against affirmative action now being waged by political, judicial, and intellectual elites reflect racially selective indifference, antipathy born of prejudice, or strategies that seek to capitalize on widespread racial resentments.

Motivation, however, always matters in determining the meaning of a policy, although it is not all that matters. Moreover, attentiveness to motive should be an important aspect of ongoing analysis of the affirmative action controversy for other reasons as well. The simple but basic desire to document accurately the history of our era is justification enough for inquiring into the motives animating political action. That inquiry is essential to

answering the most difficult of the questions that beset historians—the question of *why* particular actions are taken, given
decisions made. Furthermore baleful consequences attend dependence upon false records of social reality. After all, blindness
to contemporary social realities helped spawn the monstrous lie,
propagated by the Supreme Court in *Plessy* v. *Ferguson,* that
the segregation of the Negro had nothing to do with racial
oppression. Bitter experience should remind us, then, that in
matters touching race relations there is an especially pressing
need to keep the record straight.

The Case of the Reagan Administration

A good way to begin setting the record straight is by assessing
the motives of those in high public office. Suspicion characterizes the disposition with which I begin that assessment. My
suspicion stems from the recognition that racism in America is
an enormously powerful ideological institution, considerably
older than the political institutions of our republic, and has often
influenced the actions of the executive branch and indeed all
levels of government. My preexisting distrust is heightened,
however, by the particular background of the Reagan administration and, more specifically, by the political biography of Ronald
Reagan himself.

President Reagan now declares himself "heart and soul in
favor of the things that have been done in the name of civil rights
and desegregation." This commitment, he maintains, accounts
for his opposition to affirmative discrimination.[13] What justifies
skepticism toward the president's account is his long history of
suspect views on racial issues. His active opposition to racial
distinctions *benefitting* blacks is not matched by analogous
opposition to racial distinctions *harming* Negroes. Indeed, a
strikingly consistent feature of President Reagan's long political
career is his resistance to practically every major political effort
to eradicate racism or to contain its effects. During the height of
the civil rights revolution, he opposed the Civil Rights Act of
1964, the Voting Rights Act of 1965 and the Open Housing Act
of 1968, legislation that his own assistant attorney general has

rightly described as "designed to make equal opportunity a reality."

Of course, although opposition to this landmark legislation is itself tremendously revealing, limits exist to the inferences that one can properly draw from positions adopted over twenty years ago. But President Reagan has provided additional reasons for distrusting his explanation of his racial policies. Repeatedly his administration has shown callous disregard for the particular interests of blacks and resisted measures designed to erode racial hierarchy. These actions include the administration's opposition (1) to the amendments that strengthened and extended the Voting Rights Act, (2) to anything more than the most cramped reading of the Civil Rights Act of 1964, (3) to creating a national holiday honoring Dr. Martin Luther King, Jr., (4) to maintaining the integrity of agencies involved in federal enforcement of civil rights, and (5) to imposing sanctions on South Africa for its policy of apartheid.

Perhaps the most instructive episode was the position the Reagan administration took in the now infamous *Bob Jones University* case on the issue of tax exemption for private schools that discriminate against Negroes. The platform of the Republican Party in 1980 promised that its leaders would "halt the unconstitutional regulatory vendetta launched . . . against independent schools." President Reagan fulfilled that pledge by reversing the policy of the Internal Revenue Service (IRS) denying exempt status to discriminatory private schools. The administration stated that it had acted out of a desire to end the IRS's usurpation of powers beyond those authorized by Congress. Subsequent revelations called the honesty of this explanation into doubt. That apparent dishonesty—coupled with the administration's overwhelming defeat in the Supreme Court—turned the tax exemption imbroglio into one of the administration's most politically embarrassing moments. For present purposes, however, the significance of the episode lies in the stark illustration it provides of the underlying impulse behind the administration's racial policy—an impulse to protect the prerogatives of whites at the least hint of encroachment by claims of racial justice.

There are, of course, alternative explanations to the one above. One could disaggregate the record of Ronald Reagan and his administration and rationalize each position on a case-by-case basis, by reference to concerns having nothing to do with racist sentiments or strategies. Concerns about freedom of association might have prompted Reagan's opposition to the Civil Rights Act of 1964. Concerns about federalism might account for his opposition to the Voting Rights Act of 1965. Concerns about the proper allocation of responsibility between the executive and legislative branches might explain the administration's stance in the tax exemption controversy. And authentic regard for the philosophical premises of individualism might theoretically explain the administration's opposition to affirmative action.

The problem with this mode of defense is that it ignores the strong *systematic* tilt of the administration's actions. It disregards as well the political milieu in which debate over affirmative action and other racial policies has been waged over the past decade—a period during which there has been a discernible attenuation of public commitment to racial justice and, even more troubling, a startling reemergence of overt racial animosity. The Reagan administration's policies reflect, reinforce, and capitalize on widespread feelings that blacks have received an undeserved amount of the nation's attention. Unburdened by the inhibitions imposed by public office, ordinary white citizens have expressed quite openly the feelings that color their analysis of the affirmative action issue. The Reagan administration has expertly tapped these feelings for political gain by dint of arguments for race-blindness that are, in fact, exquisitely attuned to the racial sensitivities of the dominant white majority. Those who have ignored racism as an important element of the affirmative action controversy should consider SPONGE (The Society for the Prevention of Niggers Getting Everything), an organization of disaffected whites in the Canarsie section of Brooklyn, New York, whose arresting title is more revealing of at least part of the opposition to affirmative action than many commentators seem willing to acknowledge.

Conclusion

In the end, perhaps the most striking feature of the affirmative action debate is the extent to which it highlights the crisis of trust besetting American race relations. Proponents of affirmative action view their opponents with suspicion for good reason. They know that not all of their opponents are racist; they also know that many of them are. Such suspicions corrode reasoned discourse. Contending claims to truth and justice are often reduced by opposing camps to disguised grasps for power and privilege. It would be a mistake, however, to suppose that the antidote to such corrosion is willful blindness to pretext. The only thing that will enable affirmative action—or any similarly controversial policy—to be debated in an atmosphere free of suspicion is for the surrounding social context to be decisively transformed. The essential element of this transformation is the creation of a sentiment of community strong enough to enable each group to entrust its fate to the good faith and decency of the other—the sort of feeling that in the 1960s impelled groups of black and white mothers to exchange their children during civil rights marches. Only the presence of such sentiment can enable the force of persuasion to supplant the force of distrust.

At this point, *even if* a demonstration of policy and fact decisively pointed toward eliminating affirmative action, many of its proponents might well refuse to recognize such a showing and continue to support preferential treatment. Their reaction would stem in large measure from their fears regarding the ulterior motives of their opponents. This is another reason why, as a practical matter, motive is so important. As long as suspect motivation justifiably remains a point of apprehension, inquiry into "the merits" of affirmative action will play a peripheral, instrumental role in the resolution of the controversy.

4. Ethnic Tribalism and Human Personhood

By RUSSELL NIELI

Focus
Russell Nieli takes up the issue of preferential treatment in employment, and claims that such a policy is a betrayal of the highest ideals of the civil rights movement of the 1950s and early 1960s. The essence of that movement, as he sees it, was a respect for the dignity and worth of individual human beings each seen as distinct persons rather than as stereotyped representatives of racial or ethnic tribes. The 1964 Civil Rights Act, he says, is based upon a personalistic type of thinking that has both liberal and Christian roots—a fact he tries to illustrate through extensive quotations from Martin Luther King, Jr., and other supporters of the act. The policy of affirmative action, Nieli contends, reflects an essentially tribalistic mentality that has its origins in the American South. It is a policy, he says, that was instituted at the behest of militant black, Hispanic, and American Indian leaders who cared little about the injustice or injury they would be doing to others.

Nieli offers an extensive psychological account of the motives behind the upper-middle-class white male judges and bureaucrats who helped institute the affirmative action policy, and finds them driven by a combination of compassion, guilt, self-righteousness, romanticism, fear, and a desire for power. He says that affirmative action is based upon an underlying social mythology that has served to desensitize people to the great racial, ethnic, and socioeconomic diversity actually found in America. As an alternative to racially and ethnically based affirmative action, Nieli proposes a policy of treating all similarly disadvantaged underdogs as equal, and all persons as representatives of only themselves and their own past history. The article concludes with a warning of the grave social dangers of ethnic tribalism when it is not counterbalanced by a more universal principle.

Russell Nieli received his Ph.D. from Princeton University, and for the past two years has been a part-time lecturer in Princeton's Department of Politics. He has published numerous articles and is author of the book *Wittgenstein: From Mysticism to Ordinary Language.*

Deeply rooted in our religious heritage is the conviction that every man is an heir to a legacy of dignity and worth. Our Judeo-Christian tradition refers to this inherent dignity of man in the Biblical term 'the image of God.' . . . Every human being has etched in his personality the indelible stamp of the Creator. Every man must be respected because God loves him. The worth of an individual does not lie in the measure of his intellect, his racial origin or his social position. Human worth lies in relatedness to God. An individual has value because he has value to God. Whenever this is recognized, 'whiteness' and 'blackness' pass away as determinants in a relationship and 'son' and 'brother' are substituted.—MARTIN LUTHER KING, JR. (1967).

You guys have been practicing discrimination for years. Now it is our turn.—Justice THURGOOD MARSHALL (1974) [discussing the *DeFunis* case with William O. Douglas].

Civil rights laws were not passed to give civil rights protection to all Americans.—MARY FRANCES BERRY and BLANDINA CARDENAS RAMIREZ (1985).

DURING THE LENGTHY debate over the 1964 Civil Rights Bill (HR 7192) a number of southern opponents of the bill, in an attempt to raise public fears, claimed that the section of the bill outlawing discrimination in employment would lead to the imposition by federal enforcement agencies of racial "quota" hiring in order to achieve a desirable "racial balance." The term "discrimination," it was pointed out, was not specifically defined in the bill, and so, it was held, might be interpreted by federal authorities to mean the lack of proportional representation of the members of various racial and ethnic groups in a given employer's workforce. This contention of the southern opponents was, of course, nothing more than a scare tactic, as the clear wording of the bill precluded any such interpretation and made hiring based on racial or ethnic criteria of any kind, quota or otherwise, clearly illegal.[1] Relevant sections of what

A condensed version of this article appeared in *This World* (Fall 1987). Reprinted with permission of *This World*.

were to become Titles VI and VII of the Civil Rights Act of 1964 read as follows:

Section 601

No *person* in the United States shall, on the ground of race, color, or national origin, be excluded from participation in, be denied the benefits of, or be subjected to discrimination under any program or activity receiving Federal financial assistance (emphasis added).

Section 703

(a) It shall be an unlawful employment practice for an employer:

(1) to fail or refuse to hire or to discharge *any individual,* or otherwise to discriminate against *any individual* with respect to his compensation, terms, conditions, or privileges of employment, because of *such individual's* race, color, religion, sex, or national origin; or

(2) to limit, segregate, or classify his employees in any way which would deprive or tend to deprive *any individual* of employment opportunities or otherwise adversely affect his status as an employee, because of *such individual's* race, color, religion, sex, or national origin.

(b) It shall be an unlawful employment practice for an employment agency to fail or refuse to refer for employment, or otherwise to discriminate against *any individual* because of his race, color, religion, sex, or national origin, or to classify or refer for employment *any individual* on the basis of his race, color, religion, sex, or national origin.

(c) It shall be an unlawful employment practice for a labor organization:

(1) to exclude or to expel from its membership, or otherwise to discriminate against *any individual* because of his race, color, religion, sex, or national origin;

(2) to limit, segregate, or classify its membership, or to classify, or fail to refuse to refer for employment *any individual,* in any way which would deprive or tend to deprive *any individual* of employment opportunities, or would limit such employment opportunities or otherwise

adversely affect his status as an employee or as an applicant for employment, because of *such individual's* race, color, religion, sex, or national origin;

(d) It shall be an unlawful employment practice for any employer, labor organization, or joint labor-management committee . . . to discriminate against *any individual* because of his race, color, religion, sex, or national origin in admission to, or employment in, any program established to provide apprenticeship or other training (emphasis added).

The language of the bill was clearly the language of persons and of individuals, and guaranteed to each and every one of them the right to be considered for employment and promotion on a strictly race-, ethnicity-, gender-, and religion-neutral basis. Here, of course, the law was continuing in the tradition of the Fourteenth Amendment to the federal Constitution, which had also spoken of persons ("No State shall . . . deprive any person of life, liberty, or property, without due process of law; nor deny to any person within its jurisdiction the equal protection of the laws"), as well as of the many state fair employment practice laws after which Title VII of the 1964 Civil Rights Act was patterned.

In order to counter the scare tactics of the southern senators, the supporters of the bill, led by Majority Whip Hubert Humphrey, and the two floor captains of Title VII, Senators Joseph Clark and Clifford Case, went on record again and again to reassure their colleagues that Title VII's guarantees against hiring discrimination applied to all people equally and not just to blacks or members of any particular racial or ethnic group. They also went on to stress the fact that any attempt to maintain a racial balance would not only *not* be required by the bill, but would be clearly illegal according to its provisions. Senator Humphrey was particularly forceful in speaking out against what he called at one point the "uninterrupted flow of nightmarish propaganda" and "wholesale distortions" that were attempting to mislead the public concerning the nature of the proposed bill and were responsible, in Humphrey's view, for the strong showing George Wallace had recently made in the Wisconsin presidential primary (110 *Cong. Rec.,* pp. 11846-47). In order to counter these distortions, Humphrey had his staff draft a carefully worded interpretive statement dealing with all the major provisions of the bill, and had the statement read and approved by all of the bill's floor managers in both houses of Congress. On the question of Title VII, the statement addressed itself specifically to the southern charge that the bill would require the preferential hiring of blacks:

> [Title VII] does not provide that any preferential treatment in employment shall be given to Negroes or to any other persons or groups. It does not provide that any quota system may be established to maintain racial balance in employment. In fact, the title would prohibit preferential treatment for any particular group, and *any person,* whether or not a member of any minority group, would be permitted to file a complaint of discriminatory employment practices (110 *Cong. Rec.,* p. 11848, emphasis added).

Senators Clark and Case had stressed earlier that Title VII would prohibit any attempt to maintain a racial balance, since this would involve hiring on the basis of race and would thus discriminate against individuals:

> There is no requirement in Title VII that an employer maintain a racial balance in his work force. On the contrary, any deliberate attempt to maintain a racial balance, whatever such a balance may be, would involve a violation of Title VII because maintaining such a balance would require an employer to hire or to refuse to hire on the basis of race. It must be emphasized that discrimination is prohibited as to *any individual* (110 *Cong. Rec.,* p. 7213, emphasis added).

Senator Clark also had the Justice Department draw up a statement specifically addressing itself to a number of charges that had been made against Titles VI and VII of the bill by Senator Lister Hill of Alabama. In regard to the charge that the proposed law would require employees to maintain a racial balance, the Justice Department's memorandum offered the following rebuttal:

> Finally it has been asserted Title VII would impose a require-
> ment for "racial balance." This is incorrect. . . . No employer
> is required to hire an individual because that individual is a
> Negro. No employer is required to maintain any ratio of
> Negroes to whites, Jews to Gentiles, Italians to English, or
> women to men. . . . On the contrary, any deliberate attempt
> to maintain a given balance would almost certainly run afoul
> of Title VII because it would involve a failure or refusal to
> hire some *individual* because of his race, color, religion, sex,
> or national origin (110 *Cong. Rec.,* p. 7207, emphasis added).[2]

While the criticisms of the southern senators lacked all substance, and were essentially a tactical maneuver designed to
instill fear and doubt into the public mind, they nevertheless
reflected a peculiarly southern way of thinking—or at least a
way of thinking that was much more deeply rooted in the
American South than elsewhere—which was both incompatible
with, and hostile to, the mode of thinking that had come to
dominate American society under the impact of the civil rights
movement of the 1950s and early 1960s. These two contrasting
modes of thought might be characterized by the terms "tribalism" and "personalism."

Tribalism can be defined as that mode of consciousness that
tends to view human beings, not as unique persons, but as
stereotyped and depersonalized representatives of larger racial
or ethnic collectives, with the collectives themselves being seen
as singular or homogeneous entities, rather than as plural or
diverse ones. Personalism, on the other hand, is a mode of
consciousness that seeks to view human beings as distinct and
unique individuals ("persons"), who are capable of relating to,
and communing with, others of their kind on the basis of mutual
respect and equality. The two modes of consciousness are
mutually incompatible, with the latter, personalistic mode, representing a higher, more differentiated type of thinking than the
former, insofar as its terms and conceptual structures can be

used to explain and criticize the tribalistic mode of thought, but the reverse is not the case. The personalistic mentality can understand—and criticize—the tribalistic, but the tribalistic cannot understand the personalistic. It is something like the relationship between John Stuart Mill's higher and lower pleasures: a Socrates can comprehend the pleasures of the pig and the fool, but the reverse is not so. For people who had grown up, as the southern opponents of the Civil Rights Act had, in a legally segregated and highly race-conscious society, where people tended to be viewed less as individual persons than as representatives of racial or ethnic tribes, it was not easy to comprehend a law in which individual persons were each respected as such, and racial and ethnic tribal associations given no recognition whatever. When one views what has transpired in America since the late 1960s and early 1970s, particularly in regard to the government policy known as "affirmative action," it must certainly be seen as one of the grim ironies of modern American history that the southern tribalistic mode of consciousness would not only come to dominate much of the country, but would do so under the leadership of a national elite that claimed to be furthering the cause of "civil rights."

Personalism Explained

According to the personalistic philosophy human beings are each individually centers of Meaning and Mystery. They are not Hegelian moments in a collective group history, nor are they faceless, depersonalized abstractions upon which to project one's stereotyped image of a group, be this image positive, negative, or some combination of the two. In claiming that each human being is a center of Meaning, personalism contends that human societies are not to be viewed as single, unified, collective worlds, but as pluralities of many separate personal worlds, each interacting with other separate personal worlds, in an ongoing drama of human history. While one can speak meaningfully of many collective and communal activities that these personal worlds engage in, each world remains in and of itself a separate and distinct unit of meaning, each with its own unique experiences, its own unique struggles, and its own personal time-frame of reference. Human persons according to the personalistic philosophy, have an indissolvable unity to their being, to their life and thoughts, their actions and feelings, which groups of human beings simply cannot have, not even the most intimate group of the family.

When personalism contends that human beings are centers of Mystery, what is meant is that every person has a dimension of Depth to his being, and a private relationship to this dimension of Depth, which has about it something that is sacred. It is this dimension of Depth in each person, and the special relationship that each person has to this dimension, that forms the basis of our public claims to a respect for privacy, a respect for conscience, and a respect for personal religious belief. The Depth in each person enters into a region that is mysterious and unfathomable, and that the public has no right to enter.[3]

It is sometimes charged that the personalistic philosophy is "atomistic" or "antisocial," but this is based upon a complete misunderstanding. Persons are centers of Meaning and Mystery, and they are also centers of creativity and energy. From their vital centers outward then, persons engage other persons in society on various levels of intimacy and concern. Such social engagements can range anywhere from mutually self-interested business relationships up to the most intimate relationships of interpersonal love (e.g., Buber's I-Thou relationships). Various social virtues, including charity, civic-mindedness, brotherly love, and certain forms of patriotism, are in no way antithetical to the personalistic perspective. The personalistic perspective, however, is incompatible with any kind of group-think that attempts to wrench the center of Meaning and Mystery out of individual persons, and transfer it to a nation, a tribe, a class, or any other collective entity conceived of as a mysterious Super-Person. Personalism holds that whenever Meaning and Mystery are wrenched out of the Depth of individual souls and transferred to a collective entity of any kind an ultimate violation is committed, with absurdity and mystification being the inevitable results, as one can readily discern from all the claptrap that has been written about a *Volksgeist,* a Race-Soul, the General Will, the National Destiny, and the like. The personalistic philosophy is hostile to any type of collective self-worship, to any type of group-deification, and to any and all types of political and social movements that demand of their adherents that they rate their nationality, their ethnicity, or their class affiliations higher than their individual humanity.[4]

Personalism, at least of the type outlined here, is thus the very opposite of "atomistic individualism." Atomized individuals are not persons, they are not centers of Meaning and Mystery; rather, they are people who for one reason or another have been cut off from the deepest sources of their own unique personhood and, as a result, lack all sense of individual wholeness and human worth. In fact, atomized individuals are the very kind of people who tend to become ethnic tribalists. Lacking all sense of their own personal meaning and worth, cut off from the Depth of their own being, atomized individuals will often try to fill the existential vacuum that they experience in themselves through the desperate appropriation of a group identity. This group identity then comes to take the place of the missing Depth in their lives, and is worshipped as if it were a divinity.

American Personalism: Liberal and Christian Roots

The type of personalistic thinking embodied in the 1964 Civil Rights Act grew out of two complementary strains in American thought, the first being the Judeo-Christian religious tradition (and the closely related tradition of New England transcendentalism), the second being the liberal-Jeffersonian tradition, especially as this was embodied in the Declaration of Independence. From the Jewish-Christian religious tradition, personalism took over the idea that each human being is loved by God and has a separate inner relationship to God irrespective of whatever social relationships such a person may have. God, according to the Jewish-Christian tradition, judges all men on the basis of their individual moral excellencies and personal qualities, and this is the way men are to view one another. Personalism also took over from the Western religious tradition the idea that each human being is created in the "image of God" and thus manifests in some way a godlike nature that commands the respect of all people. A final idea that was taken over from the religious tradition was that all human beings are children of God and members of a single human family.

From the Declaration of Independence and the liberal tradition, personalism took over the notion that all human beings have individual human rights that are conferred equally upon all, and that it is the responsibility of government to protect these rights. The key passage in the Declaration, of course, comes after the words "we hold these truths" ("We hold these truths to be self-evident, that all men are created equal, that they are endowed by their Creator with certain unalienable rights . . . that to secure these rights governments are instituted among men"). The liberal tradition also provided personalism with the important idea of the citizen, and of the equality of rights of all citizens.

The influence of both these traditions, the Judeo-Christian and the liberal-Jeffersonian, on the personalistic outlook of many of the supporters of the Civil Rights Act can be well illustrated by remarks taken from three key figures in the struggle for the law's passage: President Lyndon Johnson, Senator Joseph Clark, and the Reverend Martin Luther King, Jr. Shortly before signing the Civil Rights Bill into law on July 2, 1964, President Johnson went on national television to explain to the American public the nature and purpose of the new law. His remarks began with an allusion to the Declaration of Independence: "One hundred and eighty-eight years ago this week [i.e., July 4, 1776]," he stated, "a small band of valiant men began a long struggle for freedom. They pledged their lives, their fortunes, and their sacred honor . . . not only for political independence but for personal liberty." A few paragraphs later, Johnson drew attention to the great discrepancy that existed between the principles of the American founding and the actual status of the dispossessed in America, particularly the black man.

> We believe that all men are created equal, yet many are denied equal treatment. We believe that all men have certain unalienable rights, yet many Americans do not enjoy these rights. We believe that all men are entitled to the blessings of liberty, yet

millions are being deprived of those blessings, not because of their own failures but because of the color of their skin.

Further on in the speech, Johnson invoked important tenets of the common religious tradition, suggesting that men who are equal before God should also be equal before the law and have an equal access to public accommodations and jobs:

The purpose of this law is simple . . . It does not give special treatment to any citizen. . . . It does say that those who are equal before God shall now also be equal in the polling booths, in the classrooms, in the factories, and in hotels and restaurants, and movie theatres, and other places that provide service to the public.

Finally, at the close of his address, Johnson again invoked the religious tradition, offering as a counter to the racial hatred in the land, the ideal that all men are the children of God and members of the same human family:

Let us close the springs of racial poison. . . . Let us hasten that day when our unmeasured strength and our unbounded spirit will be free to do the great works ordained to this nation by the just and wise God who is the Father of us all.

Senator Joseph Clark, like many other supporters of the Civil Rights Bill, saw the bill as involving one of the key moral issues of the day. He went on the floor of the Senate in early April 1964 to explain to his colleagues just how central the moral issue was to him personally, especially in regard to Title VII, the fair employment practices section of the bill:

The primary reason why I support it [i.e., the Civil Rights Bill] and why a majority of the Senate, I am confident, support[s] it, is that it raises as clearly as any piece of legislation which has come before the Senate since I have joined it . . . the clear issue of right and wrong. This is particularly true with respect to Title VII (110 *Cong. Rec.*, p. 7203).

To support his view concerning the preeminence of the moral issue, Clark went on to quote from a statement made on behalf of over thirty different church and synagogue groups concerning the immorality of racial segregation and discrimination. The statement he quoted drew heavily from the personalistic strains in the religious tradition:

> The religious conscience of America condemns racism as blasphemy against God. It recognizes that the racial segregation and discrimination that flow from it are a denial of the worth which God has given to all persons. We hold that God is the father of all men. Consequently in every person there is an innate dignity which is the basis of human rights. These rights constitute a moral claim which must be honored both by all persons and by the state. Denial of such rights is immoral (110 *Cong. Rec.*, p. 7203).

Clark also quoted in this context an additional statement by a rabbi who had testified previously before his committee:

> The major points of our statement, Mr. Chairman, have to do with [our] concern for the immorality of discrimination in the area of employment. . . . we believe that this kind of discrimination is blasphemous, it is an affront to our religious commitment and to our religious convictions, believing as we do that man is created in the image of God (110 *Cong. Rec.*, pp. 7203–4).

Immediately following the above quotation, Clark explained how his own support of the civil rights bill was intimately linked to his commitment to the national ideals of liberty and justice for all (i.e., the liberal-Jeffersonian ideal) and to a nation of one people, under God:

> I speak only for myself when I say that if I opposed this bill, I would find it very difficult indeed at the next public meeting I attended to pledge allegiance to the flag of the United States of America and to the Republic for which it stands, one nation

under God, indivisible, with liberty and justice for all (110 *Cong. Rec.*, p. 7204).

"But By the Content of Their Character"

In the case of Martin Luther King, Jr., we have someone who was not only the most important public figure in the 1950s and early 1960s civil rights movement, but also someone who was perhaps more self-consciously committed than any other leading figure in the movement to the basic tenets of the personalistic philosophy and the personalistic mode of thought. In his book on the Montgomery bus boycott, for instance, Dr. King explained how he had first come to adopt the personalistic philosophy while a student at Boston University's School of Theology. Speaking of the impact upon his thought of two of his teachers, Edgar S. Brightman and L. Harold DeWolf, he wrote:

It was mainly under these teachers that I studied personalistic philosophy—the theory that the clue to the meaning of ultimate reality is found in personality. This personal idealism remains today my basic philosophical position. Personalism's insistence that only personality—finite and infinite—is ultimately real strengthened me in two convictions: it gave me metaphysical and philosophical grounding for the idea of a personal God, and it gave me a metaphysical basis for the dignity and worth of all human personality.

Although Dr. King drew extensively in his political thought from the liberal-Jeffersonian tradition,[5] it is clear that the most powerful source of his personalistic philosophy was that provided by the universalistic and personalistic strains in the biblical religion. In *Where Do We Go From Here: Chaos or Community*, which was published just a year before his tragic death, the Jewish and Christian roots of his thought were made unmistakably clear:

Deeply rooted in our religious heritage is the conviction that every man is an heir to a legacy of dignity and worth. Our Judeo-Christian tradition refers to this inherent dignity of man in the Biblical term "the image of God." The image of God is universally shared in equal portions by all men. . . . Every human being has etched in his personality the indelible stamp of the Creator. Every man must be respected because God loves him. The worth of an individual does not lie in the measure of his intellect, his racial origin or his social position. Human worth lies in relatedness to God. An individual has value because he has value to God. Whenever this is recognized, "whiteness" and "blackness" pass away as determinants in a relationship and "son" and "brother" are substituted.

One could hardly find a more succinct statement of the religiously grounded personalistic outlook or one more out-of-tune with the type of ethnic tribalism that sees the ethnic group itself as God and one's relatedness to this God as the major source of one's being and worth. The God of the Jewish-Christian religion is seen as a force destructive to all racial and ethnic tribalism, a force that breaks down all racial and social barriers between human beings, and unites all men in a universal brotherhood of mankind in which each is respected as a person of individual dignity and worth.[6]

Biblical religious themes as the basis of Dr. King's personalistic outlook can also be seen in the speech of August 1963. The most often quoted lines from that speech draw heavily upon the biblical theme of judgment: "I have a dream that my four little children will one day live in a nation where they will not be judged by the color of their skins, but by the content of their character." Human beings, it is wished here, will someday be able to view one another, not in terms of artificial differences such as skin color or race, but in terms of personal moral worth, the same criterion that God uses in his judgment of people.[7]

Abolitionist Personalism

The civil rights movement of the fifties and early sixties did not, of course, invent the personalistic mode of thought, nor was it original in applying biblical and liberal-Jeffersonian themes to a struggle for personal rights. Both of these ideas and practices had been taken over from the earlier antislavery movement, and it is probably safe to say that nothing did more to weaken the influence of ethnic and tribalistic modes of thought in America than New England abolitionism and the Christian-transcendentalist philosophy that often undergirded it. Two antislavery writers can be taken to illustrate some of the themes that have been heretofore discussed. The first, Samuel Sewall, was a Puritan merchant, whose "The Selling of Joseph," first published in 1700, was one of the first antislavery tracts to appear in America. The biblical teaching that all human beings are of the same blood—the doctrine derived from both the creation myth in Genesis and chapter seventeen of the Book of Acts—was seen by Sewall as incompatible with the manner in which black Africans were being treated in America. Although he apparently believed that Africans were physically quite ugly, and that they could never be integrated into white New England society, he nevertheless held that they were children of God and should be treated with a respect commensurate with their status as such:

> It is most certain that all men, as they are the sons of Adam, are co-heirs, and have equal right unto liberty, and all other outward comforts of life. God "hath given the earth . . . unto the sons of Adam" (Psalm 115.16). "And hath made of one blood, all nations of men, for to dwell on all the face of the earth . . . that they should seek the Lord. Forasmuch then as we are the offspring of God" (Acts 17:26–7).
>
> These Ethiopians, as black as they are, seeing they are the Sons and Daughters of the First Adam, the Brethren and sisters of the Last Adam, and the offspring of God. They ought to be treated with a respect agreeable.[8]

The second example is that of William Lloyd Garrison, who developed further the biblical and religious argument against slavery, though he went much further than Sewall in carrying out its implications. The fact that all men are of one blood (i.e., that they constitute a single human race), that they have all been created by a loving God, and that what counts in the eyes of this God is an individual's moral virtue rather than his wealth or skin color—all these were seen by Garrison as facts not only incompatible with the institution of slavery, but also with the many laws in free states prohibiting interracial marriage. The standard of matrimony Garrison believed should be the degree of moral worth and mutual affection of the people involved, and not their race or ancestry:

> If [the Creator] has "made of one blood all nations of men for to dwell on all the face of the earth," then they are one species, and stand on a perfect equality: their intermarriage is neither unnatural or repugnant to nature, but obviously proper and salutary, it being designed to unite people of different tribes and nations.
>
> As civilization, and knowledge, and republican feelings, and Christianity prevail in the world, the wider will matrimonial connexions extend . . . An unnatural alliance is not that which joins in wedlock an African descendant with an American, or an Indian with a European, who are equal in moral worth . . . The standard of matrimony is erected by affection and purity, and does not depend upon the height, or bulk, or color, or wealth, or poverty, of individuals.[9]

Garrison also quotes from the famous passage in Saint Paul's Letter to the Galatians, the passage often quoted in recent times by feminist writers, where all human beings are said to be one in Christ:

> I call upon the spirits of the just made perfect in heaven, upon all who have experienced the love of God in their souls here below, upon the Christian converts in India and the islands of the sea, to sustain me in the assertion that there *is* power in the religion of Jesus Christ to melt down the most stubborn prejudice, to overthrow the highest walls of partition, to break the strongest caste, to improve and elevate the most degraded, to unite in fellowship the most hostile . . . "In Christ Jesus, all are one: there is neither Jew nor Greek, there is neither bond nor free, there is neither male nor female" (Galatians 3:28).[10]

Because of his great faith in the power of the Christian religion to transform people's attitudes and behavior, Garrison, unlike Sewall, believed that black Africans, once freed from slavery, would eventually be assimilated into American society.

The liberal-Jeffersonian tradition and the themes of the American Revolution are also prominent in Garrison's writings, and can be seen, for instance, in the very first issue of the *Liberator,* where the aims and purposes of the periodical were set forth to the public:

> I determined, at every hazard, to lift up the standard of emancipation in the eyes of the nation, within sight of Bunker Hill, and the birthplace of liberty. That standard is now unfurled.
>
> Assenting to the "self-evident truth" maintained in the American Declaration of Independence, "that all men are created equal, and endowed by their Creator with certain inalienable rights—among which are life, liberty, and the pursuit of happiness," I shall strenuously contend for the immediate enfranchisement of our slave population. . . . On this subject, I do not wish to think, or speak, or write, with moderation. . . . I will not equivocate—I will not excuse—I will not retreat a single inch—AND I WILL BE HEARD.

The mixture of biblical religious themes with the spirit of '76 was, in Garrison's case, of course, a very volatile combination, and both traditions would eventually go on to inspire the Northern armies in the American Civil War. The civil rights movement of the 1950s and early 1960s absorbed much of the driving spirit of this earlier abolitionism, but it was to add to it the important additional element of Gandhi-inspired nonviolence. It was this third element, most prominently displayed in the figures of Martin Luther King, Jr., and the early members of the Student Nonviolent Coordinating Committee (SNCC), that lent to the civil rights movement of this period much of its high moral tone, and ultimately elevated it to a moral level considerably above that of most of the earlier abolitionism.[11]

Detribalization and the Immigrant Experience

The American experience after the Civil War was marked by

the influx into the country of successive waves of immigrants from many diverse lands. The immigrants generally shared the hope of advancing economically and being accepted into the larger society on an equal footing with the descendants of the older immigrants, particularly those of English, Scottish, Welsh, and German origin. The open market economy, and the corresponding opportunities it offered for personal advancement, gave birth to a peculiarly American work and achievement ethic that shared with the earlier Christian and liberal traditions the idea that individuals should be judged by what they individually do in life, rather than by what their ancestors did or by what ethnic group they belonged to. There were counterforces at work, of course, ranging from the mild genealogical "snootiness" of the Daughters of the American Revolution to the terrorist-prone WASP racism of the Ku Klux Klan. But the personalistic mode of thought had taken strong root in America, and as the children of the first generation immigrants learned to speak the English language and to adopt the ways of the American culture, they came to be accepted more and more into the general society and to be judged individually, rather than as representatives of their respective ethnic groups. This process was never complete, of course, and ethnic-tribalistic modes of consciousness always retained a considerable hold. But the personalistic viewpoint—the view that human beings are to be judged by their own characteristics and their own achievements, and not by their ethnic-tribal affiliations—was a powerful ideal that generally had at least some effect in shaping people's attitudes and actions.

The personalistic mode of thought, as it relates to the work and achievement ethic, can be well illustrated by a look at the comments of a black writer in the early 1940s. The writer in question, a prominent newspaper columnist, was objecting to the fact that while individuals in the press were generally respected as such, and not seen as representatives of their respective racial, ethnic, or religious groups, in the case of the Negro this was not so. Only in the case of Negro individuals, the writer protested, was it thought relevant or appropriate to identify a person according to race, ethnicity, or ancestry.

This [sinister policy of identifying individual Negoes as such] is a subtle form of discrimination designed to segregate these individuals in the mind of the public and thus bolster the national policy of biracialism. Thus, Paul Robeson is not a great baritone, he is a great "Negro" baritone. Dr. Carver is not just a great scientist, he is a great "Negro" scientist. Anne Brown is not merely a great soprano, she is a great "Negro" soprano. Langston Hughes is not a poet merely, he is a "Negro" poet. Augusta Savage is a "Negro" sculptor, C. C. Spaulding is a "Negro" insurance executive, R. R. Wright, Sr., is a "Negro" banker, J. A. Rogers is a "Negro" historian, Willard Townsend is a "Negro" labor leader, etc., etc., *ad infinitum.* . . . No other group in this country is so singled out for racial identification, and no one can tell me that there is not a very definite reason for it. No daily newspaper refers to Mr. Morgenthau as "Jewish" secretary of the treasury, or New York's Herbert H. Lehman as the "Jewish" governor, or Isador Lubin as a "Jewish" New Dealer. Mayor Rossi is never identified as the "Italian-American" executive of San Francisco, nor is the millionaire Giannini called an "Italian" banker. There would be considerable uproar if Senator Robert F. Wagner were termed "New York's able German-American solon," or Representative Tenerowicz dubbed "Detroit's prominent Pole." When has a Utah legislator in Washington been labeled "Mormon"?

One could go on and on, but the point is that "our" daily newspapers carefully avoid such designations except in the case of so-called Negroes. I cannot recall when I have seen a criminal referred to as a Jew, an Italian, a German or a Catholic, but it is commonplace for colored lawbreakers or suspects to be labeled "Negro."

Personally, I shall not be convinced of the sincerity of these white editors and columnists who shape America's thinking unless they begin treating the Negro in the news as they do other Americans. Those who continue this type of journalism are the worst sort of hypocrites when they write about democracy and national unity.[12]

The writer was expresssing here, of course, the same aspiration that many Jews, Italians, Poles, and others had previously expressed of being accepted as equals into a multiracial, multi-ethnic, and multireligious culture that was respectful of individual differences and individual achievements. This seems to have been the dominant aspiration of the vast majority of black Americans, along with the vast majority of other Americans, at least up until the late 1960s,[13] though a small percentage of black separatists and black nationalists, it is true, never accepted it.

The Great Contraction

The early and mid-1960s marked a high point in post-Reconstruction American history in the public understanding of, and respect for, the dignity and worth of individual human persons. It is often hard for people today to remember just what this period was like, so far have we strayed from its motivating spirit. It was a period in which progress was being made on several fronts by many black Americans, and for the vast majority of people of all races and ethnicities this progress was the source of great rejoicing. Black faces seen in banks and business enterprises where they had never been seen before gave to all people of goodwill, black and white alike, the feeling that they lived in a society that was at least a little more just and humane than the society that had existed before. A very similar feeling had been unleashed two decades previously by President Truman's order abolishing segregation in the military, and by Jackie Robinson's breaking of the color barrier in professional baseball. These were developments about which all fair-minded Americans could feel a genuine satisfaction and pride. The early and mid-1960s was also a period when questions regarding a person's race, ethnicity, and national origin were often deleted from government questionnaires, as such questions were generally viewed as irrelevant to any legitimate government purpose, and the mere solicitation of such information was frequently held to be an affront to the dignity of human persons and a threat to the principle of equality before the law.

All this, however, was to change in the late 1960s and early 1970s with the emergence of the policy known as "affirmative action." It was at this time that a radical change in consciousness was taking place, both inside and outside of the govern-

ment, which could be seen in the very terms and conceptual
structures that were thought legitimate to interpret human reality. One might characterize this change as a shift from the
personalistic language and personalistic mode of thought that
had characterized the 1964 Civil Rights Act and the black protest
movement that had preceded it, to the depersonalizing logic of
racial and ethnic tribalism. The death of Martin Luther King,
Jr., who in many ways epitomized the personalistic ideal in its
Christian form, and who, at the time of his assassination in April
1968, was organizing a march on behalf of the poor of all races,
might be taken as symbolic of the passing of his older ideal of a
universal citizenship and universal personhood. By the late
1960s a new militant spirit, one often combined with a strong
antiwhite animus, had taken hold of many black, Hispanic, and
American Indian spokesmen, and it became clear to all by this
time that the days when Italian housewives, Jewish college
students, and Irish priests would walk arm in arm with southern
blacks in defense of universal principles of justice and individual
rights were now a thing of the past.

In the 1950s and early 1960s the black protest movement had
been a genuine civil rights movement, and represented the
convergence of an ethnic-parochial interest (i.e., the social and
economic interest of black people) with a universal-human ideal
(i.e., equal rights for all, regardless of race or ethnicity). A
decade later this was no longer the case, as black groups, often
joined in coalition with Hispanic groups and women's groups,
sought favored treatment for the members of their own particular groups, regardless of what deleterious effect this might have
on other people, and regardless of how unjust or unfair these
other people might perceive this favored treatment to be. The
attitude of many of the black and Hispanic militants was essentially this: "Look, you white folks (or "white Anglos") have
been screwing us for over three hundred years now. It's about
time we started screwing you for a while." Militant feminists
often took a similar attitude in regard to white males. The
universal-human ideal, it seems, had lost most of its appeal, and
increasingly gave way to self-seeking power-politics, ruthlessly
pursued by well-organized racial, ethnic, and gender interest

groups, which cared little for those they had to step on in the pursuit of their goals.

The period of the very late sixties and early seventies proved to be a period of unprecedented ethnicization and tribalization in the American public consciousness. It was a period when many Americans desperately sought their "roots," not in a common humanity or in a universal God, nor in a common national heritage (from which many had become estranged as a result of the unpopularity of the Vietnam War), but in their respective genealogies and ethnicities. This was true not only of Americans of African, Spanish, and Asian ancestry, but of many people of white European and Mideastern backgrounds as well. With the liberal tradition in abeyance, and the universalistic strains in the Judeo-Christian religion ceasing to have any significant influence over people's minds, the net effect of the increasing interest in genealogy and ethnicity was to erect new barriers between people where previously such barriers had been greatly weakened or in some cases had not existed at all. Ethnic-tribal modes of thought were to be given a new legitimacy in America, and the practice of classifying the whole population according to racial and ethnic criteria, at one time viewed in most places outside of the South with near universal horror, and identified in the minds of many with such depraved states as Nazi Germany and South Africa, was to become the order of the day.

There was, of course, a counterattack, led both by individuals and by the organizations of those ethnic groups who found themselves placed at a disadvantage vis-à-vis those groups that were officially favored. A new convergence of ethnic-parochial interest and universal-human ideal came to be represented by Polish-American organizations, Italian-American organizations, Jewish-American organizations, and a number of other groups, with the Jewish groups being the most active and influential owing in part to bad historical memories of the effect of racial classifications and quota systems in both Europe and America. None of these groups, however, either individually or collectively, could stem the tide of racial and ethnic classification or the preferential treatment of persons based upon such classifications.

The actual policy of affirmative action in employment, it should be understood, had nothing to do with any laws passed by Congress, and indeed was (and still is) a violation of federal statutes.[14] What happened was that the federal bureaucracy, led by the Equal Employment Opportunity Commission (EEOC) and the Office of Federal Contract Compliance (OFCC), aided and abetted along the way by the federal courts, simply rewrote Titles VI and VII of the 1964 Civil Rights Act, as well as President Lyndon Johnson's antidiscrimination Executive Orders 11246 and 11375, substituting ethnic tribal categories (e.g., "Hispanic," "Oriental," "black," etc.) for the personalistic language of the documents in question. Terms such as "person," "individual," "*any* employee," "*all* qualified applicants," and the like, were cynically reinterpreted to mean in effect only those persons, individuals, or employees who were members of officially designated racial and ethnic "minority groups" as such groups were defined by the EEOC. It was only as members of certain racial and ethnic groups that individuals could claim the right of protection under legislation that was originally written to insure to all Americans that they would be treated in all employment situations, in the language of President Johnson's Executive Order 11246, "*without* regard to their race, creed, color or national origin."[15]

The federal bureaucrats, using such euphemisms and code words as "underutilization," "goals," "timetables," and the like, began to pressure employers into giving special preference to people who fit into certain racial, ethnic, and gender categories, at the expense of people who did not, and who were denied all manner of redress for such action. The approach of the federal courts was even more direct, insofar as a finding that an employer had discriminated in the past was seen as a justification, under a blatantly dishonest reading of Section 703(g) of 1964 Civil Rights Act, for the hiring of new people on a racial or ethnic quota basis. One might have supposed that being guilty of discriminating against people in the past was even more reason not to discriminate against people in the future—that, for instance, discriminating against two people in the past because they were black, and then discriminating against two people in the present because they were white, would mean that a total of four people had been discriminated against. And this is exactly what critics of affirmative action, including such black critics as Bayard Rustin, have strenuously argued. But within the logic of affirmative action, two plus two equaled zero. It is, in fact, the logic of tribal warfare.

Consider for instance the following scenario:

A small southern town is polarized by racial tension. Early on a Friday evening, members of the local Ku Klux Klan go down to the local shopping mall, abduct the first black person they see, steal his wallet, and give all his money away to the first white person to come along. Upon hearing this, members of the local black community are incensed, and many among the more militant youth vow to get even. Consequently, during the following week members of the local Black Defense League go down to the same shopping mall, abduct the first white person they see, steal *his* wallet, and give all *his* money away to the first black person to walk by.

One has in the above account an *exact* parallel to the justice and underlying mentality of affirmative action. What most affirmative action programs in employment are really saying is this: Because of the discrimination in the past against person A, which worked to the unmerited benefit of person B, it is now necessary to give special preference to person C, at the expense of person D. Person A and person C are not the same person, nor are they necessarily related to each other in any way at all, except for the fact that they both have the same black, brown, or yellow skin color, or both have ancestors who were born in foreign countries where the official language spoken was Spanish. Similarly, person B and person D are not the same person, nor are they necessarily related to each other in any way at all, except for the fact that they both have the same white skin color and their ancestors were born in foreign countries where the official language spoken was *not* Spanish.

Put in such terms, the policy sounds clearly absurd,[16] and indeed it is, though an impression to the contrary seems to have been created in the minds of the federal judges and federal bureaucrats who developed it by their tendency to view all black and Hispanic people as poor and underprivileged, and all white people, by contrast, as rich and powerful. (On this latter point, it would seem the judges and bureaucrats have generalized from their own circumstances, and apparently assumed that white people were all more or less like themselves and their friends.) The tradition of giving a break to the underdog is certainly a praiseworthy one, and on grounds of justice, at least, few would object to a hiring policy that gave some degree of preference to poor and underprivileged people over rich and privileged ones. But the great socioeconomic diversity in America, of course, does not conform to any simple ethnic or racial stereotype. According to the Census Bureau, for instance, there are two and one-half times as many poor white people in America as poor black people, and a full 25 per cent of all black families have family incomes above the national average for whites.

One can say in their favor that many of the federal judges and bureaucrats who favored affirmative action harbored a genuine sympathy for the plight of the poor and disadvantaged, especially for those who had been victims of racial and ethnic discrimination. Where they went wrong was in abandoning the suffering person as the unit of concern, and transferring their sympathy to a very heterogeneous group of people, whom they saw only in terms of a stereotyped image. Indeed, the rhetoric of affirmative action is one in which language has cut loose from flesh-and-blood reality, and has gone on to create its own world of images, symbols, and depersonalized mental abstractions. Terms such as the "black," the "white," the "Mexican American," the "Oriental," the "Puerto Rican," etc.—terms meaning everyone in the group, and yet no one—were to become the basis for a general mystification that was to desensitize people to the personal-discrete nature of all human reality and all human suffering.

Feeble Defenses

Supporters of preferential hiring on the basis of race and ethnicity will sometimes pay lip service to the older, personalistic ideal of a color-blind society, but will then try to defend race- and ethnic-conscious hiring policies as an interim or temporary measure that is supposedly necessary to bring about such a society. This idea, for instance, was expressed in a federal circuit court decision in 1973: "Our society cannot be completely color-blind in the short run if we are to have a color-blind society in the long run." It is never explained, however, just how race-conscious policies in the short run can bring about color blindness in the long run. Why, for instance, should people who have been encouraged—or indeed, required by law—to see other people, not as persons, but as group representatives, suddenly at some future date begin seeing them as individuals? The idea is absurd on its very face. Institutionalizing ethnic and color consciousness only habituates the practice, and ingrains it that much more deeply in the public mind. The idea that you can get humans beings to think of other human beings as persons in the long run by having them think of them as group representatives in the short run, is akin to the idea that you can get young males to view young females as persons—and not as sex objects—by subjecting them in their adolescent years to heavy doses of government-sponsored porn films. As Miro Todorovich, a leading critic of affirmative action in education, has remarked, it is a policy of prescribing whiskey to cure alcoholism.

The inevitable effect of race- and ethnic-conscious hiring policies is to legitimate ethnic and racial stereotyping both as a way of thinking and as a manner of human beings relating to one another. Such policies thereby serve to undermine that ongoing openness to new experience and new encounter, which alone is an antidote to a prejudicial frame of mind. In addition, such policies provoke deep resentment on the part of those persons who are not of the favored race or ethnicity, and these persons will quite frequently take out their very legitimate anger, not upon the federal judges and federal bureaucrats who instituted the policies, nor upon the various black, Hispanic, and feminist leaders who support them, but upon the individual blacks, Hispanics, and women they encounter daily, the vast majority of whom, according to most opinion polls, are opponents of affirmative action.[17]

Many people try to justify preferential hiring based on race and ethnicity as a mode of rectifying the "present effects of past discrimination." This, however, is a rather feeble defense, as preferential hiring programs are rarely, if ever, means-tested, and it is not quite clear just what "effects" are being rectified. In some cases, at least, actual beneficiaries of preferential programs would seem to have been the victims of nothing more serious than affluence.[18] But even if preferential hiring *were* means-tested and, say, the income and educational level of a job applicant's parents were taken into account in an attempt to favor the disadvantaged, it is not at all clear why such a program should be limited to those of only certain racial and ethnic backgrounds but not others. Does socioeconomic disadvantage that may arguably be attributed to racial and ethnic discrimination against one's ancestors have any greater claim to public concern than socioeconomic disadvantage that is not so attibutable? The answer would seem to be no, but even if this were not the case, it would seem that many poor Irish Americans, poor Polish Americans, poor Jewish Americans, poor Greek Americans, poor Italian Americans, poor Portuguese Americans, poor Slavic Americans, poor Hungarian Americans, poor Czech Americans, poor Ukrainian Americans, poor Arab Americans, poor Turkish Americans, poor Armenian Americans, poor Gypsy Americans, and indeed virtually every poor person in America who is of Southern European, Eastern European, North African, or Middle Eastern ethnic background would have a legitimate claim to preferential treatment, since their socioeconomic deprivation could arguably be attributed to past discrimination against their forebears.

Perhaps the most common defense of preferential hiring in recent years is the so-called role-model argument. Women, Hispanics, and particularly black people, it is said, need same-race (or same-gender) role models in various occupations in order to be convinced that they can succeed in a competitive employment world where most important positions in the past have been held by white males. It is necessary, the argument goes, to weigh the injustice done to the better-qualified applicants who are not hired because of affirmative action programs, against all the good that is done by the additional minority and women role models that are created.[19] Such an argument may at first appear to have a certain persuasiveness, but it soon breaks down once one realizes that affirmative action role models are not genuine, and are soon recognized as such by all concerned. The role that is actually modeled by affirmative action recipients is that of a patronized black, Hispanic, or female, who is of inferior qualifications in comparison to the best qualified applicant for a job or promotion, and who would not have gotten to where he or she is except for the existence of an official policy of government favoritism. Affirmative action role models, it would seem, serve only to perpetuate the prejudiced view that blacks, Hispanics, and women are congenitally inferior to Caucasian males and incapable of competing with them on an equal basis. Affirmative action role models also serve to undermine all the positive influences of those genuine role models—i.e., of those blacks, Hispanics, and women who really have competed successfully with white males—because of the inevitable tendency of observers to lump the two together.

The situation, it would seem, is particularly damaging for young blacks, who often suffer intensely from internalized feelings of inferiority, born of the many decades of the public dominance of white-supremacy thinking. Supporters of affirmative action apparently believed that such negative effects of affirmative action role models could be significantly offset by keeping preferential hiring policies secret. People, they believed, would be given preference on the basis of their race, ethnicity, or gender, but this would not be publicly admitted, and indeed would be officially denied. Dissimulation and denial have, in fact, been a characteristic feature of most affirmative action programs, but they do not seem to have had the intended effect. Most people, both those in the preferred groups and those in the nonpreferred groups, have generally understood quite well exactly what was going on. What proponents of the role-model argument have failed to grasp is that, with regards to any positive inspirational value, it is not the quantity but the quality and genuineness of a role model that really counts.

Mythologies and Pathologies

Since affirmative action in employment is blatantly illegal, and contrary to certain moral and ethical precepts that have deep roots in America's liberal and Christian past, it became necessary for supporters and defenders of the program to devise certain legitimating social and legal mythologies, which seem to have had considerable success in confusing a good number of people. The legal myth holds that affirmative action, in the sense of preferential hiring based on racial, ethnic, and gender criteria, was mandated by President Johnson in 1965 in his Executive Order No. 11246, and is provided for in Title VII of the 1964 Civil Rights Act. This, of course is the exact opposite of the case. What is true in the myth is that President Johnson did indeed use the word "affirmative action"[20] in his executive order, but the term was used in a sense directly opposite the meaning the term would take on in the 1970s. By "affirmative action" Johnson meant that contractors doing business with the federal government would make a special effort, both to advertise their nondiscrimination policies more broadly, and to ensure that all employees and applicants for employment were treated on a strictly race-, ethnicity-, and religion-neutral basis. "Affirmative action," in other words, meant affirmative nondiscrimination, i.e., scrupulous ethnic neutrality and color blindness. The relevant section of the executive order reads:

> The contractor will not discriminate against *any* employee or applicant for employment because of race, creed, color, or national origin. The contractor will take *affirmative action* to ensure that applicants are employed, and that employees are treated during employment, *without* regard to their race, creed, color, or national origin (Section 201.1; emphasis added).

Supporters of preferential hiring in the federal bureaucracy realized, however, that few people ever read presidential executive orders, and they suspected—and suspected correctly—that if they simply set down their own laws mandating preferential hiring, the federal courts would eventually back them up and would act as though a policy that was explicitly prohibited by the Civil Rights Act of 1964 was actually required by it.[21] They also suspected—and again suspected correctly—that neither Congress nor the president would do anything to interfere out of fear of being denounced in the media by the so-called "civil rights groups" either as racist bigots or, at the very least, as insensitive to the plight of "minorities." And so, in 1971, the policy of affirmative action in employment was given birth by bureaucratic fiat, the key document in question being Revised Order No. 4 of the Labor Department's OFCC. This was the document that spoke of "goals," "timetables," "deficiencies," "good-faith efforts," "underutilization," "result-oriented" policies, and the like, and helped set the style for the mystification and double talk that would become the stock-in-trade of most affirmative action programs.[22]

The social mythology that affirmative action supporters created has also been touched upon previously. It consists of at least four interrelated mythic elements, each of which is usually presented as the unspoken premise of various arguments and moral appeals, rather than as explicitly stated facts. The first element might be described as the myth of the socioeconomically homogeneous white majority. If one is going to place a person at a disadvantage because of that person's race, then it is certainly easier on one's conscience if the person put at a disadvantage is from a rich and privileged background, rather than from a poor and underprivileged one. Hence, to justify a policy of discriminating against white people, white people must be identified with wealth and privilege. The fact that there are 25 million white people in America who are below the official poverty level, and many more in lower-middle-income circumstances, and the fact that many of these people must also apply for jobs in competitive job markets were facts that the myth propagators sought to eliminate from public awareness.

The second mythic element compliments the first, and might be described as the myth of the socioeconomically homogeneous black and Hispanic minorities. To justify preferential treatment in favor of black people, Hispanic people, and certain other people officially designated as constituting a "minority group," the people in these groups naturally had to be conceived of as economically and culturally deprived. The fact that there is a sizeable black and Hispanic elite in America, and that the members of this elite are much more likely than their poorer brethren to be the ones applying for the most competitive jobs where the greatest degree of racial and ethnic preference is generally given, were once again facts that the myth creators sought to shield from public awareness.

The third element in the mythology was what might be called the myth of the ethnically homogeneous white majority. All white people, according to this myth, are ethnically more or less the same and can be adequately viewed in terms of the white Anglo-Saxon Protestant model. Since WASPs were never discriminated against in America to any significant degree, and since many WASPs in the past have enjoyed social and economic privileges that, in some cases at least, were purchased at the expense of racial and ethnic discrimination against others, the more white people could be viewed as WASPs, the easier it would be to justify the withdrawal of certain of their rights and privileges. The myth, of course, deliberately tried to obscure the fact that many present-day WASPs are quite poor, that in any event WASPs constitute a distinct minority (less than a third[23]) among the white people of America, and that America is a nation whose "white" people come from literally dozens of different ethnic and national-origin backgounds. The myth also, of course, tried to obscure the fact that, unlike most WASPs, most white immigrants to America from the various nations and regions of eastern and southern Europe, north Africa, and the Middle East, often experienced widespread ethnic discrimination in employment and other areas of life, discrimination that was widespread roughly up until the time of the Second World War.

The fouth element in the social mythology is what might be termed the myth of the ethnically homogeneous Hispanic minority. In reality, of course, as Nathan Glazer and others have stressed, Spanish-speaking people and their descendants in America do not constitute a single ethnic group, but a whole host of ethnic groups, with widely varying group histories and group traditions. Historically speaking, the amount of ethnic discrimination that was typcially experienced by the members of these different groups varied considerably from group to group, with the members of the better-off groups, such as the Spaniards, probably experiencing less discrimination on average than the members of many of the eastern European, north African, and Middle Eastern ethnic groups. But since the public "image" of Hispanics in America, at least among many non-Hispanics, is largely conditioned by the history of Mexican Americans (who on average experienced perhaps the greatest degree of ethnic discrimination), as well as by the recent history of Puerto Ricans (who, in aggregate per capita terms, are the poorest Hispanic group in America), it served the interest of the propagators of the myth to lump all Spanish-speaking people and their descendants together under a single term.

Each element in the social mythology of affirmative action, it can be seen, was intended to desensitize the mind of the observer to the vast diversity of people in America, and to the individual-personal nature of every human being and every human life. The social mythology also sought to inject into public consciousness what is perhaps the most perverse idea of the many perverse ideas that the ethnic-tribalistic mind-set has bequeathed to mankind: the idea, that is, of collective and congenital blood-guilt. Given the history of this idea, with its use, for instance, to justify Negro slavery as just punishment for the biblical sin of Ham, and to persecute Jews throughout the centuries for their alleged collective and congenital responsibility in the murder of Christ, one might have thought such an idea would have had little appeal to those who had been victims of racial and ethnic prejudice. Its success within a modern American context is something truly alarming. According to this way of thinking, all people who have white skin partake of a collective blood-guilt for all the heinous crimes that were committed in the past by white people against blacks, Hispanics, and the members of various American Indian tribes. The guilt for such crimes, according to this view, is not only transmitted along genealogical lines, but has a peculiar race-specific infectiousness about it that contaminates all people with white skin. Even the descendants of white abolitionists, for instance, would be seen to share in this blood-guilt, as would the descendants of the many millions of post-Civil War white immigrants, despite the fact that most of their ancestors had to cope with ethnic discrimination of their own, had little or nothing to do with Southern slavery, Jim Crow laws, or the persecution of Mexicans or Indians, and generally settled in areas of the country where few Mexicans, Indians, or blacks resided. The collective and congenital guilt idea, like the various other elements in the affirmative action social mythology, was rarely to be seen stated in explicit terms, but assumed a prominent background existence, usually as the unarticulated premise and assumption of various pro-affirmative action arguments and appeals.

Some of the elements in the social mythology can be well-illustrated by a few quotations from the famous Kerner Commission report on the causes of the urban rioting of the late 1960s. This report was written at the very beginning of the period when influential intellectuals and government bureaucrats were considering the desirability of abandoning the national policy of race and ethnic neutrality in hiring, and substituting instead one of racial and ethnic favoritism. The document is invaluable for understanding the psychology and motivation of the type of guilt-ridden, self-hating, upper-middle-class white "liberal"[24] who helped to institute the policy of affirmative action, and contains one of the earliest uses of the actual term "affirmative action" in a sense that would seem to be at least approaching the meaning that the term would later acquire.[25]

The conclusion of the Kerner Commission was set forth in the now-famous sentence in the introduction to its report, in a line allegedly penned by commission vice-chairman John Lindsay, which stated:

Our nation is moving toward two societies, one black, one white—separate and unequal.

Here, of course, one can see the tendency toward the racial stereotyping of the population that would become a characteristic feature of affirmative action programs. One ethnically and socioeconomically homogeneous white group, that is thought of as rich and privileged, is pictured as standing over against an equally socioeconomically and ethnically homogeneous black group, which is thought of as uniformly poor and underprivileged. Social status and economic well-being are seen to run along strict racial lines, with little consciousness of the vast diversity to be found among the enormous black and white populations actually found in America.

The commission also set forth its view regarding the collective guilt of "white society" for the deplorable conditions in the inner-city ghettos where many Negro Americans were forced to live:

> What white Americans have never fully understood—but what the Negro can never forget—is that white society is deeply implicated in the ghetto. White institutions created it, white institutions maintain it, and white society condones it.

Now if one asks in this context, just *who* is white society?, the answer is, of course, all white people. All white people are seen as collectively responsible for the degradation and despair in the black urban ghetto, and are supposed to feel guilty for their past sins in having created it. The sin and guilt is not personal, but collective and congenital. It is a racial guilt. The commission fully realized, as indicated in the first line of the quotation, that many "white Americans" were rather far removed from the situation in the inner city ghetto, and had little understanding of its problems. But in the commission's view this fact served only to heighten their guilt, as it rendered them less concerned about the evil conditions that lurked there, for which all white people were seen as collectively responsible.

When we try to understand the motivations of the supporters of affirmative action, certainly the easiest motive to grasp is that of the leaders of various black, Hispanic, and women's groups. These groups, in their support for preferential hiring, were simply playing the typical American game of interest-group politics. They sought special favors for the members of their respective clienteles, with little regard for the rights of those who would have to be shoved aside, much as labor unions and business associations do when attempting to promote the self-interest of their respective members. Other ethnic groups in the past had acted in a similar manner (the Irish, for instance, in Boston and other northern cities), and however regrettable this may have been—however sickening the fact that these ethnic and gender interest groups often spoke in the name of "civil rights"[26]—the motivation of their members was certainly transparent enough for all to see.

The situation is much more complicated, however, when we consider the motivation of the high-ranking federal bureaucrats and judges who instituted the affirmative action policy, as well as their supporters among the intellectual elite in the universities and the news media, the great majority of whom are, of course, white males. It is the psychology of the contemporary upper-middle-class white male "liberal" that is so complicated, yet an understanding of it is crucial in order to grasp how a policy such as affirmative action could have come into being.

The upper-middle-class white "liberal" who supported affirmative action seems to have been stirred initially by two very different passions. The first of these was a genuine sympathy and compassion for the plight of the black poor in America—for those who were at the very bottom of the socioeconomic ladder, and who had often suffered in their own lifetimes from the meanest prejudices and the vilest of social practices. This sympathy and compassion was then extended by the white "liberal" to cover black people in general and, subsequently, the members of certain other ethnic groups as well, particularly Mexican Americans, Puerto Ricans, and American Indians.

The second force at work in the mind of the upper-middle-class white "liberal" was a deeply rooted sense of guilt. This sense of guilt in most cases had nothing to do with any awareness of any specific wrong that either the white "liberal" himself or any of his ancestors had actually committed against black people or the members of any other ethnic group. In many cases, of course, no such specific wrongs existed. The source of the white "liberal's" sense of guilt, rather, was something much more immediate, and had to do with the moral uneasiness that he felt over his own privileged position in society. Growing up amidst relative wealth and privilege, and discovering so many in radically different circumstances, the upper-middle-class white "liberal," like any morally sensitive person, felt a sense of guilt and uneasiness over his own personal circumstances and the fact that he was no more deserving of his relative wealth and privilege than the poor and degraded were deserving of their poverty and degradation. Even people from very modest circumstances will frequently have similar feelings when confronting, for instance, a terribly wretched beggar on a city street.

This combination of guilt over one's own privileged socioeconomic position, and compassion for the plight of the poor and downtrodden, can often, of course, lead to morally laudable activities that can be of the greatest benefit to society. A person motivated by such feelings, for instance, might decide that it was his obligation to give away much of his wealth and earnings to those more in need of them than himself; or he might decide to dedicate his spare time and energy to any number of charitable activities. With regard to underprivileged blacks, for instance, he might choose to make large contributions to the United Negro College Fund or to other black charities; he might decide to adopt a black orphan, or at least spend time as a tutor or a Big Brother to a fatherless black child in need of personal attention; he might lend large sums of money to promising black enterprises in need of start-up capital; or he might reach out in any number of ways to help individual black people in distress. But the compassion and concern for the downtrodden of the typical affirmative-action-supporting white "liberal" was to stop at that very point where any significant degree of his own personal sacrifice was called for. It was at this point that he was seized by what can only be described as a kind of demonic self-righteousness and hypocrisy, which induced him to try to expiate his own sense of guilt, not by giving up any of his own wealth or privilege—not for instance by giving up his own job or promotion entitlement and recruiting a poor black or Hispanic person to take his place—but by using government power to force other people, usually people considerably less well-off than himself, to sacrifice *their* jobs, *their* lives, and *their* promotion entitlements. And when these other people then complained about such treatment—when the Brian Webers, that is, the Stuart Marshes, the Wendy Wygants, the Memphis fire fighters, and the like, complained of the discrimination against them— they were denounced by the affirmative action-supporting white "liberal" for their insensitivity to the plight of the poor and oppressed. In the fifty-third chapter of the biblical Book of Isaiah, we read of a Suffering Servant who took upon himself the burden of the entire world's sin and guilt, in order that man might be restored to God through his great personal suffering and sacrifice. The affirmative-action-supporting white "liberal," one might say, took upon himself the sin and guilt, if not of the "world," at least of "white society," but when it came to the question of great personal suffering and sacrifice, he delegated that task to others, whom he would then confront as his moral inferiors.

In addition to the three forces of guilt, compassion, and self-righteous hypocrisy, two other forces come into play in the motivation of the upper-middle-class white "liberal," which might be designated by the terms "romanticism" and "fear." Both forces are intimately related to one another and proceed from the peculiar manner in which poor and oppressed people have frequently been viewed in Western society, particularly by those on the leftward side of the political spectrum.[27] Poor and oppressed people are, of course, exactly that—they are poor and oppressed. They are not necessarily noble people, or virtuous people, or wise people. Indeed, they are sometimes the very opposite, as the effect of poverty and oppression is frequently to brutalize people, to keep them in ignorance, and to fill them with hatreds and animosities, which they not infrequently take out both on fellow sufferers and upon innocent third parties who did them no wrong. But the upper-middle-class white "liberal" tends to romanticize the victims of poverty and oppression, and to see them as possessing a certain inner moral purity that elevates them in his mind above the general lot of better-off people, almost endowing them with a kind of secular holiness. The culmination of this type of thinking, of course, is to be found in Marxism, where the masses of poor and oppressed factory workers are seen as nothing less than the saviors and redeemers of mankind. The idea that something said by such people could be mean-spirited, or misinformed, or simply nonsense, is seen by the white "liberal," and even more so by his compatriots on the far Left, as bordering on a profanation. What is said by the poor and oppressed—or more typically, by those not-so-poor-and-oppressed people who claim to be their spokesmen—is treated with a special deference and generally exempted from the moral and intellectual scrutiny that would be accorded to statements made by almost anyone else. Indeed, many a white "liberal" and his far-Left brethren are so lacking in any cultivation of their own inner faculties of moral and spiritual discernment that morality and justice will not infrequently come to be associated in their minds with whatever spokesmen for poor and oppressed people demand.

The upper-middle-class white "liberal," one might say, views the poor and oppressed much the way medieval Catholics tended to view the orders of priests and monks. In just thinking about them, he can experience a sense of his own unworthiness and guilt, and he fears nothing more than being outside of their good graces. This fear is particularly strong when attention is turned to black people, whose disapproval the white "liberal" fears with an intensity bordering on horror.[28] The thought of a black person conjures up in his mind all the imagery and symbolism of the Civil War crusade against slavery, as well as of the subsequent struggles against the Ku Klux Klan and Jim Crow. Opposition to what black people or their spokesmen demand is thus closely associated in the white ' liberal's" mind with evil and the forces of extreme depravity. The thought that black people or their spokesmen might disapprove of him, that they might think of him, for instance, as a racist or a bigot—or merely as lacking sufficient concern to extirpate racism and bigotry—is enough to shake the white "liberal" to his foundations and instill terror in his soul.[24] It is roughly equivalent to the medieval Christian's fear of being denounced by the clergy as a heretic, excommunicated from the church, and denied access to the holy sacraments. It was the successful exploitation of this fear, it would seem, that was at least partially responsible for the incredible success of black and Hispanic groups, both in muting opposition to affirmative action, and in gaining such tremendous leverage over important segments of the federal bureaucracy and federal judiciary.

To the five forces of compassion, guilt, self-righteous hypocrisy, romanticism, and fear, a sixth would have to be added in the case of federal bureaucrats, which is simply a desire for power. A vast bureaucratic empire has been built up to enforce the policy of affirmative action, with the mandarins who rule over this empire wielding a degree of power and influence that would be the envy of many a petty prince. Almost every major corporation and university in the country has been brought under the control of this empire, which successfully intimidates employers into maintaining in their workforces whatever racial, ethnic, or gender balance the government bureaucrats deem appropriate. When the human will-to-power, the *libido dominandi,* combines with the other five forces mentioned, the result can be a potent mixture indeed.

Personalism and Public Policy

When discussing the issue of preferential hiring, both supporters and opponents of affirmative action almost invariably wind up in a position of appearing to give at least tacit approval to the materialistic-careeristic ethic that exerts so powerful a force in modern American life. One might characterize this ethic as one in which higher and better paying jobs are sought, not merely for the increase they provide in the ease and conveniences of life, or for the more challenging and fulfilling nature of the tasks they offer, but as ends in themselves and for the status and social prestige that go along with them. In premodern times, materialistic and careeristic attitudes were at least partially kept in check by the counter-pressure of the dominant religious ethic, which had always condemned the pursuit of wealth as an end in itself and viewed status-seeking as a form of vanity that constituted both a moral and social evil. Part of the reason why the affirmative action debate has generated so much heat in American society is precisely because these older religio-ethical restraints have largely been abandoned in modern times, allowing questions of material and career advancement to assume a hypertrophic significance in many people's lives totally out of proportion to the actual importance of such questions in the overall scheme of things.

There are, to be sure, numerous criticisms that can and should be made of modern Western careerism and materialism, particularly in their tendency to equate the value and worth of human beings with their degree of economic and careerist "success." But having made such criticisms, it is still necessary to have guidelines for a fair employment policy once one accepts the basic proposition that there is something radically wrong with any policy, such as the current policy of affirmative action, that encourages hiring on the basis of race and ethnicity. The present writer would like to suggest three fundamental principles, each closely related to the other, which can serve as a guide to evaluating any future government policy in the area of employment, or indeed, in any number of other areas as well. All three principles are closely in tune with the basic thrust of the 1950s and early 1960s civil rights movement and are based on the key idea of the human person as the inviolable unit of public policy concern. The three principles might be designated: 1) the self-representation-only principle; 2) the underdog-equality principle; and 3) the ethnicity-indifference principle.

The self-representation-only principle holds that in the eyes of the government each person is to be seen as representing only himself and his own personal history, rather than anyone else or anyone else's history, or any group of people or any group's history. What this means in terms of any government ameliorative or compensatory program is that no one who is himself privileged is to be considered underprivileged merely because many *other* people of the same race or ethnicity are underprivileged; nor is any person who is genuinely underprivileged to be considered privileged merely because many other people of the same race or ethnicity are privileged. The self-representation-only principle holds that the only human deprivation that public policy has any business concerning itself about is that deprivation, in terms of economic, educational, or cultural disadvantage, which is actually borne by actually deprived human be-ings.[30]

The second principle, the underdog-equality principle, holds that all involuntarily disadvantaged people, commensurate with their degree of disadvantage, have an equal claim to government compassion and concern, and an equal right to the benefits of any government program designed either to improve their life opportunities or alleviate their individual distress. The under-dog-equality principle also holds that the historical reason or reasons for a person's deprivation—whether, for instance, it can arguably be attributed to racial or ethnic discrimination rather than to some other cause or causes—is not a relevant consider-ation. The underdog-equality principle explicitly rejects racial and ethnic criteria as a basis for determining underdog status, on the grounds that all such criteria are both overinclusive and underinclusive, allowing many top-dogs to claim status as under-dogs, while denying to many genuine underdogs the right to claim title as such.

The third principle, the ethnicity-indifference principle, holds that racial and ethnic identities are strictly private affairs, which are to be accorded no official status in public law. The principle holds that all persons born or naturalized in the United States are to be viewed equally as citizens thereof, and are to enjoy all rights and benefits under public law *without* regard to race or ethnicity.

All of the three enumerated principles, as applied to a prefer-ential government hiring program, can be seen at work in the various programs that have existed in the past on state and local levels to encourage the hiring of the physically handicapped. Such programs might be taken as models for any government policy designed to improve the life-situation of the economically and culturally deprived. One obviously has no claim to special consideration because one's grandfather was physically handi-capped, or because one belongs to the same ethnic group as someone else who is physically handicapped, or because the ethnic group to which one belongs has a substantially higher percentage of physically handicapped persons than the public at large. And so it might be with a government policy to encourage employers to give special breaks to economic and cultural underdogs. While competency and ability should certainly be the main consideration for most job hiring, it would not seem to be inconsistent, either with our sense of justice or with the demands of economic efficiency, for government policy to encourage, at least on a voluntary basis, small deviations from the meritocratic principle in order to give a slight preference to those most in need of a job, or to those for whom a given employment position would represent the greatest step up the economic ladder. Such preference, however, would have to be given on a strictly race- and ethnicity-neutral basis.

Conclusion

It is important to keep in mind, in discussing the affirmative action debate, that the issues go much deeper than the simple question of employment policy, and touch the very roots of the American social order. And that social order, like any social order, is inherently precarious. The poison of ethnic tribalism brought chaos to the Balkans and to other areas of Eastern Europe in the early years of this century; it has led to bloodbaths in Armenia, India, Nigeria, Burundi, Uganda, Lebanon, Sri Lanka, and many other nations of Asia and Africa; it has periodically convulsed such otherwise stable nations as Belgium and Canada; and in the form of German National Socialism, it was to lead to one of the most brutal and genocidal regimes that the world has ever known.[31] America must not think that it is automatically immune to the fate of these other lands.[32] One simple fact can be extracted from all these tragic histories, and that simple fact is this: the principle of ethnic tribalism, if not counter-balanced by a more universal-human principle—such as that all men are created equal, that we are all part of the same *human* race, that in the eyes of God there is no Jew or Greek— is a principle of social chaos, and ultimately, a formula for civil war.

5. Why I Believe in Affirmative Action

By PAUL R. SPICKARD

Focus Despite the fact that as a white male he has been twice victimized by it, Paul R. Spickard explains why he supports the policy of affirmative action. Speaking as a Christian, Spickard says that his religion enjoins its followers to put the welfare of others ahead of their own welfare, and he sees the policy of affirmative action as one way of doing this. He describes how his own family, who came over on the *Mayflower,* profited from the slave trade, and how, through an inheritance, he himself has profited from the discriminatory behavior of his forbears. Affirmative action is seen by Spickard as an important tool for helping blacks, Hispanics, Asians, and white women who have little opportunity in life, and although he says that "some white males will get the short end of the stick," this is seen by him as a legitimate counterweight to the privileges white males have reaped in the past. "We," he says, "have given the short end to others for dozens of generations." His reaction to affirmative action should be compared with that of Lee Nisbet (selection 6).

Paul R. Spickard has taught history at Bethel College in Saint Paul, Minnesota, and is currently associate director of research at the Cultural Development Institute in Aromas, California.

SINCE THE LATE 1960s, the federal government has required those with whom it does business to act positively to hire and promote people from groups that have been discriminated against. And affirmative action has helped bring a noticeable improvement in the life chances of many blacks, Hispanics, Asians, and white women.

More recently, Attorney General Edwin Meese mounted a campaign against affirmative action, calling it "reverse discrimination." Although the Supreme Court handed him a defeat in July 1986, Justice Sandra Day O'Connor's concurring opinion and the Justice Department's hedging comments showed that Meese was unlikely to surrender.

I, a white male, have suffered from affirmative action. In 1976, with degrees from Harvard and the University of California, and a teacher's credential, I applied to teach the history of China and Japan. I was told, "I think we'll hire an Asian American." That stung. I was highly qualified: I spoke Japanese, had lived in Asia, and had studied Asian history for years. What would an American of Asian descent know about Asian history that I did not? The school could not find a qualified Asian, and I drove a truck for a living.

Five years later it happened again. A major university told me they would love to hire me. But the department was all white and all male, and they were looking to hire a minority woman.

I have been denied the chance to make a living because I am white and male. Yet I remain convinced that affirmative action is good social policy.

It is also a scriptural imperative in our social situation. Why? My understanding begins with Philippians 2:3–6, where Paul reminds us that Jesus did not look to his own benefit but spent himself for us, and he tells us that as Christians we have a responsibility to look out for other people's welfare before our own. Affirmative action is an appropriate way to do that.

This article originally appeared in *Christianity Today* (October 3, 1986). Reprinted with permission of the author.

America's initial push for equal opportunity resulted in very little progress. Blacks and others had not just been shut out of jobs, but had also been shut out of the education necessary to qualify for jobs.

Then Lyndon Johnson argued that an equal race is not necessarily a fair one. You don't starve somebody for a month, break both legs, put him at the starting line and say, "May the best man win." The long history of oppression had left some categories of people unable to compete.

Fortunately, the federal government's commitment to affirmative action created a mentality in society that it was valuable to hire minorities. This wider conviction has played an important part in improving the life chances of some women and minorities.

Isn't this unfair? It felt like discrimination to me. But consider: I come from generations of moderate wealth. My family came over on the *Mayflower* and made money in the slave trade. Doctors, lawyers, judges, and comfortable business people go back several generations in my clan. I was never wealthy, but I could not have devoted myself to college and graduate school without support from my family and a timely inheritance. I am standing on the shoulders of my ancestors and their discriminatory behavior.

Contrast my experience with that of a Chicago friend, whose immigrant father had a fourth-grade education and ran a grocery store. Without affirmative action and the social commitment it symbolizes, my friend might not have gone to Amherst, nor to Stanford law school. He might not have found a job with a major law firm, nor as a congressional aide. He is talented and has worked hard, but without affirmative action he might well be back in Modesto pumping gas. Our society would be poorer for the loss of his skills.

Affirmative action's job is not yet done. Black men still earn only about 76 per cent as much as white men in the same job categories. The gap between white males and others is far from closed.

Everything costs something. In the 1960s, when the economy was expanding, affirmative action seemed painless. But in the middle 1970s we realized that if some were to gain then others must lose. That was when affirmative action began to be called "reverse discrimination" (implying that there is a normal, proper direction for discrimination), and we white males began to defend our privileges.

Of course, affirmative action cannot do the whole job. It can do little about residential, religious, and educational segregation. But if genuine equal opportunity is to be achieved, affirmative action must be part of the picture. Some white males will get the short end of the stick, just as we have given the short end to others for dozens of generations.

Affirmative action may not always be fair. But I am willing to take second best if overall fairness is achieved. After all, for Christians, fairness—often translated in our Bibles as "justice" or "righteousness"—is a fundamental principle by which God calls us to live. And affirmative action is an appropriate part of a larger program aimed at achieving the godly goal of putting other's welfare before our own.

6. *Affirmative Action: A Liberal Program?*

By LEE NISBET

Focus Despite his superior qualifications, Lee Nisbet was denied a job at the University of North Carolina at Asheville because of affirmative action pressure placed upon the university by the federal Department of Health, Education, and Welfare. In the following article, written in the form of a commentary upon an article he had previously published, Nisbet attacks the policy of affirmative action as illiberal, unintelligent, and nonprogressive. Liberalism, he says, has always concerned itself with the welfare of individuals as individuals, not as the members of masses or classes "or other such linguistic abstractions." Racial, ethnic, and sexual groups, he says, do not apply for jobs; only individuals apply for jobs. Only individuals can perpetrate job discrimination, or suffer its effects. Nisbet protests most strongly against the type of thinking that would hold all white males guilty of discrimination—and therefore deserving of official disfavor—because other white males in the past have discriminated. Such thinking, he says, is not only illiberal, but morally unintelligible. Like Russell Nieli (selection 4), Nisbet sees much of the enthusiastic support that has been given to affirmative action by those whose own jobs are comfortable and secure as the very height of moral hypocrisy. "If faculties

111

are going to support quotas," he says, "it would seem only fair that *they* resign and search for minority candidates to replace themselves."

Nisbet's views should be compared with those of another scholar who suffered from affirmative action, Paul Spickard (selection 5).

Lee Nisbet has taught philosophy at Alfred University and at Medaille College, and has served on the editorial staff of the *Humanist* and *Free Inquiry* magazine.

A SHORT ARTICLE ON reverse discrimination, authored by myself appeared in the *Humanist* magazine in 1977. The reaction it provoked provides the opportunity to reflect not only on affirmative action but on some disturbing trends in contemporary "liberal" or "progressive" thinking.

The article, entitled "Reverse Discrimination—A Personal Encounter," said, among other things,

> Fair-minded persons applaud all efforts to make equal employment opportunities a reality. Affirmative action programs that contain racial, ethnic, or sex quotas or goals end up, however, in denying such opportunity. Consider as evidence excerpts from the following letter that I received last spring from a department chairman at the University of North Carolina at Asheville: "It is with considerable regret that I have to let you know that we are not offering you the position in our department. As you know, there is considerable pressure from HEW (Health, Education, and Welfare) to hire members of minority groups. We have offered the place to [Ms.—], the one who was here just a few days before you arrived. We all felt, of all the candidates we had checked into, you and [Ms.—]were at the top of the list. You have had more experience in teaching and already have your doctoral degree in hand. Her teaching experience is rather limited, and she will not get her degree until sometime this fall. Yet, under the circumstances, it was thought wise to offer her the position."
>
> At the bottom of the page was inscribed: "An Equal Opportunity Employer."
>
> The irony and hypocrisy of the message hardly needs comment. Appeals to HEW, articles carried in the *New York Times* and *Change* magazine by sympathetic scholars came to nought. This affair suggests that the principle of justice on which this social order *operates* is: When one group is unfairly

This excerpted article originally appeared in *Reverse Discrimination*, edited by Barry R. Gross. Reprinted with permission of Prometheus Books, 700 East Amherst Street, Buffalo, N.Y.

treated remedy the situation by unfairly treating another group. The new victim need not, however, have been the actual offender. White male graduate students looking for positions played no part in formulating university hiring practices, but they suffer sanctimonious punishment from the very academicians who did. If faculties are going to support quotas, it would seem only fair that *they* resign and search for minority candidates to replace themselves. Widespread support for this idea among academics has not yet been heard.

The consequences of reverse discrimination touch not only employer and potential employees, but also the many students who will be denied the attention of a better qualified educator. Worse yet are the political and social implications of official sanction of reverse discrimination. Creative work-oriented individuals can hardly be willing to sacrifice themselves for injustices they did not perpetrate. Sympathy for the just grievance of individuals discriminated against in the past and present will vanish if it becomes clear that these persons are advancing themselves unfairly. If the movement for political and social reforms shows itself *in practice* to be perpetrating further injustice, this social order is in for some very nasty times. In sum, it is not clear that affirmative action affirms much that is worth affirming.

A substantial number of letters to the editor followed. *All* of the correspondents were critical, some were outraged. Consider these excerpts from representative letters:

[A woman] . . . There is no "fair" way to bring about (relatively) equal opportunity in the short run, but if it is to be accomplished in the long run there is no way to avoid some injustice now. Or does Mr. Nisbet prefer to ignore three hundred years of injustice and not try to correct it? . . . Until we can gainfully employ everyone who wishes to work, some device—call it affirmative action, or anything else—is going to have to be used to distribute slices of pie more equitably.

[A man] If discrimination were directed only against isolated individuals, then the problem would be much simpler. Mr. Nisbet ignores the fact that, in social situations, none is truly innocent. How many of the white male graduate students

who are now having to bear this burden are the direct or
indirect beneficiaries of racist, sexist, or classist social policies? . . . What then is, or should be, the goal of a government-
sponsored, equal-opportunity, and affirmative-action program? In part, it is to provide relief from injustice to those
individuals who have suffered discriminatory treatment. In
the short run it can help to insure that all members of society
have an equal chance at job and promotion opportunities. But
such justifications fail to address the real problem, to provide
a solution that will, ultimately, obviate the need for affirmative
action. Such a solution requires that one not think just in
terms of individuals, but that one have an awareness of the
importance of class or group membership. Affirmative action,
to be worth the trouble and effort that it requires, must be
dedicated to creating a social setting where the power of the
white, middle-class male is broken. . . . When those who are
now the victims of the social order have their fair share of
power—and power is the name of the game—then we will
have moved closer to a just social arrangement. It is true that
those who are the beneficiaries of an unjust social order will
consider its alteration to be yet another injustice from the
personal point of view, but this cannot be helped.

In other letters, males proclaimed readiness to sacrifice career
aspirations to women, and white women professed willingness
to do the same for blacks—all in the name of reparations for
past injustice. Besides letters, disapproval was expressed in
more direct ways. Many of my friends, comrades in political
philosophy and causes, expressed surprise and dismay over my
new found "conservatism." The entire affair provoked the
following reflections.

Too much of so-called liberal or progressive thinking today is
in fact illiberal, unprogressive, and unintelligent. The essence of
liberalism has always been concern with the welfare, rights, and
responsibilities of *individuals qua individuals,* not the masses or
classes or other such linguistic abstractions. Furthermore, although there has been disagreement among liberals as to what
social arrangements might best liberate individual capacities, no
disagreement exists with the thesis that illiberal means, means

that impose *avoidable* injustices on individuals, cannot achieve just ends.

Therefore, when my letter-writing liberal or radical critics and friends explain that "in social situations no one is truly innocent," or that "power is the name of the game," or that, in effect, if one is a white male he is "guilty" of job discrimination because other white males have so discriminated and therefore "reparations" are justified and required—something seems peculiar. We find here no concern for the individual. What the person *did* as a person is irrelevant. His gender and race in some mysterious way render him guilty of offenses and deserving of admittedly unfair treatment. It hardly needs to be said that such proposals are neither liberal nor intelligent, much less morally intelligible.

Commonsensically, racial, ethnic, or sexual classes do not seek employment; individuals do. Commonsensically, discrimination is making racial, ethnic, or sexual classifications relevant criteria for jobs in which such criteria are clearly irrelevant to performing the task. As we know, the consequences of making such classifications conditions for employment have been amply and notoriously experienced by individuals who are black, female, Mexican American, or other. To claim now that these criteria *are* relevant to employment when they are used to even the score for the "good guys" is literally doublethink. The proposal that such doublethink can serve as a principle of social and economic justice is a classic example of the foolish attempt to secure just ends (equal job opportunity) through unjust means (reverse discrimination). Yet now we face the specter of a government-administered program trying to accomplish this impossible feat and thereby perpetuating the very abuses that genuinely progressive people have labored so long to eliminate.

I conclude, therefore, that labeling support of affirmative action programs of the sort discussed "liberal" or "progressive" is not only mistaken, but slanderous.

7. Affirmative Action Under Attack

By ROBERT F. DRINAN

Focus During the first term of the Reagan administration, the Department of Justice, led by Assistant Attorney General William Bradford Reynolds, filed a number of legal briefs in certain key court cases in an attempt to roll back some of the inroads that had been made by various race-, ethnicity-, and gender-based hiring programs. Although the administration's efforts were usually unsuccessful, Reynolds's activities touched off a considerable amount of controversy and debate, particularly in Washington. Robert F. Drinan criticizes the efforts of the Reagan Justice Department to abandon affirmative action. Although he concedes that the idea of affirmative action has been conceptually quite murky, he maintains that in practice the policy has had the advantage of flexibility and has been very effective in breaking down racial and gender stereotypes. Universities, businesses, and professional organizations, he contends, have accepted the policy quite willingly, and have sought to make their work forces reflect more accurately the percentage of minorities in their local populations. A vast body of law, custom, and accepted practice has been built up around the policy of affirmative action over the last fifteen years, Drinan argues, and it would be most unwise and destructive to dismantle it. According to Drinan, affirmative action has been adopted as an "interim strategy," during which time blacks and women are to be brought into the mainstream of American life. The policy, he concludes, may be in need of clarification, but it should not be abandoned.

Robert F. Drinan, a Jesuit priest, has served as a Democratic congressman from Massachusetts and is currently a professor of law at the Georgetown University Law Center in Washington, D.C.

THE REAGAN ADMINISTRATION has declared war on the concept of affirmative action in almost every one of its applications. In briefs filed in the U.S. Supreme Court, the Justice Department has claimed that the city of Detroit may not constitutionally follow a plan of hiring an equal number of black and white persons for Detroit's police force until the number of blacks in the force is 50 per cent. The assistant attorney general in charge of civil rights, William Bradford Reynolds, insisted that this plan discriminates against whites and is based on unconstitutional "quotas." On January 9, 1984, the Supreme Court declined to review the Detroit case, thus letting stand a lower court decision upholding the legality of the Detroit plan; a similar case involving fire fighters in Memphis, Tennessee, is still pending. But the administration will continue to pursue its conviction that affirmative action is neither required by nor consistent with the Constitution.

It is difficult to understand why the Reagan administration is so adamantly opposed to affirmative action. Nor is it possible to perceive any alternative it offers. In a recent debate with Mr. Reynolds I, and even some of the audience at the conservative Heritage Foundation, where the debate was held, had difficulty in comprehending where Mr. Reynolds stood on the key Supreme Court decisions on affirmative action.

Affirmative action was born as a result of the Civil Rights Act of 1964. Implementing the purposes and spirit of that law, federal agencies tried to make it clear that employers should reach out to minorities by "affirmative action." Their mandate was to bring the number of minorities in their work force more or less up to the percentage of minorities in the local community. Goals, targets, and timetables became the watchwords of officials at the Equal Employment Opportunity Commission and the Department of Labor, as these agencies sought to rectify the thousands

Reprinted by permission from the February 4, 1984, issue of *America* (© 1984 by America Press, Inc.).

of situations where minorities had obviously been discriminated against for a long time. The term "quota," used benignly or otherwise, has been generally avoided.

President Johnson explained the purpose of his Executive Order 11246 in a speech at Howard University in 1965: "You do not take a person who, for years, has been hobbled by chains and liberate him, bring him up to the starting line of a race and then say, 'You are free to compete with all of the others.' "

Guidelines issued in 1972 by the Department of Health, Education, and Welfare made it clear that Executive Order 11246 requires two things: (1) nondiscrimination or "the elimination of all existing discriminatory conditions whether purposeful or inadvertent," and (2) "affirmative action," which requires "the employer to make additional efforts to recruit, employ, and promote qualified members of groups formerly excluded."

Breaking Down Stereotypes

Professional and business groups have responded conscientiously and sometimes courageously to the challenges of affirmative action. Universities and others proudly proclaim that they are "affirmative action employers." The concept has entered the marketplace and has been accepted as fair and desirable.

The American Association of University Professors explained the concept of affirmative action in these words in 1973: "What is sought is essentially the revision of standards and practices to assure that institutions are in fact drawing from the largest marketplace of human resources in staffing their faculties and a critical review of appointment and advancement criteria to ensure that they do not inadvertently foreclose consideration of the best qualified persons by untested presuppositions which operate to exclude women and minorities."

The idea of affirmative action has always been conceptually difficult. It does not openly state that there has been overt discrimination in the past. It does not necessarily assume that racism or sexism has been operating. It is based on the painful phenomenon that blacks and women are grossly underrepresented in almost every occupation above those involving the least skilled persons. Affirmative action is designed to counter the negative action that brought about the exclusion of millions of persons because of their race or sex. Affirmative action does not say that unqualified persons must be hired but suggests that obviously many qualified persons have been excluded from positions because of a negative attitude toward them by those who do the hiring.

A dramatic example of affirmative action can be seen in the fact that President Carter in four years appointed more black lawyers to the federal bench than all other presidents together had ever done before. Why were not more black attorneys appointed to the federal bench prior to the Carter administration? That is the question that the administrators of affirmative action programs ask with respect to almost every category of workers in America.

Affirmative action programs operate with the hope that by education and example corporations and public agencies will voluntarily correct the racial and gender imbalances in their employment profile. But numerical and time goals are frequently necessary if an employer is to attain some substantial progress within a reasonable period. Hence, federal and state programs offer goals and timetables to employers and sometimes mandate them. Most employers are willing, even eager, to have outside help to break the pattern of a predominantly white or male work force. Remarkable progress has been made in the roughly fifteen years during which affirmative action has been the accepted practice of agencies that carry out the civil rights laws of the nation.

It is therefore baffling when the Justice Department insists that it is opposed in principle to affirmative action. It is, Mr. Reynolds insists, an attempt to cure discrimination by more discrimination. In its brief submitted in the Detroit case, the Justice Department stated that it "has profound doubts whether the Constitution permits governments to adopt remedies involving racial quotas to benefit persons who are not themselves the victims of discrimination—at least in the absence of a clear statement by Congress itself." This approach seeks to evade the fact of the massive underrepresentation of blacks in certain occupations by saying that "persons who are not themselves the victims of discrimination" have no claim on society. The idea of affirmative action was created precisely to reach those situations where overt racism did not necessarily exist but the results are the same as if it did exist. Affirmative action, in other words, is designed to reach the unconscious bias and the adherence to an unexamined custom that only whites should be waitresses or plumbers or police officers.

Mr. Reynolds further obscures what is actually the thinking of the Reagan administration when he insists that employment decisions should be color-blind. This approach, of course, would blot out many of the most helpful and healthy developments in the law of race relations over the past generation. Affirmative action assumes that public and private officials in the areas of education, housing, and employment can and should be color-sensitive. Mr. Reynolds seems so convinced that judgments arrived at with attention to color are undesirable that he has raised a serious question about the constitutionality of many color-conscious consent decrees entered into by the Justice Department in previous administrations.

The Supreme Court

In the three decisions in which the U.S. Supreme Court has ruled on affirmative action, it has not given support to the approach to affirmative action embraced by the Reagan administration. It has not, on the other hand, cleared up the conceptual or constitutional ambiguities inherent in the idea of hiring persons on criteria not exclusively related to their competence.

The 5-to-4 decision in 1978 requiring the University of California Medical School at Davis to admit Allan Bakke disallowed the relatively crude method of affirmative action employed by the admission officials at Davis. But the *Bakke* decision did not outlaw the use of race or minority status as one of the criteria for admission to a college. The Court, in fact, went out of its way to praise the Harvard plan where race, along with other facts, such as the ability to play the tuba, can be factored into the sophisticated formula employed for admissions. The majority decision in *Bakke,* moreover, approved of the use of race

since it conceded that ethnic diversity is a legitimate and constitutionally acceptable goal of a university. Although the result
and reasoning in *Bakke* are not free from ambiguity, that decision does not support the apparent position of the administration
that affirmative action itself is neither required nor allowed.

The Supreme Court in 1979 in a 6-to-3 vote held that Brian F.
Weber, a white employee of the Kaiser Aluminum & Chemical
Corporation who had lost his place in a training program to a
black, had no constitutional right to complain against the pact
between labor and management that reserved half the openings
in the training program for black employees. Mr. Reynolds
denies that he ever said that the *Weber* decision was wrongly
decided, but somehow he claims that the agreement to pursue
affirmative action in the Weber situation would not be constitutional if it were pursued by public employers.

In 1980, the Supreme Court sustained a provision in a public-
works program enacted by Congress by which 10 per cent of the
work had to be granted (with some exceptions) to contracting
companies controlled by minorities. The ruling in this case
should probably be limited to the unique facts of this now
discontinued federal program that was enacted, the Supreme
Court noted, by a coequal branch of government in order to deal
with an acute crisis in the economy. But again there is no
indication by the Court that affirmative action or color-
conscious programs are violations of the Constitution.

If the Supreme Court had decided to review the Detroit case
and rule on the constitutionality of laying off white police
officers with seniority over blacks in order to protect the objectives of affirmative action, it would have faced the toughest
question yet. Federal Judge Damon J. Keith who presided at the
Detroit trial held in a seventy-three-page opinion that Detroit
had for more than three decades used examinations and personnel tests that discriminated against black officers. Consequently,
he ruled to sustain the affirmative action program even though
this "upsets the expectations of white workers."

Blacks in Memphis won a similar victory where both the trial
and appellate courts concluded that Memphis could not follow
the "last-hired, first-fired" seniority rule because the objectives

of affirmative action prevent the firing of recently hired blacks. This case has produced dozens of briefs by national organizations on both sides of the controversy. The AFL-CIO took the position of the Justice Department and urged that courts should not be allowed to displace "employees of one race who have done no wrong . . . to make room for persons of another race who have not been the victims of discrimination."

Retaining the Present Policy

Up until the present time, it has been possible to continue to support the goals of affirmative action by holding that no whites will be hurt by it. Perhaps it will be possible to continue with that belief and conviction. An expanding economy makes it more possible to do so. But if jobs are phased out for any reason, hard choices between the rights of seniority and the rights obtained through affirmative action may have to be made. But to take an adamant position that all decisions made on affirmative action must yield to rights acquired by seniority is neither necessary nor required by the Constitution. Clearly, such a repudiation of affirmative action violates the spirit and even the letter of that vast body of law, custom, and practice that has developed since 1965. That body of law was designed to change the America that the Kerner Commission saw: two nations, "one white, one black."

The nation adopted affirmative action as an interim strategy for a period during which sex-based and race-rooted discrimination will gradually fade away. Affirmative action would not be needed if society would cure itself of treating women and blacks by stereotypes or by carefully concealed prejudices. Affirmative action is a technique designed to break the blindness of bias that has helped to produce a society with vast areas in which women and blacks are separated from the mainstream. To abolish affirmative action at this time is premature, unwise, and destructive.

There are some legal and constitutional commentators who continue to raise hypothetical questions about a possible Pandora's box if affirmative action is pressed too far. Not all of these critics were satisfied by the careful restraints imposed by the *Bakke* decision.

There are others who are opposed to affirmative action because they fear that a black or a woman will be placed ahead of them in the agency or corporation where they work. These fears are also present where there is a question of a minority challenge for places in schools or housing. But the remarkable thing about affirmative action is that it has worked as well as it has. Society has engaged in programs without requiring that everyone concede that the government and all of us owe restitution and reparation to black Americans because of what was done to them and to their ancestors for some 300 years. Affirmative action has remained fluid and flexible; it has requested voluntary compliance rather than requiring official submission; it has so raised the consciousness of Americans that institutions are chagrined if their personnel are inordinately white or male. It seems unwise to press Congress or the courts at this time for a definitive answer to the ultimate and enormously complicated questions involved, which are as difficult to articulate as to resolve. If white persons or males are being hurt—and there is little if any evidence of this—individual adjustments can be attempted. If unqualified blacks or women are being hired—and again the evidence is virtually nonexistent—training programs and modifications can be arranged.

Affirmative action recognizes that society must attempt to do something to correct the monumental mistakes made by generations of Americans toward blacks and women. This calls for a sensitivity to the institutionalized prejudice whose existence cannot be denied. What this country did in tolerating slavery from 1619 to 1865 has distorted reality for millions of Americans. What it did by requiring segregated schools up to 1954 has further confused that reality. Affirmative action, however ambiguous and nebulous, is one answer to all of the many misconceptions that Americans have about blacks and women. It should be clarified and refined, not scorned and abandoned.

8. *The Underhandedness of Affirmative Action*

By Harvey C. Mansfield, Jr.

Focus   Affirmative action policy is most frequently attacked for its alleged injustice and unfairness. Harvey C. Mansfield, Jr., says, however, that it is the underhandedness and duplicity of affirmative action policy, more than its injustice, that poses the real danger to democratic society. The policy of affirmative action, says Mansfield, was underhanded from its very conception, since it was clearly at odds with the 1964 Civil Rights Act and the intentions of its legislative architects. Moreover, Mansfield charges, this underhandedness carried over into the institutional implementation of the policy, since a candid acknowledgment of individual racial preference would tend to insult the policy's supposed beneficiaries and undermine the basis for their pride and self-esteem. A constitutional democracy, according to Mansfield, is based upon the principles of public discussion, persuasion, and the consent of the governed, but the current policy of affirmative action violates these basic principles. Affirmative action, he says, "never made its way through the legislative process with public notice and debate," and its proponents have treated citizens as though they need not be persuaded and their views are unworthy of being heard. Mansfield contends that our government, in pursuit of what it considers to be justice—but what the great majority of citizens consider to be injustice—"becomes ever more intrusive even as it increasingly shirks the task of persuasion." Mansfield concludes his article with some reflections on what he sees as the special mission of black Americans within the American constitutional polity. Blacks, he says, have a very special contribution to make to American society, for "they have been the victims of democratic injustice and have seen freedom from underneath." "They know what most other Americans can hardly imagine, that democratic majorities can do terrible wrong." This, Mansfield suggests, is a very valuable lesson for democratic polities to learn.

Harvey C. Mansfield, Jr., is a professor of government at Harvard University. His books include *The Spirit of Liberalism* and *Machiavelli's New Modes and Orders.*

A FFIRMATIVE ACTION IS settling down in our constitutional
  polity like a determined guest seeking to establish squat-
ter's rights. Though the issue is far from settled, controversy
has subsided. The Supreme Court has pronounced indecisively
on several occasions and in several voices. The Democratic
party, trying to exist on a faded and confused memory of itself,
has lost its early enthusiasm for affirmative action, but remains
"committed" to it in the routine sense of that word—stuck with
it. And the Reagan administration, elected in a spirit hostile to
affirmative action, has found it necessary, or merely convenient,
to tolerate it, even to truckle to it.

Former Interior Secretary James Watt's fatal remark about a
coal-leasing board he himself had appointed ("a black, a woman,
two Jews, and a cripple") helped to bring the administration's
attitude to public attention. Secretary Watt should have been
ashamed of himself, and perhaps under his boastful cynicism he
was. But, in the usual manner of shame, he seemed to put the
blame on others, on the groups clamoring for such treatment.
To supporters of affirmative action, this was "insensitive," and
insulting. Secretary Watt should have appointed the same people, minus the Jews, but without saying why. He should have
known that because everyone knows it; the concealment and the
lies are all the more necessary because everyone knows the
truth.

Affirmative action is obviously a way of helping people who
are considered insufficiently capable of helping themselves. But
just as obviously, this fact cannot be admitted. Or, if it is
admitted in general—as when Justice Marshall said in the *Bakke*
case that "meaningful equality remains a distant dream for the
Negro"—it must be denied in all particular cases. The reason
for wanting to help people is that we hold them to be equal in

some sense, hence deserving of equal treatment, but if we help them, we imply that they are unequal in some sense, hence undeserving of equal treatment. Government and management must therefore give help through affirmative action while denying that they give it, indeed *by* denying that they give it, in order not to hurt the pride of the beneficiaries. Their pride, and America's recognition of their pride, is not beside the point: it is the point.

Affirmative action *is* a question of pride, more than has been realized on either side of the debate. So far, most of the argument has been about its justice. Proponents say that because of past injustices, blacks, women, and others on a lengthening list deserve to get a break—partly for revenge, and partly because their suffering has left them unprepared to take advantage of the opportunities that it is admitted they now have. Opponents have replied that past injustice will not be remedied by new injustice of a similar kind, in which people are treated as representatives of groups rather than as individuals. The justice of affirmative action is affirmed by a majority of intellectuals and denied by a majority of the American people. In such a contest, I have no doubt where my sympathies lie. But the injustice or wrongness of affirmative action does not reach the depth of its evil.

The problem of affirmative action appears less grave than it is because its proponents present it as a matter of mere justice: they merely ask us to live by the principles we profess. They pass over the means to get us to live by our principles, and opponents of affirmative action have been content, for the most part, to dispute them over principles rather than means. But the underhandedness of affirmative action is what is worst in it. Even if justice were secured by such means, the result would not be compatible with the dignity or pride of free citizens. Such means, moreover, whether or not declared unconstitutional by the Supreme Court, are a threat to constitutional government, which is concerned as much with means as with ends—and the threat is all the greater for not being widely understood.

A Recipe for Resentment

To understand that threat, let us return to the necessity that affirmative action conceal the help it renders its beneficiaries.

As a policy, it cannot claim success, because to announce an "affirmative action appointment" as such is to insult the recipient by implying that he would not have got it on merit. It is a peculiar policy indeed where the administrator cannot admit he has done nothing, since this is hardly "action," yet cannot boast of doing something, lest his actions insult the beneficiary. Since the beneficiaries—blacks, women, and others protected by affirmative action—cannot admit that they are incapable and undeserving, the only remaining solution, it seems, is to accuse the American people, or what is left of it after the protected groups have been subtracted, of discriminating against their fellow citizens on grounds of race, sex, or national origin. The unprotected must admit their guilt so that the protected do not have to admit their incapacity.

But the unprotected include many white males who favor affirmative action; they cannot be guilty of racism and sexism. White males who oppose affirmative action must be the guilty ones, responsible for all the ills that affirmative action seeks to correct. Not that those guilty white males *do* anything discriminatory; any overt action to discriminate would be illegal without affirmative action. Rather, it is their bad attitude. Those white males glare balefully at the protected groups, wounding and disabling them with negative vibrations and looking out for any chance to do them in by wishing them ill.

This ludicrous picture of America, according to which opportunities for blacks and women have multiplied while racism and sexism have continued to run rampant, is what supporters and beneficiaries of affirmative action are required to believe. If opportunities were not open, we could not know that affirmative action beyond opening opportunities was needed; but since affirmative action is needed, the same Americans who opened them must secretly desire to close them. At a time when no American can publicly defend segregation, the most powerful Americans are supposed to desire it and to have succeeded in imposing it. Accusing one's fellow citizens of racism and sexism has become so routine, to be sure, that the seriousness of the charge has been forgotten. But to make a serious charge lightly is so far from an excuse as to be an aggravation. To accuse a group of "institutional racism" reveals a frivolous attitude in the accuser that is worse than the casual malice of which he complains.

None of this is meant to deny that prejudice exists in America. In one way prejudice is much greater than we know: since we live in a democracy, prejudice exists not only against those held inferior but also against people we suspect of superiority. But affirmative action, under the guise of opposing racism and sexism, inflates those attitudes by imputing them to other citizens as the sole cause of remaining inequalities. Although affirmative action claims to be a temporary policy, it has a vested interest in the continuation of prejudice. "Progress" in race and gender relations is made doubtful because each advance occurs not by the gradual disappearance of prejudice but with a triumph over it. The beneficiaries are encouraged to think that they got jobs or promotions not on merit but as punitive compensation, like the recovery of stolen goods from thieves. This may be cause for satisfaction in the beneficiaries, but it cannot be occasion for pride. The unprotected Americans—the "guilty" ones—are not ashamed; they are humiliated. They are not asked to live up to their ideals; they are forced to do so because it is assumed that they have not done so and will not do so on their own. This is a recipe for resentment.

Soft and Hard Modes of Bureaucratic Pressure

To combat the prejudice it inflates, affirmative action has two modes, which Nathan Glazer has distinguished as hard (quotas) and soft (pressure without quotas). These are two modes of the same policy rather than two policies. Affirmative action with quotas will often be opposed because it is too blatant, although the policy as such is by no means so honest that its proponents will admit that merit is no longer the first consideration. Instead, they try to redefine merit: it no longer means the best, or the best available; it is made to mean acceptable, or beyond a certain minimum. Sometimes "merit" is defined as what society needs, and society's needs are more big shots who are blacks and women; ergo, promoting them is promoting merit. They serve as "role models," and the role they model is that of being patronized by white males.

Still, despite these evasions, quotas are too blatant. They have been tagged as "reverse discrimination," not to say racism and sexism. Affirmative action therefore retreats to less obvious methods that, it is hoped, will save face for both employer and employed. For example, in my "place of employment"—Harvard University—affirmative action is said to amount to no more than an earnest attempt to "identify and consider" the protected candidates. Similarly, according to Justice Powell's majority opinion in the *Bakke* case, universities may "consider race" for admissions, but may not "use" it explicitly.

But this soft mode does not persist either. After time has passed, noses are counted, and if too many are found to be of the wrong color or sex, the order comes down to quit stalling, lest quotas be imposed. This order comes down, but does not go out. Soft and hard modes of affirmative action agree in their lack of candor; they vary only in the degree of pressure, as push differs from shove.

To manage its two modes, to coordinate the uses of insinuation and threat, affirmative action has its very own bureaucracy. Affirmative action officers are to be found in the employ of almost every large company and university. They are paid by the employer but they do not work for him. They work toward the achievement of affirmative action, no matter what that does to their employer, because their job is to see that their employer abides by federal regulations. Their job is not like that of a lawyer who might advise his employer on how to stay within the law while keeping his best interests in view; nor is it like that of a policeman, who enforces the law impartially and is paid by the government. Like everything else about affirmative action, its officers are in between. Their job is neither to advise nor to enforce, but to exert pressure.

It goes without saying that affirmative action officers must be members of protected groups. No white male could be trusted to have the necessary impartiality for that position, not even if he were a proponent of affirmative action. He might wish to do his best, but some tincture of bias would surely inhibit him in

question our capacity to take advantage of it. Most liberals seem not to appreciate fully that affirmative action does not add to previous reform but criticizes it, and that the reform being criticized is liberal reform. They are used to thinking of progress in reform, by which one reform, inadequate or incomplete by itself, suggests another. With the advent of affirmative action, however, previous reform is declared ineffectual, not merely inadequate, and progress itself becomes dubious.

Abolishing Prejudice By Inflating It

Those who favor affirmative action do not profess that they are abandoning equal opportunity; on the contrary, they promise to make opportunities really equal for the first time. They say that the natural endowments of the disadvantaged cannot overcome their histories right now, but at some time in the future, when those disadvantaged histories have been overcome by affirmative action, merit can once again be our standard and quotas be discarded. Affirmative action is thus professedly not an abandonment but a temporary postponement of equal opportunity. To say otherwise would be to admit that races and genders are permanently unequal.

But how long will it take to equalize the histories of blacks and women. At Harvard, the official policy is to continue affirmative action "until we have demonstrated to our own collective satisfaction that hiring decisions are absolutely color-blind and sex-neutral." *Absolutely* is a word not often heard at Harvard, where many people commonly say they do not believe in "absolutes." But the extremism of this absolute, which is necessary to the idea of affirmative action, has to be savored to be appreciated. It is not enough for us to decide, as best we can, on the basis of merit; each of us must be blind to his own color, neutral as to his sex. None of us can be trusted to decide on merit until each of us has repressed in himself any qualities that might possibly cause him not to decide on merit.

How is this marvelous repression to be achieved? Well, precisely by feeding the pride of race and sex in blacks and women, and guilt of the same in white males. One state of mind—being absolutely color-blind and sex-neutral—is to be achieved by practicing its contrary. This is what is meant when we are asked to live up to our principles, to "close the gap between reality and ideals" (as the Harvard policy puts it). Since the goal is absolute, the policy adopted to get there will take a very long time to succeed, if it can ever succeed. And since the means used by the policy contradict the goals, even progress is unlikely. Affirmative action begins with the assertion that despite civil rights legislation, prejudice continues and has got worse; then it concludes that despite the strength of prejudice, prejudice can and ought to be abolished; and last, it decides that abolition of prejudice can be accomplished by inflating it.

Some might think that the cure for the underhandedness of affirmative action is "open government," a policy of keeping nothing secret from the people. Not in the least! Under affirmative action the same thing happens as under open government generally. A visible action that is at first taken as a *sign* of morality becomes a morality *itself*. A visible affirmative action taken to overcome racism, such as appointing a black to office, instead of being understood as a sign that racism is gone, is mistaken for a blow at racism. Attention is thus shifted from motive to result ("equality of result"), and it is wrongly concluded that we can destroy racism by appointing blacks—only the result matters, not the means. What begins as an attempt to infuse our public and private lives with morality ends as indifference to the means so long as the end is achieved; it ends as indifference to morality. The gap between reality and our ideals is not closed; it is merely papered over—with bureaucratic forms, in which empty accusations are answered by insincere protestations. The perfect example of this immoral moralism is the "consent decree"—an oxymoron if there ever was one—describing the treatment of a defendant who does not admit he is guilty but agrees under compulsion to act as if he were.

Persuasion and Consent: The Requirements of a Free Society

It would be going too far to say that, in the matter of affirmative action, government by consent decree is replacing government by consent. But we have perhaps plumbed the depth of the harm done by affirmative action when we understand how it negates the principle of government by consent. The right to consent to government is often presented as a matter of justice, and rightly, because it is justice to count each person as one. But the right to consent is also a matter of dignity, because each person must *count* for something in order to be counted as one. It is the right to be treated as a person worthy of being taken seriously, as a rational creature capable of choice, who deserves to be persuaded and not taken for granted.

One cannot presume, therefore, how the right to consent will be exercised. One cannot suppose, for example, that blacks, because they are blacks, must want this and not want that. Of course, it is not always practicable to take a vote. It may be defensible to presume tacit consent in a situation from which one draws benefits, but consent that is presumed because of one's social and economic characteristics is an outrage. Whereas the first presumption declares what you have apparently consented to, leaving intact your right to withdraw consent, the second says what you *would* have consented to, thus making actual consent unnecessary and bothersome. It is hardly suprising, and not reprehensible, that blacks should vote for blacks, but for them to do so automatically is no merit and deserves no praise. For the government to presume, as a matter of law, that blacks will do so is no mere prediction of how they will vote but an unthinking usurpation of their right to consent.

In the recent extension of the Voting Rights Act (1982), Congress flirted with the idea of affirmative action consent that would have given protected groups the representation it presumed they would and should vote for. According to this bright idea, the government should no longer confine itself to guaranteeing the right to vote, but should now look to see how that right is exercised in case voting by one method or another should deprive a minority of its fair share of representation, *as calculated without reference to elections*. This was an attempt at mandated racist voting, and it was narrowly and only partially defeated.

Living together in freedom requires more than justice, for after justice has been exacted, people are not always in a mood to live together. To put ourselves in the right mood for free society we must recognize the dignity of other citizens. We must treat them, to repeat, as worthy of being persuaded. This morality of consent requires us to consent, for the sake of our morality, to a gap between reality and our ideals. It also provides a necessary check on our moralism, when we try to rush into reform too confident that those who are opposed are merely prejudiced. Moralism gives morality a bad name and makes free citizens angry and impatient with one another.

Properly understood, the right to consent neither prevents us from resorting to compulsion when necessary nor disables us from attempting reform when desirable. In this proper understanding, consent has its forms and procedures whose observance makes it necessary to persuade one's fellow citizens. Consent must be registered in legal elections to offices in bodies established by law so that it is clear who are the winners and losers. The point is to leave the majority capable of action after the minority has been heard. A person's right to consent is not violated when he has been outvoted, and his dignity has not been denied when he has been outargued. The forms and procedures of a free government give definition to the dignity of free citizens. It knows when it can act, and we know when we have been consulted.

All these forms and procedures, together with the spirit in which they are practiced, have been called constitutionalism. They ensure respect for the means by which the right of consent is exercised, and thereby they secure respect for the right of consent. They *constitute* a free society; without such forms a society might be tempted to believe that freedom is doing as one pleases, or doing what one thinks is required by justice.

Affirmative action has no regard for the forms and procedures that serve as protection of the right of consent. It has no patience with them when they seem to get in the way of justice, and no compunction about multiplying them when they are thought to advance justice. Any old procedure may be added: all that matters is the result. Thus, our government becomes ever more intrusive even as it increasingly shirks the task of persuasion.

The Special Contribution of Blacks

Those who agree with some, or most, or all of what I have said against affirmative action may still think that something needs to be done, and I believe they are right. In the first place, the case of blacks should be separated from those of all the rest. They are the only ones who were brought to America against their will and then enslaved. True, they were later freed, but still they were held down as second-class citizens. How can they be made into first-class citizens? But is it not evident that this question should be rephrased as, "How can they make themselves into first-class citizens?" To which the immediate answer must be; not by affirmative action; not by receiving justice from others so much as by claiming their own places in the name of pride.

Blacks should look more at what they contribute to America, less at what they want from it. Their wants make them dependent and force them to accentuate the negative, so that they humiliate themselves in the very act of demanding their due. They should consider what they have done in America and whether this is worthy of being continued. They should transform their predilections into conscious deliberation, and consider what they can and should do with their lives, given their choices and the range of opportunities America provides.

To claim 11 per cent of every activity on the principle of affirmative action is to say that blacks make no contribution of their own, and that America would have lost nothing distinctive if it had sent all its freed slaves back to Africa. But blacks have one sure contribution to make, a valuable addition to their other valuable contributions to our culture. They have been the victims of democratic injustice and have seen freedom from underneath, and in consequence they know what most other Americans can hardly imagine, that democratic majorities can do terrible wrong. This is valuable information for a free people.

In considering what they can do, and want to do, the primary responsibility should be on blacks themselves. The policy I suggest is as far from "benign neglect" as from intrusive interference. It is that blacks should be asked to affirm their own actions.

9. Why We Need Race Consciousness

By CHARLES KRAUTHAMMER

Focus
If affirmative action policy is thought to involve some degree of injustice to those who are involuntarily required to bear its costs, does this necessarily mean that the policy should be abandoned? Charles Krauthammer answers this question with an emphatic no. Racially based affirmative action, says Krauthammer, is a "breach of justice" and should be acknowledged as such. Nevertheless, the policy is seen by Krauthammer as furthering the valuable social purpose of rapid black advancement and integration and for this reason, he believes, should be retained. "It is not clear," says Krauthammer, "that correcting [the breach of justice that is affirmative action] is any more morally compelling than redressing the historic injustice done to blacks." Krauthammer considers the possibility that affirmative action policy may actually backfire and harm its intended black beneficiaries by negative psychological effects that reinforce a black sense of inferiority, but he concludes that on balance affirmative action policy is much more likely to help its intended beneficiaries than to harm them.

To the charge that affirmative action wrongfully disadvantages many blameless individuals and does not treat people equally, Krauthammer acknowledges that this is indeed the case, but he says that it is nothing unique to affirmative action policy. "We constantly enact social policies," Krauthammer says, "that favor certain groups at the expense of others," and as an example he mentions a government-induced recession to cure inflation. Such a recession, he says, causes suffering—"suffering that we know well in advance will be borne disproportionately by the poor and working class." Yet such policies are pursued nevertheless, for "we continually ask one group or another to bear special burdens for the sake of the community as a whole." Thus affirmative action policy, while inducing suffering, is seen by Krauthammer as fully justified by the worthy and necessary social purpose it seeks to further.

Charles Krauthammer is a senior editor of the *New Republic*.

A S RECENTLY AS three years ago Nathan Glazer noted with dismay the inability, or unwillingness, of the most conservative American administration in fifty years to do anything about the growing entrenchment, in law and in practice, of racial quotas. It seemed that officially sanctioned race consciousness was becoming irrevocably woven into American life.

Glazer's pessimism was premature. In the last two years a revolution has been brewing on the issue of affirmative action. It is marked not by the pronouncements of Clarence Pendleton, or the change in composition and ideology of the U.S. Commission on Civil Rights. That is for show. It is marked by a series of court rulings and administration actions that, step by step, will define affirmative action out of existence.

How far this process had gone was dramatized by the leak of a draft executive order that would outlaw in federal contracting not only quotas and statistical measures but any preference "on the basis of race, color, religion, sex, or national origin . . . with respect to any aspect of employment." Although this appeared as a bolt from a blue August sky, it was, in fact, the culmination of a process that has been building over the last several years. It amounts to a counterrevolution in stages on the issue of race-conscious social policy.

The counterrevolution has occured in what is probably the most crucial domain of affirmative action: employment. Classic affirmative action mandates preference for blacks (and women and other favored groups) at all four steps in the employment process: recruitment, hiring, promotion, and firing. The counterrevolution has attacked such preferences at each step of the way, beginning at the end.

The first major breach in the edifice of affirmative action was the Supreme Court's Memphis fire fighters decision of June 1984. The city of Memphis had been under a court-ordered consent decree to increase the number of blacks in the fire department. When layoffs came in 1981, a U.S. district court ruled that last-hired blacks could not be the first fired, as the seniority system dictated. Three whites were laid off instead. The Supreme Court reversed that decision. It ruled that in a clash between a bona fide seniority system and affirmative action, seniority prevails.

You cannot fire by race. But can you promote? Can you hire? The next, more tentative, step in the counterrevolution occurred in 1985 in the District of Columbia. A suit originally filed in the waning days of the Carter administration had resulted in mandated preferential hiring and promotions for minorities in the city's fire departments. In March, the D.C. fire chief, according to one of the judge's directives in the case, ordered that five black fire fighters be promoted over whites who had scored higher than they had.

The union immediately filed suit to block the promotions. And the Justice Department joined the suit on the union's side. The judge in the case then rendered a Solomonic decision prohibiting race consciousness in promotion, but permitting it in hiring.

The case is under appeal and no one knows how it will come out. The reason is that no one knows how to interpret *Memphis*. Did this ruling apply only to layoffs, as suggested by civil rights groups trying to limit their losses? Or did it apply also to hiring and/or promotion, the other crucial career choke points? You can read *Memphis* either way, and everyone is waiting for the Court to say.

Everyone, that is, except William Bradford Reynolds, head of the Justice Department's Civil Rights Division, and leading *contra*. Reynolds is a conservative in a hurry. Invoking *Memphis* as his authority, he ordered fifty-one jurisdictions from New York to Los Angeles to cleanse existing consent decrees (which mandated goals—quotas—in hiring) of any hint of group or racial preference. Not only would preferences be outlawed from now on, but existing decrees would have to be revised to reflect the new dispensation.

Reynolds's target is to root out race consciousness in toto, from firing to promotion to hiring. Everything, it seems, except recruitment. Last June, at the start of Reynolds's confirmation hearings for the number three job at Justice (he was eventually turned down), he sent a letter to Senator Edward Kennedy stating that he favored affirmative action in recruitment. He argued that it is the only permissible affirmative action; in fact, it is how you determine its success. Its success could be "measured," he wrote, "in the number of persons who are recruited to apply."

Recruiting, it seems, would be the last refuge for affirmative action. Or so it seemed, until the final step: draft Executive Order 11246 revising the affirmative action order that since 1965 has mandated race consciousness and statistical norms (quotas) in employment for government contractors. The draft executive order would repeal it all: goals, timetables, statistical norms, and other forms of racial preference.

It appears to do so even for Reynolds's cherished exception, recruitment. Hard to tell, though. The first section of the draft order seems to define affirmative action, as Reynolds likes to, as exclusively applicable to recruitment. "Each government contractor . . . shall engage in affirmative recruitment . . . to . . . expand[ing] the number of qualified minorities and women who receive full consideration for hiring and promotion." But the very next section continues: "Nothing in this executive order shall be interpreted to require . . . any preference . . . on the basis of race . . . with respect to any aspect of employment, including . . . recruitment."

Either the drafters are exceedingly careless, or the internal administration debate over whether to go the very last mile in eradicating race consciousness has yet to be decided. In either case, recruitment poses a logical problem for Reynolds & Company (if race consciousness is in principle unjust, how can it be okay for recruitment?). But it is not, in practice, a serious issue. If preferential treatment is outlawed for firing, promotion, and hiring, then recruitment really is the last mile: affirmative action expires long before it is reached. The administration and its civil rights opponents seem to agree that if this program—renegotiating the consent decrees and draft Executive Order 11246—is enacted, recruitment or not, race-conscious affirmative action is dead.

They disagree about whether that would be a good thing. Is race-conscious affirmative action worth saving?

There are three arguments in favor. The first, marshaled principally against Reynolds's revisionist consent decree, is profoundly conservative. It says that at this late date things are working out well, whatever the merits. Let well enough alone. The Justice Department would "disturb the acquiescence of the community in the new systems established after much travail and effort under the consent decrees," charged the NAACP. It will "threaten social peace for the sake of ideology," said the *Washington Post*. "Don't stick your nose in cases that have already been resolved," said Representative Don Edwards, one of five representatives who wrote to the attorney general asking him to cease and desist.

The irony here, of course, is that the NAACP is relatively new to the cause of "settledness." Not always has it argued that justice should be deferred so as not to "disturb the acquiescence of the community" in existing social arrangements. That was the segregationist case. And in that case, it was argued, correctly, that although settledness and social peace have some claim to make, they cannot prevail over the claims of justice.

It works, argues William H. Hudnut, the Republican mayor of Indianapolis, of his city's consent decree setting aside a quarter of its police and fire fighting slots for minorities. Why fix what ain't broke?

Because justice is not interested in what's broke and what's not; it is interested in justice. Hence the second argument for affirmative action, the familiar argument that while color blindness may be a value, remedying centuries of discrimination through (temporary) race consciousness is a higher value.

Does the right of the disadvantaged to redress (through preferential treatment) override the right of individuals to equal treatment? *Memphis* and the D.C. fire fighters decision begin to parse the issue. The logic of these decisions is that in layoffs and promotion the aggrieved whites have, by dint of service, acquired *additional* individual claims that outweigh the historical claims of blacks. But what about unadorned individual claims? When hired, you bring your citizenship with you and nothing else. Shouldn't that be enough to entitle you to equal, color-blind treatment?

It is not clear how to adjudicate the competing claims, that of an historically oppressed community for redress, and of the blameless individual for equal treatment. One side claims the mantle of—indeed, it defines itself as the side of—civil rights. But that is surely a semantic claim. The movement began, of course, as a civil rights movement. But when, for example, the D.C. Office of Human Rights declares that its primary mission is to ensure that blacks end up in city jobs in proportion "equal to their group representation in the available work force," the issue has ceased to be rights. It is group advancement.

The other side claims the mantle of individual rights and equal treatment. That is not a semantic claim. But it is not an absolute one either. After all, either by design or default, we constantly enact social policies that favor certain groups at the expense of others, the individuals in neither group having done anything to deserve their fate. One routine and devastating exercise in social engineering is the government-induced recession, periodically applied to the economy to curb inflation. The inevitable result is suffering, suffering that we know well in advance will be borne disproportionately by the poor and working class.

Is this discrimination by class? Certainly. It is not admitted to be so, and it is certainly not the primary effect. But it is an inevitable and predictable side effect. Yet in the face of an overriding national priority—saving the currency—we adopt policies that disproportionately injure a recognized class of blameless individuals. (Similarly, the draft discriminates by age, the placement of toxic waste dumps by geography, etc. We continually ask one group or another to bear special burdens for the sake of the community as a whole.)

If controlling inflation is a social goal urgent and worthy enough to warrant disproportionate injury to a recognized class of blameless individuals, is not the goal of helping blacks rapidly gain the mainstream of American life? This suggests a third, and to my mind most convincing, line of defense for affirmative

action. It admits that the issue is not decidable on the grounds
of justice. It argues instead a more humble question of policy:
that the rapid integration of blacks into American life is an
overriding national goal, and that affirmative action is the means
to that goal.

To be sure, affirmative action has myriad effects. They even
include such subtle negative psychological effects on blacks as
the "rumors of inferiority" studied by Jeff Howard and Ray
Hammond. The calculation is complex. But it is hard to credit
the argument that on balance affirmative action actually harms
blacks. Usually advanced by opponents of affirmative action,
this argument is about as ingenuous as Jerry Falwell's support
of the Botha regime out of concern for South African blacks.
One needs a willing suspension of disbelief to maintain that a
policy whose essence is to favor blacks hurts them. Even the
Reagan administration admits (in a report sent to Congress in
February 1985) that Executive Order 11246 has helped skilled
black men.

The Reagan counterrevolutionaries want to end the breach of
justice that is affirmative action. A breach it is, and must be
admitted to be. It is not clear, however, that correcting this
breach is any more morally compelling than redressing the
historic injustice done to blacks. In the absence of a compelling
moral case, then, the Reagan counterrevolution would retard a
valuable social goal: rapid black advancement and integration.
Justice would perhaps score a narrow, ambiguous victory.
American society would suffer a wide and deepening loss.

PART TWO

Constitutional Issues

10. Preferential Admissions and the Equal Protection Clause

By WILLIAM O. DOUGLAS

Focus The Fourteenth Amendment to the U.S. Constitution guarantees that no state shall deny to any person the equal protection of its laws, and the due process provision of the Fifth Amendment has generally been interpreted in recent times to hold actions of the federal government to a similar standard. Is preferential treatment for the members of certain stipulated racial and ethnic minority groups, when engaged in by a governmental entity, a denial of this basic constitutional right to equal protection for those people who are not members of such groups? This question has been at the heart of court challenges to the legitimacy of affirmative action programs, and the opinions of federal judges on the matter have varied widely. Indeed, the issue has been one of the most controversial and most divisive that federal courts have taken up in recent years.

The *DeFunis* case (1974), which dealt with the question of preferential admissions to a state law school, was the first occasion the U.S. Supreme Court had to address the issue of affirmative action in higher education. The majority of the Court, however, chose not to decide the matter, since the petitioner (Marcc DeFunis), who had initially won at the state superior court level, only to have the decision overturned by the state supreme court, was about to graduate from the University of Washington Law School, and thus the outcome of the case would have had no effect upon him. Justice William O. Douglas, however, dissented from the Court's decision to declare the case moot, and went on to write what many critics of affirmative action have seen as one of the most forceful, sensitive, and eloquent attacks upon the policy of preferential treatment based upon race.

Douglas's opinion challenges the view of those who claim that preferential treatment according to race does not have the effect of stigmatizing its intended beneficiaries. Despite contrary intentions, "a segregated admissions process," says Douglas, "creates suggestions of stigma and caste no less than a segregated classroom," and conveys the idea that the beneficiaries of such programs "cannot make it on their individual merit." That, he says, "is a stamp of inferiority that a state is not permitted to place on any lawyer." While Douglas is highly critical of the great weight law school admissions committees have traditionally placed on the Law School Admission Test (LSAT) score, and while he believes that admissions committees should take full account of all social, economic, or cultural disadvantage under which an applicant has had to labor, the Constitution, he says, mandates that all applicants to state law schools be treated in a neutral manner in regard to their race and ethnicity.

William O. Douglas was an associate justice of the Supreme Court from 1939 to 1975.

THE EDUCATIONAL POLICY choices confronting a university admissions committee are not ordinarily a subject for judicial oversight; clearly it is not for us but for the law school to decide which tests to employ, how heavily to weigh recommendations from professors or undergraduate grades, and what level of achievement on the chosen criteria are sufficient to demonstrate that the candidate is qualified for admission. What places this case in a special category is the fact that the school did not choose one set of criteria but two, and then determined which to apply to a given applicant on the basis of his race. The committee adopted this policy in order to achieve "a reasonable representation" of minority groups in the law school.

The Equal Protection Clause did not enact a requirement that law schools employ as the sole criterion for admissions a formula based upon the LSAT and undergraduate grades, nor does it proscribe law schools from evaluating an applicant's achievements in light of the barriers that he had to overcome. A black applicant who pulled himself out of the ghetto into a junior college may thereby demonstrate a level of motivation, perseverance, and ability that would lead a fair-minded admissions committee to conclude that he shows more promise for law study than the son of a rich alumnus who achieved better grades at Harvard. That applicant would be offered admission not because he is black, but because as an individual he has shown he has the potential, while the Harvard man may have taken less advantage of the vastly superior opportunities offered him. Because of the weight of the prior handicaps, that black applicant may not realize his full potential in the first year of law school, or even in the full three years, but in the long pull of a legal career his achievements may far outstrip those of his classmates whose earlier records appeared superior by conventional criteria. There is currently no test available to the admis-

This is an excerpted version of Douglas's dissenting opinion in the case of *DeFunis* v. *Odegaard*, 416 U.S. 312 (1974).

sions committee that can predict such possibilities with assurance, but the committee may nevertheless seek to gauge it as best as it can, and weigh this factor in its decisions. Such a policy would not be limited to blacks, or Chicanos or Filipinos or American Indians, although undoubtedly groups such as these may in practice be the principal beneficiaries of it. But a poor Appalachian white, or a second generation Chinese in San Francisco, or some other American whose lineage is so diverse as to defy ethnic labels, may demonstrate similar potential and thus be accorded favorable consideration by the committee. The difference between such a policy and the one presented by this case is that the committee would be making decisions on the basis of individual attributes, rather than according a preference solely on the basis of race.

The key to the problem is the consideration of each application *in a racially neutral way.* Since the LSAT reflects questions touching on cultural backgrounds, the admissions committee acted properly in my view in setting minority applications apart for separate processing. These minorities have cultural backgrounds that are vastly different from the dominant Caucasian. Minorities in our midst who are to serve actively in our public affairs should be chosen on talent and character alone, not on cultural orientation or leanings. The presence of an LSAT test is sufficient warrant for a school to put racial minorities into a separate class in order better to probe their capacities and potentials. The reason for the separate treatment of minorities as a class is to make more certain that racial factors do not militate *against an applicant or on his behalf.*

There is no constitutional right for any race to be preferred. The years of slavery did more than retard the progress of blacks. Even a greater wrong was done the whites by creating arrogance instead of humility and by encouraging the growth of the fiction of a superior race. There is no superior person by constitutional standards. A DeFunis who is white is entitled to no advantage by reason of that fact; nor is he subject to any disability, no matter his race or color. Whatever his race, he had a constitutional right to have his application considered on its individual merits in a racially neutral manner.

Favored-Minority Eligibility

The slate is not entirely clean. First, we have held that *pro rata* representation of the races is not required on juries or in public schools. We reviewed the contempt convictions of pickets who sought by their demonstration to force an employer to prefer Negroes to whites in his hiring of clerks, in order to ensure that 50 per cent of the employees were Negro. In finding that California could constitutionally enjoin the picketing there involved, we quoted from the opinion of the California Supreme Court:

> If petitioners were upheld in their demand then other races, white, yellow, brown, and red, would have equal rights to demand discriminatory hiring on a racial basis. . . . To deny to California the right to ban picketing in the circumstances of this case would mean that there could be no prohibition of the pressures of picketing to secure proportional employment on ancestral grounds of Hungarians in Cleveland, of Poles in Buffalo, of Germans in Milwaukee, or Portuguese in New Bedford, of Mexicans in San Antonio, of the numerous minority groups in New York, and so on through the whole gamut of racial and religious concentrations in various cities.

The reservation of a proportion of the law school class for members of selected minority groups is fraught with similar dangers, for one must immediately determine which groups are to receive such favored treatment and which are to be excluded, the proportions of the class that are to be allocated to each, and even the criteria by which to determine whether an individual is a member of a favored group. There is no assurance that a common agreement can be reached, and first the schools, and then the courts, will be buffeted with the competing claims. The University of Washington included Filipinos, but excluded Chinese and Japanese; another school may limit its program to blacks, or to blacks and Chicanos. Once the Court sanctioned racial preferences such as these, it could not then wash its hands of the matter, leaving it entirely in the discretion of the school. . . . But what standard is the Court to apply when a rejected applicant of Japanese ancestry brings suit to require the University of Washington to extend the same privileges to his group? The committee might conclude that the population of Washington is now 2 per cent Japanese, and that Japanese also constitute 2 per cent of the bar, but that had they not been handicapped by a history of discrimination, Japanese would now constitute 5 per cent of the bar, or 20 per cent. Nor obviously will the problem be solved if next year the law school included only Japanese and Chinese, for then Norwegians and Swedes, the Poles and the Italians, the Puerto Ricans and the Hungarians, and all other groups that form this diverse nation would have just complaints.

The key to the problem is consideration of such applications *in a racially neutral way*. Abolition of the LSAT test would be a start. The invention of substitute tests might be made to get a measure of an applicant's cultural background, perception, ability to analyze, and his or her relation to groups. There is, moreover, no bar to considering an individual's prior achievements, in the light of the racial discrimination that barred his way, as a factor in attempting to assess his true potential for a successful legal career. Nor is there any bar to considering on an individual basis, rather than according to racial classifications, the likelihood that a particular candidate will more likely employ his legal skills to service communities that are not now adequately represented than will competing candidates. Not every student benefited by such an expanded admissions program would fall into one of the four racial groups involved here, but it is no drawback that other deserving applicants will also get an opportunity they would otherwise have been denied. Certainly such a program would substantially fulfill the law school's interest in giving a more diverse group access to the legal profession. Such a program might be less convenient administratively than simply sorting students by race, but we have never held administrative convenience to justify racial discrimination.

The state may not proceed by racial classification to force strict population equivalencies for every group in every occupation, overriding individual preferences. The Equal Protection

Clause commands the elimination of racial barriers, not their creation in order to satisfy our theory as to how society ought to be organized. The purpose of the University of Washington cannot be to produce black lawyers for blacks, Polish lawyers for Poles, Jewish lawyers for Jews, Irish lawyers for the Irish. It should be to produce good lawyers for Americans and not to place First Amendment barriers against anyone. That is the point at the heart of all our school desegregation cases. A segregated admissions process creates suggestions of stigma and caste no less that a segregated classroom, and in the end it may produce that result despite its contrary intentions. One other assumption must be clearly disapproved, that blacks or browns cannot make it on their individual merit. That is a stamp of inferiority that a state is not permitted to place on any lawyer.

If discrimination based on race is constitutionally permissible when those who hold the reins can come up with "compelling" reasons to justify it, then constitutional guarantees acquire an accordion-like quality. It may well be that racial strains, racial susceptibility to certain diseases, racial sensitiveness to environmental conditions that other races do not experience may in an extreme situation justify differences in racial treatment that no fair-minded person would call "invidious" discrimination. Mental ability is not in this category. All races can compete fairly at all professional levels. So far as race is concerned, any state-sponsored preference of one race over another in that competition is in my view "invidious" and violative of the Equal Protection Clause.

majority, takes the view that any classification based on race that works to the detriment of anyone because of race is subject to the more severe of the two levels of scrutiny that are commonly used in equal protection cases—i.e., to the "compelling-state-interest" standard rather than the much looser "rational-basis" test. A racial classification, according to Mosk, is justified only when it serves a truly compelling governmental interest, and then only if no other reasonable means is available to achieve the same goal in a manner not constitutionally suspect. Mosk specifically rejects the view that racial classifications that disadvantage a majority race are subject to any less scrutiny under the Fourteenth Amendment than those that disadvantage the members of a minority race.

Like William O. Douglas, Mosk holds that a university may interpret the grades and test scores of applicants who come from disadvantaged backgrounds in the light of the disadvantage they have had to overcome, and it may also consider relevant nonquantitative factors; but whatever standard is applied, he says, it must be applied equally without regard to race.

Although Mosk views the shortage of physicians in many minority communities as the most compelling problem the medical school had sought to address by means of its minority admissions program, there are better means available to identify those likely to serve in such communities, he believes, than a racial test. No race, says Mosk, has a monopoly on humanitarian service to society any more than on selfish acquisitiveness.

Stanley Mosk has been a justice for the California State Supreme Court since 1964.

I T IS PLAIN that the special admission program at the Medical School of the University of California at Davis denies admission to some white applicants solely because of their race. Of the 100 admission opportunities available in each year's class, 16 are set aside for disadvantaged minorities, and the committee admits applicants who fall into this category until these 16 places are filled. The combined numerical rating assigned by the committee to each applicant who is granted an interview includes not only an evaluation of his academic scores but an assessment of all factors that the committee considers relevant to the successful pursuit of medical studies, such as an applicant's motives, character, and academic grades. Bakke claims that minority status is not a relevant consideration in determining whether an applicant is qualified for admission, and that admission decisions must be made without regard to the racial or ethnic background of a prospective student. The rating of some students admitted under the special program in 1973 and 1974 was as much as thirty points below that assigned to Bakke and other nonminority applicants denied admission. Furthermore, white applicants in the general admission program with grade-point averages below 2.5 were, for that reason alone, summarily denied admission, whereas some minority students in the special program were admitted with grade-point averages considerably below 2.5. In our view, the conclusion is inescapable that at least some applicants were denied admission to the medical school solely because they were not members of a minority race.

The fact that all the minority students admitted under the special program may have been qualified to study medicine does not significantly affect our analysis of the issues. In this context the only relevant inquiry is whether one applicant was more qualified than another. Bakke alleged that he and other nonminority applicants were *better* qualified for admission than the

This selection is excerpted from the decision of the California State Supreme Court, *Regents of the University of California* v. *Bakke,* 553 P.2d 1152 (1976).

161

minority students accepted under the special admission program, and the question we must decide is whether the rejection of better-qualified applicants on racial grounds is constitutional.

Two distinct inquiries emerge at this point. First, what test is to be used in determining whether the program violates the Equal Protection Clause. Second, does the program meet the requirements of the applicable test. The general rule is that classifications made by government regulations are valid "if any state of facts reasonably may be conceived" in their justification. This yardstick, generally called the "rational-basis" test, is employed in a variety of contexts to determine the validity of government action. But in some circumstances a more stringent standard is imposed. Classification by race is subject to strict scrutiny, at least where the classification results in detriment to a person because of his race. In the case of such a racial classification, not only must the purpose of the classification serve a "compelling state interest," but it must be demonstrated by rigid scrutiny that there are no reasonable ways to achieve the state's goals by means that impose a lesser limitation on the rights of the group disadvantaged by the classification.

The university asserts that the appropriate standard to be applied in determining the validity of the special admission program is the more lenient "rational-basis" test. It contends that the "compelling-interest" measure is applicable only to a classification that discriminates against a minority, reasoning that racial classifications are suspect only if they result in invidious discrimination; and that invidious discrimination occurs only if the classification excludes, disadvantages, isolates, or stigmatizes a minority or is designed to segregate the races. The argument is that white applicants denied admission are not stigmatized in the sense of having cast about them an aura of inferiority; therefore, it is sufficient if the special admission program has a rational relation to the university's goals.

We cannot agree with the proposition that deprivation based upon race is subject to a less demanding standard of review under the Fourteenth Amendment if the race discriminated against is the majority rather than a minority. We have found no case so holding, and we do not hesitate to reject the notion that racial discrimination may be more easily justified against one race than another, nor can we permit the validity of such discrimination to be determined by a mere census count of the races. Regardless of its historical origin, the Equal Protection Clause by its literal terms applies to "any person," and its lofty purpose, to secure equality of treatment to all, is incompatible with the premise that some races may be afforded a higher degree of protection against unequal treatment than others.

Admissions Programs

The university seeks to justify the program on the ground that the admission of minority students is necessary in order to integrate the medical school and the profession. The presence of a substantial number of minority students will not only produce diversity in the student body, it is said, but will influence the students and the remainder of the profession so that they will become aware of the medical needs of the minority community and be encouraged to assist in meeting those demands. Minority doctors will, moreover, provide role models for younger persons in the minority community, demonstrating to them that they can overcome the residual handicaps inherent from past discrimination. Furthermore, the special admission program will assertedly increase the number of doctors willing to serve the minority community, which is desperately short of physicians. Finally, it is urged, black physicians would have a greater rapport with patients of their own race and a greater interest in treating diseases that are especially prevalent among blacks, such as sickle cell anemia, hypertension, and certain skin ailments.

We reject the university's assertion that the special admission program may be justified as compelling on the ground that minorities would have more rapport with doctors of their own race and that black doctors would have a greater interest in treating diseases prevalent among blacks. The record contains no evidence to justify the parochialism implicit in the latter assertion; and as to the former, we cite as eloquent refutation to racial exclusivity the comment of Justice Douglas in *DeFunis*: "The purpose of the University of Washington cannot be to produce black lawyers for blacks, Polish lawyers for Poles, Jewish lawyers for Jews, Irish lawyers for Irish. It should be to produce good lawyers for Americans.''

Aims of the Medical School

The two major aims of the university are to integrate the student body and to improve medical care for minorities. In our view, the university has not established that a program that discriminates against white applicants because of their race is necessary to achieve either of these goals. We observe and emphasize in this connection that the university is not required to choose between a racially neutral admission standard applied strictly according to grade-point averages and test scores, and a standard that accords preference to minorities because of their race. In practice, colleges and universities generally consider matters other than strict numerical ranking in admission decisions. The university is entitled to consider that low grades and test scores may not accurately reflect the abilities of some disadvantaged students; and it may reasonably conclude that although their academic scores are lower, their potential for success in the school and the profession is equal to or greater than that of an applicant with higher grades who has not been similarly handicapped.

In addition, the university may properly, as it in fact does, consider other factors in evaluating an applicant, such as the personal interview, recommendations, character, and matters relating to the needs of the profession and society, such as an applicant's professional goals. In short, the standards for admission employed by the university are not constitutionally infirm except to the extent that they are utilized in a racially discriminatory manner. Disadvantaged applicants of all races must be eligible for sympathetic consideration, and no applicant may be rejected because of his race, in favor of another who is less qualified, as measured by standards applied without regard to race. In addition to flexible standards, the university might increase minority enrollment by instituting aggressive programs to identify, recruit, and provide remedial schooling for disadvantaged students of all races who are interested in pursuing a medical career and have an evident talent for doing so. Another ameliorative measure that may be considered is to increase the number of places available in the medical school.

Conclusion

None of the foregoing measures can be related to race, but they will provide for consideration and assistance to individual applicants who have suffered previous disabilities, regardless of their surname or color. So far as the record discloses, the university has not considered the adoption of these or other nonracial alternatives to the special admission program.

The need for more doctors to serve the minority community is perhaps the most serious of the problems that the university seeks to correct by means of its program. We do not doubt that amelioration of this societal infirmity is one of the most urgent tasks of the medical schools and the medical profession. We question, however, whether the university has established that the special admission program is the least intrusive or even the most effective means to achieve this goal. The university concedes it cannot assure that minority doctors who entered under the program, all of whom expressed an "interest" in practicing in a disadvantaged community, will actually do so. It may be correct to assume that some of them will carry out this intention, and that it is more likely they will practice in minority communities than the average doctor. Nevertheless, there are more precise and reliable ways to identify applicants who are genuinely interested in the medical problems of minorities than by race. An applicant of whatever race who has demonstrated his concern for disadvantaged minorities in the past and who declares that practice in such a community is his primary professional goal would be more likely to contribute to alleviation of the medical shortage than one who is chosen entirely on the basis of race and disadvantage. In short, there is no empirical data to demonstrate that any one race is more selflessly socially oriented or by contrast that another is more selfishly acquisitive.

Moreover, while it may be true that the influence exerted by minorities upon the student body and the profession will persuade some nonminority doctors to assist in meeting these

munities; they can help to further a better understanding for the special customs, habits, and medical needs of the members of minority communities; they will increase educational diversity in medical colleges; and they will provide important role models and sources of leadership for other members of their respective racial and ethnic groups. None of these legitimate and important goals can be achieved, Sobol contends, by any of the alternative, nonracial means suggested by the California Supreme Court. Neither increasing recruitment, expanding the size of the medical school, according special consideration to the disadvantaged, nor relying more heavily on nonquantitative criteria is likely to increase minority enrollment to any significant extent, he says.

Richard B. Sobol is a Washington, D.C.-based attorney.

JUST AS THE Fourteenth Amendment "does not enact Mr. Herbert Spencer's Social Statics," it does not enact the values of competitive selection The requirements of equal protection do not prohibit a state from considering the needs of the society and the needs of minorities in distributing the valuable resources of a professional education.

The fundamental analytical error of the court was its conclusion that the petitioner's special admissions program created a "suspect" classification, subject to review under a "strict-scrutiny" standard. Thus, the university's voluntary efforts to further racial equality were misjudged by standards developed to protect disadvantaged minorities from majoritarian governmental action that stigmatizes, separates, injures, or discriminates against them on the basis of race.

Apart from the decision, the strict-scrutiny doctrine has never been applied to thwart governmental efforts to redress deprivations suffered by minorities. To the contrary, this Court's decisions make clear that a classification is "suspect" only when it disadvantages a class entitled to special protection under the Fourteenth Amendment. A classification designed to benefit a disadvantaged class in their efforts to overcome the effects of past discrimination, and incidentally, which limits in a small way the benefits available to everyone else, is not a "suspect" classification and is not subject to "strict scrutiny."

Special Admissions Program Meets Strict Standards

For the reasons stated, *amici* believe this Court should explicitly reject the notion that governmental efforts intended to assist minorities in achieving full equality should be viewed as presumptively unconstitutional and tested under a compelling-interest standard. Nevertheless, the program in this case meets even the strictest standard of review. The Davis medical school's

This selection is excerpted from an *Amicus Curiae* brief of the National Council of Churches of Christ in the United States of America, et al.

169

efforts to include minorities in its student body is justified by a compelling social interest.

As a result of pervasive historic discrimination, there is a vast underrepresentation of certain minorities among physicians in the United States today. In 1972, when 12 per cent of all Americans were black, only 4,478 or 1.7 per cent of the 320,903 active physicians were black. There was one physician for every 649 persons in the general population; but only one black physician for every 4,298 blacks.

Before special admissions programs were inaugurated in medical schools throughout the United States, minority enrollment promised no improvement in this situation. As a result of special admissions programs, there has been a substantial increase in minority enrollment, but still far below the proportions of these groups in the population at large. By the 1974–75 school year, the percentage of black medical students rose to 6.3 per cent, of American Indians to 0.3 per cent, and of Mexican Americans to 1.2 per cent.

The Davis medical school opened in 1968. In that year there were no black or Chicano students in the school. From 1970–74, fifty-seven black and Chicano students were admitted under special admissions, but only seven were admitted under the regular admissions program. It is thus clear that absent special admissions, there would be only token black and Chicano enrollment in the medical school today.

There is a health care crisis in disadvantaged minority communities in California and throughout the United States. The infant mortality rate for black babies in America is almost double that of whites, and, in fact, approximates the rates in the developing countries. The maternal mortality rate for blacks is three times that for whites, and is on the rise. Minority babies who survive birth are twice as likely as white babies to die in infancy. White life expectancy is substantially higher. The figures go on and on.

Studies have established that minority professionals tend, to a very substantial extent, to practice in minority communities, and that they do so to a far greater extent than do white doctors. And, of course, statistical likelihood is enhanced by expressed intention. Every single student admitted to Davis under the special admissions program expressed an intention to serve disadvantaged communities upon graduation. Given the direct link between minority physicians and improved delivery of health care services in minority communities, there is obviously a compelling societal interest in programs to include minorities in medical college.

There are other compelling reasons for special admissions at Davis. First, there is the essential fairness, in a state with a 22 per cent black and Chicano population, to include minority students in a publicly supported medical school.

Second, the admission of minorities diversifies the student body and permits faculty and students alike to derive the benefits of an integrated education, inclusive of minority-group students who have a special appreciation for the customs, habits, and medical needs of their own people. "The purpose of racial integration is to benefit the community as a whole, not just certain of its members" [*Otero* v. *New York Housing Authority*, (2nd Cir. 1973)].

Third, increased numbers of minority professionals are a countervailing force to racial polarization, because minority professionals are a source of leadership to minority communities, and are able to assume positions of importance and power in the society at large. Moreover, to black and Chicano youths, professionals of their own race, and functioning in their own communities, serve as role models, and demonstrate the feasibility of educational and professional advancement.

The Court suggests that race-conscious measures are not permissible unless there has been a history of past discrimination and unless the remedy is imposed by the courts after a finding of unlawful conduct. But reason does not support such a rule and there are strong reasons to the contrary.

It may be that in this case the Davis medical school did not itself practice racial discrimination prior to the adoption of its special admissions program, but the medical school is an agency of the state of California. And there has been substantial racial discrimination against minorities in California in connection with elementary and secondary education. It cannot reasonably be

doubted that the relative absence of minorities in the Davis
student body prior to the adoption of the special admissions
program was a result of this discrimination. In these circumstances, the Fourteenth Amendment gives wide range to voluntary measures designed to include minorities in the medical
college.

Where a university determines voluntarily to redress near-
total absence of minority group members from its student body,
its efforts should be welcomed and not denied. Whites are
accorded more places in the Davis medical school than their
proportion of the California population. Nothing in the Constitution demands the virtual exclusion of minorities in pursuit of
a policy of social Darwinism.

Alternatives to a Race-Conscious Policy

As discussed above, the court applied the "strict-scrutiny"
equal protection test in this case. Although that court was willing
to assume that the Davis special admissions policy is justified by
a compelling state interest, it invalidated the policy on the
ground that the interest could be served without resorting to
race-conscious admissions. Because, under this court's decisions, the strict scrutiny test should not be applied to a benign
policy intended to help overcome the present effects of past
discrimination against minority groups, it is not the university's
burden to establish that there are no color-blind means of
achieving the same purpose. If the policy adopted by the state is
justifiable, that is the end of the inquiry.

But apart from the invalidity of the inquiry into possible
alternatives, we think it is clear that the alternative policies
suggested by the California Supreme Court would each be
ineffective or impractical. None is in any sense supported by the
record in this case or by any empirical experience.

First, the lower court suggested additional recruitment of
minorities. The medical school already engages in intensive
minority recruitment, and there is simply no reason to believe,
and indeed every reason to doubt, that additional recruitment
would produce minority candidates who meet regular admissions standards.

Next, the California court suggested that the size of the school be expanded in the hope that a larger entering class would include a large number of minorities. But the expansion of medical school facilities is enormously costly, and funds for this purpose have not been made available. Moreover, given the more than 3,700 applications for the 100 spaces in the 1974 entering class at Davis and the large number of white candidates with excellent credentials, it is doubtful that even doubling of the size of the medical school would have any significant impact on regular minority admissions.

The California court placed most emphasis on a policy of affording special consideration to economically "disadvantaged" applicants rather than to minority applicants. But many black applicants are not "disadvantaged" in terms of economic status, and most economically disadvantaged applicants are white. This approach would cut off the source of many of the most qualified black applicants—those from middle-class families who are most likely to seek professional training—and require the admission of large numbers of additional white applicants to achieve the goal of more minority students. This approach would be awkward, unmanageable, and of dubious efficacy in achieving the goal of increased numbers of minority professionals.

Lastly, the California court suggested more flexible admissions standards, which would emphasize personal interviews, recommendations, and other nonscore data. But unless such a program is intended to provide a mechanism for surreptitious consideration of race, there is no reason to believe it would significantly increase the admission of minority candidates. There are white as well as black candidates with impressive nonscore credentials, and many of the whites have impressive score credentials as well. Given the great preponderance of whites among the applicant pool, it seems reasonable to conclude that a truly nonracial implementation of such a program would not significantly increase admissions of minority candidates.

We submit that Davis's special admissions policy is narrowly drawn, is fair to white applicants, and is effective to achieve a

his application was not judged on merit, or that he was not judged as an individual, or that he was made to suffer because of his race, Dworkin answers that such charges neglect the crucial fact that the Davis admissions policy had no intention of subjecting Bakke's race to public insult or contempt. Racial exclusion is usually seen as immoral, Dworkin contends, primarily because historically it has been used to express prejudice and contempt for various races or religions. Bakke was excluded from the Davis medical school, however, not because of prejudice or contempt against the white race, "but because of a rational calculation about the socially most beneficial use of limited resources for medical education." The purpose of the special admission program, Dworkin believes, is a noble one, and one in which Bakke himself, along with the rest of society, can take pride.

Ronald Dworkin is a professor of jurisprudence at Oxford University, and a professor of law at New York University. His books include *Taking Rights Seriously, A Matter of Principle,* and *Law's Empire.*

O N OCTOBER 12, 1977, the Supreme Court heard oral argument in the case of *The Regents of the University of California* v. *Allan Bakke*. No lawsuit has ever been more widely watched or more thoroughly debated in the national and international press before the Court's decision. Still, some of the most pertinent facts set before the Court have not been clearly summarized.

The medical school of the University of California at Davis has an affirmative action program (called the "task force program") designed to admit more black and other minority students. It sets sixteen places aside for which only members of "educationally and economically disadvantaged minorities" compete. Allan Bakke, white, applied for one of the remaining eighty-four places; he was rejected but, since his test scores were relatively high, the medical school has conceded that it could not prove that he would have been rejected if the sixteen places reserved had been open to him. Bakke sued, arguing that the task force program deprived him of his constitutional rights. The California Supreme Court agreed, and ordered the medical school to admit him. The university appealed to the Supreme Court.

The Davis program for minorities is in certain respects more forthright (some would say cruder) than similar plans now in force in many other American universities and professional schools. Such programs aim to increase the enrollment of black and other minority students by allowing their race to count affirmatively as part of the case for admitting them. Some schools set a "target" of a particular number of minority places instead of setting aside a flat number of places. But Davis would not fill the number of places set aside unless there were sixteen minority candidates it considered clearly qualified for medical education. The difference is therefore one of administrative strategy and not of principle.

Decreasing the Importance of Race

So the constitutional question raised by *Bakke* is of capital importance for higher education in the United States, and a large number of universities and schools have entered briefs *amicus curiae* urging the Court to reverse the California decision. They believe that if they are not free to use explicit racial criteria in their admissions programs, they will be unable to fulfill what they take to be their responsibilities to the nation.

It is often said that affirmative action programs aim to achieve a racially conscious society divided into racial and ethnic groups, each entitled as a group to some proportionable share of resources, careers, or opportunities. That is a perverse description. American society is currently a racially conscious society; this is the inevitable and evident consequence of a history of slavery, repression, and prejudice. Black men and women, boys and girls, are not free to choose for themselves in what roles—or as members of which social groups—others will characterize them. They are black, and no other feature of personality or allegiance or ambition will so thoroughly influence how they will be perceived and treated by others, and the range and character of the lives that will be open to them.

The tiny number of black doctors and other professionals is both a consequence and a continuing cause of American racial consciousness, one link in a long and self-fueling chain reaction. Affirmative action programs use radically explicit criteria because their immediate goal is to increase the number of members of certain races in these professions. But their long-term goal is to *reduce* the degree to which American society is overall a racially conscious society.

The programs rest on two judgments. The first is a judgment of social theory: that the United States will continue to be pervaded by racial divisions as long as the most lucrative, satisfying, and important careers remain mainly the prerogative of members of the white race, while others feel themselves systematically excluded from a professional and social elite. The second is a calculation of strategy: that increasing the number of blacks who are at work in the professions will, in the long run, reduce the sense of frustration and injustice and racial self-consciousness in the black community to the point at which blacks may begin to think of themselves as individuals who can succeed like others through talent and initiative. At that future point the consequences of nonracial admissions programs, whatever these consequences might be, could be accepted with no sense of racial barriers or injustice.

It is therefore the worst possible misunderstanding to suppose that affirmative action programs are designed to produce a balkanized America, divided into racial and ethnic subnations. They use strong measures because weaker ones will fail; but their ultimate goal is to lessen not to increase the importance of race in American social and professional life.

According to the 1970 census, only 2.1 per cent of American doctors were black. Affirmative action programs aim to provide more black doctors to serve black patients. This is not because it is desirable that blacks treat blacks and whites treat whites, but because blacks, through no fault of their own, are now unlikely to be well served by whites, and because a failure to provide the doctors they trust will exacerbate rather than reduce the resentment that now leads them to trust only their own. Affirmative action tries to provide more blacks as classmates for white doctors, not because it is desirable that a medical school class reflect the racial makeup of the community as a whole, but because professional association between blacks and whites will decrease the degree to which whites think of blacks as a race rather than as people, and thus the degree to which blacks think of themselves that way. It tries to provide "role models" for future black doctors, not because it is desirable for a black boy or girl to find adult models only among blacks, but because our history has made them so conscious of their race that the success of whites, for now, is likely to mean little or nothing for them.

The history of the campaign against racial injustice since 1954, when the Supreme Court decided *Brown* v. *Board of Education,* is a history in large part of failure. We have not succeeded in reforming the racial consciousness of our society by racially neutral means. We are therefore obliged to look upon the arguments for affirmative action with sympathy and an open mind. Of course, if Bakke is right that such programs, no matter how effective they may be, violate his constitutional rights, then they cannot be permitted to continue. But we must not forbid them in the name of some mindless maxim, like the maxim that it cannot be right to fight fire with fire, or that the end cannot justify the means. If the strategic claims for affirmative action are cogent, they cannot be dismissed on the ground that racially explicit tests are distasteful. If such tests are distasteful, it can only be for reasons that make the underlying social realities the programs attack more distasteful still.

It is said that in a pluralistic society, membership in a particular group cannot be used as a criterion of inclusion or exclusion from benefits. But group membership is, as a matter of social reality rather than formal admission standards, part of what determines inclusion or exclusion for us now. If we must choose between a society that is in fact liberal and an illiberal society that scrupulously avoids formal racial criteria, we can hardly appeal to the ideals of liberal pluralism to prefer the latter.

Archibald Cox of Harvard Law School, speaking for the University of California in oral argument, told the Supreme Court that this is the choice the United States must make. As things stand, he said, affirmative action programs are the only effective means of increasing the absurdly small number of black doctors. The California Supreme Court, in approving Bakke's claim, had urged the university to pursue that goal by methods that do not explicitly take race into account. But that is unrealistic. We must distinguish, Cox said, between two interpretations of what the California court's recommendation means. It might mean that the university should aim at the same immediate goal, of increasing the proportion of black and other minority students in the medical school, by an admissions procedure that on the surface is not racially conscious. .

That is a recommendation of hypocrisy. If those who administer the admissions standards, however these are phrased, understand that their immediate goal is to increase the number of blacks in the school, then they will use race as a criterion in making the various subjective judgments the explicit criteria will require, because that will be, given the goal, the only right way to make those judgments. The recommendation might mean, on the other hand, that the school should adopt some nonracially conscious goal, like increasing the number of disadvantaged students of all races, and then hope that that goal will produce an increase in the number of blacks as a by-product. But even if that strategy is less hypocritical (which is far from plain), it will almost certainly fail because no different goal, scrupulously administered in a nonracially conscious way, will significantly increase the number of black medical students.

Cox offered powerful evidence for that conclusion, and it is supported by the recent and comprehensive report of the Carnegie Council on Policy Studies in Higher Education. Suppose, for example, that the medical school sets aside separate places for applicants "disadvantaged" on some racially neutral test, like poverty, allowing only those disadvantaged in that way to compete for these places. If the school selects those from that group who scored best on standard medical school aptitude tests, then it will take almost no blacks, because blacks score relatively low even among the economically disadvantaged. But if the school chooses among the disadvantaged on some basis other than test scores, just so that more blacks will succeed, then it will not be administering the special procedure in a nonracially conscious way.

So Cox was able to put his case in the form of two simple propositions. A racially conscious test for admission, even one that sets aside certain places for qualified minority applicants exclusively, serves goals that are in themselves unobjectionable and even urgent. Such programs are, moreover, the only means that offer any significant promise of achieving these goals. If these programs are halted, then no more than a trickle of black students will enter medical or other professional schools for another generation at least.

If these propositions are sound, then on what ground can it be thought that such programs are either wrong or unconstitutional? We must notice an important distinction between two different sorts of objections that might be made. These programs are intended, as I said, to decrease the importance of race in the United States in the long run. It may be objected, first, that the programs will harm that goal more than they will advance it. There is no way to prove that that is not so. Cox conceded in his argument that there are costs and risks in these programs.

Affirmative action programs seem to encourage, for example, a popular misunderstanding, which is that they assume that racial or ethnic groups are entitled to proportionate shares of opportunities, so that Italian or Polish ethnic minorities are, in theory, as entitled to their proportionate shares as blacks or Chicanos or American Indians are entitled to the shares the present programs give them. That is a plain mistake: the programs are not based on the idea that those who are aided are entitled to aid, but only on the strategic hypothesis that helping them is now an effective way of attacking a national problem. Some medical schools may well make that judgment, under certain circumstances, about a white ethnic minority. Indeed it seems likely that some medical schools are even now attempting to help white Appalachian applicants, for example, under programs of regional distribution.

So the popular understanding is wrong, but so long as it persists it is a cost of the program because the attitudes it encourages tend to a degree to make people more rather than less conscious of race. There are other possible costs. It is said, for example, that some blacks find affirmative action degrading; they find that it makes them more rather than less conscious of prejudice against their race as such. This attitude is also based on a misperception, I think, but for a small minority of blacks at least it is a genuine cost.

In the view of the many important universities that have such programs, however, the gains will very probably exceed the losses in reducing racial consciousness overall. This view is hardly so implausible that it is wrong for these universities to seek to acquire the experience that will allow us to judge whether they are right. It would be particularly silly to forbid these experiments if we know that the failure to try will mean, as the evidence shows, that the status quo will almost certainly continue. In any case, this first objection could provide no argument that would justify a decision by the Supreme Court holding the programs unconstitutional. The Court has no business substituting its speculative judgment about the probable consequences of educational policies for the judgement of professional educators.

Fundamental Rights

So the acknowledged uncertainties about the long-term results of such programs could not justify a Supreme Court decision making them illegal. But there is a second and very different form of objection. It may be argued that even if the programs *are* effective in making our society less a society dominated by race, they are nevertheless unconstitutional because they violate the individual constitutional rights of those, like Allan Bakke, who lose places in consequence. In the oral argument Reynold H. Colvin of San Francisco, who is Bakke's lawyer, made plain that his objection takes this second form. Mr. Justice White asked him whether he accepted that the goals affirmative action programs seek are important goals. Colvin acknowledged that they were. Suppose, Justice White continued, that affirmative action programs are, as Cox had argued, the only effective means of seeking such goals. Would Colvin nevertheless maintain that the programs are unconstitutional? Yes, he insisted, they would be, because his client has a constitutional right that the programs be abandoned, no matter what the consequences.

Colvin was wise to put his objections on this second ground; he was wise to claim that his client has rights that do not depend on any judgment about the likely consequences of affirmative action for society as a whole, because if he sustains that claim, then the Court must give him the relief he seeks.

But can he be right? If Allan Bakke has a constitutional right so important that the urgent goals of affirmative action must yield, then this must be because affirmative action violates some fundamental principle of political morality. This is not a case in which what might be called formal or technical law requires a decision one way or the other. There is no language in the Constitution whose plain meaning forbids affirmative action.

Only the most naive theories of statutory construction could argue that such a result is required by the language of any earlier Supreme Court decision or of the Civil Rights Act of 1964 or of any other congressional enactment. If Colvin is right, it must be because Allan Bakke has not simply some technical legal right but an important moral right as well.

What could that right be? The popular argument frequently made on editorial pages is that Bakke has a right to be judged on his merit. Or that he has a right to be judged as an individual rather than as a member of a social group. Or that he has a right, as much as any black man, not to be sacrificed or excluded from any opportunity because of his race alone. But these catch phrases are deceptive here, because, as reflection demonstrates, the only genuine principle they describe is the principle that no one should suffer from the prejudice or contempt of others. And that principle is not at stake in this case at all. In spite of popular opinion, the idea that the *Bakke* case presents a conflict between a desirable social goal and important individual rights is a piece of intellectual confusion.

Consider, for example, the claim that individuals applying for places in medical school should be judged on merit, and merit alone. If that slogan means that admissions committees should take nothing into account but scores on some particular intelligence test, then it is arbitrary and, in any case, contradicted by the long-standing practice of every medical school. If it means, on the other hand, that a medical school should choose candidates that it supposes will make the most useful doctors, then everything turns on the judgment of what factors make different doctors useful. The Davis medical school assigned to each regular applicant, as well as to each minority applicant, what it called a "benchmark score." This reflected not only the results of aptitude tests and college grade averages, but a subjective evaluation of the applicant's chances of functioning as an effective doctor, in view of society's present needs for medical service. Presumably the qualities deemed important were different from the qualities that a law school or engineering school or business school would seek, just as the intelligence tests a medical school might use would be different from the tests these other schools would find appropriate.

There is no combination of abilities and skills and traits that constitutes "merit" in the abstract; if quick hands count as "merit" in the case of a prospective surgeon, this is because quick hands will enable him to serve the public better and for no other reason. If a black skin will, as a matter of regrettable fact, enable another doctor to do a different medical job better, then that black skin is by the same token "merit" as well. That argument may strike some as dangerous; but only because they confuse its conclusion—that black skin may be a socially useful trait in particular circumstances—with the very different and despicable idea that one race may be inherently more worthy than another.

Consider the second of the catch phrases I have mentioned. It is said that Bakke has a right to be judged as an "individual," in deciding whether he is to be admitted to medical school and thus to the medical profession, and not as a member of some group that is being judged as a whole. What can that mean? Any admissions procedure must rely on generalizations about groups that are justified only statistically. The regular admissions process at Davis, for example, set a cutoff figure for college grade-point averages. Applicants whose averages fell below that figure were not invited to any interview, and therefore rejected out of hand.

An applicant whose average fell one point below the cutoff might well have had personal qualities of dedication or sympathy that would have been revealed at an interview, and that would have made him or her a better doctor than some applicant whose average rose one point above the line. But the former is excluded from the process on the basis of a decision taken for administrative convenience and grounded in the generalization, unlikely to hold true for every individual, that those with grade averages below the cutoff will not have other qualities sufficiently persuasive. Even the use of standard Medical College Admission Test (MCAT) as part of the admissions procedure requires judging people as part of groups, because it assumes that test scores are a guide to medical intelligence, which is in turn a guide to medical ability. Though this judgment is no doubt true statistically, it hardly holds true for every individual.

Allan Bakke was himself refused admission to two other medical schools, not because of his race but because of his age: these schools thought that a student entering medical school at the age of thirty-three was likely to make less of a contribution to medical care over his career than someone entering at the standard age of twenty-one. Suppose these schools relied, not on any detailed investigation of whether Bakke himself had abilities that would contradict the generalization in his specific case, but on a rule of thumb that allowed only the most cursory look at applicants over (say) the age of thirty. Did these two medical schools violate his right to be judged as an individual rather than as a member of a group?

The Davis medical school permitted whites to apply for the sixteen places reserved for members of "educationally or economically disadvantaged minorities," a phrase whose meaning might well include white ethnic minorities. In fact several whites have applied, though none has been accepted, and the California court found that the special committee charged with administering the program had decided, in advance, against admitting any. Suppose that decision had been based on the following administrative theory: it is so unlikely that any white doctor can do as much to counteract racial imbalance in the medical professions as a well-qualified and trained black doctor can do that the committee should for reasons of convenience proceed on the presumption no white doctor could. That presumption is, as a matter of fact, more plausible than the corresponding presumption about medical students over the age of thirty, or even the presumption about applicants whose grade-point averages fall below the cutoff line. If the latter presumptions do not deny the alleged right of individuals to be judged as individuals in an admissions procedure, then neither can the former.

Contempt and Public Insult

Colvin, in oral argument, argued the third of the catch phrases I mentioned. He said that his client had a right not to be excluded from medical school because of his race alone, and this as a statement of constitutional right sounds more plausible than claims about the right to be judged on merit or as an individual. It sounds plausible, however, because it suggests the following more complex principle. Every citizen has a constitutional right that he not suffer disadvantage, at least in the competition for any public benefit, because the race or religion or sect or other natural or artificial group to which he belongs is the object of prejudice or contempt.

That is a fundamentally important constitutional right, and it is that right that was systematically violated for many years by racist exclusions and anti-Semitic quotas. Color bars and Jewish quotas were not fair because they made race or religion relevant or because they fixed on qualities beyond individual control. It is true that blacks or Jews do not choose to be blacks or Jews. But it is also true that those who score low in aptitude or admissions tests do not choose their levels of intelligence. Nor do those denied admission because they are too old, or because they do not come from a part of the country underrepresented in the school, or because they cannot play basketball well, choose not to have the qualities that made the difference.

Race seems different because exclusions based on race have historically been motivated not by some instrumental calculation, as in the case of intelligence or age or regional distribution or athletic ability, but because of contempt for the excluded race or religion as such. Exclusion by race was in itself an insult, because it was generated by and signaled contempt.

Bakke's claim, therefore, must be made more specific than it is. He says he was kept out of medical school because of his race. Does he mean that he was kept out because his race is the object of prejudice or contempt? That suggestion is absurd. A very high proportion of those who were accepted (and, presumably, of those who run the admissions program) were members of the same race. He therefore means simply that if he had been black he would have been accepted, with no suggestion that this would have been so because blacks are thought more worthy or honorable than whites.

That is true: no doubt he would have been accepted if he were black. But it is also true, and in exactly the same sense, that he would have been accepted if he had been more intelligent, or made a better impression in his interview, or, in the case of other schools, if he had been younger when he decided to become a doctor. Race is not, in *his* case, a different matter from these other factors equally beyond his control. It is not a different matter because in his case race is not distinguished by the special character of public insult. On the contrary, the program presupposes that his race is still widely if wrongly thought to be superior to others.

In the past it made sense to say that an excluded black or Jewish student was being sacrificed because of his race or religion; that meant that his or her exclusion was treated as desirable in itself, not because it contributed to any goal in which he as well as the rest of society might take pride. Allan Bakke is being "sacrificed" because of his race only in a very artifical sense of the word. He is being "sacrificed" in the same artifical sense because of his level of intelligence, since he would have been accepted if he were more clever than he is. In both cases he is being excluded not by prejudice but because of a rational calculation about the socially most beneficial use of limited resources for medical education.

It may now be said that this distinction is too subtle, and that if racial classifications have been and may still be used for malign purposes, then everyone has a flat right that racial classifications not be used at all. This is the familiar appeal to the lazy virtue of simplicity. It supposes that if a line is difficult to draw, or might be difficult to administer if drawn, then there is wisdom in not making the attempt to draw it. There may be cases in which that is wise, but those would be cases in which nothing of great value would as a consequence be lost. If racially conscious admissions policies now offer the only substantial hope for bringing more qualified black and other minority doctors into the profession, then a great loss is suffered if medical schools are not allowed voluntarily to pursue such programs. We should then be trading away a chance to attack certain and present injustice in order to gain protection we may not need against speculative abuses we have other means to prevent. And such abuses cannot, in any case, be worse than the injustice to which we would then surrender.

Conclusion

We have now considered three familiar slogans, each widely thought to name a constitutional right that enables Allan Bakke to stop programs of affirmative action no matter how effective or necessary these might be. When we inspect these slogans, we find that they can stand for no genuine principle except one. This is the important principle that no one in our society should suffer because he is a member of a group thought less worthy of respect, as a group, than other groups. We have different aspects of that principle in mind when we say that individuals should be judged on merit, that they should be judged as individuals, and that they should not suffer disadvantages because of their race. The spirit of that fundamental principle is the spirit of the goal that affirmative action is intended to serve. The principle furnishes no support for those who find, as Bakke does, that their own interests conflict with that goal.

It is regrettable when any citizen's expectations are defeated by new programs serving some more general concern. It is regrettable, for example, when established small businesses fail because new and superior roads are built; in that case people have invested more than Bakke has. And they have more reason to believe their businesses will continue than Bakke had to suppose he could have entered the Davis medical school at thirty-three, even without a task force program.

There is, of course, no suggestion in that program that Bakke shares in any collective or individual guilt for racial injustice in the United States; or that he is any less entitled to concern or respect than any black student accepted in the program. He has been disappointed, and he must have the sympathy due that disappointment, just as any other disappointed applicant—even one with much worse test scores who would not have been accepted in any event—must have sympathy. Each is disappointed because places in medical schools are scarce resources and must be used to provide what the more general society most needs. It is not Bakke's fault that racial justice is now a special need—but he has no right to prevent the most effective measures of securing that justice from being used.

14. Remedying Past Discrimination

By WILLIAM J. BRENNAN, JR.

Focus
When the Supreme Court in 1978 finally handed down its decision in the *Bakke* case, four justices said that the Davis admissions program was a clear violation of Title VI of the 1964 Civil Rights Act, though they refused to address the constitutional question. Four other justices said that the Davis program was clearly constitutional and concluded from this fact that it must also be legal under Title VI. Justice Lewis Powell then negotiated between these two blocks and wrote the opinion for the Court (see selection 15). Justice Brennan, representing the second group of justices, defends here the constitutionality of Davis's admissions program on the basis of a standard of constitutional review somewhere between the very loose standard of a "rational basis," and the much stricter standard of a "compelling state interest." Racial classifications that seek to aid members of racial minority groups that in the past have been victimized by widespread social discrimination are not to be subject to the strictest level of constitutional scrutiny, according to Brennan, because those nonminority people who may be disadvantaged have recourse to the protection of the majoritarian political process, and in any event, they are not thereby stigmatized as inferior. Allan Bakke's rejection by the Davis medical school, says Bren-

nan, will "not affect him throughout his life in the same way as the segregation of the Negro school children" in the *Brown* case.

Racial classifications and preferences of the type used by the Davis medical school nevertheless must be scrutinized to some extent, Brennan contends, especially since the possibility exists that such practices may inadvertently lead to racial separatism and the stamping of those who benefit from them as inferior. Unlike William O. Douglas, however, Brennan does not find that a dual-track admissions system, or at least the particular one used at Davis, adversely stigmatizes minority admittees because, he says, all the students sit in the same classes, have the same instructors, and must meet the same requirements for a degree. Thus minority graduates, he asserts, "cannot justifiably be regarded as less well qualified than nonminority graduates." Like Richard B. Sobol (see selection 12), Brennan also contends that there is no practical alternative means of increasing minority enrollment without racial classification and racial preference. Giving preference to students from disadvantaged backgrounds is not likely to increase minority enrollment very much, he explains, because there are many more disadvantaged white people than disadvantaged minority group members, and the test scores of the disadvantaged white applicants tend to be higher than those of the disadvantaged minority applicants.

William J. Brennan, Jr., has served as an associate justice on the U.S. Supreme Court since 1956.

O UR NATION WAS founded on the principle that "all men are created equal." Yet candor requires acknowlegdment that the framers of our Constitution, to forge the thirteen colonies into one nation, openly compromised this principle of equality with its antithesis: slavery. The consequences of this compromise are well known and have aptly been called our "American Dilemma." Against this background, claims that law must be "color-blind" or that the datum of race is no longer relevant to public policy must be seen as aspiration rather than as description of reality. We cannot let color blindness become myopia, that masks the reality that many "created equal" have been treated within our lifetimes as inferior both by the law and by their fellow citizens. The assertion of human equality is closely associated with the proposition that differences in color or creed, birth or status, are neither significant nor relevant to the way in which persons should be treated. Nonetheless, the position that such factors must be "constitutionally an irrelevance," summed up by the shorthand phrase "our Constitution is color-blind," has never been adopted by this Court as the proper meaning of the Equal Protection Clause. Indeed, we have expressly rejected this proposition on a number of occasions.

We have held that a government practice or statute that restricts "fundamental rights" or that contains "suspect classifications" is to be subjected to "strict scrutiny" and can be justified only if it furthers a compelling government purpose and, even then, only if no less restrictive alternative is available. But no fundamental right is involved here. Nor do whites as a class have any of the "traditional indicia of suspectness: the class is not saddled with such disabilities, or subjected to such a history of purposeful unequal treatment, or relegated to such a position of political powerlessness as to command extraordinary protection from the majoritarian political process." On the other hand,

---

This is excerpted from William J. Brennan, Jr.'s, opinion in *Regents of the University of California* v. *Bakke,* 438 U.S. 265 (1978).

the fact that this case does not fit neatly into our prior analytic framework for race cases does not mean that it should be analyzed by applying the very loose rational-basis standard of review that is the very least that is always applied in equal protection cases. Instead, a number of considerations lead us to conclude that racial classifications designed to further remedial purposes "must serve important governmental objectives and must be substantially related to achievement of those objectives."

First, race, like "gender-based classifications too often [has] been inexcusably utilized to stereotype and stigmatize politically powerless segments of society." While a carefully tailored statute designed to remedy past discrimination could avoid these vices, we nonetheless have recognized that the line between honest and thoughtful appraisal of the effects of past discrimination and paternalistic stereotyping is not so clear.

Second, race, like gender and illegitimacy, is an immutable characteristic that its possessors are powerless to escape or set aside. While a classification is not *per se* invalid because it divides classes on the basis of an immutable characteristic, it is nevertheless true that such divisions are contrary to our deep belief that "legal burdens should bear some relationship to individual responsibility or wrongdoing," and that advancement sanctioned, sponsored, or approved by the state should ideally be based on individual merit or achievement, or at the least on factors within the control of an individual. In sum, because of the significant risk that racial classifications established for ostensibly benign purposes can be misused, causing effects not unlike those created by invidious classifications, it is inappropriate to inquire only whether there is any conceivable basis that might sustain such a classification. Instead, to justify such a classification an important and articulated purpose for its use must be shown. In addition, any statute must be stricken that stigmatizes any group or that singles out those least well represented in the political process to bear the brunt of a benign program.

Properly construed our prior cases unequivocally show that a state government may adopt race-conscious programs if the purpose of such programs is to remove the disparate racial impact its actions might otherwise have and if there is reason to believe that the disparate impact is itself the product of past discrimination, whether its own or that of society at large. There is no question that Davis's program is valid under this test.

Davis's Admission Program

Certainly, on the basis of the undisputed factual submissions before the Court, Davis had a sound basis for believing that the problem of underrepresentation of minorities was substantial and chronic and that the problem was attributable to handicaps imposed on minority applicants by past and present discrimination. Until at least 1973, the practice of medicine in this country was, in fact, if not in law, largely the prerogative of whites. In 1950, for example, while Negroes comprised 10 per cent of the total population, Negro physicians constituted only 2.2 per cent of the total number of physicians. Moreover, Davis had very good reason to believe that the national pattern of underrepresentation of minorities in medicine would be perpetuated if it retained a single admissions standard. For example, the entering classes in 1968 and 1969, the years in which such a standard was used, included only one Chicano and two Negroes out of 100 admittees.

The second prong of our test—whether the Davis program stigmatizes any discrete group or individual and whether race is reasonably used in light of the program's objectives—is clearly satisfied by the Davis program. It is not even claimed that Davis's program in any way operates to stigmatize or single out any discrete and insular, or even any identifiable nonminority group. Nor will harm comparable to that imposed upon racial minorities by exclusion or separation on grounds of race be the likely result of the program. It does not, for example, establish an exclusive preserve for minority students apart from and exclusive of whites. Rather, its purpose is to overcome the effects of segregation by bringing the races together.

Nor was Bakke in any sense stamped as inferior by the medical school's rejection of him. Indeed, it is conceded by all

that he satisfied those criteria regarded by the school as generally relevant to academic performance better than most of the
minority members who were admitted. Moreover, there is absolutely no basis for concluding that Bakke's rejection as a result
of Davis's use of racial preference will affect him throughout his
life in the same way as the segregation of the Negro school
children in *Brown* would have affected them.

In addition, there is simply no evidence that the Davis program discriminates intentionally or unintentionally against any
minority group that it purports to benefit. The program does not
establish a quota in the invidious sense of a ceiling on the
number of minority applicants to be admitted. Nor can the
program reasonably be regarded as stigmatizing the program's
beneficiaries or their race as inferior. The Davis program does
not simply advance less-qualified applicants; rather it compen-
sates applicants, whom it is uncontested are fully qualified to
study medicine, for educational disadvantage that it was reasonable to conclude was a product of state-fostered discrimination.
Once admitted, these students must satisfy the same degree
requirements as regularly admitted students; they are taught by
the same faculty in the same classes; and their performance is
evaluated by the same standards by which regularly admitted
students are judged. Under these circumstances, their performance and degrees must be regarded equally with the regularly
admitted students with whom they compete for standing.

Conclusion

We disagree with the lower court's conclusion that the Davis
program's use of race was unreasonable in light of its objectives.
First, as petitioner argues, there are no practical means by which
it could achieve its ends in the foreseeable future without the
use of race-conscious measures. With respect to any factor
(such as poverty or family educational background) that may be
used as a substitute for race as an indicator of past discrimination, whites greatly outnumber racial minorities simply because
whites make up a far larger percentage of the total population
and therefore far outnumber minorities in absolute terms at

every socioeconomic level. For example, of a class of recent medical school applicants from families with less than $10,000 income, at least 71 per cent were white. Moreover, while race is positively correlated with differences in GPA and MCAT scores, economic disadvantage is not. Thus, it appears that economically disadvantaged whites do not score less well than economically advantaged whites, while economically advantaged blacks score less well than do disadvantaged whites.

Second, the Davis admissions program does not simply equate minority status with disadvantage. Rather, Davis considers on an individual basis each applicant's personal history to determine whether he or she has likely been disadvantaged by racial discrimination. The record makes clear that only minority applicants likely to have been isolated from the mainstream of American life are considered in the special program; other minority applicants are eligible only through the regular admissions program. True, the procedure by which disadvantage is detected is informal, but we have never insisted that educators conduct their affairs through adjudicatory proceedings, and such insistence here is misplaced. A case-by-case inquiry into the extent to which each individual applicant has been affected, either directly or indirectly, by racial discrimination, would seem to be, as a practical matter, virtually impossible, despite the fact that there are excellent reasons for concluding that such effects generally exist. When individual measurement is impossible or extremely impractical, there is nothing to prevent a state from using categorical means to achieve its ends, at least where the category is closely related to the goal.

Finally, Davis's special admissions program cannot be said to violate the Constitution simply because it has set aside a predetermined number of places for qualified minority applicants rather than using minority status as a positive factor to be considered in evaluating the applications of disadvantaged minority applicants. For purposes of constitutional adjudication, there is no difference between the two approaches. In any admissions program that accords special consideration to disadvantaged racial minorities, a determination of the degree of preference to be given is unavoidable, and any given preference that results in the exclusion of a white candidate is no more or less constitutionally acceptable than a program such as that at Davis.

15. Race as a 'Plus' Factor

By LEWIS F. POWELL, JR.

Focus   Shortly before his retirement, Justice Lewis Powell said that his decision for the Court in the *Bakke* case was, of all his opinions, the one of which he was most proud. In his *Bakke* decision, Powell affirms the view that rights guaranteed under the Fourteenth Amendment are personal rights and that they apply equally to all individuals regardless of race or ethnicity. Powell also affirms the view that all racial and ethnic classifications, regardless of whether those injured by such classifications are members of a discrete and insular minority group or not, are inherently suspect and thus, subject to the most exacting standard of constitutional scrutiny. The view of those who would apply different equal protection standards to the members of different racial and ethnic groups is specifically rejected. "The guarantee of equal protection," says Powell, "cannot mean one thing when applied to one individual and something else when applied to a person of another color. If both are not accorded the same protection, then it is not equal." Even if it were constitutionally permissible to accord different standards of judicial scrutiny to legislation depending upon the racial and ethnic groups it affected, it would not be possible, Powell contends, for a court to devise such standards given the enormous ethnic diversity of America. America, he stresses, has become "a nation of minorities" as a result of post-Civil War immigration; one cannot simply divide the population into "Negro" and "white."

Powell scrutinizes four of the justifications given for Davis's preferential admissions program, and finds serious problems with each of the first three. The fourth justification, however, which emphasizes the educational benefit that comes from an ethnically diverse student body, is seen to have considerable merit since it involves the rights of academic freedom that are protected by the First Amendment. Powell was particularly impressed by the justification given for the program of preferential admissions at Harvard College: "A farm boy from Idaho can bring something to Harvard College that a Bostonian cannot offer. Similarly, a black student can usually bring something that a white person cannot offer." The dual admissions program at the Davis medical school, however, is seen by Powell as going far beyond any legitimate purpose that an educational institution might have in an ethnically diverse student body, and is therefore declared by him to be in violation of the Fourteenth Amendment. Race and ethnicity may be taken into account to add to the cultural diversity of an institution, but must be weighed fairly along with other relevant modes of individual diversity that would enhance the educational experience that an institution provides.

Lewis F. Powell, Jr., was a U.S. Supreme Court associate justice from 1972 to 1988.

THE SPECIAL ADMISSIONS program is undeniably a classification based on race and ethnic background. To the extent that there existed a pool of at least minimally qualified minority applicants to fill the 16 special admissions seats, white applicants could compete only for 84 seats in the entering class, rather than the 100 open to minority applicants. Whether this limitation is described as a quota or a goal, it is a line drawn on the basis of race and ethnic status.

The guarantees of the Fourteenth Amendment extend to all persons. Its language is explicit: "No state shall . . . deny to any person within its jurisdiction the equal protection of the laws." It is settled beyond question that the "rights created by the first section of the Fourteenth Amendment are, by its terms, guaranteed to the individual. The rights established are personal rights" (*Shelley* v. *Kraemer*, 1948). The guarantee of equal protection cannot mean one thing when applied to one individual and something else when applied to a person of another color. If both are not accorded the same protection, then it is not equal.

Nevertheless, petitioner argues that the court below erred in applying strict scrutiny to the special admissions programs because white males, such as respondent, are not a "discrete and insular minority" requiring extraordinary protection from the majoritarian political process. This rationale, however, has never been invoked in our decisions as a prerequisite to subjecting racial or ethnic distinctions to strict scrutiny. Nor has this Court held that discreteness and insularity constitute necessary preconditions to a holding that a particular classification is invidious. Racial and ethnic distinctions of any sort are inherently suspect and thus call for the most exacting judicial examination.

This perception of racial and ethnic distinctions is rooted in our nation's constitutional and demographic history. The

This is an excerpt from Lewis F. Powell, Jr.'s, opinion in *Regents of the University of California* v. *Bakke*, 435 U.S 265 (1978).

Court's initial view of the Fourteenth Amendment was that its "one pervading purpose" was "the freedom of the slave race, the security and firm establishment of that freedom, and the protection of the newly made freeman and citizen from the oppressions of those who had formerly exercised dominion over him" (*Slaughterhouse Cases*, 1873). The Equal Protection Clause, however, was "virtually strangled in infancy by post-Civil War judicial reactionism." It was relegated to decades of relative desuetude while the Due Process Clause of the Fourteenth Amendment, after a short germinal period, flourished as a cornerstone in the Court's defense of property and liberty of contract. It was only as the era of substantive due process came to a close, that the Equal Protection Clause began to attain a genuine measure of vitality.

By that time it was no longer possible to peg the guarantees of the Fourteenth Amendment to the struggle for equality of one racial minority. During the dormancy of the Equal Protection Clause, the United States had become a nation of minorities. Each had to struggle—and to some extent struggles still—to overcome the prejudices not of a monolithic majority, but of a "majority" composed of various minority groups of whom it was said—perhaps unfairly in many cases—that a shared characteristic was a willingness to disadvantage other groups. As the nation filled with the stock of many lands, the reach of the clause was gradually extended to all ethnic groups seeking protection from official discrimination.

Although many of the framers of the Fourteenth Amendment conceived of its primary function as bridging the vast distance between members of the Negro race and the white "majority," the amendment itself was framed in universal terms, without reference to color, ethnic origin, or condition of prior servitude. Indeed, it is not unlikely that among the framers were many who would have applauded a reading of the Equal Protection Clause that states a principle of universal application and is responsive to the racial, ethnic, and cultural diversity of the nation.

Petitioner urges us to adopt for the first time a more restrictive view of the Equal Protection Clause and hold that discrimination against members of the white "majority" cannot be suspect if its purpose can be characterized as "benign."[1] The clock of our liberties, however, cannot be turned back to 1868. It is far too late to argue that the guarantee of equal protection to *all* persons permits the recognition of special wards entitled to a degree of protection greater than that accorded others. "The Fourteenth Amendment is not directed solely against discrimination due to a 'two-class theory'—that is, based upon differences between 'white' and Negro."

Once the artificial line of a "two-class theory" of the Fourteenth Amendment is put aside, the difficulties entailed in varying the level of judicial review according to a perceived "preferred" status of a particular racial or ethnic minority are intractable. The concepts of "majority" and "minority" necessarily reflect temporary arrangements and political judgments. As observed above, the white "majority" itself is composed of various minority groups, most of which can lay claim to a history of prior discrimination at the hands of the state and private individuals. Not all of these groups can receive preferential treatment and corresponding judicial tolerance of distinctions drawn in terms of race and nationality, for then the only "majority" left would be a new minority of white Anglo-Saxon Protestants. There is no principled basis for deciding which groups would merit "heightened judicial solicitude" and which would not. Courts would be asked to evaluate the extent of the prejudice and consequent harm suffered by various minority groups. The kind of variable sociological and political analysis necessary to produce such rankings simply does not lie within the judicial competence—even if they otherwise were politically feasible and socially desirable.

Morever, there are serious problems of justice connected with the idea of preference itself. First, it may not always be clear that a so-called preference is in fact benign. . . . Second, preferential programs may only reinforce common stereotypes holding that certain groups are unable to achieve success without special protection based on a factor having no relationship to individual worth. Third, there is a measure of inequity in forcing innocent persons in respondent's position to bear the burdens of redressing grievances not of their making.

By hitching the meaning of the Equal Protection Clause to these transitory considerations, we would be holding, as a constitutional principle, that judicial scrutiny of classifications touching on racial and ethnic background may vary with the ebb and flow of political forces. Disparate constitutional tolerance of such classifications may well serve to exacerbate racial and ethnic antagonisms rather than alleviate them. Also, the mutability of a constitutional principle, based upon shifting political and social judgments, undermines the chances for consistent application of the Constitution from one generation to the next, a critical feature of its coherent interpretation.

Petitioner's Purpose

We have held that in "order to justify the use of a suspect classification, a state must show that its purpose or interest is both constitutionally permissible and substantial, and that its use of the classification is 'necessary . . . to the accomplishment' of its purpose or the safeguarding of its interest." The special admissions program purports to serve the purpose of: (i) "reducing the historic deficit of traditionally disfavored minorities in medical schools and in the medical profession." (ii) countering the effects of societal discrimination; (iii) increasing the number of physicians who will practice in communities currently underserved; and (iv) obtaining the educational benefits that flow from an ethnically diverse student body. It is necessary to decide which, if any, of these purposes is substantial enough to support the use of a suspect classification.

If petitioner's purpose is to assure within its student body some specified percentage of a particular group merely because of its race or ethnic origin, such a preferential purpose must be rejected not as insubstantial but as facially invalid. Preferring members of any one group for no reason other than race or ethnic origin is discrimination for its own sake. This the Constitution forbids.

The state certainly has a legitimate and substantial interest in ameliorating, or eliminating where feasible, the disabling effects of identified discrimination. In the school cases, the states were required by court order to redress the wrongs worked by specific instances of racial discrimination. That goal was far more focused than the remedying of the effects of "societal discrimination," an amorphous concept of injury that may be ageless in its reach into the past. We have never approved a classification that aids persons perceived as members of relatively victimized groups at the expense of other innocent individuals in the absence of judicial, legislative, or administrative findings of constitutional or statutory violations. Without such findings of constitutional or statutory violations, it cannot be said that the government has any greater interest in helping one individual than in refraining from harming another. Thus, the government has no compelling justification for inflicting such harm. The purpose of helping certain groups whom the faculty of the Davis medical school perceived as victims of "societal discrimination" does not justify a classification that imposes disadvantages upon persons like respondent, who bear no responsibility for whatever harm the beneficiaries of the special admissions program are thought to have suffered.

Petitioner identifies, as another purpose of its program, improving the delivery of health care services to communities currently underserved. It may be assumed that in some situations a state's interest in facilitating the health care of its citizens is sufficiently compelling to support the use of a suspect classification. But there is virtually no evidence in the record indicating that petitioner's special admissions program is either needed or geared to promote that goal. Petitioner simply has not carried its burden of demonstrating that it must prefer members of particular ethnic groups over all other individuals in order to promote better health care delivery to deprived citizens. Indeed, petitioner has not shown that its preferential classification is likely to have any significant effect on the problem.

Ethnic Diversity

The fourth goal asserted by petitioner is the attainment of a diverse student body. This clearly is a constitutionally permissible goal for an institution of higher education. Academic freedom, though not a specifically enumerated constitutional right, long has been viewed as a special concern of the First Amendment. The freedom of a university to make its own judgments as to education includes the selection of its student body. Thus in arguing that its universities must be accorded the right to select those students who will contribute the most to the "robust exchange of ideas," petitioner invokes a countervailing constitutional interest, that of the First Amendment.

It may be argued that there is greater force to these views at the undergraduate level than in a medical school where the training is centered primarily on professional competency. But even at the graduate level, our tradition and experience lend support to the view that the contribution of diversity is substantial. Physicians serve a heterogeneous population. An otherwise qualified medical student with a particular background—whether it be ethnic, geographic, culturally advantaged, or disadvantaged—may bring to a professional school of medicine experiences, outlooks, and ideas that enrich the training of its student body and better equip its graduates to render with understanding their service to humanity.

Ethnic diversity, however, is only one element in a range of factors a university properly may consider in attaining the goal of a heterogeneous student body. Although a university must have wide discretion in making the sensitive judgments as to who should be admitted, constitutional limitations protecting individual rights may not be disregarded. It may be assumed that the reservation of a specified number of seats in each class for individuals from the preferred ethnic groups would contribute to the attainment of considerable ethnic diversity in the student body. But petitioner's argument that this is the only effective means of serving the interest of diversity is seriously flawed. In a most fundamental sense the argument misconceives the nature of the state interest that would justify consideration of race or ethnic background. It is not an interest in simple ethnic diversity, in which a specified percentage of the student body is in effect guaranteed to be members of selected ethnic groups, with the remaining percentage an undifferentiated aggregation of students. The diversity that furthers a compelling state interest encompasses a far broader array of qualifications and characteristics of which racial or ethnic origin is but a single though important element. Petitioner's special admissions program, focused *solely* on ethnic diversity, would hinder rather than further attainment of genuine diversity.

The experience of other university admissions programs, which take race into account in achieving the educational diversity valued by the First Amendment, demonstrates that the assignment of a fixed number of places to a minority group is not a necessary means toward that end. An illuminating example is found in the Harvard College program:

> In recent years Harvard College has expanded the concept of diversity to include students from disadvantaged economic, racial, and ethnic groups. Harvard College now recruits not only Californians or Louisianians but also blacks and Chicanos and other minority students. . . . In practice, this new definition of diversity has meant that race has been a factor in some admission decisions. The race of an applicant may tip the balance in his favor just as geographic origin or a life spent on a farm may tip the balance in other candidates' cases. A farm boy from Idaho can bring something to Harvard College that a Bostonian cannot offer. Similarly, a black student can usually bring something that a white person cannot offer. In Harvard College admissions the Committee has not set target-quotas for the number of blacks, or of musicians, football players, physicists or Californians to be admitted in a given year. . . . [But the Committee], with a number of criteria in mind, pays some attention to distribution among many types and categories of students.

In such an admissions program race or ethnic background may be deemed a "plus" in a particular applicant's file, yet it does not insulate the individual from comparison with all other candidates for the available seats. The file of a particular black applicant may be examined for his potential contribution to diversity without the factor of race being decisive when compared, for example, with that of an applicant identified as an Italian American if the latter is thought to exhibit qualities more likely to promote beneficial educational pluralism. Such qualities could include exceptional personal talents, unique work or service experience, leadership potential, maturity, demonstrated compassion, a history of overcoming disadvantage, ability to communicate with the poor, or other qualifications deemed important. This kind of program treats each applicant as an individual in the admissions process. The applicant who loses out on the last available seat to another candidate receiving a "plus" on the basis of ethnic background will not have been foreclosed from all consideration for that seat simply because he was not the right color or had the wrong surname. It would mean only that his combined qualifications, which may have included similar nonobjective factors, did not outweigh those of the other applicant. His qualifications would have been weighed fairly and competitively, and he would have no basis to complain of unequal treatment under the Fourteenth Amendment.

In summary, it is evident that the Davis special admissions program involves the use of an explicit racial classification never before countenanced by this Court. No matter how strong their qualifications, quantitative and extracurricular, including their own potential for contribution to educational diversity, applicants who are not Negro, Asian, or Chicano are never afforded the chance to compete with applicants from the preferred groups for the special admissions seats. The fatal flaw in petitioner's preferential program is its disregard of individual rights as guaranteed by the Fourteenth Amendment. In enjoining petitioner from ever considering the race of any applicant, however, the courts failed to recognize that the state has a substantial interest that legitimately may be served by a properly devised admissions program involving the competitive consideration of race and ethnic origin.

16. The Disease as a Cure

By ANTONIN SCALIA

Focus Lewis Powell's decision in the *Bakke* case (selection 15) was viewed in many quarters as a Solomonic compromise, and indeed there was something in it for each side in the affirmative action debate. Opponents of preferential admissions could point to the fact that the dual admissions system at Davis was declared unconstitutional, that Allan Bakke was to be admitted to medical school, and that the principle that the Fourteenth Amendment applied equally to everyone, regardless of race or ethnicity, was affirmed with considerable force. Supporters of preferential admissions, however, could point out that the decision explicitly allowed for race to be taken into account in the making of admissions decisions, and since few educational institutions giving preference according to race did so through so rigid and so formalized a procedure as the two-track admissions policy at the Davis Medical School, most affirmative action programs, at least those in higher education, were seen to be given a secure constitutional footing.

Antonin Scalia, while opposing racial affirmative action, agrees with many of the supporters of the policy in seeing Powell's decision as a green light to racial preference, at least if the preference is conferred in a more discrete manner than was done at the Davis medical school. Unlike Powell, Scalia finds the state's interest in cultural diver-

against discrimination by race, we have witnessed an historic trivialization of the Constitution. Justice Powell's opinion, which we must work with as the law of the land, strikes me as an excellent compromise between two committees of the American Bar Association on some insignificant legislative proposal. But it is thoroughly unconvincing as an honest, hard-minded, reasoned analysis of an important provision of the Constitution.

There is, of course, a lot of pretense or self-delusion (you can take your choice) in all that pertains to affirmative action. Does anyone really think, for example, that the situation has changed at Davis? So instead of reserving class places for minority students, the school will open all slots to all applicants, but in choosing among them, will take into account the need for diversity—piano players, football players, people from the country, minority students, etc. When it comes to choosing among these manifold diversities in God's creation, will being a piano player, do you suppose, be regarded as more important than having yellow skin? Or will coming from Oshkosh, Wisconsin, be regarded as more important than having a Spanish surname? It will be very difficult to tell.

Only two results of the *Bakke* decision are certain. First, the judgments that the Davis medical school makes in filling these 100 slots will be effectively unappealable to the courts. (There is no way to establish, for example, that the diversity value of New York City oboists has not been accorded its proper weight.) Second, when all is said and done, it is a safe bet that though there may not be a piano player in the class, there are going to be close to sixteen minority students. And I suspect that Justice Powell's delightful compromise was drafted precisely to achieve these results—just as, it has been charged, the Harvard College "diversity admissions" program, which Mr. Justice Powell's opinion so generously praises, was designed to reduce as inconspicuously as possible the disproportionate number of New York Jewish students that a merit admissions system had produced.

Examples abound to support my suggestion that this area is full of pretense or self-delusion. Affirmative action requirements under Title VI and VII are said repeatedly "not to require the hiring of any unqualified individuals." That gives one a great feeling of equal justice until it is analyzed. Unfortunately, the world of employment applicants does not divide itself merely into "qualified" and "unqualified" individuals. There is a whole range of ability—from unqualified, through minimally qualified, qualified, well qualified, to outstanding. If I cannot get Leontyne Price to sing a concert I have scheduled, I may have to settle for Erma Glatt. La Glatt has a pretty good voice, but not as good as Price. Is she unqualified? Not really—she has sung other concerts with modest success. But she is just not as good as Price. Any system that coerces me to hire her in preference to Price, because of her race, degrades the quality of my product and discriminates on racial grounds against Price. And it is no answer to either of these charges that Glatt is "qualified." To seek to assuage either the employer's demand for quality or the disfavored applicant's demand for equal treatment by saying there is no need to hire any unqualified individuals is a sort of intellectual shell game, which diverts attention from the major issue by firmly responding to a minor one.

But, of course, even the disclaimer of compulsion to hire unqualified individuals loses something when it is translated into practice by the advocates of affirmative action. Consider, for example, the following statement by Professor Edwards: "This is not to say that blacks or women must be thrust into positions for which they are not qualified; however, when the choice is between white males and other qualified or qualifiable individuals, we should open the available positions to those who formerly could not occupy them. ' Note that what begins with the ritualistic denial of any intent to foster hiring of the unqualified imperceptibly shifts to a call for hiring of the "qualifiable," which surely must be a subcategory of the unqualified. It is typical of the confused level of debate that characterizes this field.

Another example of pretense or self-delusion is the Department of Labor's regulations concerning goals for hiring to overcome "underutilization": "The purpose of a contractor's establishment and use of goals is to insure that he meets his affirmative action obligation. It is not intended and should not be used to discriminate against any applicant or employee because of race, color, religion, sex, or national origin." This is, quite literally, incredible. Once there is established a numerical figure, the failure to meet it will have material, adverse consequences; namely, the substantial risk of cutoff of government contracts and the substantial certainty of disruptive and expensive government investigations. All that we know about human nature and human motivations indicates quite clearly that discrimination often will be produced in an effort to meet or exceed the magic number. I am a businessman who has, let us say, six more jobs to fill, and I am three short of my minority "goal." Reaching the goal will render my government contracts secure and will save thousands of dollars in the expenses necessary to comply with the demands of an equal employment investigation. If I consult my self-interest, which people tend to do, I will hire three minority applicants, even if they are somewhat less qualified than others. When the results that are inevitable are compared with the results that are said to be "intended," one must conclude that the drafter of the regulation is either fooling us or fooling himself. I appreciate, of course, that any antidiscrimination law with teeth in it will generate *some* pressures to favor minority groups. But that is worlds away from the "we-need-three-more-nonwhites" attitude that is the utterly predictable result of so-called "goals."

Judge Wisdom, dissenting in the *Weber* case, makes the following statement: "The Union's duty to bargain in good faith for all its members [an obligation imposed by law] does not prevent it from fairly advancing the national policy against discrimination, even if that requires assisting some of its members more than others." One has to be reminded of the line from *Animal Farm*, to the effect that all animals are created equal but some are more equal than others. And one cannot help but think that a paraphrase of Judge Wisdom's statement would fit very nicely in the mouth of a good old-fashioned racist employer: "We favor all applicants, but we favor white applicants more than others." It is very difficult to take Judge Wisdom's argument as a serious attempt to identify and grapple with the real issue rather than as an elaborate intellectual word game.

Another pretense or self-delusion—perhaps the grandest of

all—is the notion that what was involved in the *Weber* case is voluntary private discrimination against whites. As Judge Wisdom put it: "While the government might not be able to require that restorative justice be done neither should it prevent it." Fancy that! To think that the real issue in *Weber,* and presumably all those "reverse discrimination" cases, is damnable federal regulation: whether the federal government should be able to *prevent* the discrimination against better qualified employees, which Kaiser and thousands of other businesses throughout the country are chomping at the bit to engage in! That is, of course, chimerical. Nobody really believes that Kaiser would have established the challenged program, or the union permitted it, without the "incentive" of federal administrative regulations, which in effect makes the application of what Judge Wisdom calls "restorative justice" a condition for the award of government contracts and for the avoidance of expensive litigation in and out of the courts. To discuss the issue in the fictitious context of voluntarism not only makes any intelligently reasoned decision impossible in the particular case, but poisons the well of legal discourse.

The Restorative Justice Handicapping System

That last quotation concerning "restorative justice" may explain why I feel a bit differently about these issues than, for example, Judge Wisdom or Justice Powell or Justice White. When John Minor Wisdom speaks of "restorative justice," I am reminded of the story about the Lone Ranger and his "faithful Indian companion" Tonto. If you recall the famous radio serial, you know that Tonto never said much, but what he did say was (disguised beneath a Hollywood-Indian dialect) wisdom of an absolutely Solomonic caliber. On one occasion, it seems that the Lone Ranger was galloping along with Tonto, heading eastward, when they saw coming towards them a large band of Mohawk Indians in full war dress. The Lone Ranger reigns in his horse, turns to Tonto, and asks "Tonto, what should we do?" Tonto says, "Ugh, ride-um west." So they wheel around and gallop off to the west until suddenly they encounter a large band of Sioux heading straight toward them. The Lone Ranger asks, "Tonto, what should we do?" Tonto says, "Ugh, ride-um north." So, they turn around and ride north, and, sure enough, there's a whole tribe of Iroquois headed straight towards them. The Ranger asks, "Tonto, what should we do?" And Tonto says, "Ugh, ride-um south," which they do until they see a war party of Apaches coming right for them. The Lone Ranger says, "Tonto, what should we do?" And Tonto says, "Ugh, what you mean, 'we' white man?"

I have somewhat the same feeling when John Minor Wisdom talks of the evils that "we" whites have done to blacks and that "we" must now make restoration for. My father came to this country when he was a teenager. Not only had he never profited from the sweat of any black man's brow, I don't think he had ever seen a black man. There are, of course, many white ethnic groups that came to this country in great numbers relatively late in its history—Italians, Jews, Irish, Poles—who not only took no part in, and derived no profit from, the major historic suppression of the currently acknowledged minority groups, but were, in fact, themselves the object of discrimination by the dominant Anglo-Saxon majority. If I can recall in my lifetime the obnoxious "White Trade Only" signs in shops in Washington, D.C., others can recall "Irish Need Not Apply" signs in Boston, three or four decades earlier. To be sure, in relatively recent years some or all of these groups have been the beneficiaries of discrimination against blacks, or have themselves practiced discrimination. But to compare their racial debt—I must use that term, since the concept of "restorative justice" implies it; there is no creditor without a debtor—with that of those who plied the slave trade, and who maintained a formal caste system for many years thereafter, is to confuse a mountain with a molehill. Yet curiously enough, we find that in the system of restorative justice established by the Wisdoms and the Powells and the Whites, it is precisely *these* groups that do most of the restoring. It is they who, to a disproportionate degree, are the competitors with the urban blacks and Hispanics for jobs, housing, education—all those things that enable one to scramble to the top of the social heap where one can speak eloquently (and quite safely) of restorative justice.

To remedy this inequity, I have developed a modest proposal, which I call RJHS—the Restorative Justice Handicapping System. I only have applied it thus far to restorative justice for the Negro, since obviously he has been the victim of the most widespread and systematic exploitation in this country; but a similar system could be devised for other creditor-races, creditor-sexes, or minority groups. Under my system each individual in society would be assigned at birth Restorative Justice Handicapping Points, determined on the basis of his or her ancestry. Obviously, the highest number of points must go to what we may loosely call the Aryans—the Powells, the Whites, the Stewarts, the Burgers, and, in fact (curiously enough), the entire composition of the present Supreme Court, with the exception of Justice Marshall. This grouping of north European races obviously played the greatest role in the suppression of the American black. But unfortunately, what was good enough for Nazi Germany is not good enough for our purposes. We must further divide the Aryans into subgroups. As I have suggested, the Irish (having arrived later) probably owe less of a racial debt than the Germans, who in turn surely owe less of a racial debt than the English. It will, to be sure, be difficult to draw precise lines and establish the correct number of handicapping points, but having reviewed the Supreme Court's jurisprudence on abortion, I am convinced that our justices would not shrink from the task.

Of course, the mere identification of the various degrees of debtor-races is only part of the job. One must in addition account for the dilution of bloodlines by establishing, for example, a half-Italian, half-Irish handicapping score. There are those who will scoff at this as a refinement impossible of achievement, but I am confident it can be done, and can even be extended to take account of dilution of blood in creditor-races as well. Indeed, I am informed (though I have not had the stomach to check) that a system to achieve the latter objective is already in place in federal agencies—specifying, for example, how much dilution of blood deprives one of his racial-creditor status as a "Hispanic" under affirmative action programs. Moreover, it should not be forgotten that we have a rich body of statutory and case law from the Old South to which we can turn for guidance in this exacting task.

But I think it unnecessary to describe the Restorative Justice Handicapping System any further. I trust you find it thoroughly offensive, as I do. It, and the racist concept of restorative justice of which it is merely the concrete expression, is fundamentally contrary to the principles that govern, and should govern, our society. I owe no man anything, nor he me, because of the blood that flows in our veins. To go down that road (or I should say to return down that road), even behind a banner as gleaming as restorative justice, is to make a frightening mistake. This is not to say that I have no obligation to my fellow citizens who are black. I assuredly do—not because of their race or because of any special debt that my bloodline owes to theirs, but because they have (many of them) special needs, and they are (all of them) my countrymen and (as I believe) my brothers. This means that I am entirely in favor of according the poor inner-city child, who happens to be black, advantages and preferences not given to my own children because they do not need them. But I am not willing to prefer the son of a prosperous and well-educated black doctor or lawyer—solely because of his race—to the son of a recent refugee from Eastern Europe who is working as a manual laborer to get his family ahead. The affirmative action system now in place will produce the latter result because it is based upon concepts of racial indebtedness and racial entitlement rather than individual worth and individual need; that is to say, because it is racist.

Evil Fruits of a Bad Seed

But I not only question the principle upon which racial affirmative action is based; I even question its effectiveness in achieving the desired goal of advancing a particular race. Professor Edwards, for example, states in one of his pieces that: "The continued existence of long-standing myths about the inherent inability of blacks to perform certain work has also contributed to their exclusion from significant jobs in the employment market." That strikes me as true, but one may well wonder whether the prescribed solution of affirmative action based on race will eliminate the myths rather than assure their perpetuation. When one reads the *Bakke* case, the most striking factual data is the enormous divergence in the average college grades and average test scores of the regular admittees and the special (minority) admittees of the Davis medical school for the years Bakke was rejected. In 1973 they looked like this:

| | Grade Point Average | | Medical College Admission Test | | | |
	Science	Overall	Verbal	Quanti- tative	Science	Gen'l Info.
Regular	3.51	3.49	81	76	83	69
Minority	2.62	2.88	46	24	35	33

Do you suppose the "image" of minority groups has been improved by this? I suggest that, to the contrary, the very ability of minority group members to distinguish themselves and their race has been dreadfully impaired. To put the issue to you in its starkest form: If you must select your brain surgeon from among recent graduates of Davis medical school and have nothing to go on but their names and pictures, would you not be well advised—playing the odds—to eliminate all minority group members? It is well known to the public that the outstanding institutions of higher education graduate the best and the brightest principally through the simple device of admitting only the best and the brightest. And it is obvious to the public that (to the extent these schools flunk *anyone* out) the same factor that produced special admissions will also tend to produce special retention and, ultimately, special graduation. Thus, insofar as "public image" is concerned, the immediate and predictable effect of affirmative action is to establish a second-class, "minority" degree, which is a less certain certificate of quality. In other words, we have established within our institutions of higher education (and wherever else racial affirmative action is applied) a regime reminiscent of major league baseball in the years before Jackie Robinson: a separate "league" for minority students, which makes it difficult for the true excellence of the minority star to receive his or her deserved acknowledgment. To be sure, the students' teachers, and those of us who have the opportunity of examining the students' transcripts, can tell who is or is not outstanding. But those members of the public about whom Professor Edwards is concerned—those who judge by generalities, or by "image," if you will—are they likely to think better or worse of minority graduates? The person who was so ignorant as to say "a Negro simply cannot become a truly outstanding doctor" can now plausibly add "—and the fact that he obtained a degree from one of the best medical schools in the country doesn't prove a thing."

In response to this, the advocates of racial affirmative action might say the following: "Even if, as you say, our system cannot give an increased number of minority students a first-class Davis degree—and indeed, even if it may, as you say, make it impossible for *any* minority student to obtain a first-class Davis degree—at least it gives more minority students the concrete benefits of a first-class Davis education." But that is questionable pedagogy. In grammar school, at least, where the politics of race do not yet seem to have permeated pupil assignment within schools, we do not "help" a disadvantaged student by admitting him into a faster group. Why should college and graduate school be different? During the guns-on-campus disturbances at Cornell, one-half of that school's black students were on academic probation. Why? They were neither stupid nor lazy. As a whole their test scores were in the *upper* 25 per cent of all students admitted to college. But the Cornell student body as a whole was in the upper one percent. Was it really "helping" these young men and women, either from the standpoint of their personal intellectual development or from the standpoint of their "image" as minority graduates in later life, to place them in an environment where it was quite probable (as probable as such things can ever be) that they did not belong? It solved the political problems of the school administrators, no doubt. And it may have given the administrators, faculty, and alumni the warm feeling that they were doing their part (at no expense, by and large, to their own children) for "restorative justice." But did it really help these young men and women? With few exceptions, I suspect not.

I could mention other harmful, practical effects of racial

affirmative action. It has been suggested, for example, that one consequence is to encourage the location of industries in areas where affirmative action problems are likely to be reduced; that is, away from the inner cities where the game of racial percentages produces significantly higher quotas (or, if you prefer, goals). In any case, it is a fact that statistics show an increase in the economic status of blacks in the years immediately preceding affirmative action and a decline thereafter. Whatever else the program may be, it is not demonstrably effective.

Conclusion

I am, in short, opposed to racial affirmative action for reasons of both principle and practicality Sex-based affirmative action presents somewhat different constitutional issues, but it seems to me an equally poor idea, for many of the reasons suggested above. I do not, on the other hand, oppose—indeed, I strongly favor—what might be called (but for the coloration that the term has acquired in the context of its past use) "affirmative action programs" of many types of help for the poor and disadvantaged. It may well be that many, or even most, of these benefited by such programs would be members of minority races that the existing programs exclusively favor. I would not care if *all* of them were. The unacceptable vice is simply selecting or rejecting them *on the basis of their race*.

A person espousing the views I have expressed, of course, exposes himself to charges of, at best, insensitivity or, at worst, bigotry. That is one reason these views are not expressed more often, particularly in academia. Beyond an anticipatory denial, I must content myself with the observation that it must be a queer sort of bigotry indeed, since it is shared by many intelligent members of the alleged target group. Some of the most vocal opposition to racial affirmative action comes from minority group members who have seen the value of their accomplishments debased by the suspicion—no, to be frank, the reality—of a lower standard for their group in the universities and the professions. This new racial presumption, imposed upon those who have lifted themselves above the effects of old racial presumptions, is the most evil fruit of a fundamentally bad seed. From racist principles flow racist results.

17. Minority Set-Asides

By WARREN E. BURGER

Focus The Minority Business Enterprise provision of the Public Works Employment Act of 1977 required that 10 per cent of the federal funds allocated to state and local governments for public works projects be used to procure services and supplies from businesses owned by the members of certain stipulated racial and ethnic minority groups. Those who are to benefit from this set-aside provision are limited by the act to "citizens of the United States who are Negroes, Spanish-speaking, Orientals, Indians, Eskimos, and Aleuts." In a challenge to the law, petitioners representing several associations of construction contractors argued that the minority set-aside provision not only violated various federal antidiscrimination laws, but was a clear violation of the Equal Protection Clause of the Fourteenth Amendment, and the equal protection component of the due process clause of the Fifth Amendment.

In the decision that follows, Chief Justice Burger, writing for the Supreme Court, dismissed the constitutional challenge of the petitioners, arguing that the set-aside provision was intended to remedy the present competitive disadvantage of minority-owned businesses resulting from past illegal discrimination. The statute in question, he says, is a legitimate exercise of Congress's power to regulate interstate commerce, to ensure equal protection of the laws, and to provide for the general welfare through the dispersement of public funds (spending power). While acknowledging that laws employing racial and ethnic classifications require "careful judicial evaluation" to pass constitutional muster, Chief Justice Burger holds that the set-aside program is narrowly tailored to the achievement of its legitimate remedial purpose. Though innocent nonminority parties may suffer because of the set-aside provision, this, the chief justice explains, is only an incidental consequence of the law, and in any event, a sharing of the burden by innocent parties is not necessarily a violation of the Constitution. To the charge that the set-aside program is underinclusive—i.e., that it does not include all the minority groups that may have suffered from illegal discrimination in government contracting, Burger explains that Congress may take one step at a time to remedy only part of a more extensive problem. In addition, he says that no evidence has been presented to the Court to indicate that there are other identifiable minority groups that have suffered discrimination to a degree equal to or greater than the groups stipulated in the congressional act.

Warren E. Burger was the chief justice of the U.S. Supreme Court from 1969 to 1986.

IN ENACTING THE minority business enterprise (MBE) provision, it is clear that Congress employed an amalgam of its specifically delegated powers. The Public Works Employment Act of 1977, by its very nature, is primarily an exercise of the spending power. Congress has frequently employed the spending power to further broad policy objectives by conditioning receipt of federal monies upon compliance by the recipient with federal statutory and administrative directives. This Court has repeatedly upheld against constitutional challenge the use of this technique to induce governments and private parties to cooperate voluntarily with federal policy.

The MBE program is structured within this familiar legislative pattern. The program conditions receipt of public works grants upon agreement by the state or local governmental grantee that at least 10 per cent of the federal funds will be devoted to contracts with minority businesses. It is further conditioned to require that MBE bids on these contracts are competitively priced, or might have been competitively priced but for the present effects of prior discrimination.

We turn first to the commerce power. The legislative history of the MBE provision shows that there was a rational basis for Congress to conclude that the subcontracting practices of prime contractors could perpetuate the prevailing impaired access by minority businesses to public contracting opportunities, and that this inequity has an effect on interstate commerce. Thus Congress could take necessary and proper action to remedy the situation. With respect to the MBE provision, Congress had abundant evidence from which it could conclude that minority businesses have been denied effective participation in public contracting opportunities by procurement practices that perpetuated the effects of prior discrimination. Congress has before it, among other data, evidence of a long history of marked disparity in the percentage of public contracts awarded to minority busi-

---

This opinion was excerpted from *Fullilove v. Klutznick,* 448 U.S. 448 (1980).

ness enterprises. This disparity was considered to result not from any lack of capable and qualified minority businesses, but from the existence and maintenance of barriers to competitive access, which had their roots in racial and ethnic discrimination or other unlawful conduct. Although much of this history related to the experience of minority businesses in the area of federal procurement, there was direct evidence before Congress that this pattern of disadvantage and discrimination existed with respect to state and local construction contracting as well.

Although the act recites no preambulary "findings" on the subject, we are satisfied that Congress had abundant historical basis from which it could conclude that traditional procurement practices, when applied to minority businesses, could perpetuate the effects of prior discrimination. Insofar as the MBE program pertains to the actions of state and local grantees, Congress could have achieved its objectives by use of its power under Section 5 of the Fourteenth Amendment. We conclude that in this respect the objectives of the MBE provision are within the scope of the spending power.

Racial and Ethnic Criteria

We now turn to the question whether, as a *means* to accomplish these plainly constitutional objectives, Congress may use racial and ethnic criteria, in this limited way, as a condition attached to a federal grant. Congress may employ racial or ethnic classifications in exercising its spending or other legislative powers only if those classifications do not violate the equal protection component of the Due Process Clause of the Fifth Amendment. We recognize the need for careful judicial evaluation to assure that any congressional program that employs racial or ethnic criteria to accomplish the objective of remedying the present effects of past discrimination is narrowly tailored to the achievement of that goal.

Our review of the regulations and guidelines governing administration of the MBE provision reveals that Congress enacted the program as a strictly remedial measure. As a threshold matter, we reject the contention that in the remedial context the Congress must act in a wholly "color-blind" fashion. In *Swann*

v. *Charlotte-Mecklenberg Board of Education* (1971), we rejected this argument in considering a court-formulated school desegregation remedy on the basis that examination of the racial composition of student bodies was an unavoidable starting point. And in *North Carolina Board of Education* v. *Swann* (1971), we invalidated a state law that absolutely forbade assignment of any student on account of race because it foreclosed implementation of desegregation plans that were designed to remedy constitutional violations.

Here we deal, not with the limited remedial powers of a federal court, for example, but with the broad remedial powers of Congress. It is fundamental that in no organ of government, state or federal, does there repose a more comprehensive remedial power than in the Congress, expressly charged by the Constitution with competence and authority to enforce equal protection guarantees.

A more specific challenge to the MBE program is the charge that it impermissibly deprives nonminority businesses of access to at least some portion of the government contracting opportunities generated by the act. It must be conceded that by its objective of remedying the historical impairment of access, the MBE provision can have the effect of awarding some contracts to MBEs that otherwise might be awarded to other businesses, who may themselves be innocent of any prior discriminatory actions. Failure of nonminority firms to receive certain contracts is, of course, an incidental consequence of the program, not part of its objective. It is not a constitutional defect in this program that it may disappoint the expectations of nonminority firms. When effectuating a limited and properly tailored remedy to cure the effects of prior discrimination, such "a sharing of the burden" by innocent parties is not impermissible. The actual "burden" shouldered by nonminority firms is relatively light in this connection when we consider the scope of this public works program as compared with overall construction contracting opportunities. Moreover, although we may assume that the complaining parties are innocent of any discriminatory conduct, it was within congressional power to act on the assumption that in the past some nonminority businesses may have reaped competitive benefit over the years from the virtual exclusion of minority firms from these contracting opportunities.

Another challenge to the validity of the MBE program is the assertion that it is underinclusive—that it limits its benefit to specified minority groups rather than extending its remedial objectives to all businesses whose access to government contracting is impaired by the effects of disadvantage or discrimination. Even in this context, the well-established concept that a legislature may take one step at a time to remedy only part of a broader problem is not without relevance. We are not reviewing a federal program that seeks to confer a preferred status upon a nondisadvantaged minority or to give special assistance to only one of several groups established to be similarly disadvantaged minorities. There has been no showing in this case that Congress has inadvertently effected an invidious discrimination by excluding from coverage an identifiable minority group that has been the victim of a degree of disadvantage and discrimination equal to or greater than that suffered by the groups encompassed by the MBE program.

Any preference based on racial or ethnic criteria must necessarily receive a most searching examination to make sure that it does not conflict with constitutional guarantees. This case is one that requires and has received that kind of examination. This opinion does not adopt, either expressly or implicitly, the formulas of analysis articulated in such cases as *University of California* v. *Bakke* (1978) [see selections 11–16]. Our analysis demonstrates, however, that the MBE provision would survive judicial review under either "test" articulated in the several *Bakke* opinions. The MBE provision of the Public Works Employment Act of 1977 does not violate the Constitution.

18. Minority Set-Asides Are Unconstitutional

By POTTER STEWART

Focus Chief Justice Burger's majority opinion on the set-aside issue (selection 17) encountered two vigorous dissents, one by Justice John Paul Stevens, and the other by Justice Potter Stewart. Any law that grants preference to individuals solely on the basis of the fact that they are Negroes, Spanish-speaking, Orientals, Indians, Eskimos, or Aleuts, is on its very face, according to Stewart, a violation of the equal protection guarantees of the Fifth and Fourteenth Amendments of the U.S. Constitution. The latter document, he says, mandates strict color-blindness—i.e., strict race and ethnic neutrality—in the way government deals with its citizens. "Under our Constitution," Stewart declares, "any official action that treats a person differently on account of his race or ethnic origin is inherently suspect and presumptively invalid." It is, says Stewart, a denial of equal protection for a government to take into account the racial and ethnic features of its citizens in the setting of public policy, because such features are immutable characteristics that have no necessary relationship to a person's abilities, level of socioeconomic disadvantage, or degree of moral culpability for past acts of injustice to others. Moreover, the very practice of classifying the population according to racial and ethnic criteria is, according to Stewart, an odious one that wrongly teaches the general public that it is a legitimate and even good thing to think of people in racial and ethnic terms.

Stewart suggests that the set-aside provision may actually have been passed not merely to compensate victims of past illegality, but as (1) a racial entitlement designed to assure to the members of specific racial and ethnic groups a certain percentage share of public contracting funds; and (2) as a form of compensation for social, economic, and educational disadvantage. As a racial entitlement, Stewart dismisses the law outright, saying that the Constitution protects individual persons from any such discrimination; and as a form of compensation for disadvantage he notes that social, economic, and educational disadvantages are not the monopoly of the members of any particular racial or ethnic group. Like many other critics of affirmative action programs, Stewart attacks the set-aside provision for overinclusiveness—the law, he says, paints with too broad a brush since it does not require beneficiaries to demonstrate any degree of likelihood of past victimization. The special benefits of the set-aside program are open to any and all Negroes, Spanish-speaking, Orientals, Indians, Eskimos, and Aleuts—and closed to all others—regardless of their personal circumstances.

Potter Stewart was an associate justice of the U.S. Supreme Court from 1958 to 1981.

"**O**UR CONSTITUTION IS color-blind, and neither knows nor tolerates classes among citizens. . . . The law regards man as man, and takes no account of his surroundings or of his color." Those words were written by a member of this Court eighty-four years ago (*Plessy* v. *Ferguson,* 1896, Justice Harlan dissenting). His colleagues disagreed with him, and held that a statute that required the separation of people on the basis of their race was constitutionally valid because it was a "reasonable" exercise of legislative power and had been "enacted in good faith for the promotion [of] public good." Today, the Court upholds a statute that accords a preference to citizens who are "Negroes, Spanish-speaking, Orientals, Indians, Eskimos, and Aleuts," for much the same reasons. I think today's decision is wrong for the same reason that *Plessy* v. *Ferguson* was wrong, and I respectfully dissent.

The equal protection standard of the Constitution has one clear and central meaning—it absolutely prohibits invidious discrimination by government. That standard must be met by every state under the Equal Protection Clause of the Fourteenth Amendment. And that standard must be met by the United States itself under the Due Process Clause of the Fifth Amendment. Under our Constitution, any official action that treats a person differently on account of his race or ethnic origin is inherently suspect and presumptively invalid.

The hostility of the Constitution to racial classifications by government has been manifested in many cases decided by this Court. And our cases have made clear that the Constitution is wholly neutral in forbidding such racial discrimination, whatever the race may be of those who are its victims. Under our Constitution, the government may never act to the detriment of a person solely because of that person's race. The color of a person's skin and the country of his origin are immutable facts that bear no relation to ability, disadvantage, moral culpability,

---

Excerpted from *Fullilove* v. *Klutznick,* 448 U.S. 448 (1980).

or any other characteristics of constitutionally permissible interest to government. "Distinctions between citizens solely because of their ancestry are by their very nature odious to a free
people whose institutions are founded upon the doctrine of
equality." The command of the equal protection guarantee is
simple but unequivocal: In the words of the Fourteenth Amendment, "No State shall . . . deny to *any* person . . . the equal
protection of the laws." Nothing in this language singles out
some "persons" for more "equal" treatment than others.
Rather, as the Court made clear in *Shelley* v. *Kraemer,* the
benefits afforded by the Equal Protection Clause are, by its
terms, guaranteed to the individual. [They] are personal rights."
From the perspective of a person detrimentally affected by a
racially discriminatory law, the arbitrariness and unfairness is
entirely the same, whatever his skin color and whatever the
law's purpose, be it purportedly "for the promotion of the public
good" or otherwise.

No one disputes the self-evident proposition that Congress
has broad discretion under its spending power to disburse the
revenues of the United States as it deems best and to set
conditions on the receipt of the funds disbursed. No one disputes
that Congress has the authority under the Commerce Clause to
regulate contracting practices on federally funded public works
projects, or that it enjoys broad powers under Section 5 of the
Fourteenth Amendment "to enforce by appropriate legislation"
the provisions of that amendment. But these self-evident truisms
do not begin to answer the question before us in this case. For
in the exercise of its powers, Congress must obey the Constitution just as the legislatures of all the states must obey the
Constitution in the exercise of their powers. If a law is unconstitutional, it is no less unconstitutional just because it is a product
of the Congress of the United States.

Equal Protection

On its face, the minority business enterprise (MBE) provision
at issue in this case denies equal protection of the law. The
Public Works Employment Act of 1977 directs that all project
construction shall be performed by those private contractors

who submit the lowest competitive bids and who meet established criteria of responsibility. One class of contracting firms—defined solely according to the racial and ethnic attributes of their owners—is, however, excepted from the full rigor of these requirements with respect to a percentage of each federal grant. The statute, on its face and in effect, thus bars a class to which the petitioners belong from having the opportunity to receive a government benefit, and bars the members of that class solely on the basis of their race or ethnic background. This is precisely the kind of law that the guarantee of equal protection forbids.

The Court's attempt to characterize the law as a proper remedial measure to counteract the effects of past or present racial discrimination is remarkably unconvincing. The legislative branch of government is not a court of equity. It has neither the dispassionate objectivity nor the flexibility that are needed to mold a race-conscious remedy around the single objective of eliminating the effects of past or present discrimination.

But even assuming that Congress has the power, under Section 5 of the Fourteenth Amendment or some other constitutional provision, to remedy previous illegal racial discrimination, there is no evidence that Congress has in the past engaged in racial discrimination in its disbursement of federal contracting funds. The MBE provision thus pushes the limits of any such justification far beyond the equal protection standard of the Constitution. Certainly, nothing in the Constitution gives Congress any greater authority to impose detriments on the basis of race than is afforded the judicial branch. And a judicial decree that imposes burdens on the basis of race can be upheld only where its sole purpose is to eradicate the actual effects of illegal race discrimination.

The provision at issue here does not satisfy this condition. Its legislative history suggests that it had at least two other objectives in addition to that of counteracting the effects of past or present racial discrimination in the public works construction industry. One such purpose appears to have been to assure to minority contractors a certain percentage of federally funded public works contracts. But, since the guarantee of equal protection immunizes from capricious governmental treatment "persons," not "races," it can never countenance laws that seek racial balance as a goal in and of itself.

Second, there are indications that the MBE provision may have been enacted to compensate for the effects of social, educational, and economic "disadvantage." No race, however, has a monopoly on social, educational, or economic disadvantage, and any law that indulges in such a presumption clearly violates the constitutional guarantee of equal protection. Since the MBE provision was in whole or in part designed to effectuate objectives other than the elimination of the effects of racial discrimination, it cannot stand as a remedy that comports with the strictures of equal protection, even if it otherwise could.

Moreover, even a properly based judicial decree will be struck down if the scope of the remedy it provides is not carefully tailored to fit the nature and extent of the violation. Here, assuming that the MBE provision was intended solely as a remedy for past and present racial discrimination, it sweeps far too broadly. It directs every state and local government covered by the program to set aside 10 per cent of its grant for minority business enterprises. Waivers from that requirement are permitted, but only where insufficient numbers of minority businesses capable of doing the work at nonexorbitant prices are located in the relevant contracting area. No waiver is provided for any governmental entity that can prove a history free of racial discrimination. Nor is any exemption permitted for nonminority contractors that are able to demonstrate that they have not engaged in racially discriminatory behavior. Finally, the statute makes no attempt to direct the aid it provides solely toward those minority contracting firms that arguably still suffer from the effects of past or present discrimination.

These are not the characteristics of a racially conscious remedial decree that is closely tailored to the evil to be corrected. In today's society, it constitutes far too gross an oversimplification to assume that every single Negro, Spanish-speaking citizen, Oriental, Indian, Eskimo, and Aleut potentially interested in construction contracting currently suffers from the effects of past or present racial discrimination. Since the MBE set-aside must be viewed as resting upon such an assumption, it necessarily paints with too broad a brush. Except to make whole the identified victims of racial discrimination, the guarantee of equal protection prohibits the government from taking detrimental action against innocent people on the basis of the sins of others of their own race.

[The Court has failed to consider] the ramifications of its decision. Laws that operate on the basis of race require definitions of race. Because of the Court's decision today, our statute books will once again have to contain laws that reflect the odious practice of delineating the qualities that make one person a Negro and make another white. Most importantly, by making race a relevant criterion once again in its own affairs, the government implicitly teaches the public that the apportionment of rewards and penalties can legitimately be made according to race—rather than according to merit or ability—and that people can, and perhaps should, view themselves and others in terms of their racial characteristics. Notions of "racial entitlement" will be fostered, and private discrimination will necessarily be encouraged.

There are those who think that we need a new constitution, and their views may someday prevail. But under the Constitution we have, one practice in which government may never engage is the practice of racism—not even "temporarily" and not even as an "experiment." For these reasons, I would reverse the judgment of the court of appeals.

19. Set-Asides Violate the Equal Protection Clause

By SANDRA DAY O'CONNOR

Focus

Even before the federal government passed its own set-aside law in 1977, a number of state and local governments had ordinances containing various set-aside provisions that granted to firms owned by members of certain stipulated racial and ethnic minority groups a minimum percentage of government contracting funds. By the late 1980s, over 30 states and 200 local governments had such set-aside provisions in their laws. In the important decision of *Richmond City* v. *J. A. Croson Co.* (1989), however, a majority of the members of the U.S. Supreme Court declared that racial classifications in such instances are suspect categories, that such laws must be judged by the strictest standard of constitutional review, and that the specific 30 per cent set-aside provison of the City of Richmond was an unconstitutional violation of the Equal Protection Clause of the Fourteenth Amendment. The decision clearly reflected the impact on the Court of the three Reagan-era appointees, Sandra Day O'Connor, Antonin Scalia, and Anthony Kennedy.

Justice Sandra Day O'Connor states that under the Fourteenth Amendment, Congress has certain powers for remedying past discriminatory actions that are not the same as those possessed by state and local governments. For this reason, she holds, the Court's prior justification in *Fulli-*

love of a race-based federal law is not necessarily applicable to set-aside provisions of states and localities. The city of Richmond has shown no evidence of specific discrimination against any minority contractor or subcontractor, O'Connor contends, and the mere comparison of the amount of money going to minority firms with the number of minority group members in the general population cannot establish a valid statistical case for actual discrimination in Richmond's construction industry. "Where special qualifications are necessary," says O'Connor, "the relevant statistical pool for purposes of demonstrating discriminatory exclusion must be the number of minorities qualified to undertake the particular task." Justice O'Connor specifically rejects the view that past discrimination in education, or past "societal discrimination," constitute the kind of specifically identified prior discrimination in construction contracting that would be necessary to justify a racial classification. And even if it could be demonstrated that there was specific antiblack discrimination in the past in the Richmond construction industry, Richmond's set-aside scheme, says O'Connor, is overly broad since it includes among its beneficiaries such ethnic groups as Spanish-speaking, Orientals, Indians, Eskimos, and Aleuts who were not themselves likely to have been victims of past discrimination in the Richmond area. "Under Richmond's scheme," she says, "a successful black, Hispanic, or Oriental entrepreneur from anywhere in the country enjoys absolute preference over other citizens based solely on their race." It is obvious, she says, that such a scheme "is not narrowly tailored to remedy the effects of prior discrimination."

Sandra Day O'Connor, appointed in 1981, is an associate justice of the U.S. Supreme Court.

APPELLANT (the City of Richmond) and its supporting *amici* rely heavily on *Fullilove* for the proposition that a city council, like Congress, need not make specific findings of discrimination to engage in race-conscious relief. What appellant ignores is that Congress, unlike any state or political subdivision, has a specific constitutional mandate to enforce the dictates of the Fourteenth Amendment. That Congress may identify and redress the effects of society-wide discrimination does not mean that, *a fortiori,* the states and their political subdivisions are free to decide that such remedies are appropriate. To hold otherwise would be to cede control over the content of the Equal Protection Clause to the fifty state legislatures and their myriad political subdivisons. The mere recitation of a benign or compensatory purpose for the use of a racial classification would essentially entitle the states to exercise the full power of Congress under Section 5 of the Fourteenth Amendment and insulate any racial classification from judicial scrutiny under Section 1 [the equal protection section]. We believe that such a result would be contrary to the intentions of the framers of the Fourteenth Amendment, who desired to place clear limits on the states' use of race as a criterion for legislative action.

The Equal Protection Clause of the Fourteenth Amendment provides that "No State shall . . . deny to *any person* within its jurisdiction the equal protection of the laws." As this Court has noted in the past, the "rights created by the first section of the Fourteenth Amendment are, by its terms, guaranteed to the individual. The rights established are personal rights" (*Shelly* v. *Kraemer,* 1948). The Richmond Plan denies certain citizens the opportunity to compete for a fixed percentage of public contracts based solely upon their race. To whatever racial group these citizens belong, their "personal rights" to be treated with equal dignity and respect are implicated by a rigid rule erecting race as the sole criterion in an aspect of public decisionmaking.

Excerpted from *Richmond City* v. *Croson Co., 57 LW 4132 (1989).*

239

Absent searching judicial inquiry into the justification for such race-based measures, there is simply no way of determining what classifications are "benign" or "remedial" and what classifications are in fact motivated by illegitimate notions of racial inferiority or simple racial politics. Indeed, the purpose of strict scrutiny is to "smoke out" illegitimate uses of race by assuring that the legislative body is pursuing a goal important enough to warrant use of a highly suspect tool. The test also ensures that the means chosen "fit" this compelling goal so closely that there is little or no possibility that the motive for the classification was illegitimate racial prejudice or stereotype.

Under the standard proposed by Justice Marshall's dissent, "race-conscious classifications designed to further remedial goals," are forthwith subject to a relaxed standard of review. How the dissent arrives at the legal conclusion that a racial classification is "designed to further remedial goals," without first engaging in an examination of the factual basis for its enactment and the nexus between its scope and that factual basis we are not told. One of the central arguments for applying a less exacting standard to "benign" racial classifications is that such measures essentially involve a choice made by dominant racial groups to disadvantage themselves. In this case, blacks comprise approximately 50 per cent of the population of the city of Richmond. Five of the nine seats on the city council are held by blacks. The concern that a political majority will more easily act to the disadvantage of a minority based on unwarranted assumptions or incomplete facts would seem to militate for, not against, the application of heightened judicial scrutiny in this case.

Inadequate Justifications

Appellant argues that it is attempting to remedy various forms of past discrimination that are alleged to be responsible for the small number of minority businesses in the local contracting industry. Among these the city cites the exclusion of blacks from skilled construction trade unions and training programs. This past discrimination has prevented them "from following the traditional path from laborer to entrepreneur." While there is no doubt that the sorry history of both private and public discrimination in this country has contributed to a lack of opportunities for black entrepreneurs, this observation, standing alone, cannot justify a rigid racial quota in the awarding of public contracts in Richmond, Virginia. Like the claim (in *Bakke*) that discrimination in primary and secondary schooling justifies a rigid racial preference in medical school admissions, an amorphous claim that there has been past discrimination in a particular industry cannot justify the use of an unyielding racial quota.

It is sheer speculation how many minority firms there would be in Richmond absent past societal discrimination, just as it was sheer speculation how many minority medical students would have been admitted to the medical school at Davis absent past discrimination in educational opportunities. Defining these sorts of injuries as "identified discrimination" would give local governments license to create a patchwork of racial preferences based on statistical generalizations about any particular field of endeavor. These defects are readily apparent in this case. The 30 per cent quota cannot in any realistic sense be tied to any injury suffered by anyone. There is nothing approaching a *prima facie* case of a constitutional or statutory violation by *anyone* in the Richmond construction industry. The district court relied on the highly conclusionary statement of a proponent of the plan that there was racial discrimination in the construction industry "in this area, and the state, and around the nation." It also noted that the city manager had related his view that racial discrimination still plagued the construction industry in his home city of Pittsburgh. These statements are of little probative value in establishing identified discrimination in the Richmond construction industry. A governmental actor cannot render race a legitimate proxy for a particular condition merely by declaring that the condition exists.

Reliance on the disparity between the number of prime contracts awarded to minority firms and the minority population of the city of Richmond is similarly misplaced. In the employment context, we have recognized that for certain entry-level positions or positions requiring minimal training, statistical comparisons of the racial composition of an employer's workforce to

the racial composition of the relevant population may be probative of a pattern of discrimination. But where special qualifications are necessary, the relevant statistical pool for purposes of
demonstrating discriminatory exclusion must be the number of
minorities qualified to undertake the particular task. In this case
the city does not even know how many MBEs (minority business
enterprises) in the relevant market are qualified to undertake
prime or subcontracting work in public construction projects.
Nor does the city know what percentage of total city construction dollars minority firms now receive as subcontractors on
prime contracts let by the city. Without any information on
minority participation in subcontracting, it is quite simply impossible to evaluate overall minority representation in the city's
construction expenditures.

The city and the district court also relied on evidence that
MBE membership in local contractors' associations was extremely low. Again, standing alone this evidence is not probative
of any discrimination in the local construction industry. There
are numerous explanations for this dearth of minority participation, including past societal discrimination in education and
economic opportunities as well as both black and white career
and entrepreneurial choices. Blacks may be disproportionately
attracted to industries other than construction. The mere fact
that black membership in these trade organizations is low,
standing alone, cannot establish a *prima facie* case of discrimination.

While the states and their subdivisions may take remedial
action when they possess evidence that their own spending
practices are exacerbating a pattern of prior discrimination, they
must identify that discrimination, public or private, with some
specificity before they may use race-conscious relief. In sum,
none of the evidence presented by the city points to any identified discrimination in the Richmond construction industry. We,
therefore, hold that the city has failed to demonstrate a compelling interest in apportioning public contracting opportunities on
the basis of race. To accept Richmond's claim that past societal
discrimination alone can serve as the basis for rigid racial
preferences would be to open the door to competing claims for

"remedial relief" for every disadvantaged group. The dream of a nation of equal citizens in a society where race is irrelevant to personal opportunity and achievement would be lost in a mosaic of shifting preferences based on inherently unmeasurable claims of past wrongs. We think such a result would be contrary to both the letter and spirit of a constitutional provision whose central command is equality.

Unnecessary Quotas

The foregoing analysis applies only to the inclusion of blacks within the Richmond set-aside program. There is *absolutely no evidence* of past discrimination against Spanish-speaking, Oriental, Indian, Eskimo, or Aleut persons in any aspect of the Richmond construction industry. It may well be that Richmond has never had an Aleut or Eskimo citizen. The random inclusion of racial groups that, as a practical matter, may never have suffered from discrimination in the construction industry in Richmond, suggests that perhaps the city's purpose was not, in fact, to remedy past discrimination. If a 30 per cent set-aside was "narrowly tailored" to compensate black contractors for past discrimination, one may legitimately ask why they are forced to share this "remedial relief" with an Aleut citizen who moves to Richmond tomorrow? The gross overinclusiveness of Richmond's racial preference strongly impugns the city's claim of remedial motivation.

At noted by the Court below, it is almost impossible to assess whether the Richmond Plan is narrowly tailored to remedy prior discrimination since it is not linked to identified discrimination in any way. We limit ourselves to two observations in this regard. First, there does not appear to have been any consideration of the use of race-neutral means to increase minority business participation in city contracting. Many barriers to minority participation in the construction industry relied upon by the city to justify a racial classification appear to be race neutral. If MBEs disproportionately lack capital or cannot meet bonding requirements, a race-neutral program of city financing for small firms would, *a fortiori,* lead to greater minority participation. There is no evidence in this record that the Richmond

City Council has considered any alternatives to a race-based quota.

Second, the 30 per cent quota cannot be said to be narrowly tailored to any goal, except perhaps outright racial balancing. It rests upon the "completely unrealistic" assumption that minorities will choose a particular trade in lockstep proportion to their representation in the local population. Under Richmond's scheme, a successful black, Hispanic, or Oriental entrepreneur from anywhere in the country enjoys an absolute preference over other citizens based solely on their race. We think it obvious that such a program is not narrowly tailored to remedy the effects of prior discrimination.

Even in the absence of evidence of discrimination, the city has at its disposal a whole array of race-neutral devices to increase the accessibility of city contracting opportunities to small entrepreneurs of all races. Simplification of bidding procedures, relaxation of bonding requirements, and training and financial aid for disadvantaged entrepreneurs of all races would open the public contracting market to all those who have suffered the effects of past societal discrimination or neglect. Business as usual should not mean business pursuant to the unthinking exclusion of certain members of our society from its rewards.

In the case at hand, the city has not ascertained how many minority enterprises are present in the local construction market nor the level of their participation in city construction projects. The city points to no evidence that qualified minority contractors have been passed over for city contracts or subcontracts, either as a group or in any individual case. Because the city of Richmond has failed to identify the need for remedial action in the awarding of its public construction contracts, its treatment of its citizens on a racial basis violates the dictates of the Equal Protection Clause.

20. A Giant Step Backward on Set-Asides

By THURGOOD MARSHALL

Focus The decision of the U.S. Supreme Court invalidating the racially based set-aside law of Richmond, Virginia, as a violation of the equal protection provision of the Fourteenth Amendment, encountered the vigorous dissent of Justice Thurgood Marshall. The Richmond set-aside plan, Marshall points out, was patterned after the federal set-aside law whose constitutionality was previously upheld by the Supreme Court in the case of *Fullilove* v. *Klutznick* (1980). Marshall specifically rejects the view of the court majority that the Fourteenth Amendment limits or preempts the power of state governments to take remedial measures to rectify past racial discrimination. Nothing in either the Fourteenth Amendment or the two other Reconstruction-era amendments, says Marshall, "suggests that states, exercising their police power, are in any way constitutionally inhibited from working alongside the federal government in the fight against discrimination and its effects." Contrary to the majority view of the Court, the Richmond City Council, says Marshall, had clearly demonstrated widespread discrimination in the Richmond-area construction industry. The fact that only .67 per cent of public contracting expenditures went to minority-owned contractors, that Richmond-area trade associations had almost no minority members, that discrimination in the construction industry was a pervasive national phenomenon well documented by Congress, and that not a single person who testified before the Richmond City Council denied the existence of widespread racial discrimination in the area construction industry—these facts, says Marshall, taken together, clearly demonstrate the existence of specific prior discrimination.

Justice Marshall objects strongly to the majority's use of the "strict-scrutiny" standard of constitutional review in cases of race-based measures designed to remedy previous discrimination and its effects. There is a profound difference, says Marhsall, between "governmental actions that themselves are racist, and governmental actions that seek to remedy the effects of prior racism or to prevent neutral governmental activity from perpetuating the effects of such racism." Marshall believes that an intermediate level of review somewhere between "strict scrutiny" and mere "reasonableness" is the appropriate method in deciding the constitutionality of the latter type of actions. Marshall also strongly objects to the suggestion that because five of the nine members of the Richmond City Council were black, Richmond's set-aside plan can be seen as an instance of "racial politics." This view, Marshall contends, is cynical and insulting and impugns the political maturity of the nation's locally elected black officials. "When the legislatures and leaders of cities with histories of pervasive discrimination," says Marshall, "testify that past discrimination has infected one of their industries, armchair cynicism like that exercised by the majority has no place."

Thurgood Marshall, appointed in 1967, is an associate justice of the U.S. Supreme Court.

I T IS A WELCOME symbol of racial progress when the former capital of the Confederacy acts forthrightly to confront the effects of racial discrimination in its midst. In my view, nothing in the Constitution can be construed to prevent Richmond, Virginia, from allocating a portion of its contracting dollars for businesses owned or controlled by members of minority groups. Indeed, Richmond's set-aside program is indistinguishable in all meaningful respects from—and in fact was patterned upon—the federal set-aside plan that this Court upheld in *Fullilove* v. *Klutznick* (1980).

A majority of this Court holds today, however, that the Equal Protection Clause of the Fourteenth Amendment blocks Richmond's initiative. The essence of the majority's position is that Richmond has failed to catalogue adequate findings to prove that past discrimination has impeded minorities from joining or participating fully in Richmond's construction industry. I find deep irony in second-guessing Richmond's judgment on this point. As much as any municipality in the United States, Richmond knows what racial discrimination is; a century of decisions by this and other federal courts has richly documented the city's disgraceful history of public and private racial discrimination. In any event, the Richmond City Council *has* supported its determination that minorities have been wrongly excluded from local construction contracting. Its proof includes statistics showing that minority-owned businesses have received virtually no city contracting dollars and rarely if ever belonged to area trade associations; testimony by municipal officials that discrimination has been widespread in the local construction industry; and the same exhaustive and widely publicized federal studies relied on in *Fullilove*, studies that showed that pervasive discrimination in the Nation's tight-knit construction industry had operated to exclude minorities from public contracting. These are precisely the types of statistical and testimonial evidence that, until today,

Excerpted from *Richmond City* v. *Croson Co.*, 57 LW 4132 (1989).

247

this Court had credited in cases approving of race-conscious measures designed to remedy past discrimination.

More fundamentally, today's decision marks a deliberate and giant step backward in this Court's affirmative action jurisprudence. Cynical of one municipality's attempt to redress the effects of past racial discrimination in a particular industry, the majority launches a grapeshot attack on race-conscious remedies in general. The majority's unnecessary pronouncements will inevitably discourage or prevent governmental entities, particularly states and localities, from acting to rectify the scourge of past discrimination. This is the harsh reality of the majority's decision, but it is not the Constitution's command.

As an initial matter, the majority takes an exceedingly myopic view of the factual predicate on which the Richmond City Council relied when it passed the Minority Business Utilization Plan. The majority analyzes Richmond's initiative as if it were based solely upon the facts about local construction and contracting practices adduced during the city council session at which the measure was enacted. In so doing, the majority downplays the fact that the city council had before it a rich trove of evidence that discrimination in the Nation's construction industry had seriously impaired the competitive position of businesses owned or controlled by members of minority groups. It is only against this backdrop of documented national discrimination, however, that the local evidence adduced by Richmond can be properly understood. The majority's refusal to recognize that Richmond has proven itself no exception to the dismaying pattern of national exclusion that Congress so painstakingly identified infects its entire analysis of this case.

The members of the Richmond City Council were well aware of these exhaustive congressional findings, a point the majority, tellingly, elides. The transcript of the session at which the council enacted the local set-aside initiative contains numerous references to the six-year-old congressional set-aside program, to the evidence of nationwide discrimination barriers, and to the *Fullilove* decision itself. The city council's members also heard testimony that, although minority groups made up half of the city's population, only .67 per cent of the $24.6 million that

Richmond had dispensed in construction contracts during the five years ending in March 1983 had gone to minority-owned prime contractors. They heard testimony that the major Richmond-area construction trade associations had virtually no minorities among their hundreds of members. Finally, they heard testimony from city officials as to the exclusionary history of the local construction industry. As the district court noted, not a single person who testified before the city council denied that discrimination in Richmond's construction industry had been widespread.

The majority is wrong to trivialize the continuing impact of government acceptance or use of private institutions or structures once wrought by discrimination. In my view, the interest in ensuring that the government does not reflect and reinforce prior private discrimination in dispensing public contracts is every bit as strong as the interest in eliminating private discrimination—an interest that this Court has repeatedly deemed compelling. The more government bestows its rewards on those persons or businesses that were positioned to thrive during a period of private racial discrimination, the tighter the dead-hand grip of prior discrimination becomes on the present and future.

Proof of Past Discrimination

The remaining question with respect to the "governmental-interest" prong of equal protection analysis is whether Richmond has proffered satisfactory proof of past racial discrimination to support its twin interests in remediation and in governmental nonperpetuation. The varied body of evidence on which Richmond relied provides a "strong," "firm," and "unquestionably legitimate" basis upon which the city council could determine that the effects of past racial discrimination warranted a remedial and prophylactic governmental response. The fact that just .67 per cent of public construction expenditures over the previous five years had gone to minority-owned prime contractors, despite the city's racially mixed population, strongly suggests that construction contracting in the area was rife with "present economic inequities." To the extent this enormous disparity did not itself demonstrate that discrimination had occurred, the descriptive testimony of Richmond's elected and appointed leaders drew the necessary link between the pitifully small presence of minorities in construction contracting and past exclusionary practices. That *no one* who testified challenged this depiction of widespread racial discrimination in area construction contracting lent significant weight to these accounts. The fact that area trade associations had virtually no minority members dramatized the extent of present inequities and suggested the lasting power of past discriminatory systems. In sum, to suggest that the facts on which Richmond has relied do not provide a sound basis for its finding of past racial discrimination simply blinks credibility.

Richmond's reliance on localized, industry-specific findings is a far cry from the reliance on generalized "societal discrimination," which the majority decries as a basis for remedial action. The majority also takes the disingenuous approach of disaggregating Richmond's local evidence, attacking it piecemeal, and thereby concluding that no *single* piece of evidence adduced by the city, "standing alone," suffices to prove past discrimination. But items of evidence do not, of course, "stan[d] alone" or exist in alien juxtaposition; they necessarily work together, reinforcing or contradicting each other.

In any event, the majority's criticisms of individual items of Richmond's evidence rest on flimsy foundations. There are roughly equal numbers of minorities and nonminorities in Richmond—yet minority-owned businesses receive *one seventy-fifth* the public contracting funds that other businesses receive. Where the issue is not present discrimination but rather whether *past* discrimination has resulted in the *continuing exclusion* of minorities from an historically tight-knit industry, a contrast between population and work force is entirely appropriate to help gauge the degree of the exclusion. This contrast is especially illuminating in cases like this, where a main avenue of introduction into the work force—here, membership in the trade associations whose members presumably train apprentices and help them procure subcontracting assignments—is itself grossly dominated by nonminorities. The majority's assertion that the city "does not even know how many MBEs in the relevant market are qualified" is thus entirely beside the point. If Richmond indeed has a monochromatic contracting community—a conclusion reached by the district court—this most likely reflects the lingering power of past exclusionary practices. Certainly this is the explanation Congress has found persuasive at the national level. The city's requirement that prime public contractors set aside 30 per cent of their subcontracting assignments for minority-owned enterprises, subject to the ordinance's provision for waivers where minority-owned enterprises are unavailable or unwilling to participate, is designed precisely to ease minority contractors into the industry.

The majority's perfunctory dismissal of the testimony of Richmond's appointed and elected leaders is also deeply disturbing. These officials—including council members, a former mayor, and the present city manager—asserted that race discrimination in area contracting had been widespread, and that the set-aside ordinance was a sincere and necessary attempt to eradicate the effects of this discrimination. By disregarding the testimony of local leaders and the judgment of local government, the majority does violence to the very principles of comity within our federal system that this Court has long championed. Local officials, by virtue of their proximity to, and their expertise with, local affairs, are exceptionally well qualified to make determinations of public good "within their respective spheres of authority." Had the majority paused for a moment on the facts of the Richmond experience, it would have discovered that the city's leadership is deeply familiar with what racial discrimination is. The members of the Richmond City Council have spent long years witnessing multifarious acts of discrimination, including, but not limited to, the deliberate diminution of black residents' voting rights, resistance to school desegregation, and publicly sanctioned housing discrimination When the legislatures testify that past discrimination has infected one of their industries, armchair cynicism like that exercised by the majority has no place. Disbelief is particularly inappropriate here in light of the fact that appellee Croson, who had the burden of proving unconstitutionality at trial, has *at no point* come forward with *any* direct evidence that the city council's motives were anything other than sincere.

Richmond's Set-Aside Similar to that of Fullilove

In my judgment, Richmond's set-aside plan also comports with the second prong of the equal protection inquiry, for it is substantially related to the interests it seeks to serve in remedying past discrimination and in ensuring that municipal contract procurement does not perpetuate that discrimination. The most striking aspect of the city's ordinance is the similarity it bears to the "appropriately limited" federal set-aside provision upheld in *Fullilove*. Like the federal provision, Richmond's is limited to five years in duration, and was not renewed when it came up for reconsideration in 1988. Like the federal provision, Richmond's contains a waiver provision freeing from its subcontracting requirements those nonminority firms that demonstrate that they cannot comply with its provisions. Like the federal provision, Richmond's has a minimal impact on innocent third parties. While the measure affects 30 per cent of *public* contracting dollars, that translated to only 3 per cent of overall Richmond-area contracting. Finally, like the federal provision, Richmond's does not interfere with any vested right of a contractor to a particular contract; instead it operates entirely prospectively. Richmond's initiative affects only future economic arrangements and imposes only a diffuse burden on nonminority competitors—here, businesses owned or controlled by nonminorities that seek subcontracting work on public construction projects.

The majority takes issue, however, with two aspects of Richmond's tailoring: the city's refusal to explore the use of race-neutral measures to increase minority business participation in contracting, and the selection of a 30 per cent figure. The majority's first criticism is flawed in two respects. First, the majority overlooks the fact that since 1975, Richmond has barred both discrimination by the city in awarding public contracts and discrimination by public contractors. The virtual absence of minority businesses from the city's contracting rolls, indicated by the fact that such businesses have received less than 1 per cent of public contracting dollars, strongly suggests that this ban has not succeeded in redressing the impact of past discrimination or in preventing city contract procurement from reinforcing racial homogeneity. Second, the majority's suggestion that Richmond should have first undertaken such race-neutral measures as a program of city financing for small firms, ignores the fact that such measures, while theoretically appealing, have been discredited by Congress as ineffectual in eradicating the effects of past discrimination in this very industry.

As for Richmond's 30 per cent target, the majority states that this figure "cannot be said to be narrowly tailored to any goal, except perhaps outright racial balancing." The majority ignores two important facts. First, the set-aside measure affects only 3 per cent of overall city contracting; thus, any imprecision in tailoring has far less impact than the majority suggests. But more important, the majority ignores the fact that Richmond's 30 per cent figure was patterned directly on the *Fullilove* precedent. Congress's 10 per cent figure fell "roughly halfway between the present percentage of minority contractors and the percentage of minority group members in the Nation." The Richmond City Council's 30 per cent figure similarly falls roughly halfway between the present percentage of Richmond-based minority contractors (almost zero) and the percentage of minorities in Richmond (50 per cent).

Standards of Strict Scrutiny

Today, for the first time, a majority of this Court has adopted strict scrutiny as a standard of Equal Protection Clause review of race-conscious remedial measures. In concluding that remedial classifications warrant no different standard of review under the Constitution than the most brute and repugnant forms of state-sponsored racism, a majority of this Court signals that it regards racial discrimination as largely a phenomenon of the past, and that government bodies need no longer preoccupy themselves with rectifying racial injustice. I, however, do not believe this Nation is anywhere close to eradicating racial discrimination or its vestiges. In constitutionalizing its wishful thinking, the majority today does a grave disservice not only to those victims of past and present racial discrimination in this

Nation whom government has sought to assist, but also to this Court's long tradition of approaching issues of race with the utmost sensitivity.

In my view, the "circumstances of this case," underscore the importance of *not* subjecting to a strict-scrutiny straitjacket the increasing number of cities that have recently come under minority leadership and are eager to rectify, or at least prevent the perpetuation of, past racial discrimination. In many cases, these cities will be the ones with the most in the way of prior discrimination to rectify. Richmond's leaders had just witnessed decades of publicly sanctioned racial discrimination in virtually all walks of life—discrimination amply documented in the decisions of the federal judiciary. This history of "purposefully unequal treatment" forced upon minorities, not imposed by them, should raise an inference that minorities in Richmond had much to remedy—and that the 1983 set-aside was undertaken with sincere remedial goals in mind, not "simple racial politics."

Richmond's own recent political history underscores the facile nature of the majority's assumption that elected officials' voting decisions are based on the color of their skins. In recent years, white and black council members in Richmond have increasingly joined hands on controversial matters. When the Richmond City Council elected a black mayor in 1982, for example, his victory was won with the support of the city council's four white members. The vote on the set-aside plan a year later also was not purely along racial lines. Of the four white councilmembers, one voted for the measure and another abstained. The majority's view that remedial measures undertaken by municipalities with black leadership must face a stiffer test of Equal Protection Clause scrutiny than remedial measures undertaken by municipalities with white leadership implies a lack of political maturity on the part of this nation's elected minority officials that is totally unwarranted. Such insulting judgments have no place in constitutional jurisprudence.

With respect to Section 5, our precedents have never suggested that this provision was meant to preempt or limit state police power to undertake race-conscious remedial measures. As for Section 1 it is too late in the day to assert seriously that the Equal Protection Clause prohibits states—or for that matter, the federal government, to whom the equal protection guarantee has largely been applied—from enacting race-conscious remedies. Our cases in the areas of school desegregation, voting rights, and affirmative action have demonstrated time and again that race is constitutionally germane, precisely because race remains dismayingly relevant in American life. In adopting its *prima facie* standard for states and localities, the majority closes its eyes to this constitutional history and social reality.

The three Reconstruction amendments undeniably "worked a dramatic change in the balance between congressional and state power," they forbade state-sanctioned slavery, forbade the state-sanctioned denial of the right to vote and uniquely forbade states from denying equal protection. But nothing in the amendments themselves, or in our long history of interpreting or applying those momentous charters, suggests that states, exercising their police power, are in any way constitutionally inhibited from working alongside the federal government in the fight against discrimination and its effects.

The majority today sounds a full-scale retreat from the Court's longstanding solicitude to race-conscious remedial efforts "directed toward deliverance of the century-old promise of equality of economic opportunity." The new and restrictive tests it applies scuttle one city's effort to surmount its discriminatory past, and imperil those of dozens more localities. I, however, profoundly disagree with the cramped vision of the Equal Protection Clause which the majority offers today and with its application of that vision to Richmond's laudable set-aside plan. The battle against pernicious racial discrimination or its effects is nowhere near won.

21. Race-Based Preference Violates the Fourteenth Amendment

By LEWIS F. POWELL, JR.

Focus   Wendy Wygant was one of several white school teachers employed by the Jackson, Michigan, Board of Education who were laid off from their jobs while many "minority" school teachers with lesser seniority were retained. The layoffs had been carried out in accordance with a collective bargaining agreement between the Jackson Board of Education and the local teachers' union—an agreement that, under its Article XII, sought to maintain the existing proportion of minority teachers in the Jackson school district. For purposes of the collective bargaining agreement, "minorities" were defined as "those employees who are black, American Indian, Oriental, or of Spanish descendancy." Wygant, and many of the other "nonminority" teachers who had been displaced, brought suit in federal court claiming a violation of their constitutional rights under the equal protection provision of the Fourteenth Amendment. Although losing in the lower courts, their case was eventually reviewed by the U.S. Supreme Court, which decided in their favor.

In the following decision, Justice Lewis Powell, writing for the Court majority, reaffirms the position he had taken in *Bakke* that racial and ethnic classifications are in their very nature constitutionally suspect and are justified only if they serve a truly compelling state interest. Moreover, even if they serve such an interest, the means chosen to further that interest, he says, must be properly tailored so as not to burden unduly any innocent parties. Powell rejects the view of the lower court that the desire to provide same-race role models for minority students is an important enough state interest to justify a race-based policy, and he dismisses the notion that the proportion of minority teachers must reflect the proportion of minority students in the Jackson school district. Powell also rejects the view that past "societal discrimination" constitutes a legitimate reason for increasing the number of minority teachers. Taken by itself, "societal discrimination," he contends, "is too amorphous a basis for imposing a racially classified remedy." Only prior discrimination in the employment of teachers on the part of the Jackson school board itself, Powell believes, would constitute a compelling enough reason for the employment of a race-based system of preferential employment. And even if such actual past discrimination could be shown, he says, race-based layoffs, unlike race-based hiring preferences, would not be constitutionally permissible because of the extraordinary burden layoffs impose upon those whom they adversely affect.

Lewis F. Powell, Jr., was an associate justice of the U.S. Supreme Court from 1972 to 1988.

PETITIONERS' CENTRAL claim is that they were laid off because of their race in violation of the Equal Protection Clause of the Fourteenth Amendment. Decisions by faculties and administrators of public schools based on race or ethnic origin are reviewable under the Fourteenth Amendment. The Court has recognized that the level of scrutiny does not change merely because the challenged classification operates against a group that historically has not been subject to governmental discrimination. In this case, Article XII of the [collective bargaining agreement between the teachers union and the school board] operates against whites and in favor of certain minorities, and therefore constitutes a classification based on race.

The court of appeals, relying on the reasoning and language of the district court's opinion, held that the board's interest in providing minority role models for its minority students, as an attempt to alleviate the effects of societal discrimination, was sufficiently important to justify the racial classification embodied in the layoff provision. The court discerned a need for more minority faculty role models by finding that the percentage of minority teachers was less than the percentage of minority students. This Court never has held that societal discrimination alone is sufficient to justify a racial classification. Rather, the Court has insisted upon some showing of prior discrimination by the governmental unit involved before allowing limited use of racial classifications in order to remedy such discrimination. Unlike the analysis in *Hazelwood* [an earlier employment discrimination case], the role-model theory employed by the district court has no logical stopping point. The role-model theory allows the board to engage in discriminatory hiring and layoff practices long past the point required by any legitimate remedial purpose. Moreover, because the role-model theory does not necessarily bear a relationship to the harm caused by prior discriminatory hiring practices, it actually could be used to

---

Excerpted from *Wygant* v. *Jackson Board of Education,* 476 U.S. 267 (1986).

escape the obligation to remedy such practices by justifying the small percentage of black teachers by reference to the small percentage of black students. Carried to its logical extreme, the idea that black students are better off with black teachers could lead to the very system the Court rejected in *Brown* v. *Board of Education* (1954).

Societal discrimination, without more, is too amorphous a basis for imposing a racially classified remedy. The role-model theory announced by the district court and the resultant holding typify this indefiniteness. There are numerous explanations for a disparity between the percentage of minority students and the percentage of minority faculty, many of them completely unrelated to discrimination of any kind. In fact, there is no apparent connection between the two groups. Nevertheless, the district court combined irrelevant comparisons between these two groups with an indisputable statement that there has been societal discrimination, and upheld state action predicated upon racial classifications. No one doubts that there has been serious racial discrimination in this country. But as the basis for imposing discriminatory *legal* remedies that work against innocent people, societal discrimination is insufficient and over expansive. In the absence of particularized findings, a court could uphold remedies that are ageless in their reach into the past, and timeless in their ability to affect the future.

Prior Discrimination

Respondents also now argue that their purpose in adopting the layoff provision was to remedy prior discrimination against minorities by the Jackson school district in hiring teachers. A public employer like the board must ensure that, before it embarks on an affirmative action program, it has convincing evidence that remedial action is warranted. That is, it must have sufficient evidence to justify the conclusion that there has been prior discrimination. Despite the fact that Article XII has spawned years of litigation and three separate lawsuits, no such determination ever has been made. The board now contends that, given another opportunity, it could establish the existence of prior discrimination. Although this argument seems belated at this point in the proceedings, we need not consider the question since we conclude below that the layoff provision was not a legally appropriate means of achieving even a compelling purpose.

The court of appeals examined the means chosen to accomplish the board's race-conscious purposes under a test of "reasonableness." That standard has no support in the decisions of this Court. Our decisions always have employed a more stringent standard—however articulated—to test the validity of the means chosen by a state to accomplish its race-conscious purposes. Under strict scrutiny the means chosen to accomplish the state's asserted purpose must be specifically and narrowly framed to accomplish that purpose. We have recognized that in order to remedy the effects of prior discrimination, it may be necessary to take race into account. As part of this nation's dedication to eradicating racial discrimination, innocent persons may be called upon to bear some of the burden of the remedy. [In this case] the means chosen to achieve the board's asserted purposes is that of laying off nonminority teachers with greater seniority in order to retain minority teachers with less seniority. We have previously expressed concern over the burden that a preferential-layoffs scheme imposes on innocent parties. In cases involving valid *hiring* goals, the burden to be borne by innocent individuals is diffused to a considerable extent among society generally. Though hiring goals may burden some innocent individuals, they simply do not impose the same kind of injury that layoffs impose. Denial of a future employment opportunity is not as intrusive as loss of an existing job.

Many of our cases involve union seniority plans with employees who are typically heavily dependent on wages for their day-to-day living. Even a temporary layoff may have adverse financial as well as psychological effects. A worker may invest many productive years in one job and one city with the expectation of earning the stability and security of seniority. Layoffs disrupt these settled expectations in a way that general hiring goals do not. While hiring goals impose a diffuse burden, often foreclosing only one of several opportunities, layoffs impose the entire burden of achieving racial equality on particular individuals, often resulting in serious disruption of their lives. That burden is too intrusive. We therefore hold that, as a means of accomplishing purposes that otherwise may be legitimate, the board's layoff plan is not sufficiently narrowly tailored. Other, less intrusive means of accomplishing similar purposes—such as the adoption of hiring goals—are available. For these reasons, the board's selection of layoffs as the means to accomplish even a valid purpose cannot satisfy the demands of the Equal Protection Clause.

22. Minority Teachers Serve an Important Purpose

By JOHN PAUL STEVENS III

Focus Lewis Powell's majority decision in *Wygant* (selection 21) encountered two dissents, one by Justice Thurgood Marshall, the other by Justice John Paul Stevens. Justice Stevens contends his view that race-based employment policies can be justified constitutionally for purposes other than remedying past acts of discrimination. Even if the Jackson Board of Education never engaged in employment discrimination against blacks or other minority teachers, the Jackson school board, Stevens suggests, has a legitimate purpose in hiring more minority teachers in order to enhance the ethnic diversity of the faculty. An ethnically diverse faculty, Stevens believes, will teach by its example the important truth that the diverse ethnic and cultural groups that have come together in America "do not identify essential differences among the human beings that inhabit our land." Not only the minority students, but the white students as well will benefit from an ethnically diverse faculty, Justice Stevens holds.

Since the purpose of the Jackson layoff plan, according to Stevens, is important enough to justify a race-based classification, the critical question then becomes whether the plan was instituted through a procedurally fair method and whether those adversely affected by it have been

harmed in a constitutionally impermissible manner. Regarding the first issue, Stevens asserts that
the procedures for instituting the plan were scrupulously fair, with those teachers who were eventually disadvantaged by it enjoying full participation in the plan's adoption. Regarding the second
issue, he says that the harm done to the teachers
who were laid off, while serious, was little different than the harm that would be done to disappointed applicants in a race-based hiring scheme.
Justice Stevens specifically rejects in this context
the view of Lewis Powell that "there is a distinction of constitutional significance under the Equal
Protection Clause between a racial preference at
the time of hiring and an identical preference at
the time of discharge." Neither, in Stevens's
view, is any more nor less harmful than the other,
nor is one any more constitutionally suspect than
the other. The fact that the layoff policy of the
Jackson school board was not intended to stereotype any race in a negative way, or display toward
any race a lack of respect, is very significant,
Stevens believes, in evaluating its constitutional
validity.

John Paul Stevens III has been an associate
justice on the U.S. Supreme Court since 1975.

IT IS NOT NECESSARY to find that the [Jackson] Board of Education has been guilty of racial discrimination in the past to support the conclusion that it has a legitimate interest in employing more black teachers in the future. Rather than analyzing a case of this kind by asking whether minority teachers have some sort of special entitlement to jobs as a remedy for sins that were committed in the past, we should first ask whether the board's action advances the public interest in educating children for the future. If so, we should consider whether that public interest, and the manner in which it is pursued, justifies any adverse effects on the disadvantaged group.

The Equal Protection Clause absolutely prohibits the use of race in many governmental contexts. To cite only a few: the government may not use race to decide who may serve on juries, who may use public services, who may marry, and who may be fit parents. The use of race in these situations is "utterly irrational" because it is completely unrelated to any valid public purpose; moreover, it is particularly pernicious because it constitutes a badge of oppression that is unfaithful to the central promise of the Fourteenth Amendment. Nevertheless, in our present society, race is not always irrelevant to sound governmental decisionmaking. To take the most obvious example, in law enforcement, if an undercover agent is needed to infiltrate a group suspected of ongoing criminal behavior—and if the members of the group are all of the same race—it would seem perfectly rational to employ an agent of that race rather than a member of a different racial class. Similarly, in a city with a recent history of racial unrest, the superintendent of police might reasonably conclude that an integrated police force could develop a better relationship with the community and thereby do a more effective job of maintaining law and order than a force composed only of white officers.

In the context of public education, it is quite obvious that a

Excerpted from *Wygant* v. *Jackson Board of Education,* 476 U.S. 267 (1986).

school board may reasonably conclude that an integrated faculty will be able to provide benefits to the student body that could not be provided by an all-white, or nearly all-white, faculty. For one of the most important lessons that the American public schools teach is that the diverse ethnic, cultural, and national backgrounds that have been brought together in our famous "melting pot" do not identify essential differences among the human beings that inhabit our land. It is one thing for a white child to be taught by a white teacher that color, like beauty, is only "skin deep"; it is far more convincing to experience that truth on a day-to-day basis during the routine, ongoing learning process.

In this case, the collective-bargaining agreement between the union and the board of education succinctly stated a valid public purpose—"recognition of the desirability of multi-ethnic representation on the teaching faculty," and thus "a policy of actively seeking minority group personnel." Nothing in the record—not a shred of evidence—contradicts the view that the board's attempt to employ, and to retain, more minority teachers in the Jackson public school system served this completely sound educational purpose. Thus, there was a rational and unquestionably legitimate basis for the board's decision to enter into the collective-bargaining agreement that petitioners have challenged, even though the agreement required special efforts to recruit and retain minority teachers.

Excluding Versus Including

It is argued, nonetheless, that the purpose should be deemed invalid because, even if the board of education's judgment in this case furthered a laudable goal, some other boards might claim that their experience demonstrates that segregated classes, or segregated faculties, lead to better academic achievement. There is, however, a critical difference between a decision to *exclude* a member of a minority race because of his or her skin color and a decision to *include* more members of the minority in a school faculty for that reason. The exclusionary decision rests on the false premise that differences in race, or in the color of a person's skin, reflect real differences that are relevant to a person's right to share in the blessings of a free society. The inclusionary decision is consistent with the principle that all men are created equal; the exclusionary decision is at war with that principle.

Even if there is a valid purpose to the race consciousness, however, the question that remains is whether that public purpose transcends the harm to the white teachers who are disadvantaged by the special preference the board has given to its most recently hired minority teachers. In my view, there are two important inquiries in assessing the harm to the disadvantaged teacher. The first is an assessment of the procedures that were used to adopt, and implement, the race-conscious action. The second is an evaluation of the nature of the harm itself.

In this case, there can be no question about either the fairness of the procedures used to adopt the race-conscious provision, or the propriety of its breadth. As Justice Marshall has demonstrated, the procedures for adopting this provision were scrupulously fair. The union that represents the petitioners negotiated the provision and agreed to it; the agreement was put to a vote of the membership, and overwhelmingly approved. Again, not a shred of evidence in the record suggests any procedural unfairness in the adoption of the agreement. Similarly, the provision is specifically designed to achieve its objective—retaining the minority teachers that have been specially recruited to give the Jackson schools, after a period of racial unrest, an integrated faculty.

Finally, we must consider the harm to the petitioners. Every layoff, like every refusal to employ a qualified applicant, is a grave loss to the affected individual. The undisputed facts in this case demonstrate, however, that this serious consequence to the petitioners is not based on any lack of respect for their race, or on blind habit and stereotype. Rather, petitioners have been laid off for a combination of two reasons: the economic conditions that have led Jackson to lay off some teachers and the special contractual protections intended to preserve the newly integrated character of the faculty in the Jackson schools. Thus, the same harm might occur if a number of gifted young teachers had been given special contractual protection because their specialties were in short supply and if the Jackson Board of Education faced a fiscal need for layoffs. A board decision to grant immediate tenure to a group of experts in computer technology, an athletic coach, and a language teacher, for example, might reduce the pool of teachers eligible for layoffs during a depression and therefore have precisely the same impact as the racial preference at issue here. In either case, the harm would be generated by the combination of economic conditions and the special contractual protection given a different group of teachers—a protection that, as discussed above, was justified by a valid and extremely strong public interest.[1]

We should not lightly approve the government's use of a race-based distinction. History teaches the obvious dangers of such classifications. Our ultimate goal must, of course, be "to eliminate entirely from governmental decisionmaking such irrelevant factors as the human being's race." In this case, however, I am persuaded that the decision to include more minority teachers in the Jackson, Michigan, school system served a valid public purpose, that it was adopted with fair procedures and given a narrow breadth, that it transcends the harm to petitioners, and that it is a step toward the ultimate goal of eliminating entirely from governmental decisionmaking such irrelevant factors as a human being's race.

23. The Supreme Court and Civil Rights

By ROBERT H. BORK

Focus

The first half of 1989 was a critical period for employment discrimination litigation, for it was during this time that the Supreme Court developed a clear five-vote majority that was critical of racial hiring quotas and race-based systems of employment promotion. In three important cases, one dealing with the constitutionality of state and local construction set-asides (*Richmond City* v. *J. A. Croson Co.*), another with the use of statistical evidence to demonstrate the existence of illegal employment discrimination (*Wards Cove Packing Co.* v. *Atonio*), and a third with the use of consent decrees to establish immunity from charges of reverse discrimination on the part of disadvantaged white workers (*Martin* v. *Wilks*), the Supreme Court changed or modified earlier rulings in such a way that severely restricted the use of race-conscious criteria of decisionmaking. Much of the liberal print media, along with black and Hispanic civil rights groups, were alarmed by the high court's shift away from affirmative action, and hostile editorials and opinion columns attacking the new decisions appeared in some of the nation's most influential newspapers and magazines.

Responding to these critical columns and editorials, former federal appeals court judge Robert

H. Bork says that the disputed decisions on affirmative action, far from heralding a new age of
segregation as some of their critics suggest, were
nothing more than "moderate and overdue adjustments" that would make it "harder to justify
quotas or force them upon employers." Though
supported by the American Left, most Americans
are opposed to racial and gender quotas in both
employment and education, Bork contends. If
any congressional action is taken in the wake of
these decisions, Bork says, "Congress should
specifically disapprove of quotas and avoid any
provisions that have the effect of pressuring employers to adopt them." Racial quotas and other
forms of preferential treatment based on race,
Bork believes, serve to increase destructive competition over group entitlements.

Robert H. Bork served as solicitor general in
the U.S. Justice Department during the Nixon
and Ford administrations, and was a judge on the
U.S. Court of Appeals, D.C. Circuit, from 1982
to 1988. He had previously taught for many years
at Yale Law School and is now John M. Olin
scholar at the American Enterprise Institute in
Washington, D.C.

THE SUPREME COURT has decided a series of civil rights cases this term and from much of the press reaction, as well as that of the civil rights groups, one might suppose that the justices had reinstituted segregation.

The *New York Times* editorialized that the court "displays an icy indifference . . . to the hopes of discrimination victims." A guest columnist in the *Washington Post* angrily asked, "Is the only choice now for civil rights activists between capitulation or an angry return to the streets?" Reaching an even shriller note, an editor of the *New Republic* proclaimed that in America "Race is the wound that will not heal, and the Supreme Court has just rubbed fresh salt in that wound." He invited us to behold "the dizzying moral fall from the Warren Court, a product of Eisenhower Republicanism, to the Rehnquist Court, a product of Reagan Republicanism." Something pretty savage must have happened.

What actually happened is that the court made some moderate and overdue adjustments to legal doctrine in the field of civil rights law. The real cause of the caterwauling is not that discrimination is being allowed—it isn't—but that it is now harder to justify quotas or force them upon employers. Almost all Americans want to heal the wounds of race; almost all are concerned with civil liberties; but most are opposed to racial and sexual quotas in employment, promotion, and education.

Moral Assault

But quotas are the pet solution of the American Left, which specializes not in argument but in moral assault upon those with whom it has substantive differences. Now that the moral assault is directed at the Supreme Court it is important that Americans understand what the Court has in fact done and what it has not.

The Court's January 1989 decision in *Richmond City* v. *J. A.*

Croson Co., held unconstitutional the city's minority set-aside program. The city council had adopted an ordinance requiring prime contractors on city construction contracts to subcontract at least 30 per cent of the dollar amount of the contract to businesses at least 51 per cent-owned by U.S. citizens who are "blacks, Spanish-speaking, Orientals, Indians, Eskimos, or Aleuts." It was less than clear why Richmond thought it should extend the benefits of its quota to minorities from anywhere in the United States and even less clear how Orientals, Indians, Eskimos, and Aleuts got on the favored list. The one thing that was clear was that white-owned companies were to be discriminated against. Croson Co. was.

Croson was the only bidder on a project, and the only minority supplier of fixtures willing to participate came in well over market price. The city denied requests that the minority requirement be waived or that the contract price be raised and Croson lost the contract.

The Court found a violation of the Equal Protection Clause of the Fourteenth Amendment. "The Richmond Plan," Justice O'Connor's opinion said, "denies certain citizens the opportunity to compete for a fixed percentage of public contracts based solely upon their race." The 30 per cent quota was not an allowable remedy because there was no evidence that the city or anyone in the Richmond construction industry had illegally discriminated against anyone.

The opinion is marred only by its argument that the federal government could impose quotas that the states and cities may not because the federal government has the power to "enforce" the Fourteenth Amendment. The power to enforce, however, is the power to prescribe remedies, not the power to change the substantive command of the Equal Protection Clause. Justice Kennedy said in concurring, "The process by which a law that is an equal protection violation when enacted by a state becomes transformed to an equal protection guarantee when enacted by Congress poses a difficult proposition for me." If the Court sticks to that untenable distinction, the pro-quota forces will have won more than they should.

In June, when the Court handed down *Wards Cove Packing*

Co. v. *Atonio,* the Left's moral assault moved into high gear. Eighteen years before, in *Griggs* v. *Duke Power Co.,* the Court had decided that under Title VII of the Civil Rights Act of 1964 a plaintiff need not prove intentional discrimination. Statistical imbalance in the racial composition of the work force was presumed discriminatory unless proven otherwise. The test was the *consequences* of business practices, not their motivation.

This highly questionable reading of the act produced unfortunate results. Statistical imbalances are everywhere in our society since entirely innocent social forces and cultural differences do not produce proportional representation of each ethnic group in each occupation.

Wards Cove involved Alaskan salmon canneries that had a predominantly white work force in skilled jobs and a predominantly nonwhite work force in unskilled jobs. The court of appeals had held that imbalance created a *prima facie* case against the companies. Justice White's opinion for the majority disagreed: The lower court's theory "at the very least, would mean that any employer who had a segment of his work force that was—for some reason—racially imbalanced, could be haled into court and forced to engage in the expensive and time-consuming task of defending the 'business necessity' of the methods used to select the other members of his work force." Thus, the "only practicable option for many employers will be to adopt racial quotas . . . ; this is a result that Congress expressly rejected in drafting Title VII."

The Court held that the proper comparison was between the proportion of a racial group in the work force and the proportion of qualified members of that race in the pool available to the employer. The plaintiff must also identify the employment practice alleged to be responsible for the disparity. Once that has been done, the employer must produce evidence of business justification for those practices but the ultimate burden of persuading the Court that discrimination exists remains with the plaintiff.

Civil rights activists charged that the Court had done two terrible things. One was to change the rule of *Griggs;* the other was to make it more difficult to win a discrimination case.

Neither charge has any merit. Courts modify prior decisions all of the time. Indeed, the Court the activists most admire, that headed by Earl Warren, continually jettisoned prior rulings it found politically or morally unseemly. For the present Court to modify a rule that produced results contrary to the intention of the 1964 Civil Rights Act is not only unexceptionable but praiseworthy. The fact that plaintiffs may have more difficulty winning proves nothing at all. The object of the law is not to see the plaintiffs always win. All the Supreme Court has held is that discrimination must be proved rather than assumed. Only to those who think America pervasively and incurably racist does that seem outrageous.

Also this month, *Martin* v. *Wilks* held that white firefighters in Birmingham, Alabama, were not barred by a consent decree, to which they were not parties, from challenging the preferential promotion of allegedly less qualified black firefighters. The challengers had a right to their day in court. The Court majority applied the established "general rule that a person cannot be deprived of his legal rights in a proceeding to which he is not a party." The opinion necessarily relied upon the Federal Rules of Civil Procedure to hold that the white firefighters were under no obligation to intervene in the litigation.

That *New Republic* editor found the technical language insufficiently "exalted," and quoted Justice Blackmun's dissent in *Wards Cove:* "One wonders whether the majority still believes that race discrimination—or, more accurately, race discrimination against nonwhites—is a problem in our society, or even remembers that it ever was." That attack is wide of the mark. It is not only an unjustified slur on five justices but assumes that the Court's function is to replace law with moral passion, even if that moral passion produces dubious results.

These and other decisions of the Court have prompted the civil rights groups to say they will turn to Congress to undo the Supreme Court's decisions. Since those decisions are clearly correct, it is to be hoped that Congress will not respond. President Bush has stated that he does not think new legislation is needed. But if these matters are taken up, and if new legislation is written, Congress should specifically disapprove of quotas and avoid any provisions that have the effect of pressuring employers to adopt them.

The moral passion of the dissents in these cases is imprudent on more grounds than one. For too long, in our zeal to achieve moral results, we have ignored the morality of process. A judge should have the compassion to understand the human situation before him in order to apply law intelligently and sensitively. The judge should never, however, allow compassion to control his reading of the law. The morality of process is the highest morality of the jurist.

Salt in the Wound

But there is a second objection to a morality that leads to quotas, and this objection applies no matter what arm of government approves or requires them. Race is indeed a wound that has not healed. But it is precisely the use of preferential quotas that rubs fresh salt into the wound. When nonwhite individuals who have not themselves been the victims of discrimination are preferred to white individuals who have not inflicted discrimination, racial resentments are certain to be inflamed. The problem is likely to grow more acute, for the question of race and ethnicity is no longer simply a black-white issue.

As the composition of our population changes, we see competition for group entitlements among whites of European ancestry, blacks, Hispanics, and Asians. The competition has become bitter and has led to the expression of sentiments that can only be called racist. The only possibility of avoiding a much worse situation than the one we now face is to drop the entire notion of group entitlements, which means abandoning quotas. The Supreme Court has been moving in that direction, which is fortunate both for the integrity of the law and for social policy. We must hope that the Court is not affected by the moral intimidation to which it, and we, are being subjected.

PART THREE

The Civil Rights Act of 1964

24. Racial Preference in the Factory: The Case of Brian Weber

By CARL COHEN

Focus Brian Weber was an employee of the Kaiser Aluminum and Chemical Corporation whose application for admittance to an on-the-job training program—a program that would have substantially upgraded his skills and enabled him to earn a considerably higher salary—was rejected because of an affirmative action program that granted special consideration to black workers who had less seniority. Weber filed a class action suit on behalf of himself and others charging Kaiser and the United Steelworkers Union with racial discrimination in violation of Title VII of the 1964 Civil Rights Act, and his case was eventually decided by the U.S. Supreme Court.

Carl Cohen analyzes the various arguments presented in defense of the affirmative action program at Kaiser and offers his reasons for rejecting each one of them. The meaning of Title VII's prohibition against discrimination in on-the-job training programs, Cohen says, is perfectly clear, and all citizens are granted the right under Title VII not to be disadvantaged in employment situations because of their race, religion, or national origin. Cohen also rejects the view of those who would defend the Kaiser policy as a means of compensating for past discrimination. Since, Cohen argues, this case shows that none of the black workers given preference over Weber had been the victims of past discrimination by Kaiser, and since Weber had never fortuitously benefited by Kaiser's discrimination against others, compensatory justice considerations do not apply. "If the moral ground for compensatory affirmative action," Cohen holds, "is the redress of injury, the uninjured have no claim to it." Moreover, Cohen contends, racial quotas are defective as compensatory devices under any circumstances since "they cannot make the morally crucial distinction between the blameworthy and the blameless, between the deserving and the undeserving." Any policy of compensatory justice, Cohen believes, must deal with people on an individual basis, and is properly carried out only by a legislature and a court, not by an interested private party. Cohen is particularly critical of those people who are so zealous in their defense of affirmative action that they would deny or minimize the harm that was done to Brian Weber, or would deny or minimize the importance to factory workers of individual seniority entitlements.

Carl Cohen, a professor of philosophy at the Residential College of the University of Michigan at Ann Arbor, is a former member of the Board of Directors of the American Civil Liberties Union and author of *Democracy* and *Civil Disobedience*.

THE ROLE OF RACE in assuring social justice is again squarely before the Supreme Court in a case whose full and revealing name is: *Kaiser Aluminum & Chemical Corporation and United Steelworkers of America, AFL-CIO* v. *Brian F. Weber, individually and on behalf of all other persons similarly situated.*

Weber, a white unskilled steelworker, is Bakke's analogue. The Steelworkers Union and Kaiser Aluminum are not the only forces against him. The United Auto Workers and the United Mine Workers, the National Education Association, the Coalition of Black Trade Unionists, and assorted other unions are against him. The American Civil Liberties Union is against him. Even the United States government is formally aligned against him. On Weber's side is the Anti-Defamation League of B'nai B'rith (with some associated non-Jewish ethnic groups) and, according to repeated surveys, an overwhelming majority of the American population, including a majority of the black population.

But the issues at stake here, touching the most fundamental rights of individual persons, are not to be decided by counting noses. The chief things going for Weber are the Fourteenth Amendment of the U.S. Constitution, the Civil Rights Act of 1964 as amended, and sound moral principles. Thrice is he armed who hath his quarrel just.

Weber has thus far been victorious, both in the U.S. District Court, and in the U.S. Court of Appeals (Fifth Circuit, New Orleans). His formidable opponents find it difficult to overcome the plain words of the law applied straightforwardly to the established facts of his case. The law (Title VII of the Civil Rights Act, Section 703) forbids flatly all discrimination in employment because of race. Beyond any possible doubt (as we shall see) Weber was discriminated against by his employer, and

This article originally appeared in *Commentary* (June 1979), under the title "Why Racial Preference is Illegal and Immoral." Reprinted with permission of the author.

classified by his employer, and had his status as an employee adversely affected because of his race. That the employment practice through which this was done is a violation of this federal law is an ineluctable conclusion of any rational mind.

It is not remarkable, then, that unions, industry, and government should now join in the effort to persuade the Supreme Court to evade this conclusion? Weber's opponents are neither foolish nor evil. They seek, somehow, to surmount the barriers to racially discriminatory treatment in order to achieve objectives they think good. Reflection upon this case will oblige the Supreme Court—and all citizens who would reach thoughtful judgment on these issues—to reconsider those objectives, and to appraise the means by which they have been pursued.

The *Bakke* case, and the *DeFunis* case before it, dealt with racially discriminatory practices in professional-school admissions—a matter for which the middle classes have, rightly, a tender concern. *Weber* deals with racial discrimination in blue-collar employment. The injury done Brian Weber was at least as great as that done Allan Bakke, and the class Weber formally represents is much larger, if less articulate, than that directly affected by racially preferential school admissions. It is disturbing, therefore, that the voices raised in behalf of Weber's rights, and the rights of literally millions of individual citizens in like similar circumstances, are so painfully few. Silence now from quarters that were outspoken in opposition to racial preference in higher education may lead some to infer that self-interest, more than justice, was what motivated that earlier concern.

In both spheres—school admissions and industrial employment—the same issues arise: in the allocation of scarce goods, may one's race count in one's favor? If ever, when? In *Bakke,* a racially preferential admission system at the University of California Medical School at Davis was struck down, but attention to race in the admissions process was there held permissible within certain very narrow limits: to advance the diversity of an entering class, or to remedy the condition of specific persons who had been discriminated against by the school using the racial instrument. *Weber* is in many important respects different. Here the factor of diversity does not enter; here matters pertaining to intellectual qualifications are replaced by matters pertaining to seniority. Here the stakes are greater and the underlying moral issues are presented more cleanly.

The Facts of the Case

Kaiser (Kaiser Aluminum & Chemical Corporation) and the union (United Steelworkers of America, AFL-CIO) sought to increase the number of minority workers in the skilled crafts at Kaiser's Gramercy, Louisiana, plant. To this end, in a 1974 collective-bargaining agreement. they changed the system whereby employees would enter on-the-job training for craft positions. Prior craft experience was eliminated as a requirement, and entrance ratios, by race, were established for acceptance in the job-training program. For each white worker admitted one minority worker would be admitted, until the percentage of minority craft workers in the Gramercy plant roughly approximated the percentage of the minority population in the surrounding area, then about 40 per cent. Dual seniority lists were established, one black and one white, and each two vacancies filled with the persons at the top of the two racially distinct lists.

It was an inevitable result of this system that some employees would be favored because of their race, and some would be injured because of theirs. Brian Weber was refused admission to the job-training program although his seniority was higher than some employees from the other racial list who were admitted. Weber sued on his own behalf and on behalf of all nonminority employees who applied for on-the-job training at the Gramercy plant after that labor agreement was signed. A racially preferential scheme for allocating on-the-job training opportunities, he argues, is a clear violation of the federal Civil Rights Act.

One portion of Title VII of that act deals explicitly with on-the-job training programs. That portion (subsection (d) of Section 703) reads as follows:

It shall be an unlawful employment practice for any employer, labor organization, or joint labor-management committee controlling apprenticeship or other training or retraining, *including on-the-job training programs,* to discriminate against any individual because of his race, color, religion, sex, or national origin in admission to, or employment in, any program established to provide apprenticeship or other training [emphasis added].

Was it prescience that caused the Congress to formulate this ban with language so precisely and indubitably covering the case at hand? Not at all. Title VII had as its purpose the elimination of all ethnic favoritism in employment; there had been, at the time of its adoption, plenty of experience of the ways in which racial prejudice can be given effect—one of the commonest being in job-training programs. In that form as in all forms, said the Congress in effect, racial discrimination in employment is no longer permissible.

How can Kaiser and the union (and the U.S. Department of Justice) reasonably argue that such a scheme is indeed lawful or fair? They contend that the law, properly interpreted, does not forbid this variety of racial preference, which they think justified by our history of discrimination. They contend that if the pursuit of pressing social objectives now imposes incidental costs on individuals, Weber and his like are the right persons to bear those costs. They contend that they were ordered, by the U.S. government, to introduce racial preference of precisely this kind. And they contend that Weber was not really injured by this program at all. I examine these arguments in turn.

Kaiser's Argument

"Kaiser and the union [the first argument begins] reached an agreement that was fully in accord with the spirit of Title VII. Theirs was a voluntary effort to bring a greater number of minority workers into the skilled crafts. Congress never intended to forbid such voluntary efforts. If now the product of such agreements, reached through collective bargaining, is struck down, the cause of racial justice will have been dealt a devastating blow.

"We must [this argument continues] permit management and labor to join, as in this case, to correct a racially unbalanced situation flowing from the historical and social realities of American life. Blacks have been discriminated against, cruelly and consistently, by industry and by unions. Now an effort is being made to give redress. It is an ironic inversion of the Civil Rights Act to use that act to forbid the only instruments that may effectively achieve its own intended result.

"It is true [the argument proceeds] that Title VII specifies that preferential treatment of racial minorities is not required [Section 703 (j)]. But that is not to say it is forbidden. When its aim is precisely that of the act itself, it must not be forbidden. Weber relies upon the narrowest construction of the words and misses—inadvertently or deliberately—the remedial spirit of the law and of the Kaiser program here in question."

The main pillar of Weber's opposition comes to this: "If the Court agrees that racial quotas such as this one are discriminatory, we will be kept from doing what many of us think it is necessary to do, and do quickly, in the interest of long-term justice. Let it be understood, therefore [the argument concludes], that this quota, although it does of course distinguish by race, and does, admittedly, give favor by race, does not 'discriminate' by race in the bad sense that the law condemns. When we come to realize that some plans for racial balance, while they may have adverse effects upon some white workers, are nevertheless justified by pressing societal needs, we will also see what interpretation of the law is required by justice."

To put the argument plainly is to see both its earnestness and its frailty. The requirements of the Civil Rights Act, which in turn were intended to give concrete meaning to the constitutional demand that no citizen be denied the equal protection of the laws, were aimed at bringing to a final halt all formal discrimination on the basis of race—and color, religion, sex, and national origin. It certainly was not intended, and it obviously was not formulated, to forbid only such racial discrimination as employers and unions thought objectionable, while permitting any racially discriminatory schemes that employers and unions might by agreement find worthy or convenient. What the employer and the union happen to prefer, whether their motives be honorable or crass, has absolutely no weight, says the law in effect, against the *right* of each individual citizen to be dealt with, in matters pertaining to employment, without regard to race, religion, or national origin.

A Second Argument

"But that cannot be the correct interpretation of the law," answer Kaiser and the union in chorus, "because the Supreme Court has several times, in the years since, recognized the lawfulness and wisdom of racially preferential employment schemes. Indeed, our federal courts have *ordered* the imposition of such racial preference in some cases! So it is clearly false that *all* racial preference has been forbidden. If that is so, then it is not obviously true that *this* scheme for racial preference has been forbidden."

This rejoinder brings us to the core, legal and moral, of the controversy in *Weber*. What kind of attention to race does the Civil Rights Act (and, indirectly, the Constitution) permit? And what should it permit? In the *Bakke* case, this question was complicated by the entry of First Amendment considerations pertaining to the robust exchange of ideas in the classroom; the holding in *Bakke* was tangled by the fact that Justice Powell's pivotal opinion, although condemning racial favoritism, permits attention to race to advance diversity among an entering school class. Here, in *Weber,* such First Amendment considerations are totally absent. What, if anything, remains to justify race-conscious employment practices?

There is a clear and honorable answer to this question, given forcefully by federal courts at every level. Title VII of the Civil Rights Act forbids all deliberate discrimination by race, save only in cases where racial classification is absolutely essential to give redress to *identifiable persons* injured by racial discrimination *and where the injury done them was done by the same party upon whom the numerical program is imposed.* One purpose only may justify numerical schemes using racial categories: the *making whole* of those to whom redress for racial injury is specifically owed, by those who owe it.

For example: the known victims of racial discrimination by a trucking company have been held entitled, as a remedy, to a place in the seniority lists of that company that would have been theirs if they had not been so victimized. To put them now in as good a place as they would have been in but for the discriminatory employment practice from which they can be shown to have suffered, it may be necessary to attend to race. Only in that way can the victims be made whole; they would otherwise remain subordinate to persons who, had it not been for racial discrimination in that company, would now be their subordinates. (See *Franks* v. *Bowman Transportation Co.*, 1976.) In such cases, the racially oriented remedy cannot be refused on the ground that the effect on other employees is adverse because, although the employees who suffer from the imposition of the plan are very possibly innocent themselves, they have clearly benefited, in seniority, from the specific discriminatory practice for which remedy is being given. Race-conscious remedies for the victims of illegal discrimination are lawful, consistent with Title VII, only in such circumstances.

Weber and Kaiser Aluminum are in no such circumstances. Upon examining the facts, the federal district court found that Kaiser had not been guilty of any discriminatory hiring or promotion at its Gramercy plant. Kaiser's industrial-relations superintendent at that plant testified that, prior to 1974, Kaiser had vigorously sought trained black craftsmen from the general community. Advertising in periodicals and newspapers that were published primarily for black subscribers, Kaiser found it very difficult to attract black craftsmen. The evidence established two key facts:

1. Kaiser had a serious, operational, no-discrimination hiring policy at its Gramercy plant from the day of that plant's opening in 1958.

2. Not one of the black employees who were offered on-the-job training opportunities over more senior white employees (pursuant to the 1974 labor agreement) had been subject to any prior employment discrimination by Kaiser.

From these facts it is an inescapable conclusion that the quota system at Kaiser's Gramercy plant was not an instrument for the specific redress of persons injured by racial discrimination there; it was unabashed racial preference aimed at numerical proportions having nothing to do with past conduct in that plant.

Such preference Title VII outlaws. The distinction between impermissible racial preference and permissible remedy for past discrimination is put eloquently by the circuit court of appeals in affirming Weber's rights:

> If employees who have been arbitrarily favored are deprived of benefits capriciously conferred on them in order that those who were arbitrarily deprived may receive what they should, in fairness, have had to begin with, no law is violated. This is so even if both the class whose rights are restored and the class required to "move over" are defined by race—if the original arbitrariness was defined in that manner. And the reason is that no one is being favored or disfavored, advantaged or injured, under these circumstances *because* of race; rather, those who have been unjustly deprived receive their due and those who have been arbitrarily favored surrender some of the largesse capriciously conferred on them. That these consequences end by race is a mere incident of the fact that they began that way.

But those who were favored by race at Weber's expense were admittedly not the victims of such original arbitrariness. The circuit court's support of Weber is therefore categorical: "[U]nless a preference is enacted to restore employees to their rightful places within a particular employment scheme it is strictly forbidden by Title VII."

"Societal Discrimination"

Since it is clear that the beneficiaries of this racial program were not victims of Kaiser's previous discrimination, and equally clear that the use of dual seniority lists is an explicit effort to favor blacks over whites, the defenders of this program are compelled to resort to a different justification—past "societal discrimination."

"We cannot deny [say the defenders in effect] that the two-list system deliberately favors one race over another. But we do deny that favoring this race at this time in this country is unfair. We contend that, in view of the historical discrimination against blacks (and other minorities), the racially preferential device now before us is entirely justifiable. It is justifiable not only because blacks have been so long oppressed, but because, as a corollary, whites have been unfairly *advantaged* by race prejudice. The white employees of Kaiser who are passed over by this plan may indeed be innocent of any racial discrimination themselves, but they have been and are the beneficiaries of racial discrimination by others. This is the heart of our justification. Favor to blacks now is just because of the favor whites have enjoyed until now.''

This is the principled argument by which many without selfish interests in these programs are persuaded that they are fair. One might have expected the American Civil Liberties Union, for example, to spring to the defense of the rights of an almost defenseless individual. Instead it joins the forces against Weber because the ACLU has convinced itself that his rights have not really been infringed on, even though he suffers from deliberate disadvantage because of race. How can that be?

"Racial preference in employment is justified [the argument proceeds] when it is a response to the morally legitimate demand that the *lingering effects* of past racial discrimination be remedied. The lingering effects of historical oppression include the continuing losses of decent employment, together with the money and status that it brings. But the same historical race prejudice that has systematically blocked minorities from access to decent jobs has conferred an involuntary benefit upon whites because, while the number of desirable jobs remains roughly constant, the elimination of competition by minority workers results in the availability of desirable jobs for whites in generous disproportion to their numbers. This benefit is conferred even upon those whites who may, in fact, deplore the prejudice from which they gain. Yet they did gain. Now, with racial quotas favoring blacks, they lose. Their present loss is morally justified by their earlier gain. The primary target of racially preferential programs should be those guilty of past unlawful discrimination, of course. But where those guilty parties simply cannot be identified or are no longer available to make restitution, a secondary but legitimate target is the unjust enrichment attributable to that racial discrimination. Quota plans, like the one devised by Kaiser and the union, seek to redistribute that unjust enrichment. Seen in this light, their fairness—the moral rightness of racial preference for societal rebalancing—cannot be denied.'' So reasons the ACLU explicitly, and many other honest citizens implicitly, in giving pained approval to race quotas.

The argument fails utterly upon inspection. It relies upon a premise that is clearly and admittedly false in the *Weber* case and like cases. And were all its premises true, they could still not justify the racial preference here in question.

Consider the premises first. The adverse impact on Weber is held justifiable by his unjust enrichment resulting from the bad conduct of others. But if Weber were in any way the beneficiary of past discrimination, he certainly was not unjustly enriched by employment discrimination in the Gramercy plant. In that plant, it is agreed by advocates of the quota and by the courts, there had been no refusal to hire or promote blacks or other minorities, no racial discrimination from which Weber benefited. But the injustice done to Weber is manifested in the loss of entitlements he earned by ten years of work *in that plant*—not in the Kaiser Corporation or in the workforce at large. His entitlements in this matter cannot have been acquired as the result of the historical misconduct of others. Long before Weber came to work at that plant, blacks and whites received equal employment treatment there—so the claim that simply by virtue of his having the seniority that he did in the Gramercy plant Weber was enjoying an unjust enrichment is simply false. That false premise cannot justify "redistribution." The circuit court put the matter crisply: "Whatever other effects societal discrimination may have, it has had—by the specific finding of the court below—*no effect* on the seniority of any party here. It is therefore inappropriate to meddle with any party's seniority or with any perquisites attendant upon it, since none has obtained any unfair seniority advantage at the expense of any other."

But suppose *arguendo* (what is not true) that Weber had been unfairly enriched by past racial discrimination. What would follow? The enrichment thus identified might then be a target for redistribution. Among whom? To take from Weber and give to another because Weber got his seniority "unjustly" could conceivably be justified (if ever) *only* if those to whom the redistribution were made were the same persons from whom the spoils had been taken in the first instance. The appealing argument by which so many are persuaded makes the faulty supposition that, if X has gained fortuitously but undeservedly from some unidentifiable Y, we are morally justified in taking from him and giving to a wholly different Z who suffered no loss to X's benefit, but who happens to be of the same race as that injured but unidentifiable Y. Buried in this reasoning process is the mistaken premise that the distribution of goods or opportunities is rightly made by racial categories. Z, the person now given preference over X because of race, has a right to get from him (this premise supposes) because Z is black, and blacks have been so long oppressed. But rights do not and cannot inhere in skin-color groups. Individuals have rights, not races. It is true, of course, that many persons have been cruelly deprived of rights simply because of their blackness. Whatever the remedy all such persons deserve, it is deserved by those injured and because of their injury; nothing is deserved because of the color of one's skin. This is the philosophical nub of the *Weber* case.

Compensatory Justice

So long-lasting and self-perpetuating have been the damages done to many blacks and others by discrimination that some corrective steps must be undertaken. The moral anxiety created by this need for affirmative action accounts, in part, for the willingness of some to tolerate outright racial quotas. In the passion to make social restitution, sensitive and otherwise fair-minded people have gotten the moral claims of living persons badly confused. The head of the Office of Federal Contract Compliance (OFCC) (by whom, as we shall see, Kaiser was threatened) epitomizes this confusion: "Society is trying to correct an age-old problem, and Weber is a victim of that process. There is nothing I can say to him. This is something that has to happen. The question is whether you give priority to a group that's been systematically deprived of opportunity while Brian Weber's parents and grandparents were not discriminated against. If someone has to bear the sins of the fathers, surely it has to be their children" (*New York Times Magazine,* February 25, 1979).

But deliberately visiting the sins of the fathers upon their innocent sons and grandsons, to the special advantage of persons not connected with the original sinning, is conduct neither lawful nor morally right. To suppose that both the beneficiaries of redress and those who are made to carry its burden are properly identified by race is, to be plain, racism. It is ethical racism because supposed with good will. It is simplistic because, on this view, race by itself—without consideration of the nature or degrees of past injuries, present advantages, or future pains—is sufficient to trigger the preferential device. The mistaken view in question is therefore properly entitled *simplistic ethical racism.*

Injuries are suffered in fact, claims made and burdens carried, by individual persons. Civil society is constituted to protect the rights of individuals; the sacrifice of fundamental individual rights cannot be justified by the desire to advance the well-being of any ethnic group. Precisely such justification is precluded by the Fourteenth Amendment of our Constitution, whose words— no state "shall deny to any person within its jurisdiction the equal protection of the laws"—express no mere legalism but a philosophical principle of the deepest importance. Explicating that clause, in a now famous passage, the Supreme Court wrote: "The rights created by the first section of the Fourteenth Amendment are, by its terms, guaranteed to the individual. The rights established are personal rights. . . . Equal protection of the laws is not advanced through indiscriminate imposition of inequalities (*Shelly* v. *Kraemer,* 1948).

The nature and degree of the injury done to many Americans because they were black or brown or yellow varies greatly from case to case. Some such injuries may justify compensatory advantage now to those injured. But the calculation of who is due what from whom is a very sticky business; compensatory instruments are likely to compound injustice unless the individual circumstances of all involved—those who were originally hurt, those who benefit now, and those who will bear the cost—

are carefully considered. Whatever compensatory advantage may be given—in employment or elsewhere—it must be given to all and only those who have suffered like injury, without regard to their race. What we may not do, constitutionally or morally, is announce in effect: "No matter that you, X, were innocent and gained no advantage; you are white and therefore lose points. No matter whether you, Z, were damaged or not; you are black and therefore gain points." If the moral ground for compensatory affirmative action is the redress of injury, the uninjured have no claim to it, and all those individuals of whatever ethnic group who have suffered the injury in question have an equal claim to it.

Racially based numerical instruments have this grave and unavoidable defect: they cannot make the morally crucial distinctions between the blameworthy and the blameless, between the deserving and the undeserving. As compensatory devices they are underinclusive in failing to remedy the same damage when it has been done to persons of the nonfavored races; they are overinclusive in benefiting some in the favored categories who are without claims, often at substantial cost to innocent persons. Except in those cases where the discriminatory policy of the employer is established, and the identity of injured applicants or employees determinable, racial preference in employment is intolerably blunt, incapable of respecting the rights of individuals.

This unsuitability of the racial means to the compensatory end partly explains the queasiness of language with which the advocates of "numerical instruments" defend their schemes. Although they believe their aims are good, there is yet widespread shame among them that they resort to racial preference to advance them. Hence the use of euphemisms like "disadvantaged" in identifying the beneficiaries of racial programs, when what is really meant is "black" or "minority." Not all minorities are disadvantaged, and not all those disadvantaged are minorities, obviously. But it is tempting to hide the racial character of a program that, if exposed, would be legally and morally intolerable.

"Affirmative action"—a phrase that now pervades our language—has commonly been used in the same duplicitous way. Affirmative steps to eliminate racially discriminatory practices rightly win the assent of all. Affirmative efforts to recruit fairly (whether for on-the-job training programs or for professional schools), affirmative inquiry to determine whether testing is job-related and to insure that evaluation of performance is not racially infected—in such forms affirmative action is of unquestionable merit. But when, in the name of affirmative action for racial equality, the deliberately unequal treatment of the races is introduced, we suffer a national epidemic of double-speak. Employment advertisements everywhere exhibit this duplicity with an almost ritualized motto: "An equal opportunity/affirmative action employer." The very term "affirmative action" has lost its honor and has become, for most, a euphemism for racial preference.

The unsavory character of their means is recognized by the advocates of racial instruments; that recognition is revealed by an inclination to be covert in conduct and to equivocate in language. Unsavoriness is tolerated here, however, even by organizations whose normal pride it is to expose immoral expedience in the body politic. Nothing is more indicative of the true spirit of a community than the character of the instruments it permits, and of those it precludes, in advancing public policy. Police surveillance to root out spies, the suppression of speech (radical or conservative) to protect the peace—all such instruments are rejected in a decent society. Civil libertarians wisely insist that we forswear instruments that invade the rights of individuals, even when forswearing proves inconvenient. The use of such instruments is precluded, forbidden not just to evil people but to all people. Preference by race is one of these forbidden instruments. The very high priority given to this exclusionary principle, and its applicability to all including the state itself, marks it as *constitutional* in the most profound sense.

Efforts to cut constitutional corners—however well intentioned—corrupt a civil society. The means we use penetrate the ends we achieve; when the instrument is unjust, the outcome will be infected by that injustice This lesson even civil libertarians have always to be relearning.

The Double-Bind Argument

The inconsistency between racially preferential means and the end of honestly equal treatment is exquisitely exhibited in one aspect of the *Weber* case upon which Kaiser and the union place much emphasis. "We are caught [say they] in a monstrous double bind. What will you have us do? Desegregate, you say. Integrate your workforce; show us that you mean to undo, affirmatively, the wrongs earlier done. We do it, making serious efforts to increase the number of minorities in craft jobs through advertisement, recruitment, encouragement. We get some results, but they are not dramatic. Then you—the nation speaking through your regulatory agencies—tell us that what we have done is not enough. You threaten us! Of course we take action in response to your threat—and having done so, we are threatened at law on the other side! Such inconsistency is unbearable. You, the body politic, must speak with one tongue!"

What is that first threat of which Kaiser complains? It came from the Office of Federal Contract Compliance whose regulations mandate "affirmative action" by all government contractors. The withdrawal of all federal contracts was the price Kaiser might have had to pay if, to avoid being found in "noncompliance," racial preference for minorities had not been introduced. Whence does the OFCC get the authority to make such threats? From an order of the president of the United States, say they, Executive Order 11246. This order requires federal contractors to take affirmative action to prevent low employment of women and minorities in their workforces, on the assumption that most disproportionately low employment is the result of discrimination. Since the racial instrument agreed upon was a direct response to federal authority exercised under that valid order, it is outrageous now, say Kaiser and the union, to attack us for violation of the Civil Rights Act.

This response to official inconsistency cannot help but evoke some sympathy. But as a defense of racial quotas it is worthless. The argument fails on two levels. First, Executive Order 11246 does not require and cannot justify racial quotas in cases like this one, in which the conduct of the employer has not been unlawfully discriminatory. The order says nothing about numerical ratios. Indeed, its plain words *forbid* all racial preference. The relevant passage of that order reads: "The contractor will take affirmative action to insure that applicants are employed, and that employees are treated during employment, without regard to their race, color, religion, sex, or national origin."

Some numerical plans to protect employment for minorities have been upheld by the courts as valid executive actions—but they have been so upheld as responses to specifically identified violations by those upon whom the remedy was imposed. The so-called Philadelphia Plan was held permissible under Title VII, but that holding was explicitly tied to prior exclusionary practices by the six trade unions controlling the workforce in the construction industry in Philadelphia. Whatever tools the Office of Federal Contract Compliance may think itself entitled to employ, it has no authority in law, and certainly none in morals, to press for a racial quota in cases where, as here, those getting preference under the scheme had not been injured by that employer, and those injured by the scheme had not benefited from any misconduct of that employer.

The argument fails at a second level as well. If Executive Order 11246 be interpreted so as to authorize the OFCC to require racial quotas in cases like this one, the executive order itself is plainly unlawful, an illegitimate exercise of administrative authority in conflict with federal statute. The Civil Rights Act specifically prohibits racial classification in admission to on-the-job training programs (Section 703 (d)). The quota plan devised by Kaiser and the union is, as we have seen, patently in violation of this section. When the law and an executive order clash, there can be no doubt of the outcome. Writes the circuit court: "If Executive Order 11246 mandates a racial quota for admission to on-the-job training by Kaiser, *in the absence of any prior hiring or promotion discrimination,* the executive order must fall before this direct congressional prohibition."

Only by resolutely enforcing the rights of citizens can the insolence of office be restrained. Individual workers, without power or money, need to be protected against civil servants who take it upon themselves to threaten in order to be able to report numerical ratios they think desirable, claiming only to be following the orders of their superiors.

The Evils of Racial Preference

Defenses of racial preference—by efforts to reinterpret the law, by confused arguments based on "societal discrimination," by claim of executive order—all collapse. It is important to see why they *should* collapse. The defenders, conscious of their own righteous pursuit of racial justice, little doubt that the tools they wish to employ would have the good consequences they hope for. To question the merit of those tools is for them almost a betrayal of the oppressed in whose behalf they claim to battle. In their eyes the conflict is only over whether they are to be permitted to do a good deed—i.e., give preference to racial minorities—not whether it is a good deed, or whether its consequences will be good.

Decency of motivation, however, does not insure the goodness of the immediate object, or the goodness of its consequences. Racial justice is an aim that all share; it is distorted when transformed into formulas for ethnic proportionality in workforces and professions based (as in this case) upon ethnic populations in the surrounding area. What accounts for this transformation? Motives honorable in their general statement are blended with a vision of cultural homogeneity that is profoundly unhealthy. The objectives then sought in making that blend operational often prove inconsistent with the original aim. It is this inchoate vision of homogeneity—made concrete in numerical proportions—that lies behind racial instruments like the one at issue in *Weber*. Federal appellate courts have not been oblivious to the evils that ensue:

There are good reasons why the use of racial criteria should be strictly scrutinized and given legal sanction only where a compelling need for remedial action can be shown. . . . Government recognition and sanction of racial classifications may be inherently divisive, reinforcing prejudices, confirming perceived differences between the races, and weakening the government's educative role on behalf of equality and neutrality. It may also have unexpected results, such as the development of indicia for placing individuals into different racial categories. Once racial classifications are imbedded in the law, their purpose may become perverted: a benign preference under certain conditions may shade into malignant preference at other times. Moreover, a racial preference for members of one minority might result in discrimination against another minority, a higher proportion of whose members had previously enjoyed access to a certain opportunity (*Associated General Contractors of Massachusetts Inc.* v. *Altshuler*, 1973).

In this spirit three federal circuit courts have repeatedly refused to approve racial quotas in the absence of proved past discriminatory practice dictating that specific remedy.

Racial classifications have insidious long-term results: anger and envy flowing from rewards or penalties based on race; solidification of racial barriers and the encouragement of racial separatism; inappropriate entry of race into unrelated intellectual or economic matters; the indirect support of condescension and invidious judgments among ethnic groups—in sum, the promotion of all the conditions that produce racial *dis*harmony and racial *dis*integration. What Kaiser and the union defend is very far from an innocuous good deed.

Some of the damage, direct and substantial, is done to those, like Weber and Bakke, who bear the immediately resulting burden. "Society" does not pay; the "white majority" does not pay; individual citizens pay. The penalty to them is great and undeserved. One notable feature of the *Bakke* decision, almost entirely overlooked by commentators and the press, is the fact that all nine Supreme Court justices agreed that, as a result of the quota system used by the medical school at Davis, Allan Bakke was done a constitutional injury—that is, an injury he should not have to suffer unless it can be well justified. Even the four justices who thought the injury could be justified took the hurt done to him very seriously. One of those four (that is, one of the group who did *not* side with Bakke), Justice Blackmun, refers to the injury done to Bakke as an "ugly" one. The other five justices struck down that racially preferential program; Powell among them condemns the damage such programs do. The Washington Supreme Court, too, in deciding against Marco DeFunis in an analogous case, did not deny that he had been seriously hurt, and candidly rejected the claim that such quotas are "benign." A program giving special favor to racial minorities, say they, "is certainly not benign with respect to nonminority students replaced by it" (*DeFunis* v. *Odegaard, 1974*). *Reverse discrimination* is not an invention or a hypothesis yet to be confirmed; it is a sociological and legal fact.

Private Compensatory Justice

The reality of the evils flowing from racial instruments introduces one of the most intriguing aspects of the *Weber* case. A dispute arises between the district and the circuit court beneath which lies a momentous philosophical issue. Numerical remedies based on race do damage, the two courts agree; they further agree that this is a case in which the imposition of such a numerical remedy cannot be justified because there has been, in fact, no previous unlawful discrimination by the employer here. In those cases in which such remedy might prove justifiable (previous discriminatory practice in that setting being alleged), however, the following question arises: may that numerical instrument of redress be devised and executed on the authority of the employer and union acting jointly? Or is a racial quota permissible as remedy only on the express authority of the judiciary? The district court not only found the remedy unjustifiable, but held in addition that such painful remedies would in no case be in the province of unions and management to impose. The circuit court, agreeing on the first point, did not agree on the second. Voluntary remedial action (said they) is preferable to court action; therefore, to insist upon judicial imposition of remedies would interfere unduly with reasonable private amelioration. The underlying issue here is the locus of authority in resolving questions of justice. Which court is the wiser?

In permitting numerical remedies to be imposed (if at all) only by the judiciary, the district court, I submit, is deeply right. The reasons for this are several and complicated.

First, the question of whether the circumstances are such as to justify the imposition of a numerical remedy (a question that must be answered affirmatively if any such remedy is to be lawful) is precisely the kind of question that cannot be answered fairly by employers and unions acting in their joint interests. Individuals will bear the burden; if the case were of a kind to justify the imposition of that burden on Weber and his like, past discrimination by that employer in that context must be proved or admitted. No employer is likely to make that admission. To do so would invite a host of very expensive lawsuits in behalf of those injured. Employers will therefore enter such agreements only with the understanding that no past discrimination has been proved or admitted. That very understanding (however arguable it may be) on which an employer might be willing to enter an agreement with a union to give racial preference to minorities is precisely the understanding which, if reflecting the facts truly, shows that racial preference unjustly injurious and unlawful.

This peculiar feature of "voluntary" racial instruments is admitted—even emphasized, ironically—by the United Auto Workers, the National Education Association, and other assorted unions. If (they argue) voluntary racial preference is permissible only when the employer's past conduct would be found in violation of Title VII, there will be no voluntary race-conscious action. For, as they agree: "[I]t is usually difficult to predict whether or not [previous] discrimination would be found" (associated unions, brief *amici,* p. 13). Indeed! For this reason precisely it is a question of such a kind that no answer to it reached as part of a labor-management agreement could be trusted.

The aggregated unions continue: "Moreover, the employer would, by taking voluntary action, put itself in a no-win situation in a suit such as this. Either its past conduct will be determined to be unlawful, thereby inviting litigation by discriminatees, or the remedial action will be found unlawful, and liability to white employees will exist" (Ibid.). Just so! But the authors of this candid statement apparently do not see where their argument leads. They would like the courts to conclude that, since the present standard (that "voluntary" racial quotas suppose the same finding of unlawful discrimination that alone might justify court-imposed remedies) effectively precludes "voluntary" quotas altogether, we should permit the introduction of a new standard, one that would allow "voluntary" quotas under some factual circumstances that—as they admit—would not justify a court in imposing them! What could serve as such a standard? The lone dissenting judge of the circuit court, pursuing the same line, is driven to propose an astonishing answer: A "voluntary" quota plan should be upheld, he suggests, if it is "a *reasonable remedy* for an *arguable violation* of Title VII" (p. 230, emphasis added).

This standard is neither feasible in practice, nor morally acceptable if it were. As a practical matter, such notions as "reasonable remedy" and "arguable violation" have virtually no objective content. Only the courts could resolve, on a case-by-case basis, disputed claims about "arguable violations" and about the reasonableness of remedy. Endless litigation could not be avoided—but it is the elimination of time-consuming litigation that is alleged to be the great merit of "voluntary" racial instruments. The increase in court involvement that would result undercuts any proposed justification of "voluntary" quotas on grounds of efficiency.

More important than its inefficiency, however, is the fact that the proposed standard (that a voluntary quota plan should be upheld if it is "a reasonable remedy for an arguable violation of Title VII") is morally unacceptable. Just remedies presuppose some determinable wrongs for which they give redress and by which they are justified. It is confusion of mind to propose a *remedy* for an *arguable* violation: one cannot put right what might prove on more judicious examination to have been no wrong at all.

Voluntary Programs and Individual Rights

All "voluntary" quotas (i.e., those introduced without court imposition) presuppose reliance upon some standard that must encounter essentially the same problem. The philosophical dimensions of the dispute between the two courts here emerge. The circuit court's position exhibits irremediable moral defect: by permitting racially preferential programs without the backing of judicial authority, it permits the delegation of questions of justice to private hands that are neither equipped, nor disposed, nor authorized to resolve them fairly.

To resolve a matter of individual right the bargaining process between labor and management is almost the worst imaginable tool. The impartial determination of facts without regard to interest, and the honest application of principles without regard to advantage, are essential in adjudicating questions of right—but the elimination of regard for self-interest and advantage is precisely what is impossible at the bargaining table.

Even if the needed impartiality were possible there, it would be inappropriate, uncommon, and surely could not be relied upon. Union and management bargainers are duty-bound to press for the advantage of the units they represent. The process is designed to deal with issues of pay and working conditions, not with the protection of individual rights. Justice entails giving to each his due—whether or not he or others can negotiate for it successfully.

Most important, the authority to resolve questions of justice cannot lie in a labor-management bargain. Individual rights *may not*—as a matter of law or morals—be bargained away. As a matter of constitutional principle, the Supreme Court has spoken definitively on this issue. A union, they agree, may waive some of its rights to *collective* activity, such as the right to strike, in a bargaining agreement made with the aim of economic advantage for its members. The Court continues:

> Title VII, on the other hand, stands on plainly different ground; *it concerns not majoritarian processes, but an individual's right to equal employment opportunities.* Title VII's strictures are absolute and represent a congressional command that *each* employee be free from discriminatory practices. Of necessity, *the rights conferred can form no part of the collective bargaining process* since waiver of these rights would defeat the paramount congressional purpose behind

Title VII. In these circumstances, an employee's rights under Title VII are not susceptible of prospective waiver (*Alexander* v. *Gardner-Denver Co.*, 1974, emphasis added).

Contracts reached through collective bargaining may, of course, introduce different terms of employment for different groups of employees in the light of the relevant conditions of those groups. Race, however, is never relevant in that sense. Because racial discrimination invariably touches the nonbargainable rights of all individuals adversely affected, race itself has been identified as an inappropriate criterion for the classification of employees.

In sum: the courts have repeatedly held that, in compromising with an employer, a union may not take race into account. Programs like the one at issue in *Weber* explicitly take race into account. The conclusion of this syllogism is inescapable.

The unions take another tack. "You fail to note [they rejoin in effect] that this is a *voluntary* program. Weber and his fellows may be said to have relinquished their rights in this matter because, when the plan was devised, they were adequately represented by their union. The union has a duty to represent all of its members; its bargainers are selected democratically; and since white workers constitute a majority of the bargaining unit, the union process may be relied upon to reach no agreement that will violate the rights of individual white members."

It is hard to take this argument seriously. Union process is often genuinely democratic; negotiators for unions generally do seek to represent the interests of all the members of the bargaining unit. But the most sympathetic review of union process could not rationally conclude that the fairness of unions to their members over the long term has been such as to justify the delegation, to bargainers, of matters of fundamental individual right. The current flow of complaints about reverse discrimination in employment contracts in itself provides substantial evidence that the bargaining process, notwithstanding its general fairness, cannot be depended upon in this sphere. "Voluntary" is an appealing word. But its use here suggests what is not true— that those who were injured by the racial instruments devised in the contract did themselves volunteer to carry the burden. To call Weber's sacrifice "voluntary" is most inappropriate.

This defense of "voluntary" racial instruments (even if unions were invariably sensitive to matters of individual right) avoids the key question of legitimate authority. At stake here are the rights of individuals to the most fundamental of democratic conditions—equal treatment under the law—and, moreover, their rights to that equal treatment as it bears upon the most suspect of all categorical distinctions, race. Even legislators, it may be argued, however powerful their assembly, honorable their election, and dutiful their conduct, may not take from individual citizens certain fundamental rights. With the noblest of intentions, it is not within their authority to pursue public policy at the cost of compromising the individual citizen's right not to be discriminated against because of his race or religion. Philosophers will differ about the grounds of legislative authority, but few will seriously deny that upon such authority there must be some hard limits. Unequal treatment because of race is as clear an example as there is of the violation of those limits.

If the principle here expressed were somehow mistaken, if it were sometimes just, in the cause of racial redress, to sacrifice the rights of some blameless nonbeneficiaries to advantage others who had not been injured, even so it would at least be certain that no such decision could be properly made by any save the legislature of highest authority, subject to the review of the court of highest jurisdiction. The notion that, to encourage "voluntary affirmative action plans," we may bypass the body politic, investing unions and management with the authority to bargain with fundamental human rights, makes the prospect of a reversal in the *Weber* case very distressing. Not substantive entitlements alone are at issue here, but also the procedural rights of working people to have questions of justice decided by legislatures and courts.

A Comparison with Bakke

Weber and *Bakke* are closely analogous in this procedural regard. Weber's right to equal treatment was infringed on by a union-management agreement, Bakke's by a medical school admissions committee. Legitimate authority was exceeded in both cases. When it was asked, in *Bakke,* for what purposes a university might consider race in admissions, Justice Powell replied, in his decisive opinion, that it may be considered for the sake of student diversity (to support the exchange of ideas in accord with First Amendment concerns), or, conceivably, as redress for the specific victims of specific injustices. "Societal discrimination" as a ground for racial preference he explicitly considered and rejected. Powell wrote:

We [i.e., the Supreme Court] have never approved a classification that aids persons perceived as members of relatively victimized groups at the expense of other innocent individuals, in the absence of judicial, legislative, or administrative findings of constitutional or statutory violations [references omitted]. After such findings have been made, the governmental interest in preferring members of the injured groups at the expense of others is substantial, since the legal rights of the victims must be vindicated. In such a case the extent of the injury and the consequent remedy will have been judicially, legislatively, or administratively defined. Also, the remedial action usually remains subject to continuing oversight to assure that it will work the least harm possible to other innocent persons competing for the benefit. Without such findings of constitutional or statutory violations it cannot be said that the government has any greater interest in helping one individual than in refraining from harming another. Thus the government has no compelling justification for inflicting such harm [*University of California Regents* v. *Bakke,* 1978].

But findings of constitutional or statutory violations is not the business of private bodies—unions, or managements, or medical-school committees—to make. Powell continued:

Petitioner [the Regents of the University] does not purport to have made, *and is in no position to make,* such findings. . . . [Even] isolated segments of our vast governmental structures are not competent to make those decisions, at least in the absence of legislative mandates and legislatively determined

criteria [references omitted]. Before relying upon these sorts
of findings in establishing a racial classification, a governmental body must have the authority and capability to establish, in the record, that the classification is responsive to
identified discrimination (emphasis added).

Powell's point is that a medical school admissions committee
(even though indirectly an agent of the state) is entirely without
the requisite authority. Kaiser and the union have a far weaker
claim to the needed authority than did they. An admissions
committee is not competent to make the findings that might
justify racial preference, granted. But if the admissions committee had sought to present such findings of identified discrimination at the Davis medical school (discrimination that, in fact, the
university specifically denies), they might conceivably contend
that as one agent of one arm of one element of the state, it was
within their province to do so—and thus might conceivably seek
to justify their racial program as remedy. That claim must fail,
the mission of the medical school and all its subsidiary elements
being educative, not judicial. Any analogous claim made by
Kaiser and the union—that they are authorized to make findings
of "societal discrimination" that will justify inflicting harm on
Weber and other blameless parties—is totally without warrant.

If the Facts Had Been Different

In the absence of any showing or admission of previous illegal
discrimination at the Gramercy plant, every defense of racially
preferential remedy must prove unsatisfactory. Sensitive to this
point, the American Civil Liberties Union argues at length that
the factual circumstances of this case have been misunderstood,
that Kaiser Aluminum *did* discriminate against minorities. The
pattern of employment by Kaiser at other plants in earlier years
is reviewed, and much is made of the racially disproportionate
impact, at the Gramercy plant, of a "purportedly neutral criterion." Using the percentage of the minority population in the
surrounding parishes of Louisiana as benchmark, the argument
concludes that Kaiser's workforce at the Gramercy plant in
skilled-craft positions was "severely under-representative."

Putting aside the question of how "representativeness" might rationally be established or, if it had been established, what bearing that would have upon the lawfulness of Kaiser's previous conduct, it is important to note that the entire thrust of this argument is misdirected. The *Weber* case presents an appeal to our highest court on a matter of fundamental principle. That principle must be argued on the basis of a factual record properly established at trial in a responsible federal district court. Appellate courts, and the Supreme Court, face the question of principle *given that record*. Even the district court could analyze only the facts brought before it by the parties. Kaiser testified to its nondiscriminatory practices at the Gramercy plant from its opening, and of its efforts to recruit black craftsmen from the general community. They would not and could not report otherwise. If (as some now claim) the record should have shown hidden unlawful conduct by Kaiser, such findings could only have entered the record at the trial level. At this point the issue is, supposing the record complete and accurate, whether, *without* such previous violations established, this racial quota is permissible.

To contend that the facts of the matter *could* be viewed differently is to blind oneself to the essence of the controversy. Had the courts found, after examining all testimony, that Kaiser had previously discriminated against minorities in its Gramercy plant, the issue now to be decided here would not even have arisen.

Seniority Entitlements

All arguments thus far explored incorporate the realization that individuals are indeed injured when disadvantaged solely because of their race. Brian Weber did not get the job-training opportunity he was entitled to. Most ordinary people, and most judges, have no difficulty in seeing that. So zealous are some of the advocates of racial preference, however, that they claim not to see it. Weber was never really hurt, say they. He has a legitimate complaint only if he was discriminated against unfairly. But he was not discriminated against at all! Hence he has no case.

Puzzling though this claim appears on its face, it is honestly defended, in two ways. First, it is argued, Weber has lost nothing more than seniority entitlements. But seniority systems may be altered by labor-management agreement, and in any event, seniority rights are not vested in the individual employee but in the collective-bargaining unit. Therefore, when a voluntary quota plan results in Weber's getting less than he expected in view of his greater seniority, he loses nothing that belonged to him in the first place. The injury done to him (it is contended) is apparent, not real.

This argument is twice faulty. It underplays the importance of individual seniority entitlements in the industrial context; and it does not face up to the discriminatory nature of the seniority deprivation in this case.

In allocating scarce opportunities and goods in the industrial world, seniority is critically important. For very many workers a host of matters—job security, opportunities for advanced training, vacation and retirement benefits—depend chiefly upon the number of years of service they have given. Nothing remains to them after years of service but their seniority claims. To deny that harm is done to an unskilled worker on an hourly wage when he is deprived of entitlements flowing normally from ten years' seniority shows gross moral insensitivity. Seniority does not insure qualification for positions demanding special talents, of course; but where qualifications are roughly equal, or not distinguishable, seniority above all other considerations will be relied upon in the interests of fairness.

Seniority entitlements are tied to individuals, not just to the bargaining unit. In matters of job assignment, transfer, layoff and recall, and job training, opportunities must be distributed among competing employees. Competitive-status seniority is therefore of great moral as well as practical importance, and directly affects individuals more importantly than it does the bargaining collective. Noncompetitive benefits also—pensions, sick leave, paid vacations—are commonly determined in part by length of service and therefore must be tied to individuals. Seniority, the Supreme Court writes, "has become of overriding importance, and one of its major functions is to determine who gets or who keeps an available job" (*Humphrey* v. *Moore*, 1964). The "who" in this passage refers to individual persons, not to groups.

Seniority systems are bargainable, true. It does not follow, however, that all seniority rights are bargainable. It is essential not to confuse the *system* of seniority with individual *entitlements* under a given system in force. Once a seniority system has become a reality in rule and practice, a worker's rights and expectations under that system are his and very previous to him. It is callous to minimize the injury done when such rights are not respected.

When the ground of that disrespect is race, the injury is particularly offensive. Entitlements in themselves minor (which an opportunity for on-the-job training is not) become matters of grave concern when manipulated for racial reasons. Where one must sit on a bus or go to the toilet understandably becomes a source of rage and an issue of constitutional proportions when the determination is made by race. Protests over segregated lunch counters had as their target not the culinary opportunities denied, but the immoral character of the ground of their denial. Even if Weber's seniority expectations be thought trivial, the racial ground of the unequal treatment he received is very far from trivial.

Some who understand very clearly why Allan Bakke was injured when excluded from medical school in a racially discriminatory way fail to see that the injury done to Brian Weber is equally unjust. Applicants to a competitive program, they appreciate, have a right to evaluation on some set of relevant criteria— past performance, intellectual promise, character, or whatever—and if deserving on the basis of those criteria, ought not be deprived of place because of race. But if the performance qualifications of all applicants are roughly equal (as were those of Weber and the minority workers chosen in his place), where they ask, is the injustice?

The injustice lies in the deprivation, on improper grounds, of what one is otherwise entitled to. The basis for the entitlement will be different in different contexts. Scarce places in medical or law schools are rightly allocated to persons best exhibiting the characteristics that have been determined relevant to the studies or profession to be pursued. Scarce on-the-job training opportunities are rightly allocated to those having certain seniority entitlements. The bases of Weber's and Bakke's claims to that of which they were deprived are very different; but both were wrongly denied what they would have received if the scarce available goods had been distributed in accord with established criteria in a morally just way. Both were the plain victims of racial discrimination, losing out because of the color of their skin.

Persons concerned about such injustice when done in the academic world ought seriously to consider the wisdom of remaining silent when essentially the same injustice (although with respect to different entitlements) is done in the industrial world. If preference by race should be found, in the *Weber* case, to justify the deprivation of what is fairly earned by a laborer, the security of what is fairly earned by anyone in any sphere is similarly threatened.

Beyond Seniority

If the damage to Weber cannot reasonably be minimized, can it be wholly denied? This is the second line of defense to which Kaiser and the union fall back in the effort to show that Weber was not discriminated against at all. Weber's rights were not infringed on, they say, because he never had any seniority rights to job training here. The argument goes like this: "Where admission to a training program is properly a function of seniority, and seniority, like Weber's, is untainted by the employer's previous discrimination, he would be damaged if race were allowed to supervene. But Weber errs in thinking that seniority gives him any claim under *this* quota program, which was initiated in 1974, by Kaiser and the union, specifically to increase minority representation in the craft employments. New rights were then created, Kaiser and the union agreeing to use seniority only for the distribution of available slots *within* the two racial lists, black and white. If, in the new plan, they had agreed to use the lottery method—two separate lotteries, one for whites and one for blacks—it would be obvious that seniority was not the real issue here. They could have done just that. Weber's claim that he was deprived of seniority rights is a red herring, because the mode of selecting from each racial pool is irrelevant. So the Kaiser plan, as the dissenting judge wrote, 'stands or falls on its separation of workers into two racial pools for assignment to job training.' "

This argument is a compound of perceptivity and blindness. Seniority was the system deliberately adopted by Kaiser and the union—but they did not make that choice at random. Years of past work in the very plant where those training opportunities were to arise was thought the fairest consideration in allocating scarce places to otherwise equally qualified workers. Seniority was adopted as a relevant and rational principle. To create two seniority lists, black and white, and then choose the top person from each list, even if he has less seniority than the fourth or twentieth person on the other list, is to override the seniority principle with race. If the basis chosen for the fair distribution of scarce opportunities had not been seniority, but (say) a lottery, then the just application of the lottery principle would require that *it* not be overriden by race. It is therefore perceptive to note that the real issue here goes beyond seniority—that the plan fails simply because it separates the workers into two *racial* pools—every such separation being necessarily invidious. Any system used to distribute opportunities among the members of each racial pool, even if of itself fair, must be distorted by that antecedent racial classification. Whatever besides seniority might prove just as a ground for the distribution of goods, skin color is not it.

Is it correct to say, then, that Weber had no seniority rights here at all? No. When it is agreed by union and employer that, for allocating these job-training opportunities, length of service is the appropriate basis, employees acquire entitlements on that basis. The injustice of racial favoritism manifests itself, in this case, in the deprivation of those entitlements. Were a worker's entitlements based on some other feature of his circumstances— his experience or his performance on a competitive examina- tion—then the injustice of racial favoritism might be manifested in the deprivation of entitlements flowing from those. Weber has a right to nondiscriminatory treatment. To contend that he never had any rights in this matter because the respect in which he was discriminated against is not the only respect in which he might have been discriminated against is a last-ditch effort to obscure the wrong that was done him.

25. The Civil Rights Act Permits Voluntary Affirmative Action

By WILLIAM J. BRENNAN, JR.

Focus Brian Weber eventually lost his case when, in 1979, the U.S. Supreme Court overturned the decision of the Fifth Circuit Court of Appeals, which had earlier ruled in his favor. The majority opinion in his case was written by Justice William J. Brennan, Jr. Although conceding that "a literal construction" of Title VII of the Civil Rights Act would tend to support Weber's claim that the Kaiser/United Steelworkers affirmative action plan was unlawful, Justice Brennan stresses in his decision that the Civil Rights Act must be read within the context of its legislative history and the purpose for which it was enacted. He quotes from the congressional testimony of Senators Clark and Humphrey, as well as a statement of President Kennedy, to the effect that the Civil Rights Act was needed to alleviate the grave unemployment problem of Negro workers in America. Given this legislative history, says Brennan, "we cannot agree with respondents that Congress intended to prohibit the private sector from taking effective steps to accomplish the goal that Congress designed Title VII to achieve." Title VII, he says, should not be interpreted to prohibit "all voluntary, private, race-conscious efforts to abolish traditional patterns of racial segregation and hierarchy."

Brennan also points to the prohibition in Section 703(j) of Title VII as lending support to the majority interpretation. Section 703(j) says that the Civil Rights Act shall not be interpreted to require an employer to grant preferential treatment to any group because of a racial imbalance in the employer's work force. Had Congress intended to outlaw all race-conscious affirmative action, Brennan argues, it could have said in Section 703(j) that Title VII must not be interpreted either to require or to *permit* racial preference. Since Congress did not do this, "the natural inference," says Brennan, "is that Congress chose not to forbid all voluntary race-conscious affirmative action." Brennan also argues that the Kaiser affirmative action policy is temporary and is not intended to *maintain* a racial balance—a practice that congressional supporters of the Civil Rights Bill had seen as impermissible—but to eliminate an existing racial imbalance. Preferential treatment of black trainees will end, says Brennan, "as soon as the percentage of black skilled craft workers in the Gramercy, Louisiana, plant approximates the percentage of blacks in the local labor force."

William J. Brennan, Jr., appointed in 1956, is an associate justice of the U.S. Supreme Court.

THIS CASE AROSE from the operation of [the affirmative action plan] at Kaiser's plant in Gramercy, Louisiana. Until 1974 Kaiser hired as craft workers for that plant only persons who had had prior craft experience. Because blacks had long been excluded from craft unions, few were able to present such credentials. As a consequence, prior to 1974 only 1.83 per cent (5 out of 273) of the skilled craft workers at the Gramercy plant were black, even though the work force in the Gramercy area was approximately 39 per cent black. Pursuant to the national agreement Kaiser altered its craft hiring practice in the Gramercy plant. Rather than hiring already trained outsiders, Kaiser established a training program to train its production workers to fill craft openings. Selection of craft trainees was made on the basis of seniority, with the proviso that at least 50 per cent of the new trainees were to be black until the percentage of black skilled craft workers in the Gramercy plant approximated the percentage of blacks in the local labor force.

During 1974, the first year of the operation of the Kaiser-USWA affirmative action plan, thirteen craft trainees were selected from Gramercy's production work force. Of these, seven were black and six white. The most junior black selected into the program had less seniority than several white production workers whose bids for admission were rejected. Thereafter one of those white production workers, respondent Brian Weber, instituted this class action in the U.S. District Court for the Eastern District of Louisiana. The complaint alleged that the filling of craft-trainee positions at the Gramercy plant pursuant to the affirmative action program had resulted in junior black employees receiving training in preference to more senior white employees, thus discriminating against respondent and other similarly situated white employees in violation of Sections 703(a) and (d) of Title VII.

Excerpted from *United Steelworkers of America* v. *Weber*, 443 U.S. 193 (1979).

We emphasize at the outset the narrowness of our inquiry. Since the Kaiser-USWA plan does not involve state action, this case does not present an alleged violation of the Equal Protection Clause of the Constitution. Further, since the Kaiser-USWA plan was adopted voluntarily, we are not concerned with what Title VII requires or with what a court might order to remedy a past proven violation of the act. The only question before us is the narrow statutory issue of whether Title VII *forbids* private employers and unions from voluntarily agreeing upon bona fide affirmative action plans that accord racial preferences in the manner and for the purpose provided in the Kaiser-USWA plan. That question was expressly left open in *McDonald* v. *Santa Fe Trail Trans. Co.* (1976), which held, in a case not involving affirmative action, that Title VII protects whites as well as blacks from certain forms of racial discrimination.

Respondent argues that Congress intended in Title VII to prohibit all race-conscious affirmative action plans. Respondent's argument rests upon a literal interpretation of Sections 703(a) and (d) of the act. Those sections make it unlawful to "discriminate . . . because of . . . race" in hiring and in the selection of apprentices for training programs. Since, the argument runs, *McDonald* v. *Sante Fe Trans. Co.* settled that Title VII forbids discrimination against white employees solely because they are white, it follows that the Kaiser-USWA plan violates Title VII.

Respondent's argument is not without force. But it overlooks the significance of the fact that the Kaiser-USWA plan is an affirmative action plan voluntarily adopted by private parties to eliminate traditional patterns of racial segregation. In this context respondent's reliance upon a literal construction of Sections 703(a) and (d) and upon *McDonald* is misplaced. It is a "familiar rule, that a thing may be within the letter of the statute and yet not within the statute, because not within its spirit, nor within the intention of its makers." The prohibition against racial discrimination in Sections 703(a) and (d) of Title VII must therefore be read against the background of the legislative history of Title VII and the historical context from which the act arose. Examination of those sources makes clear that an interpretation of the sections that forbade all race-conscious affirmative action would "bring about an end completely at variance with the purpose of the statute" and must be rejected.

Congress's primary concern in enacting the prohibition against racial discrimination in Title VII of the Civil Rights Act of 1964 was with "the plight of the Negro in our economy" (110 *Cong. Rec.* 6458, remarks of Senator Humphrey). Because of automation the number of such jobs was rapidly decreasing. As a consequence "the relative position of the Negro worker [was] steadily worsening. In 1947 the nonwhite unemployment rate was only 64 per cent higher than the white rate; in 1963 it was 124 per cent higher" (Ibid., at 6547, remarks of Senator Humphrey). Congress considered this a serious social problem. As Senator Clark told the Senate:

> The rate of Negro unemployment has gone up consistently as compared with white unemployment for the past fifteen years. This is social malaise and a social situation which we should not tolerate. That is one of the principle reasons why this bill should pass.

Congress feared that the goals of the Civil Rights Act—the integration of blacks into the mainstream of America society—could not be achieved unless this trend were reversed. And Congress recognized that that would not be possible unless blacks were able to secure jobs "which have a future" (Ibid., at 7204, remarks of Senator Clark). As Senator Humphrey explained to the Senate:

> What good does it do a Negro to be able to eat in a fine restuarant if he cannot afford to pay the bill? What good does it do him to be accepted in a hotel that is too expensive for his modest income? How can a Negro child be motivated to take full advantage of integrated-educational facilities if he has no hope of getting a job where he can use that education?
>
> Without a job, one cannot afford public convenience and accommodations. Income from employment may be necessary to further a man's education, or that of his children. If

his children have no hope of getting a good job, what will motivate them to take advantage of educational opportunities?

These remarks echoed President Kennedy's original message to Congress upon the introduction of the Civil Rights Act in 1963:

There is little value in a Negro's obtaining the right to be admitted to hotels and restaurants if he has no cash in his pocket and no job.

Accordingly, it was clear to Congress that "the crux of the problem [was] to open employment opportunities for Negroes in occupations which have been traditionally closed to them," (Ibid., at 6548, remarks of Senator Humphrey), and it was to this problem that Title VII's prohibition against racial discrimination in employment was primarily addressed.

It plainly appears from the House Report accompanying the Civil Rights Act that Congress did not intend wholly to prohibit private and voluntary affirmative action efforts as one method of solving this problem. The report provides:

No bill can or should lay claim to eliminating all of the causes and consequences of racial and other types of discrimination against minorities. There is reason to believe, however, that national leadership provided by the enactment of federal legislation dealing with the most troublesome problems *will create an atmosphere conducive to voluntary or local resolution of other forms of discrimination* (emphasis supplied).

No Absolute Prohibition

Given this legislative history, we cannot agree with respondent that Congress intended to prohibit the private sector from taking effective steps to accomplish the goal that Congress designed Title VII to achieve. The very statutory words intended as a spur or catalyst to cause "employers and unions to self-examine and to self-evaluate their employment practices and to endeavor to eliminate, so far as possible, the last vestiges of an unfortunate and ignominious page in this country's history,''(*Albemarle* v. *Moody, 1975*), cannot be interpreted as an absolute prohibition against all private, voluntary race-conscious affirmative action efforts to hasten the elimination of such vestiges. It would be ironic indeed if a law triggered by a nation's concern over centuries of racial injustice and intended to improve the lot of those who had "been excluded from the American dream for so long," (110 *Cong. Rec.,* at 6552, remarks of Senator Humphrey), constituted the first legislative prohibition of all voluntary, private, race-conscious efforts to abolish traditional patterns of racial segregation and hierarchy.

Section 703(j)

Our conclusion is further reinforced by examination of the language and legislative history of Section 703(j) of Title VII. Opponents of Title VII raised two related arguments against the bill. First, they argued that the act would be interpreted to *require* employers with racially imbalanced work forces to grant preferential treatment to racial minorities in order to integrate. Second, they argued that employers with racially imbalanced work forces would grant preferential treatment to racial minorities, even if not required to do so by the act. Had Congress meant to prohibit all race-conscious affirmative action, as respondent urges, it easily could have answered both objections by providing that Title VII would not require or *permit* racially preferential integration efforts. But Congress did not choose such a course. Rather, Congress added Section 703(j), which addresses only the first objection. The section provides that nothing contained in Title VII "shall be interpreted to *require* any employer . . . to grant preferential treatment . . . to any group because of the race . . . of such . . . group on account of" a de facto racial imbalance in the employer's work force. The section does *not* state that "nothing in Title VII shall be interpreted to *permit*" voluntary affirmative efforts to correct racial imbalances. The natural inference is that Congress chose not to forbid all voluntary race-conscious affirmative action.

The reasons for this choice are evident from the legislative record. Title VII could not have been enacted into law without substantial support from legislators in both Houses who traditionally resisted federal regulation of private business. Those legislators demanded as a price for their support that "management prerogatives and union freedoms . . . be left undisturbed to the greatest extent possible." Section 703(j) was proposed by Senator Dirksen to allay any fears that the act might be interpreted in such a way as to upset this compromise. The section was designed to prevent Section 703 of Title VII from being interpreted in such a way as to lead to undue "federal government interference with private businesses because of some federal employee's ideas about racial balance or imbalance" (110 *Cong. Rec.*, at 14314, remarks of Senator Miller). Clearly, a prohibition against all voluntary, race-conscious, affirmative action efforts would disserve these ends. Such a prohibition would augment the powers of the federal government and diminish traditional management prerogatives while at the same time impeding attainment of the ultimate statutory goals. In view of this legislative history and in view of Congress's desire to avoid undue federal regulation of private businesses, use of the word "require" rather than the phrase "require or permit" in Section 703(j) fortifies the conclusion that Congress did not intend to limit traditional business freedom to such a degree as to prohibit all voluntary, race-conscious affirmative action.

We need not today define in detail the line of demarcation between permissible and impermissible affirmative action plans. It suffices to hold that the challenged Kaiser-USWA affirmative action plan falls on the permissible side of the line. The purposes of the plan mirror those of the statute. Both were designed to break down old patterns of racial segregation and hierarchy. Both were structured to "open employment opportunities for Negroes in occupations which have been traditionally closed to them" (110 *Cong. Rec.* 6548, remarks of Senator Humphrey).

At the same time the plan does not unnecessarily trammel the interests of the white employees. The plan does not require the discharge of white workers and their replacement with new black hires. Nor does the plan create an absolute bar to the advancement of white employees; half of those trained in the program will be white. Moreover, the plan is a temporary measure; it is not intended to maintain racial balance, but simply to eliminate a manifest racial imbalance. Preferential selection of craft trainees at the Gramercy plant will end as soon as the percentage of black skilled craft workers in the Gramercy plant approximates the percentages of blacks in the local labor force.

26. Title VII Not Intended to Lock-In Minorities

By HARRY A. BLACKMUN

Focus Justice Brennan's decision in the *Weber* case (selection 25) gave rise to two dissenting opinions—one by Chief Justice Warren E. Burger, the other by Justice William Rehnquist—both of which accused the Court majority of intellectual dishonesty in its reading of the legislative history of Title VII. Rehnquist's dissent was particularly spirited, and accused the Court of a cynicism and disregard for truth that was Orwellian. It also set forth by quotation after quotation from the congressional debates on Title VII, what it believed to be the clear legislative intent of Congress on the issue of racial preference. Justice Brennan's decision, however, was supported by a concurring opinion of Justice Blackmun, which, oddly enough, began with an expression of sympathy for some of the points raised in the Rehnquist dissent.

"The Court's expansive approach is somewhat disturbing for me," Blackmun writes in his opinion, "because, as Mr. Justice Rehnquist points out, the Congress that passed Title VII probably thought it was adopting a principle of nondiscrimination that would apply to blacks and whites alike." Despite his misgivings about the intent of Congress, however, Blackmun believes that the majority decision can be justified on the basis of fundamental equity. "Strong considerations of equity," he says, "support an interpretation of Title VII that would permit affirmative action to reach where Title VII itself does not." Title VII, he says, should not be interpreted so as to lock-in "the effects of segregation for which Title VII provides no remedy." Although Blackmun is willing to accept the expanded role for affirmative action-type racial preference as envisioned in the Brennan decision, he clearly has much sympathy for a narrower interpretation expounded by Judge Wisdom of the Fifth Circuit Court of Appeals. According to this narrower "arguable-violations" approach, a company could hire blacks on a preferential basis, without fear of lawsuits from whites, if it believed it may have violated Title VII in the past, even though such violation has not been demonstrated or proven. Blackmun nevertheless is willing to go along with the much broader Brennan view, which would permit affirmative action-type racial preference—even in the absence of "arguable violations" of Title VII—wherever there has been a "societal history of purposeful exclusion of blacks" from a given job category if such exclusion has resulted in "a persistent disparity between the proportion of blacks in the labor force and the proportion of blacks among those who hold jobs within the category."

Harry A. Blackmun, appointed in 1970, is an associate justice of the U.S. Supreme Court.

W HILE I SHARE some of the misgivings expressed in Mr. Justice Rehnquist's dissent concerning the extent to which the legislative history of Title VII clearly supports the result the Court reaches today, I believe that additional considerations, practical and equitable, only partially perceived, if perceived at all, by the Eighty-eighth Congress, support the conclusion reached by the Court today, and I therefore join its opinion as well as its judgment.

In his dissent from the decision of the U.S. Court of Appeals for the Fifth Circuit, Judge Wisdom pointed out that this case arises from a practical problem in the administration of Title VII. The broad prohibition against discrimination places the employer and the union on what he accurately described as a "high tightrope without a net beneath them." If Title VII is read literally, on the one hand they face liability for past discrimination against blacks, and on the other they face liability to whites for any voluntary preferences adopted to mitigate the effects of prior discrimination against blacks.

In this case, Kaiser denies prior discrimination but concedes that its past hiring practices may be subject to question. Although the labor force in the Gramercy, Louisiana, area was approximately 39 per cent black, Kaiser's work force was less than 15 per cent black, and its craft work force was less than 2 per cent black.

Respondent's reading of Title VII, endorsed by the court of appeals, places voluntary compliance with Title VII in profound jeopardy. The only way for the employer and the union to keep their footing on the "tightrope" it creates would be to eschew all forms of voluntary affirmative action. Even a whisper of emphasis on minority recruiting would be forbidden. Because Congress intended to encourage private efforts to come into compliance with Title VII, Judge Wisdom concluded that em-

Excerpted from *United Steelworkers of America* v. *Weber,* 443 U.S. 193 (1979).

325

ployers and unions who had committed "arguable violations" of Title VII should be free to take reasonable responses without fear of liability to whites. Preferential hiring along the lines of the Kaiser program is a reasonable response for the employer, whether a court, on these facts, could order the same step as a remedy. The company is able to avoid identifying victims of past discrimination, and so avoids claims for backpay that would inevitably follow a response limited to such victims. If past victims should be benefited by the program, however, the company mitigates its liability to those persons.

The "arguable-violation" theory has a number of advantages. It responds to a practical problem in the administration of Title VII not anticipated by Congress. It draws predictability from the outline of present law, and closely effectuates the purpose of the act. Both Kaiser and the United States urge its adoption here. Because I agree that it is the soundest way to approach this case, my preference would be to resolve this litigation by applying it and holding that Kaiser's craft-training program meets the requirement that voluntary affirmative action be a reasonable response to an "arguable violation" of Title VII.

The Court, however, declines to consider the narrow "arguable-violation" approach and adheres instead to an interpretation of Title VII that permits affirmative action by an employer whenever the job category in question is "traditionally segregated." The sources cited suggest that the Court considers a job category to be "traditionally segregated" when there has been a societal history of purposeful exclusion of blacks from the job category, resulting in a persistent disparity between the proportion of blacks in the labor force and the proportion of blacks among those who hold jobs within the category.

"Traditionally segregated job categories," where they exist, sweep far more broadly than the class of "arguable violations" of Title VII. The Court's expansive approach is somewhat disturbing for me because, as Mr. Justice Rehnquist points out, the Congress that passed Title VII probably thought it was adopting a principle of nondiscrimination that would apply to blacks and whites alike. A closer look at the problem, however, reveals that in each of the principle ways in which the Court's "traditionally-segregated-job-categories" approach expands on the "arguable-violations" theory, still other considerations point in favor of the broad standard adopted by the Court, and make it possible for me to conclude that the Court's reading of the statute is an acceptable one.

Strong considerations of equity support an interpretation of Title VII that would permit affirmative action to reach where Title VII does not. The bargain struck in 1964 with the passage of Title VII guaranteed equal opportunity for white and black alike, but where Title VII provides no remedy for blacks, it should not be construed to foreclose private affirmative action from supplying relief. It seems unfair for respondent Weber to argue, as he does, that the asserted scarcity of black craftsmen in Louisiana, the product of historic discrimination, makes Kaiser's training program illegal because it ostensibly absolves Kaiser of all Title VII liability. Absent compelling evidence of legislative intent, I would not interpret Title VII itself as a means of "locking in" the effects of segregation for which Title VII provides no remedy. Such a construction, as the Court points out, would be "ironic," given the broad remedial purposes of Title VII.

The dissent, while it focuses more on what Title VII does not require than on what Title VII forbids, cites several passages that appear to express an intent to "lock in" minorities. In mining the legislative history anew, however, the dissent, in my view, fails to take proper account of our prior cases that have given that history a much more limited reading than that adopted by the dissent. In short, the passages marshaled by the dissent are not so compelling as to merit the whip hand over the obvious equity of permitting employers to ameliorate the effects of past discrimination for which Title VII provides no direct relief.

I also think it significant that, while the Court's opinion does not foreclose other forms of affirmative action, the Kaiser program it approves is a moderate one. The opinion notes that the program does not afford an absolute preference for blacks and that it ends when the racial composition of Kaiser's craft work force matches the racial composition of the local population. It thus operates as a temporary tool for remedying past discrimination without attempting to "maintain" a previously achieved balance.

27. *Justice Debased*

By CARL COHEN

Focus Responding to the Supreme Court's decision in the *Weber* case, Carl Cohen finds that arguments of the majority collapse upon closer inspection. By its clear wording, says Cohen, Title VII of the Civil Rights Act outlaws all racial preference in employment situations, including specifically on-the-job training programs. That, he says, is all one needs to know to see that the action committed against Brian Weber was unlawful. Legislative intent, he holds, is first and foremost to be discerned from the wording of a law, and only if that wording is ambiguous, or if a situation arises not envisioned by the law, is a court ever justified in turning to legislative history. But even if one does turn to the legislative history of Title VII, says Cohen, one sees that the intent of Congress in 1964 was just as clear as the statute it passed: Congress explicitly intended to outlaw through Title VII all racial preference in employment, regardless of which race was being preferred. Cohen, in this context, quotes extensively from the congressional debates in both the House and the Senate. In the entire protracted debate over the Civil Rights Bill, says Cohen, not a single representative or senator expressed the intent to permit voluntary racial preference that the Court majority seeks to ascribe to the entire Congress. Cohen also rejects the majority view that Congress intended to permit the achievement of a racial balance though not the maintaining of such a balance once achieved. The Court's distinction between "achieving" and "maintaining" a racial balance, says Cohen, is a grasp at a straw, and was never part of the understanding of the legislature that adopted the Civil Rights Act.

To the Court's argument that Congress intended to allow racial preference, Cohen replies that Section 703(j) was directed at enforcement officials, not at those who came under the provisions of the law, and had a very specific purpose in mind in overcoming one specific type of objection to the Civil Rights Bill. The fact that racial preference in employment was not specifically outlawed in *that* section, says Cohen, in no way negates the fact that it was explicitly outlawed in other sections of the law, specifically in Sections 703(a) and (d), which were directed at private employers.

Carl Cohen is a professor of philosophy at the Residential College of the University of Michigan at Ann Arbor. He is a former member of the Board of Directors of the American Civil Liberties Union and author of *Democracy* and *Civil Disobedience*.

A RACIAL QUOTA IN the allotment of on-the-job training opportunities among competing employees, instituted by the
management-union agreement, was held lawful by the Supreme
Court in the recent case of *United Steelworkers of America* v.
Weber. This was an important decision, and a very bad one. Its
badness lies not only in the substantive result, upholding preference in employment by race, but also in the reasons given by
the Court in defending that result, and in the abuse of judicial
discretion manifested.

The precise question decided was this: does Title VII of the
Civil Rights Act of 1964 forbid employers and unions in the
private sector from adopting racially preferential employment
programs like the one adopted by Kaiser Aluminum and the
steelworkers union? The answer was no. The evaluation of that
answer requires a brief description of the quota plan approved,
and a brief review of the statute in question.

The plan, adopted as part of a collective-bargaining agreement
between Kaiser Aluminum & Chemical Corporation and the
United Steelworkers of America, provides that, in filling apprentice and craft jobs, "at a minimum not less than one minority
employee will enter for every nonminority employee entering"
until the percentage of blacks in craft jobs equals the percentage
of blacks in the local work force—about 39 per cent at the
Gramercy, Louisiana, plant where Brian Weber works. Seniority in the plant was the criterion on which employees competing
for admission to on-the-job training vacancies were ranked. But
two seniority lists were maintained pursuant to this agreement,
one for whites and one for blacks; vacancies were filled alter-
nately from the top of the two lists. Weber, a white employee
with about five years' seniority in that plant at that time, was
refused admission to three different training programs—although, because of the quota plan in force, some nonwhite
employees having less seniority than Weber were admitted.

Reprinted with permission of the author. This excerpted article originally
appeared in *Commentary* (September 1979).

Believing that he had been displaced only because he was white, Weber brought suit against Kaiser and the union, in behalf of himself and all white employees at that plant similarly situated. His target was the racial preference in that job-training scheme.

The law in question, Title VII of the Civil Rights Act of 1964, reads in pertinent part as follows:

It shall be an unlawful employment practice for an employer—
(1) to fail or refuse to hire or discharge any individual, or otherwise to discriminate against any individual with respect to his compensation, terms, conditions, or privileges of employment, because of such individual's race, color, religion, sex, or national origin; or
(2) to limit, segregate, or classify his employees or applicants for employment in any way which would deprive any individual of employment opportunities or otherwise adversely affect his status as an employee, because of such individual's race, color, religion, sex, or national origin.

It seems hardly possible to deny that this statute does plainly prohibit racially preferential programs of the kind described above. Thus, as one would expect, Weber won his case in the federal district court, and won again, on appeal, in the federal circuit court.

That result has now been reversed by the Supreme Court. The opinion of the five-member majority, delivered by Justice Brennan [see selection 25], is devoted almost entirely to an explanation of why, in their view, Title VII does not prohibit the plan in question. This explanation cries out for response. Response is given in two dissenting opinions, one by Chief Justice Burger, which is crisp and condemnatory, a second by Justice Rehnquist, which is scathing and detailed. Justice Rehnquist's tightly woven, thirty-seven page treatise, to which I will be referring, utterly demolishes the majority position. Its cogency is acknowledged by the majority itself.

The Majority Argument

On what grounds does the majority reach its result? The *intent* of Congress, say they, in enacting Title VII, was not to forbid

racial preference having the wholesome purpose this program
did. The key to the problem, says the majority, is not the
"literal" meaning of the statute, but its "spirit." If, by studying
the history of the act, one can discover the purposes of Congress
in its adoption, and if this plan advances those purposes, the
plan will be, if not "within the letter of the statute," yet still
"within its spirit," "within the intentions of its makers." Now
the aims of Congress in passing this legislation can be readily
discovered. In a nutshell, Congress aimed to counteract black
unemployment, to protect and promote the opportunities of
blacks to get decent jobs. In legislative debate Senators Humphrey, Clark, and others contended that, without such a bill,
discrimination against blacks would become a source of social
unrest and intolerable injustice. The majority's defense of their
interpretation of Title VII rests principally upon the fact that the
proponents of the bill repeatedly insisted upon the importance
of jobs for minority groups. That having been the goal, they
continue, it cannot have been the case that Congress intended
to prohibit private parties "from taking effective steps to accomplish the goal that Congress designed Title VII to achieve."

The argument of the majority, in effect, is this: "We know the
purpose of Congress; we know the purpose of this plan; they are
fully consonant. It must be, therefore, that Congress did not
intend to forbid this plan. If the literal language of Congress says
otherwise, we must interpret that language to mean what it did
not say, while saying what it did not mean."

Purpose versus Intent

What Congress really did intend with this statute is a matter
about which I shall have much to say. Before turning to that
historical question, however, I want to say something about the
logic of the majority's argument. The majority blunders seriously by confusing *purpose* with *intent*. That the purpose of
Congress was to promote employment opportunities for blacks
is beyond doubt. It certainly does not follow that any special
scheme having that purpose was intended to be permitted.
Different persons, or different pieces of legislation, may share
the same aim yet differ greatly in what are believed the wise or

the just steps properly taken to achieve that aim. This simple but important point is what underlies the common homily: "The end doesn't justify the means." The aphorism is imperfect, of course; ends do serve to justify means. But the moral point of the aphorism is sound: ends, even very good ones, don't justify *any* means that may be thought effective in achieving them. That ends are shared is no proof that there will be agreement on the justice or the desirability of particular instruments or programs for their attainment.

Consider this hypothetical example, also in the sphere of legislative action. Suppose funds were appropriated to explore alternative sources of energy, one of the major purposes of the appropriation being, in the minds of most members of Congress, to reduce dependence on foreign oil. By adopting some measures clearly having that objective Congress would not warrant the inference that every measure having the same tendency had thereby been permitted. Suppose the expenditure of the funds appropriated for the exploration of alternative energy sources, although having the larger aim of energy independence, were also restricted by the provision that these funds were not to be spent on the development of nuclear energy. It would not then have been rational to conclude that a plan to spend the funds on the development of nuclear energy was "within the intentions" of the legislature because (as Justice Brennan says of the racial quota in *Weber*) "the purposes of the plan mirror those of the statute." To find out whether Congress intended to advance its larger purposes in that way we would have had to read the enacted statute. If they were to have said: "It shall be unlawful to expend any of these funds on the development of nuclear energy," we might or might not have thought them wise in that restriction. But it does not take great profundity to distinguish between their *purpose* in legislating and their *intent* in that law— between what they would have hoped to accomplish and what they would actually have proposed to do.

In seeking to advance employment opportunities for blacks in 1964, Congress adopted legislation forbidding *all* racial discrimination in employment. To argue, as the majority does, that they cannot have intended to forbid all discrimination because some racial discrimination might also serve their larger purposes, does not do credit to a high appellate court.

The Meaning of Title VII

What opens the question of congressional intent? Under what circumstances is it appropriate for any court to inquire into the intent of a legislature in enacting the legislation being applied? When the applicability of the language of the statute is unclear, or its wording is ambiguous, that inquiry may be very much in order. Such circumstances commonly arise. New conditions, unforeseen by the legislature at the time of a law's enactment, may create issues of interpretation that cannot be resolved by its language alone. A court may then be obliged to construe what the legislative intent might most reasonably have been in order to determine fairly the bearing of the statutory language upon the new conditions. Sometimes, in a different vein, legislation may be formulated in deliberately ambiguous language for assorted political reasons. Courts may later be obliged to apply that language to cases treated equivocally in the statute, having then to construe some reasonable legislative intent to guide them.

Nothing like either of these circumstances arises in the present case. The language of Title VII, as Chief Justice Burger observes, exhibits "no lack of clarity, no ambiguity." The Kaiser quota plan, as all agree, discriminates against individual white employees seeking admission to on-the-job training programs simply because they are white. That, under the very plain language of the statute, is "an unlawful employment practice."

Could it be, perhaps, that the operative meaning of the language of the statute is unclear because it has been sometimes construed by the Court, in past instances, to prohibit discrimination against blacks, but not discrimination against whites? No, that was put out of the question by this Supreme Court in 1976, explicitly interpreting this title of this statute. White employees who were dismissed after being charged with misappropriating company property brought suit under Title VII because black employees, similarly charged, had not been dismissed. This Supreme Court then concluded, from the "uncontradicted legislative history," that "Title VII prohibits racial discrimination against the white petitioners in this case upon the same standards as would be applicable were they Negroes" (*McDonald* v. *Santa Fe Trail Transportation Co.*, 427 U.S. 273, at 280).

So there is no doubt that Title VII does—or did!—apply equally to all races. That is what the Supreme Court has repeatedly affirmed. Title VII, they earlier insisted, "prohibits *all* racial discrimination in employment, without exception for any group of particular employees" (ibid., p. 283, emphasis in original). A few years earlier, in a landmark interpretation of Title VII, the Supreme Court had agreed unanimously on a definitive account of the legislative intent of Title VII: "The objective of Congress in the enactment of Title VII is plain from the language of the statute. It was to achieve equality of employment opportunity. . . . Discriminatory preference for any group, minority or majority, is precisely and only what Congress has proscribed" (*Griggs* v. *Duke Power Co.*, 1971). And just one year before *Weber* the very same point was hammered home by the same Court in the context of employment ratios. "It is clear beyond cavil that the obligation imposed by Title VII is to provide an equal opportunity for *each* applicant regardless of race, without regard to whether members of the applicant's race are already proportionately represented in the work force" (*Furnco Construction Corp.* v. *Waters*, 1978; emphasis in original).

There is no vestige, no trace of ambiguity or unclarity, either in the language of the statute or in the interpretation repeatedly given to that language, respecting the question whether Title VII protects whites as well as nonwhites. There is, therefore, no justification for entering the question of legislative intent. Justice Rehnquist, understandably infuriated, calls attention to the Court's oft-repeated principle applied in another case just as *Weber* was being decided: "Our duty is to construe rather than rewrite legislation."

The Legislative History of Title VII

Beyond opening the question of legislative intent where that is not proper, and beyond the muddling of congressional intent with congressional purpose, the majority has given an unbelievably obtuse reading of that legislative intent. Though it is not appropriate in this case even to ask whether Congress intended to permit some racial discrimination with Title VII, the task of answering that factual, historical question is exceedingly easy. The lengthy debates in the House and the Senate are open to us in the *Congressional Record;* majority and minority committee reports of the House on the proposed bill are also open to us; a lengthy, scholarly study of the legislative history of precisely this title of this act is available to us.

The study referred to, used both by Justice Rehnquist and myself, is by Francis J. Vaas, "Title VII: Legislative History," in volume 7 of the *Boston College Industrial and Commercial Law Review,* pp. 431–58. Vaas records the tortuous path of the Civil Rights Act through Congress with meticulous attention to detail, and makes this striking comment: "Seldom has similar legislation been debated with greater consciousness of the need for 'legislative history,' or with greater care in the making thereof, to guide the courts in interpreting and applying the law" (p. 444). There can be no genuine doubt—in the mind of one who has examined these materials—about the intent of the Congress in choosing the language they did choose. Democrats and Republicans *both,* conservatives and liberals *both,* insisted repeatedly and at great length, illustrating their explanations with detailed examples, that H. R. 7152 (which eventually became the Civil Rights Act of 1964) would forbid *all* racial preference for *any* race.

In the House of Representatives the bill was amended by the Committee on the Judiciary to include Title VII because no compulsory provisions to deal with private discrimination in employment had been included in its original form. It was added, the committee noted, "to eliminate . . . discrimination in employment based on race, color, religion, or national origin" (*H.R. Reports,* No. 914, p. 26). That title was further amended on the floor of the House to include a Section, 703(d), which specifically addressed the prohibition against discrimination (already formulated in 703(a) quoted above) to on-the-job training. Section (d) of 703 reads as follows:

It shall be an unlawful employment practice for any employer, labor organization, or joint labor-management committee controlling apprenticeship or other training or retraining, *including on-the-job training programs,* to discriminate against any individual because of his race, color, religion, sex, or national origin in admission to, or employment in, any program established to provide apprenticeship or other training (emphasis added).

Included with the report of the Judiciary Committee were the lengthy "Additional Views on H.R. 7152" of a group of its advocates, Representative McCulloch and others, which incorporated a passage referred to by Vaas as fairly stating the consensus of the civil-rights proponents as they guided the bill toward adoption. This representative passage includes these sentences:

Internal affairs of employers and labor organizations must not be interfered with [under Title VII] except to the limited extent that correction is required in discrimination practices. Its [the Equal Opportunity Employment Commission's] primary task is to make certain that the channels of employment are open to persons regardless of their race and that jobs in companies or membership in unions are strictly filled on the basis of qualification (*H.R. Reports,* No. 914, pt. 2, p. 29; Vaas, p. 437).

The major objection faced by Title VII in the House (and again later in the Senate) was the claim that under it racial proportionality in employment might subsequently be required by some federal agency, acting under color of that law. This fear was epitomized in the Minority Report that suggested, as one serious concern, that an employer, under Title VII, "*may be forced to hire according to race,* to 'balance racially' those who work for him *in every job classification* or be in violation of federal law" (*H.R. Reports,* No. 914, p. 69; emphasis in original). That fear had to be allayed; proponents of the bill strenuously and repeatedly reassured their colleagues that no such racial balancing was contemplated, and that none would be required or even permitted under this title.

Representative Celler, one of the sponsors of the bill and chairman of the Committee on the Judiciary, at the opening gun of the debate in the House, made the intent of the language of 703 (a) unmistakable. The fear that it would require or permit hiring or promotion on the basis of race resulted, he said, from a description of the bill that was "entirely wrong." He continued:

Even . . . the court could not order that any preference be given to any particular race, religion or other group, but would be limited to ordering an end to discrimination. The statement that a federal inspector could order the employment and promotion only of members of a specific racial or religious group is therefore patently erroneous.

The bill would do no more than prevent a union, as it would prevent employers, from discriminating against or in favor of workers because of their race, religion, or national origin.

It is likewise not true that the Federal Employment Opportunity Commission [established by Title VII] would have power to rectify existing "racial or religious imbalance" in employment by requiring the hiring of certain people without regard to their qualifications simply because they are of a given race or religion. Only actual discrimination could be stopped (110 *Cong. Rec.*, p. 1518).

This theme was echoed repeatedly in the course of the debate in the House of Representatives. Representative Lindsay of New York, among others, took up the defense of Title VII:

This legislation . . . does not, as has been suggested heretofore both on and off the floor, force acceptance of people in schools, jobs, housing, or public accommodations because they are Negro. It does not impose quotas or any special privileges of seniority or acceptance. There is nothing whatever in the bill about racial balance. . . . What the bill does do is prohibit discrimination because of race (110 *Cong. Rec.*, p. 1540).

With that clear understanding the bill passed the House, 290 to 130, on February 10, 1964.

In the Senate

In the Senate, the expression of legislative intent was voluminous and unequivocal. Again the fear of opponents was that some federal inspector might one day impose racial balance under color of this law. Again—and again and again and again— the defenders of the bill replied with reassurance, insisting vehemently that such fears were totally unfounded. The key term, "discrimination," appearing in Sections 703(a) and 703(d) and elsewhere in the bill, was examined minutely on the Senate floor. Could it be taken to mean (the critics asked) only numerical imbalance? Answer: definitely not. Could it have been, for the framers of the legislation, a technical term, whose hidden meaning was "discrimination against blacks" but not "discrimination against whites"? No, definitely not. Senator Humphrey put that suggestion permanently to rest: "[T]he meaning of racial or religious discrimination is perfectly clear. . . . [I]t means a distinction in treatment given to different individuals because of their different race, religion, or national origin" (110 *Cong. Rec.,* p. 5423). The only freedom of employers that the bill limits, he emphasized, is the freedom to take action based on race, religion, sex, or national origin.

When the Senate took up the substance of the act directly, after deciding not to submit it to committee, it again became essential for the bill's advocates to answer the complaint that the bill would lead to racial preference. Not so, they insisted. Senator Humphrey again:

That bugaboo has been brought up a dozen times; but it is nonexistent. In fact, the very opposite is true. Title VII prohibits discrimination. In effect, it says that race, religion, and national origin are not to be used as the basis for hiring and firing. Title VII is designed to encourage hiring on the basis of ability and qualifications, not race or religion.

In the same speech Senator Humphrey gives a series of examples that "makes clear what is implicit throughout the whole title; namely, that employers may hire and fire, promote and refuse to promote for any reason, good or bad, provided only that individuals may not be discriminated against because of race, religion, sex, or national origin." He repeats himself so that even the deaf may hear: "The truth is that this title forbids discriminating against anyone on account of race. This is the simple and complete truth about Title VII" (110 *Cong. Rec.,* p. 6549). Humphrey was majority whip and the floor leader for the Civil Rights Act in the Senate. In his support rose senator after senator to give the same explanatory assurances about the intent of the legislation.

Senator Kuchel, the minority whip, emphasized that the seniority rights of workers already employed would not be affected by Title VII. He said:

> Employers and labor organizations could not discriminate in favor or against a person because of his race, his religion, or his national origin. In such matters, the Constitution, and the bill now before us drawn to conform to the Constitution, is color-blind (110 *Cong. Rec.,* p. 6564).

Senators Clark and Case were floor captains in the Senate for Title VII specifically. To them fell the task of explaining that title, what it meant and did not mean, what it permitted and what it prohibited. Their chief task was to refute the charge that Title VII would result in preference for racial minorities. In a memorandum prepared for the Senate they expressed the intent of Title VII unequivocally:

> [A]ny deliberate attempt to maintain a racial balance, whatever such a balance may be, would involve a violation of Title VII because maintaining such a balance would require an employer to hire or to refuse to hire on the basis of race. It must be emphasized that discrimination is prohibited as to any individual (110 *Cong. Rec.,* p. 7213).

A different memorandum, prepared by the U.S. Department of Justice at Senator Clark's request, also makes the point that there is no need to fear employers' being required to maintain racial balance:

> No employer is required to maintain any ratio of Negroes to whites, Jews to Gentiles, Italians to English, or women to men. The same is true of labor organizations. On the contrary, any deliberate attempt to maintain a given balance would almost certainly run afoul of Title VII because it would involve a failure or refusal to hire some individual because of his race, color, religion, sex, or national origin. What Title VII seeks to accomplish, what the civil rights bill seeks to accomplish is equal treatment for all (110 *Cong. Rec.,* p. 7207).

Senators Smathers and Sparkman, granting that the bill did not require the use of hiring quotas, put the attack against Title VII more subtly. Under it, they suggested, employers might be *coerced,* by federal agencies, into giving preference by race. Would that not be permitted under this law? The answer, this time from Senator Williams, was an emphatic negative. Opponents, he replies,

> persist in opposing a provision which is not only not contained in the bill, but is *specifically excluded* from it. Those opposed to H.R. 7152 should realize that to hire a Negro solely because he is a Negro is racial discrimination, just as much as a "white-only" employment policy. *Both forms of discrimination are prohibited by Title VII of this bill.* The language of that title simply states that race is not a qualification for employment. . . . [A]ll men are to have an equal opportunity to be considered for a particular job. Some people charge that H.R. 7152 favors the Negro, at the expense of the white majority. But how can the language of equality favor one race or one religion over another? Equality can have only one meaning, and that meaning is self-evident to reasonable men. Those who say that equality means favoritism do violence to commonsense (110 *Cong. Rec.,* p. 8921; emphasis added).

Still the fear that racially preferential hiring would somehow be encouraged or permitted under Title VII would not die down. Once again the floor leader, Humphrey, took up the battle:

The title [Title VII] does not provide that any preferential treatment in employment shall be given to Negroes or to any other persons or groups. It does not provide that any quota systems may be established to maintain racial balance in employment. *In fact, the title would prohibit preferential treatment for any particular group,* and any person, whether or not a member of any minority group, would be permitted to file a complaint of discriminatory employment practices (110 *Cong. Rec.,* p. 11848; emphasis added).

Maintaining versus Achieving Racial Balance

How could the majority of the Supreme Court, in *Weber,* escape the force of this parade of unequivocal accounts marching across the printed record of the process of its adoption? Could they contend, perhaps, that although racial preference was indeed prohibited, that prohibition did not bear upon efforts to overcome the effects of *past* discrimination upon the seniority rights of employees? At one point, conceding that it was the intent of the Senate to forbid the maintenance of racial balance, the majority grasps at a straw: this Kaiser quota plan was not introduced to maintain racial balance, they contend, but to "eliminate a manifest racial imbalance." Can the net of clear congressional intent be thus eluded, by making the distinction between "maintaining" racial balance and "eliminating" racial imbalance, holding that Title VII forbids the former but not the latter?

Not a chance. Explicating Title VII, its most thorough congressional students, Senators Clark and Case, wrote in their joint memorandum:

Title VII would have no effect on established seniority rights. *Its effect is prospective and not retrospective.* Thus, for example, if a business has been discriminating in the past and as a result has an all-white working force, when the title comes into effect the employer's obligation would be simply to fill future vacancies on a nondiscriminatory basis. He would not be obliged—*or indeed, permitted*—to fire whites in order to hire Negroes, or *to prefer Negroes for future vacancies,* or, *once Negroes are hired, to give them special seniority rights at the expense of the white workers hired earlier* (110 *Cong. Rec.*, p. 7213; emphasis added).

The Justice Department had earlier drawn the same conclusion: Title VII could not be used to alter seniority entitlements because of discrimination in employment before its adoption:

Title VII would have no effect on seniority rights existing at the time it takes effect. . . . This would be true even in the case where owing to discrimination prior to the effective date of the title, white workers had more seniority than Negroes. . . . [A]ssuming that seniority rights were built up over a period of time during which Negroes were not hired, these rights would not be set aside by the taking effect of Title VII. Employers and labor organizations would simply be under a duty not to discriminate against Negroes because of their race (110 *Cong. Rec.*, p. 7207).

The distinction between "maintaining" and "achieving" racial balance was, manifestly, never part of the understanding of the legislature that adopted Title VII.

That distinction, moreover, would have been and is specious from the point of view both of advocates and critics of racial preference. If, after the achievement of racial balance through racial preference, craft jobs again were to become predominantly white, the advocates of racial preference would certainly not be content. Convinced that such imbalance is in itself wrong, they would, understandably, then insist that if racial preference be permitted for the achievement of racial balance, it must be permitted for its reachievement. The claim that such instruments are only "temporary" is a fiction. It will be of little consequence to its advocates that the majority in *Weber* leaned on a tenuous distinction that it will be in their interest to ignore. And the opponents of racial preference—including the Eighty-eighth Congress of 1964—may rightly insist that if preference by race is in principle wrong, it is no less wrong in the one case than in the other. Indeed, both the Justice Department and the floor captains for Title VII in the Senate very carefully pointed out that maintaining racial balance would be forbidden "*because* it would involve a failure or refusal to hire some individual because of his race" (emphasis added). The reference in these arguments is to the actual words of Section 703(a). Adverse effects upon an employee or applicant because of race would result whether the goal had been the maintenance of racial balance or the achieving of it.

The argument that the Congress intended Title VII to permit racial preference in achieving racial balance, but forbade it for maintaining racial balance, and that therefore once proportionality is achieved all such preference will cease, is unworthy of the Supreme Court; it is a sop designed to placate critics with unreliable assurances that the instrument approved will be only "temporary." In fact ethnic preference, once ensconced, is likely to be nearly impossible to eradicate. To mitigate its unfairness more and different ethnic preferences will be introduced—as already they are being introduced.

Those who condemn racial favoritism condemn it both for achieving and for maintaining racial balance; those who support racial favoritism will not object to its use in either role. That distinction cannot serve to render plausible the majority's interpretation of congressional intent in enacting Title VII of the Civil Rights Act.

Section 703(j)

As debate over the Civil Rights Act continued in the Senate it became evident that the bill would have to be amended to make absolutely clear the fact that it could not later serve as the justification, by any federal agency, of the imposition of racial preference. Only thus might the repeated objections of its most implacable opponents be successfully met. A bipartisan coalition, made up of Senators Dirksen, Mansfield, Humphrey, and Kuchel, cooperating with leaders in the House of Representatives, devised the Dirksen-Mansfield amendment, ultimately adopted. Among the changes thus introduced was a clarifying addition, Section 703 (j), very specifically addressing the critics' fears of imposed racial balancing. This section provides that nothing in the entire title shall be interpreted to require the giving of preferential treatment to any individual because of race. It reads:

> Nothing contained in this subchapter shall be interpreted to require any employer, employment agency, labor organization, or joint labor-management committee subject to this subchapter to grant preferential treatment to any individual or to any group because of the race, color, religion, sex, or national origin of such individual or group on account of an imbalance which may exist with respect to the total number or percentage of persons of any race, color, religion, sex, or national origin employed by any employer, referred or classified by any employment agency or labor organization, or admitted to, or employed in, any apprenticeship or other training program, in comparison with the total number of persons of such race, color, religion, sex, or national origin in any community, state, section, or other area, or in the available work force in any community, state, section, or other area.

Now, in an ironic and extraordinary turn, the Supreme Court majority in *Weber* uses the language of this section to infer (relying upon what Justice Burger calls a "negative pregnant") that since it bars the requirement of racial preference, but does not specifically prohibit racial preference, it must have been the intention of Congress not to prohibit it! The majority writes:

> The section does *not* state that "nothing in Title VII shall be interpreted to *permit*" voluntary affirmative efforts to correct racial imbalances. The natural inference is that Congress chose not to forbid all voluntary race-conscious affirmative action (emphasis in original).

This inference is either disingenuous or obtuse. The objection this added section was designed specifically to meet was that racial preference would somehow be required. No one thought it would or could be introduced voluntarily because "voluntary" racial preference precisely had been forbidden by the plain language of the earlier key section, 703 (a). Debate in the Senate went on for almost three full months. Never in that entire period was it argued, *by either side,* that employers could, of their own accord, give preference by race. Both proponents and opponents made perfectly clear their understanding that voluntary racial preference by employers, for blacks or for whites, was entirely precluded by the flat and unambiguous wording of those earlier passages, forbidding *any* employment practice that would "discriminate against any individual" because of that individual's race. To add that prohibition yet again, in 703(j), would have been entirely redundant—and more importantly, it might have diluted the intended force of that particular passage, aimed narrowly at the objection that racial preference would otherwise someday be imposed by government.

That it was so aimed is made exquisitely clear by the difference in the phrasing of 703(j) from that of the earlier, central sections of the title. The earlier sections, prohibiting racial discrimination in employment universally, are directed specifically at the employer, and therefore begin: "It shall be an unlawful employment practice for an employer." Section 703(j) is directed specifically *at possible federal enforcement agencies,* commissions, or courts, and therefore begins with language indicating that kind of target: "Nothing contained in this subchapter shall be interpreted." Now to infer, from the fact that this section does not repeat the prohibition already several times explicit in earlier sections, that it was the intention of Congress not to prohibit racial preference, is a transparently unsound defense of so grave a decision.[1]

Lest there be any doubt, however, about the intent of the Congress *after* the addition of 703(j), we can return to the debate itself. Senator Saltonstall, defending the Dirksen-Mansfield amendment including 703(j), says of it, very plainly: "The legislation before us today provides no preferential treatment for any group of citizens. In fact, it specifically prohibits such treatment" (110 *Cong. Rec.,* p. 12691).

And yet again, in defending the amended bill against Senator Ervin's criticism that it "would make the members of a particular race special favorites of the laws," Senator Clark answers: "The bill does not make anyone higher than anyone else. It establishes no quotas." Employers, labor unions, employment agencies, remain free, Clark points out, to use normal judgment in their business activity—but:

> All this is subject to one qualification, and that qualification is to state: "In your activity as an employer, as a labor union, as an employment agency, you must not discriminate because of the color of a man's skin. . . ." That is all this provision does. . . . It merely says, "When you deal in interstate commerce, you must not discriminate on the basis of race."

In the event this be somehow misunderstood, he repeats himself in that speech:

> All it [Title VII] does is to say that no American, individual, labor union, or corporation, has the right to deny any other American the very basic civil right of equal job opportunity (110 *Cong. Rec.*, pp. 13079–80).

Senator Cooper, anxious to make the force of what was soon to become law unmistakably clear, also responds to Senator Ervin's concerns, saying:

> As I understand Title VII, an employer could employ the usual standards which any employer uses in employing—in dismissing, in promoting, or in assigning those who work for him. There would be only one limitation: he could not discriminate, he could not deny a person a job, or dismiss a person from a job, or promote on the sole ground of his color, or his religion, other factors being equal (110 *Cong. Rec.*, p. 13078).

Additional Considerations

But how, one asks, can the majority not have been fully aware of all this? They must have seen the draft of Justice Rehnquist's dissent, which makes the same points vividly. Did they, perhaps, find other evidence within the record of the debates in Congress, evidence that has here been left unmentioned, which might somehow permit a reading of congressional intent to permit racial preference? No, no evidence has been suppressed here. Like Vaas and Justice Rehnquist, upon whose guidance I have relied, I have scoured the pages of the *Congressional Record;* like them I have registered only a fraction of the evidence against the majority's interpretation. If, in all those pages, there were evidence that *any* senator or congressman had the intent that the majority ascribes to the whole Congress, we may be certain it would have been dug up and registered within the majority opinion. No such evidence appears there. Here again we may indeed rely upon a negative pregnant. In this majority opinion, in which every quotation from the congressional debates is presented that might contribute, even with arguments far-fetched or unsound, to an excessively strained interpretation of congressional intent, the absence of any passages that actually express that intent is very revealing.

The plainest proof that the members of the majority in *Weber* cannot have been in ignorance of the actual intent of Congress, and after searching could find no evidence of contrary intent, is given by Justice Marshall himself. In a 1976 opinion, writing for the Court, he presents a careful analysis of the intent of Congress in Title VII. He quotes Representative Celler, saying Title VII was intended to "cover white men and white women and all Americans" (110 *Cong. Rec.,* p. 2578). He cites Senator Humphrey, Senator Clark, Senator Case, and Senator Williams in passages like those quoted above. Justice Marshall concludes that "Its [Title VII's] terms are not limited to discrimination against members of any particular race." He then substantiates this judgment by extended reference to the interpretation of Title VII given by the Equal Employment Opportunity Commission:

> The EEOC, whose interpretations are entitled to great deference, . . . *has consistently interpreted Title VII to proscribe racial discrimination in private employment against whites on the same terms as racial discrimination against nonwhites,* holding that to proceed otherwise would "constitute a derogation of the commission's congressional mandate to eliminate all practices which operate to disadvantage the employment opportunities of any group protected by Title VII, including Caucasians.

Justice Marshall explains, representing the Court, that the history of legislative intent in adopting Title VII is *"uncontradicted"* (*McDonald* v. *Santa Fe Trail Transportation Co.*, 427 U.S. 273, at 278–80, 283; emphasis added).

Members of the House and Senate are quoted by the majority, to be sure. But the quotations serve to establish matters only tenuously related to the central point at issue. Repeated citations from the debates are given to establish that it was the larger purpose of Congress, in tackling this legislation, to promote employment opportunities for blacks. That, as we have seen, is not at issue, and does not speak to the question of what prohibitions were intended. Several citations are given to show, correctly, that one major concern in the Senate when introducing Section 703(j), which precludes the requirement of racial preference by the enforcers, was to reduce the likelihood of federal interference with private business. That was an aim of many senators; but showing that does not prove, or even tend to confirm the thesis, that Title VII as a whole was designed to permit nongovernmental racial preference.

One other citation by the majority deserves attention. To give credence to the claim that the distinction between private racial favoritism and federally required racial favoritism was before the congressional mind, the majority quotes from the House Committee report favoring the original bill. The passage says that "the enactment of federal legislation dealing with the most troublesome problems [of social discrimination] will create an atmosphere conducive to voluntary or local resolution of other forms of discrimination." The majority fastens on this sentence, even adds emphasis to the final phrase, suggesting that it proves that a voluntary racial quota in employment is one of those "other forms" for which the Civil Rights Act had created the atmosphere.

Fallacious would be the gentlest way to describe this argument—in view of the failure, not likely to be accidental, to quote the lines immediately following the cited passage. An explanation is given there of the distinction between "the most serious types of discrimination" and those other varieties for which voluntary attention might be encouraged. The serious types,

types this House Report there suggests *will* be dealt with by this bill, specifically include voting, public accommodation, *and employment*. The omitted passage reads:

> It is, however, possible and necessary for the Congress to enact legislation which prohibits and provides the means of terminating the most serious types of discrimination. This H.R. 7152, as amended, would achieve in a number of related areas. . . . It would prohibit discrimination in employment (*H. R.,* No. 914, p. 18).

The forms of discrimination it was hoped might yield to voluntary action were those *other* than discrimination in employment, voting, and the like. Indeed, employment discrimination is mentioned repeatedly in the report as being of the most serious kind, the kind for whose prevention this legislation was specifically designed.

There is not a shred of evidence in this passage that the report actually envisaged voluntary racial *preference* of any kind, or that would have suggested to the House that such preference—especially in employment—was permissible under this act.

Final Consideration

One hates to flog a dead horse. But this horse came to life in an extraordinary opinion of a Supreme Court majority—so I report, finally, the understanding of the Civil Rights Act of 1964 as that understanding was registered in the final hours of debate on the Senate floor—after which it was returned to the House and approved as amended. The legislative decision was at hand. The advocates of the bill, now under cloture, had to give their final defenses and interpretations. On the point at issue here their remarks were unmistakably clear.

Senator Muskie:

> It has been said that the bill discriminates in favor of the Negro at the expense of the rest of us. It seeks to do nothing more than to lift the Negro from the status of inequality to one of equality of treatment (110 *Cong. Rec.,* p. 14328).

Senator Moss:

> The bill does not accord to any citizen advantage or prefer-
> ence—it does not fix quotas of employment or school popula-
> tion—it does not force personal association. What it does is
> to prohibit public officials and those who invite the public
> generally to patronize their businesses or to apply for employ-
> ment, to utilize the offensive, humiliating, and cruel practice
> of discrimination on the basis of race. In short, the bill does
> not accord special consideration; it establishes equality (110
> *Cong. Rec.*, p. 14484).

Very self-consciously, aware that it was making history, the
Senate passed the amended Civil Rights Act on June 19, 1964,
by 73 to 27, every member voting. The struggle in that body, as
Vaas describes it, had been "titanic and protracted." The meaning and force of every line, every phrase in the bill had been
intensely scrutinized and explained with scrupulous care. The
legislators knew precisely what they were prohibiting with this
legislation, and we know exactly what they understood themselves to be doing because they took care, very deliberately, to
put their explanatory accounts on record.

No impartial judge, properly attentive to the abundant evidence that establishes dispositively the true intent of Congress,
could honestly conclude that its intent was to permit private
racial preference in employment. Yet that is what the majority
has concluded, in a decision that is, taken all in all, simply
shocking.

28. Consent Decrees Cannot Bind Nonconsenting Parties

By WILLIAM H. REHNQUIST

Focus Over the past two decades one of the most important means of resolving claims of racial discrimination under Title VII of the Civil Rights Act of 1964 has been through the use of the "consent decree"—i.e., a voluntary agreement between the parties to a dispute that has been approved of by a federal court. In employment discrimination cases consent decrees have frequently involved the use of racial hiring and promotion quotas, and until the important Supreme Court case of *Martin* v. *Wilks* (1989), employers could use the fact that they were acting under the terms of a consent decree as a successful legal defense against "reverse discrimination" charges on the part of disadvantaged whites. In *Martin* v. *Wilks,* however, a majority of the members of the Supreme Court declared that people who have not been parties to a consent decree have the right to challenge the legality of the decree under federal antidiscrimination statutes and the provisions of the Constitution. Like the earlier decision in the Richmond, Virginia, set-aside case (selections 19 and 20), the *Martin* ruling clearly reflects the impact of the three Reagan-era appointees, and indicates greater sympathy on the part of the new Court for claims of discrimination on the part of plaintiffs who are not members of officially designated racial and ethnic minority groups.

Writing for the Court majority, Chief Justice Rehnquist declares in his decision that the immunization of the parties to a consent decree from attacks by third parties who believe they have been victims of discrimination under the terms of the decree "contravenes the general rule that a person cannot be deprived of his legal rights in a proceeding to which he is not a party." "A voluntary settlement in the form of a consent decree between one group of employees and their employer cannot possibly 'settle,' voluntarily or otherwise, the conflicting claims of another group of employees who do not join in the agreement." The only way, according to Rehnquist, that parties can bind other parties to the outcome of the lawsuit is through a process of legal "joinder," whereby potentially affected parties are first identified and then legally joined from the outset as official parties to the dispute. The *Martin* case grew out of charges of discrimination on the part of white fire fighters in the city of Birmingham, Alabama.

William H. Rehnquist was an associate justice of the Supreme Court from 1972 to 1986, and is currently the chief justice.

A GROUP OF WHITE fire fighters sued the city of Birmingham, Alabama, and the Jefferson County Personnel Board alleging that they were being denied promotions in favor of less-qualified black fire fighters. They claimed that the city and the board were making promotion decisions on the basis of race in reliance on certain consent decrees, and that these decisions constituted impermissible racial discrimination in violation of the Constitution and federal statute. The district court held that the white firefighters were precluded from challenging employment decisions taken pursuant to the decrees, even though these firefighters had not been parties to the proceedings in which the decrees were entered. We think this holding contravenes the general rule that a person cannot be deprived of his legal rights in a proceeding to which he is not a party.

The litigation in which the consent decrees were entered began in 1974, when the Ensley, Alabama, branch of the NAACP and seven black individuals filed separate class-action complaints against the city and the board. They alleged that both had engaged in racially discriminatory hiring and promotion practices in various public-service jobs in violation of Title VII of the Civil Rights Act of 1964 and other federal law. After a bench trial on some issues, but before judgment, the parties entered into two consent decrees, one between the black individuals and the city and the other between them and the board. These proposed decrees set forth an extensive remedial scheme, including long-term and interim annual goals for the hiring of blacks as fire fighters. The decrees also provided for goals for promotion of blacks within the department.

[Following unsuccessful challenges by the Birmingham Fire Fighters Association and a group of seven white fire fighters] a new group of white fire fighters, the *Wilks* respondents, then brought suit against the city and the board in district court. They too alleged that, because of their race, they were being denied

Excerpted from *Martin* v. *Wilks*, 57 LW 4616 (1989).

promotions in favor of less-qualified blacks in violation of federal law. The board and the city admitted to making race-conscious employment decisions, but argued the decisions were unassailable because they were made pursuant to the consent decrees. A group of black individuals, the *Martin* petitioners, were allowed to intervene in their individual capacities to defend the decrees. The defendants moved to dismiss the reverse discrimination cases as impermissible collateral attacks on the consent decrees. After trial the district court granted the motion to dismiss. On appeal, the eleventh circuit reversed. It held that "because . . . [the *Wilks* respondents] were neither parties nor privies to the consent decrees, . . . their independent claims of unlawful discrimination are not precluded."

We now affirm the eleventh circuit's judgment. All agree that "it is a principle of general application in Anglo-American jurisprudence that one is not bound by a judgment *in personam* in a litigation in which he is not designated as a party or to which he has not been made a party by service of process." This rule is part of our "deep-rooted historic tradition that everyone should have his own day in court." A judgment or decree among parties to a lawsuit resolves issues as among them, but it does not conclude the rights of strangers to those proceedings. Petitioners argue that, because respondents failed to timely intervene in the initial proceedings, their current challenge to actions taken under the consent decree constitutes an impermissible "collateral attack." They argue that respondents were aware that the underlying suit might affect them and if they chose to pass up an opportunity to intervene, they should not be permitted to later litigate the issues in a new action. The position has sufficient appeal to have commanded the approval of the great majority of the federal courts of appeals, but we agree with the contrary view expressed by the Court of Appeals for the Eleventh Circuit in this case.

[According to rules 19 and 24 of the Federal Rules of Civil Procedure] a party seeking a judgment binding on another cannot obligate that person to intervene; he must be joined. Joinder as a party, rather than knowledge of a lawsuit and an opportunity to intervene, is the method by which potential parties are subjected to the jurisdiction of the court and bound by a judgment or decree. The parties to a lawsuit presumably know better than anyone else the nature and scope of relief sought in the action, and at whose expense such relief might be granted. It makes sense, therefore, to place on them a burden of bringing in additional parties where such a step is indicated, rather than placing on potential additional parties a duty to intervene when they acquire knowledge of the lawsuit. The linchpin of the "impermissible-collateral-attack" doctrine is therefore quite inconsistent with rule 19 and rule 24.

Petitioners contend that a different result should be reached because the need to join affected parties will be burdensome and ultimately discouraging to civil rights litigation. Even if we were wholly persuaded by these arguments as a matter of policy, acceptance of them would require a rewriting rather than an interpretation of the relevant rules. But we are not persuaded that their acceptance would lead to a more satisfactory method of handling cases like this one. Petitioners' alternative does not eliminate the need for, or difficulty of, identifying persons who, because of their interests, should be included in a lawsuit. It merely shifts that responsibility to less able shoulders. Petitioners also urge that the congressional policy favoring voluntary settlement of employment discrimination claims also supports the "impermissible-collateral-attack" doctrine. [But] a voluntary settlement in the form of a consent decree between one group of employees and their employer cannot possibly "settle," voluntarily or otherwise, the conflicting claims of another group of employees who do not join in the agreement.

29. Leave Consent Decrees Alone

By JOHN PAUL STEVENS III

Focus Like the earlier decision in the Richmond, Virginia, set-aside case, the decision of the Supreme Court majority in *Martin* v. *Wilks* touched off a storm of protest within much of the mainline civil rights community. The decision was handed down just a week after the high Court, in a much-criticized decision involving workers in the Alaskan cannery industry, had limited the type of statistical evidence that could be used to establish a *prima facie* case of racial discrimination under Title VII. Critics of the new direction the Court was taking charged that the new Court majority in the area of affirmative action (a majority consisting of Chief Justice Rehnquist along with Justices White, O'Connor, Scalia, and Kennedy) was uprooting important precedents and procedures that had worked very well in the past and were of long standing. Justice John Paul Stevens wrote two of the dissenting opinions against the Court's new direction, one in the Alaskan cannery case (*Wards Cove Packing Co.* v. *Atonio*), the other in *Martin* v. *Wilks*.

In his dissenting opinion in *Martin*, Justice Stevens suggests that there is an important legal distinction to be made between various benefits that employees are guaranteed as a matter of legal right, and those practical advantages that may be affected by third-party lawsuits to which they have no special legal entitlement. The consent decree in the case of the Birmingham fire fighters, says Stevens, "obviously could not deprive [the white fire fighters] of any contractual rights, such as seniority, or accrued vacation pay, or of any other legal rights." "There is no reason, however, why the consent decrees might not produce changes in conditions at the white fire fighters' place of employment that, as a practical matter, may have a serious effect on their opportunities for employment or promotion even though they are not bound by the decrees in any legal sense." Since the voluntary agreements that are entered into by the parties to a consent decree may have a great impact on the interests of a variety of third parties, it is imperative, says Stevens, that these third parties join in the original litigation if they want to protect their individual interests. If they choose to sit on the sidelines, and do not intervene in a timely fashion, however, they have no right, according to Stevens, to appeal from a consent-decree settlement even though they may be seriously harmed by it. Only in very limited circumstances, such as cases involving fraud, collusion, duress, lack of jurisdiction, or facial invalidity, do nonintervening parties have the right to relitigate the settled judgment of a consent decree, Stevens contends. To hold otherwise, Stevens believes, would subject large employers to never-ending litigation and would undermine the beneficial effects of consent decrees in remedying past discrimination.

John Paul Stevens III, appointed in 1975, is an associate justice of the U.S. Supreme Court.

A S A MATTER OF LAW there is a vast difference between persons who are actual parties to litigation and persons who merely have the kind of interest that may, as a practical matter, be impaired by the outcome of a case. Persons in the first category have a right to participate in a trial and to appeal from an adverse judgment. Persons in the latter category have a right to intervene in the action in a timely fashion, or they may be joined as parties against their will. But if they remain on the sidelines, they may be harmed as a practical matter even though their legal rights are unaffected. One of the disadvantages of sideline-sitting is that the bystander has no right to appeal from a judgment no matter how harmful it may be.

In this case, the Court quite rightly concludes that the white fire fighters who brought the second series of Title VII cases could not be deprived of their legal rights in the first series of cases because they had neither intervened nor been joined as parties. The consent decrees obviously could not deprive them of any contractual rights, such as seniority, or accrued vacation pay, or of any other legal rights, such as the right to have their employer comply with federal statutes like Title VII. There is no reason, however, why the consent decrees might not produce changes in conditions at the white fire fighters' place of employment that, as a practical matter, may have a serious effect on their opportunities for employment or promotion even though they are not bound by the decrees in any legal sense. The fact that one of the effects of a decree is to curtail the job opportunities of nonparties does not mean that the nonparties have been deprived of legal rights.

Persons who have no right to appeal from a final judgment—either because the time of appeal has elapsed or because they never became parties to the case—may nevertheless collaterally attack a judgment on certain narrow grounds. If the court had no jurisdiction over the subject matter, or if the judgment is the

Excerpted from *Martin* v. *Wilks*, 57 LW 4616 (1989).

product of corruption, duress, fraud, collusion, or mistake, under limited circumstances it may be set aside in an appropriate collateral proceeding. This rule not only applies to parties to the original action, but also allows interested third parties collaterally to attack judgments. In both civil and criminal cases, however, the grounds that may be invoked to support a collateral attack are much more limited than those that may be asserted as error on direct appeal. Thus, a person who can foresee that a lawsuit is likely to have a practical impact on his interests may pay a heavy price if he elects to sit on the sidelines instead of intervening.

Regardless of whether the white fire fighters were parties to the decrees granting relief to their black co-workers, it would be quite wrong to assume that they could never collaterally attack such a decree. If a litigant has standing, he or she can always collaterally attack a judgment for certain narrowly defined defects. On the other hand, a district court is not required to retry a case—or to sit in review of another court's judgment—every time an interested nonparty asserts that *some* error that might have been raised on direct appeal was committed. Such a broad allowance of collateral review would destroy the integrity of litigated judgments, would lead to an abundance of vexatious litigation, and would subvert the interest in comity between courts.

In a case such as this in which there has been no showing that the decree was collusive, fraudulent, transparently invalid, or entered without jurisdiction, it would be "unconscionable" to conclude that obedience to an order remedying a Title VII violation could subject a defendant to additional liability. Assuming that the district court's findings of fact were not clearly erroneous—which of course is a matter that is not before us—it seems perfectly clear that its judgment should have been affirmed. Any other conclusion would subject large employers who seek to comply with the law by remedying past discrimination to a never-ending stream of litigation and potential liability. It is unfathomable that either Title VII or the Equal Protection Clause demands such a counterproductive result.

The predecessor to this litigation was brought to change a

pattern of hiring and promotion practices that had discriminated against black citizens in Birmingham for decades. The white respondents in this case are not responsible for that history of discrimination, but they are nevertheless beneficiaries of the discriminatory practices that the litigation was designed to correct. Any remedy that seeks to create employment conditions that would have obtained if there had been no violations of law will necessarily have an adverse impact on whites, who must now share their job and promotion opportunities with blacks. Just as white employees in the past were innocent beneficiaries of illegal discriminatory practices, so is it inevitable that some of the same white employees will be innocent victims who must share some of the burdens resulting from the redress of the past wrongs.

There is nothing unusual about the fact that litigation between adverse parties may, as a practical matter, seriously impair the interests of third persons who elect to sit on the sidelines. Indeed, in complex litigation this Court has squarely held that a sideline-sitter may be bound as firmly as an actual party if he has adequate notice and a fair opportunity to intervene and if the judicial interest in finality is sufficiently strong. The city of Birmingham, in entering into and complying with this decree, has made a substantial step toward the eradication of the long history of pervasive racial discrimination that has plagued its fire department. The district court, after conducting a trial and carefully considering respondents' arguments, concluded that this effort is lawful and should go forward. Because respondents have thus already had their day in court and have failed to carry their burden, I would vacate the judgment of the court of appeals.

PART FOUR

The Impact on Blacks

30. Rumors of Inferiority

By JEFF HOWARD AND RAY HAMMOND

Focus Despite enormous advances over the past twenty years, black people on average continue to lag far behind white people and Asian people in their performance on many standardized tests even when allowances are made for differences in social, economic, and educational background. Jeff Howard and Ray Hammond argue that black people have internalized the "image of black intellectual inferiority [that has been] projected by the larger society," and that this internalized image of inferiority produces a self-defeating fear and avoidance of intellectual competition. Many black people do not perform up to their potential, the authors contend, because they subconsciously believe that they lack the required aptitude to succeed in intellectual competition with whites.

Although Howard and Hammond do not take up the issue of racial preference in this article—they would seem to support at least some types of affirmative action programs—the issues they raise obviously have enormous implications for the affirmative action debate. If the psychic mechanisms they describe are indeed as powerful in creating obstacles to black achievement as suggested, both supporters and opponents of affirmative action must address the question of whether the current policies of racial preference tend to feed into these mechanisms or to thwart them. Many opponents of affirmative action (see, for example, Ernest van den Haag, selection 31, Charles Murray, selection 32, and Thomas Sowell, selection 34) argue that a policy of racial preference will only confirm the general belief in black inferiority and prevent blacks from escaping from its paralyzing grasp. Supporters of affirmative action, on the other hand (see, for instance, Derek Bok, selection 33, Randall Kennedy, selection 3, and Ronald Dworkin, selection 13) believe that black feelings of inferiority would be greatly increased by the abandonment of the current policy of racial preference, since this would necessarily result in a drastic reduction in the number of blacks in the most prestigious universities, in the professions, and in many other important institutions of American society.

Jeff Howard is a social psychologist.

Ray Hammond is an ordained minister and a physician.

Today's black Americans are the beneficiaries of great historical achievements. Our ancestors managed to survive the brutality of slavery and the long history of oppression that followed emancipation. Early in this century they began dismantling the legal structure of segregation that had kept us out of the institutions of American society. In the 1960s they launched the civil rights movement, one of the most effective mass movements for social justice in history. Not all of the battles have been won, but there is no denying the magnitude of our predecessors' achievement.

Nevertheless, black Americans today face deteriorating conditions in sharp contrast to other American groups. The black poverty rate is triple that of whites, and the unemployment rate is double. Black infant mortality not only is double that of whites, but may be rising for the first time in a decade. We have reached the point where more than half of the black children born in this country are born out of wedlock—most to teenage parents. Blacks account for more than 40 per cent of the inmates in federal and state prisons, and in 1982, the probability of being murdered was six times greater for blacks than for whites. The officially acknowledged high school dropout rate in many metropolitan areas is more than 30 per cent. Some knowledgeable observers say it is over 50 per cent in several major cities. These problems not only reflect the current depressed state of black America, but also impose obstacles to future advancement.

The racism, discrimination, and oppression that black people have suffered and continue to suffer are clearly at the root of many of today's problems. Nevertheless, our analysis takes off from a forward-looking, and we believe optimistic, note: we are convinced that black people today, because of the gains in education, economic status, and political leverage that we have won as a result of the civil rights movement, are in a position to improve substantially the conditions of our communities using the resources already at our disposal. Our thesis is simple: the progress of any group is affected not only by public policy and by the racial attitudes of society as a whole, but by that group's capacity to exploit its own strengths. Our concern is about factors that prevent black Americans from using those strengths.

It is important to distinguish between the specific circumstances a group faces and its capacity to marshal its own resources to change those circumstances. Solving the problems of black communities requires a focus on the factors that hinder black people from more effectively managing their own circumstances. What are some of these factors?

Intellectual Development

Intellectual development is the primary focus of this article because it is the key to success in American society. Black people traditionally have understood this. Previous generations decided that segregation had to go because it relegated blacks to the backwater of American society, effectively denying us the opportunities, exposure, and competition that form the basis of intellectual development. Black intellectual development was one of the major benefits expected from newly won access to American institutions. That development, in turn, was expected to be a foundation for future advancement.

Yet now, three decades after *Brown* v. *Board of Education,* there is pervasive evidence of real problems in the intellectual performance of many black people. From astronomical high school dropout rates among the poor to substandard academic and professional performance among those most privileged, there is a disturbing consistency in reports of lagging development. While some black people perform at the highest levels in every field of endeavor, the percentages who do so are small. Deficiencies in the process of intellectual development are one effect of the long-term suppression of a people; they are also, we believe, one of the chief causes of continued social and economic underdevelopment. Intellectual underdevelopment is one of the most pernicious effects of racism, because it limits the people's ability to solve problems over which they are capable of exercising substantial control.

Black Americans are understandably sensitive about discussions of the data on our performance, since this kind of information has been used too often to justify attacks on affirmative action and other government efforts to improve the position of blacks and other minorities. Nevertheless, the importance of this issue demands that black people and all others interested in social justice overcome our sensitivities, analyze the problem, and search for solutions.

The Performance Gap

Measuring intellectual performance requires making a comparison. The comparison may be with the performance of others in the same situation, or with some established standard of excellence, or both. It is typically measured by grades, job performance ratings, and scores on standardized and professional tests. In recent years a flood of articles, scholarly papers, and books have documented an intellectual performance gap between blacks and the population as a whole.

In 1982 the College Board, for the first time in its history, published data on the performance of various groups on the Scholastic Aptitude Test (SAT). The difference between the combined median scores of blacks and whites on the verbal and math portions of the SAT was slightly more than 200 points. Differences in family income do not explain the gap. Even at incomes over $50,000, there remained a 120-point difference. These differences persisted in the next two years.

In 1983 the NCAA proposed a requirement that all college athletic recruits have a high school grade-point average of at least 2.0 (out of a maximum of 4.0) and a minimum combined SAT score of 700. This rule, intended to prevent the exploitation of young athletes, was strongly opposed by black college presidents and civil rights leaders. They were painfully aware that in recent years less than half of all black students have achieved a combined score of 700 on the SAT.

Asian Americans consistently produce a median SAT score

140 to 150 points higher than blacks with the same family income.

The pass rate for black police officers on New York City's sergeant's exam is 1.6 per cent. For Hispanics, it is 4.4 per cent. For whites, it is 10.6 per cent. These are the results *after* $500,000 was spent, by court order, to produce a test that was job-related and nondiscriminatory. No one, even those alleging discrimination, could explain how the revised test was biased.

Florida gives a test to all candidates for teaching positions. The pass rate for whites is more than 80 per cent. For blacks, it is 35 to 40 per cent.

This is just a sampling. All these reports demonstrate a real difference between the performance of blacks and other groups. Many of the results cannot be easily explained by socioeconomic differences or minority status *per se*.

What is the explanation? Clear thinking about this is inhibited by the tendency to equate performance with ability. Acknowledging the performance gap is, in many minds, tantamount to inferring that blacks are intellectually inferior. But inferior performance and inferior ability are not the same. Rather, the performance gap is largely a behavioral problem. It is the result of remediable tendency to avoid intellectual engagement and competition. Avoidance is rooted in the fears and self-doubt engendered by a major legacy of American racism: the strong negative stereotypes about black intellectual capabilities. Avoidance of an intellectual competition is manifested most obviously in the attitudes of many black youths toward academic work, but it is not limited to children. It affects the intellectual performance of black people of all ages and feeds public doubts about black intellectual ability.

The performance gap damages the self-confidence of many black people. Black students and professional people cannot help but be bothered by poor showings in competitive academic and professional situations. Black leaders too often have tried to explain away these problems by blaming racism or cultural bias in the tests themselves. These factors have not disappeared, but for many middle-class black Americans who have had access to educational and economic opportunities for nearly twenty years, the traditional protestations of cultural deprivation and educational disadvantage ring hollow. Given the cultural and educational advantages that many black people now enjoy, the claim that all blacks should be exempt from the performance standards applied to others is interpreted as a tacit admissions of inferiority. This admission adds further weight to the questions, in our own minds and in the minds of others, about black intelligence.

The traditional explanations—laziness or inferiority on the one hand; racism, discrimination, and biased tests on the other—are inaccurate and unhelpful. What is required is an explanation that accounts for the subtle influences people exert over the behavior and self-confidence of other people.

Developing an explanation that might serve as a basis for corrective action is important. The record of the last twenty years suggests that waiting for grand initiatives from the outside to save the black community is futile. Blacks will have to rely on our own ingenuity and resources. We need local and national political leaders. We need skilled administrators and creative business executives. We need a broad base of well-educated volunteers and successful people in all fields as role models for black youths. In short, we need a large number of sophisticated, intellectually developed people who are confident of their ability to operate on an equal level with anyone. Chronic mediocre intellectual performance is deeply troubling because it suggests that we are not developing enough such people.

The Competitive Process

Intellectual development is not a fixed asset that you either have or do not have. Nor is it based on magic. It is a process of expanding mental strength and reach. The development process is demanding. It requires time, discipline, and intense effort. It almost always involves competition as well. Successful groups place high value on intellectual performance. They encourage the drive to excel and use competition to sharpen skills and stimulate development in each succeeding generation. The developed people that result from this competitive process become the pool from which leadership of all kinds is drawn. Competition, in other words, is an essential spur to development.

Competition is clearly not the whole story. Cooperation and solitary study are valuable, too. But of the various keys to intellectual development, competition seems to fare worst in the estimation of many blacks. Black young people, in particular, seem to place a strong negative value on intellectual competition.

Black people have proved to be very competitive at some activities, particularly sports and entertainment. It is our sense, however, that many blacks consider intellectual competition to be inappropriate. It appears to inspire little interest or respect among many youthful peer groups. Often, in fact, it is labeled "grade grubbing," and gives way to sports and social activity as a basis for peer acceptance. The intellectual performance gap is one result of this retreat from competition.

The Psychology of Performance

The need to avoid intellectual competition is a psychological reaction to an image of black intellectual inferiority that has been projected by the larger society, and to a less than conscious process of internalization of that image by black people over the generations.

The rumor of black intellectual inferiority has been around for a long time. It has been based on grounds as diverse as twisted biblical citations, dubious philosophical arguments, and unscientific measurements of skull capacity. The latest emergence of this theme has been in the controversy over race and IQ. For fifteen years magazines and television talk shows have enthusiastically taken up the topic of black intellectual endowment. We have watched authors and critics debate the proposition that blacks are genetically inferior to whites in intellectual capability.

Genetic explanations have a chilling finality. The ignorant can be educated, the lazy can be motivated, but what can be done for the individual thought to have been born without the basic equipment necessary to compete or develop? Of course the allegation of genetic inferiority has been hotly disputed. But the debate has touched the consciousness of most Americans. We are convinced that this spectacle has negatively affected the way both blacks and whites think about the intellectual capabilities of black people. It also has affected the way blacks behave in intellectually competitive situations. The general expectation of black intellectual inferiority, and the fear this expectation generates, cause many black people to avoid intellectual competition.

Our hypothesis, in short, is this. (1) Black performance problems are caused in large part by a tendency to avoid intellectual competition. (2) This tendency is a psychological phenomenon that arises when the larger society projects an image of black intellectual inferiority and when that image is internalized by black people. (3) Imputing intellectual inferiority to genetic causes, especially in the face of data confirming poorer performance, intensifies the fears and doubts that surround this issue.

Clearly the image of inferiority continues to be projected. The internalization of this image by black people is harder to prove empirically. But there is abundant evidence in the expressed attitudes of many black youths toward intellectual competition; in the inability of most black communities to inspire the same commitment to intellectual excellence that is routinely accorded athletics and entertainment; and in the fact of the performance gap itself—especially when that gap persists among the children of economically and educationally privileged households.

Expectancies and Performance

The problem of black intellectual performance is rooted in human sensitivity to a particular kind of social interaction known as "expectancy communications." These are expressions of belief—verbal or nonverbal—from one person to another about the kind of performance to be expected. "Mary, you're one of the best workers we have, so I know that you won't have any trouble with this assignment." Or, "Joe, since everyone else is busy with other work, do as much as you can on this. When you run into trouble, call Mary." The first is a positive expectancy; the second, a negative expectancy.

Years of research have clearly demonstrated the powerful impact of expectancies on performance. The expectations of teachers for their students have a large effect on academic achievement. Psychological studies under a variety of circumstances demonstrate that communicated expectations induce people to believe that they will do well or poorly at a task, and that such beliefs very often trigger responses that result in performance consistent with the expectation. There is also evidence that "reference-group expectancies"—directed at an entire category of people rather than a particular individual—have a similar impact on the performance of members of the group.

Expectancies do not always work. If they come from a questionable source or if they predict an outcome that is too inconsistent with previous experience, they will not have much effect. Only credible expectancies—those that come from a source considered reliable and that address a belief or doubt the performer is sensitive to—will have a self-fulfilling impact.

The widespread expectation of black intellectual inferiority—communicated constantly through the projection of stereotyped images, verbal and nonverbal exchanges in daily interaction, and the incessant debate about genetics and intelligence—represents a credible reference-group expectancy. The message of the race/IQ controversy is: "We have scientific evidence that blacks, because of genetic inadequacies, cannot be expected to do well at tasks that require great intelligence." As an explanation for past black intellectual performance, the notion of genetic inferiority is absolutely incorrect. As an expectancy communication exerting control over our present intellectual strivings, it has been powerfully effective. These expectancies raise fear and self-doubt in the minds of many blacks, especially when they are young and vulnerable. This has resulted in avoidance of intellectual activity and chronic underperformance by many of our most talented people.

The powerful effect of expectancies on performance has been proved, but the way the process works is less well understood. Expectancies affect behavior, we think, in two ways. They affect performance behavior; the capacity to marshal the sharpness and intensity required for competitive success. And they influence cognition: the mental processes by which people make sense of everyday life.

Behavior and Cognition

As anyone who has experienced an "off day" knows, effort is variable; it is subject to biological cycles, emotional states, and motivation. Most important for our discussion, it depends on levels of confidence going into a task. Credible expectancies influence performance behavior. They affect the intensity of effort, the level of concentration or distractibility, and the willingness to take reasonable risks—a key factor in the development of self-confidence and new skills.

Expectations also influence the way people think about or explain their performance outcomes. These explanations are called "attributions." Research in social psychology has demonstrated that the causes to which people attribute their successes and failures have an important impact on subsequent performance.

All of us encounter failure. But a failure we have been led to expect affects us differently from an unexpected failure. When people who are confident of doing well at a task are confronted with unexpected failure, they tend to attribute the failure to inadequate effort. The likely response to another encounter with the same or a similar task is to work harder. People who come into a task expecting to fail, on the other hand, attribute their failure to lack of ability. Once you admit to yourself, in effect, that "I don't have what it takes," you are not likely to approach that task again with great vigor.

Indeed, those who attribute their failures to inadequate effort are likely to conclude that more effort will produce a better outcome. This triggers an adaptive response to failure. In contrast, those who have been led to expect failure will attribute their failures to lack of ability, and will find it difficult to rationalize the investment of greater effort. They often, in fact, feel depressed when they attempt to work, since each attempt represents a confrontation with their own feared inadequacy.

This combined effect on behavior and cognition is what makes expectancy so powerful. The negative expectancy first tends to generate failure through its impact on behavior, and then induces the individual to blame the failure on lack of ability, rather than the actual (and correctable) problem of inadequate effort. This misattribution in turn becomes the basis for a new negative expectancy. By this process the individual, in effect, internalizes the low estimation originally held by others. This internalized

negative expectancy powerfully affects future competitive behavior and future results.

The process we describe is not limited to black people. It
affects individuals from all groups. It helps to explain the superiority of some groups at some areas of endeavor, and the
mediocrity of those same groups in other areas. What makes
black people unique is that they are singled out for the stigma of
genetic intellectual inferiority.

The expectation of intellectual inferiority accompanies a black
person into each new intellectual situation. Since each of us
enters these tests under the cloud of predicted failure, and since
each failure reinforces doubts about our capabilities, all intellectual competition raises the specter of having to admit a lack of
intellectual capacity. But this particular expectancy goes beyond
simply predicting and inducing failure. The expectancy message
explicitly ascribes the expected failure to genes, and amounts to
an open suggestion to black people to understand any failure in
intellectual activity as confirmation of genetic inferiority. Each
engagement in intellectual competition carries the weight of a
test of one's own genetic endowment and that of black people
as a whole. Facing such a terrible prospect, many black people
recoil from any situation where the rumor of inferiority might be
proved true.

For many black students this avoidance manifests itself in a
concentration on athletics and socializing, at the expense of
more challenging (and anxiety-provoking) academic work. For
black professionals, it may involve a tendency to shy away from
competitive situations or projects, or an inability to muster the
intensity—commit the time—necessary to excel. This sort of
thinking and behavior certainly does not characterize all black
people in competitive settings. But it is characteristic of enough
to be a serious problem. When it happens, it should be understood as a less-than-conscious reaction to the psychological
burden of the terrible rumor.

The Intellectual Inferiority Game

There always have been constraints on the intellectual exposure and development of black people in the United States, from

laws prohibiting the education cf blacks during slavery to the Jim Crow laws and "separate-but-equal" educational arrangements that persisted until very recently. In dismantling these legal barriers to development, the civil rights movement fundamentally transformed the possibilities for black people. Now, to realize those possibilities, we must address the mental barriers to competition and performance.

The doctrine of intellectual inferiority acts on many black Americans the way that a "con" or a "hustle" like three-card monte acts on its victim. It is a subtle psychological input that interacts with characteristics of the human cognitive apparatus—in this case, the extreme sensitivity to expectancies—to generate self-defeating behavior and thought processes. It has reduced the intellectual performance of millions of black people.

Intellectual inferiority, like segregation, is a destructive idea whose time has passed. Like segregation, it must be removed as an influence in our lives. Among its other negative effects, fear of the terrible rumor has restricted discussion by all parties, and has limited our capacity to understand and improve our situation. But the intellectual inferiority game withers in the light of discussion and analysis. We must begin now to talk about intellectual performance, work through our expectations and fears of intellectual inferiority, consciously define more adaptive attitudes toward intellectual development, and build our confidence in the capabilities of all people.

The expectancy/performance process works both ways. Credible positive expectancies can generate self-confidence and result in success. An important part of the solution to black performance problems is converting the negative expectancies that work against black development into positive expectancies that nurture it. We must overcome our fears, encourage competition, and support the kind of performance that will dispel the notion of black intellectual inferiority.

The Commitment to Development

In our work with black high school and college students and with black professionals, we have shown that education in the psychology of performance can produce strong performance improvement very quickly. Black America needs a nationwide effort, now, to ensure that all black people—but especially black youths—are free to express their intellectual gifts. That effort should be built on three basic elements:

(1) Deliberate control of expectancy communications. We must begin with the way we talk to one another: the messages we give and the expectations we set. This includes the verbal and nonverbal messages we communicate in day-to-day social intercourse, as well as the expectancies communicated through the educational process and media images.

(2) Definition of an "intellectual work ethic." Black communities must develop strong positive attitudes toward intellectual competition. We must teach our people, young and mature, the efficacy of intense, committed effort in the arena of intellectual activity and the techniques to develop discipline in study and work habits.

(3) Influencing thought processes. Teachers, parents, and other authority figures must encourage young blacks to attribute their intellectual successes to ability (thereby boosting confidence) and their failure to lack of effort. Failures must no longer destroy black children's confidence in their intelligence or in the efficacy of hard work. Failures should be seen instead as feedback indicating the need for more intense effort or for a different approach to the task.

The task that confronts us is no less challenging than the task that faced those Americans who dismantled segregation. To realize the possibilities presented by their achievement, we must silence, once and for all, the rumors of inferiority.

Expectations of black inferiority are communicated, consciously or unconsciously, by many whites, including teachers, managers, and those responsible for the often demeaning representations of blacks in the media. These expectations have sad consequences for many blacks, and those whose actions lead to such consequences may be held accountable for them. If the people who shape policy in the United States, from the White House to the local elementary school, do not address the problem of performance and development of blacks and other minorities, all Americans will face the consequences: instability, disharmony, and a national loss of the potential productivity of more than a quarter of the population.

When economic necessity and the demands of social justice compel us toward social change, however, those who have the most to gain from change—or the most to lose from its absence—should be responsible for pointing the way.

It is time that blacks recognize our own responsibility. When we react to the rumor of inferiority by avoiding intellectual engagement, and allow children to do so, black people forfeit the opportunity for intellectual development that could extinguish the debate about capacities, and set the stage for group progress. Blacks must hold ourselves accountable for the resulting waste of talent—and valuable time. Black people have everything to gain—in stature, self-esteem, and problem-solving capability—from a more aggressive and confident approach to intellectual competition. We must assume responsibility for our own performance and development.

31. Jews and Negroes

By ERNEST VAN DEN HAAG

Focus
Though the official policy of the federal government from the mid-1960s to the early 1970s was to encourage strict nondiscrimination (i.e., racial and ethnic neutrality) in employment and university admission, by the late 1960s many private institutions, particularly universities, began adopting on a voluntary basis their own informal policies of granting preference to black people.

In 1969, Ernest van den Haag criticized such policies as psychologically destructive to their intended Negro beneficiaries. His analysis takes the form of a comparison of the histories of Negroes and Jews. Before the Second World War, van den Haag explains, Jews were often discriminated against in American universities both as students and as professors, insofar as it was generally required that Jews have higher qualifications than their Gentile counterparts. While not intended to benefit Jews, such policies actually had the effect, van den Haag argues, of enhancing the Jewish self-image and the image of Jews among non-Jews. Since the typical Jewish student or Jewish professor really *was* superior intellectually to his Gentile counterpart—he had to be to get where he was—intellectual superiority, van den Haag says, came to be seen by many non-Jews as a characteristic Jewish trait.

A policy of preferential treatment for Negroes, van den Haag predicts, will have the exact opposite effect. Since the typical Negro who a white person encounters as a student, colleague, or client, will, as a result of preferential policies, be less qualified than his white counterpart, the view that Negroes are intellectually inferior to whites will receive strong empirical confirmation. "Just as the Jewish image," says van den Haag, "was largely created by the superiority of the most visible Jews to Gentile colleagues . . . so the Negro image will be influenced strongly by the inferiority of the most visible Negroes to white colleagues." The psychological effect of preferential advancement upon the Negro self-image, van den Haag concludes, will be utterly disastrous, as it will serve to reinforce the deeply rooted sense of inadequacy and inferiority from which many Negroes suffer.

Ernest van den Haag is the John M. Olin Professor of Jurisprudence at Fordham University and a practicing psychoanalyst.

WHEN JEWS WERE FINALLY accepted into American society, they were allowed to succeed or fail according to their individual merits as others did—almost. They mostly succeeded.

Until the Second World War, some extra merit was still required for promotion and recognition to come to Jews. Their achievement had to be both undeniable and extraordinary to gain the recognition that might come to Gentiles of ordinary merit. Jewish lawyers became Supreme Court justices in spite of Jewish origin; Jewish physicians became members of medical faculties; Jewish scholars attained professorial rank. It would be tedious to prolong the listing, and redundant, as well as pedantic, to document the point. Since Jews were held to be in some general way inferior—a survival of the historical Christian viewpoint, which enabled Gentiles to look upon them as unredeemed social pariahs—special gifts, merits, or abilities were required to offset the assumed inferiority: to be granted parity, Jews had to be superior to their peers.

The extra barriers Jews had to overcome for promotion and recognition, and the extra merits and efforts required to do so, were—need it be said?—inequitable. Nonetheless, the effect, unintended and unanticipated by those who built barriers to Jews to make sure that their status remained inferior, was to create an aura of superiority, which ever since has surrounded Jews.

Over a fairly long period, only Jews who actually were quite superior to their professional or scholary peers obtained recognition and promotion. Thus Jews achieved prominent positions that made them highly visible to Gentiles only if they actually were superior to their Gentile colleagues. Unavoidably Jews came to be regarded as usually having abilities superior to those of Gentiles.

It was Gentile pressure and Gentile laws [in medieval Europe] that drove Jews into the cities, and into occupations such as money lending and international trade, which, though necessary, useful, and profitable, were undertaken by Gentiles only with reluctance and in some cases were regarded as sinful by them. With the development of an industrial society, their specialization in these occupations gave Jews an indirect power. This power seemed mysterious—inconsistent as it was with their low social position and their lack of political power. The mystery added to their ambivalent prestige. Most important, their specialization and their lack of a vested interest in the agricultural and feudal order made the adjustment of Jews to the modern, urban, and industrial world easier than that of any other group— and, therefore, helped them play a leading role in it. This development, largely due to discrimination against them, in the end added as well to the belief in the superiority of Jews.

As might be expected, the public image of Jewish cleverness and superiority that was unwittingly created, or at least confirmed, by anti-Semitic practices, had ambivalent effects. In Germany, it contributed to a defensive reaction: let us kill those who, by possibly being superior, may confront us with our own inadequacy and threaten our dominant position as well as our feeling of superiority. In the United States, which does not have a homogeneous group that feels threatened (and where the threat to WASPs come from more than one quarter), the reaction has been more along the lines of: if you can't beat them, join them. The joining has accelerated in the last few decades. In America the fear of and the desire for the (true or imagined) Jewish superiority has been dealt with by absorbing the Jews, making them part of the American self-image. We have given a Jewish flavor to whatever was cooked in the melting pot. Other ingredients were more sizable. But the Jews were the spice that came to dominate the flavor most of the time.

Discrimination In Favor of Negroes

At present, we witness the attempts of Negroes to be fully accepted as equals in America, to be considered each on his individual merits alone. As their history differs from Jewish history, so does the attempt of Negroes to be recognized as equals in America differ from that of Jews, and so does the response.

Negroes are neither recent nor voluntary immigrants. They were brought to America forcibly; they were oppressed; they were made to live in, but not allowed to be of, the society that used them for centuries. Unlike Jews, they lived in rural areas far from the city slums to which they now are migrating. In these "ghettos" they engage in occupations most often shunned by whites. But these are not now finance and commerce—the occupations Gentiles left to Jews—but low-paying, menial jobs with little chance for advancement or independence. The Gentile leftovers that the Jews had to be content with turned out to be the mainstays of the age that was to come. But what was left for Negroes was whatever tended to become obsolete and actually had been left by whites for newer and better occupations.

Most importantly, the tribal cultures Negroes possessed, even their language, as well as their religion, were destroyed in slavery. The Negro family itself was impaired. Had they not been destroyed, their original tribal cultures still could not have prepared Negroes for the civilization to which they were suddenly and forcibly removed. The absence of a viable tradition of any endogenous culture of their own, and their low status in American society, often led to a self-image of inadequacy that reduces and distorts motivation even when opportunity is present.

The present attempt of Negroes to enter American society, unlike that of other groups, is bitter and resentful as often as eager, violent as often as diligent. The reaction of the white environment also differs. Often it is guilt-ridden; in the past it was openly hostile; and it threatens to become so once more as the lower-middle classes feel threatened by Negroes, even if that threat more often flows from the rhetoric of militants than from any actual power shift. For a long time, the relation between Negroes and whites is likely to be felt, at best, as an antagonistic symbiosis.

Now successful and accepted, Jews are quite frequently in positions to lead; and they feel guilty about Negroes. Unlike the guilt feelings of WASPs, those of Jews do not spring from having been oppressors in the past, but rather from having been oppressed as well. Jews identify with the oppressed and deprived Negro treated by his white environment in a way all too familiar to them—a way that cannot but recall the memory of their own oppression, deprivation, and ghettoization. Now that they are successful, Jews feel that they have the obligation to help those who suffer, as they did, from discrimination; those who are considered, as the Jews were, as inferior; those who are, as they were, oppressed and held in contempt; those who so often are stereotyped, to whom so many unfavorable characteristics are ascribed, as they were to Jews.

The identification, to be sure, is topological only: Negroes occupy a social spot once occupied by Jews (often they actually occupy the formerly Jewish areas of cities); they do not resemble Jews in background, attitude, character, or characteristics. Above all, they lack the cohesive culture, the religion, the self-image Jews managed to create and preserve, and their family relationship to Christian culture. Never mind; the guilt feeling is genuine enough. Yet, however necessary it may be as motivation, I do not think that this Jewish guilt feeling (shared by many non-Jews as well) is a useful guide to action. On the contrary, the actions prompted by it threaten to make matters worse—particularly "reverse discrimination": discrimination in favor of Negroes. Many Negroes, and nearly all their spokesmen, now claim this favorable discrimination as a right.

Jews, as mentioned, had to be better than Gentiles to attain equal rank, to be promoted in spite of being Jewish. Thus the Jews who became notable and were regarded as representative, who created the public image, not to say the stereotype, were usually better qualified than their Gentile colleagues. "Reverse discrimination," however, means that Negroes often are promoted not *despite* being Negroes, but *because* they are, and regardless of merit. Because they are Negroes they are accepted as students and given scholarships, even when less qualified than white competitors. Perhaps such "compensatory opportunity" can be justified when it is combined with special help to allow the students selected to catch up with their fellow students.

Negroes are also sought out, however, and asked to join faculties over more-qualified white competitors. Anyone familiar with the situation knows that colleges look high and low for Negro students and faculty members and accept them over better-qualified white ones. This holds not only for universities, but for many institutions, corporations, and for many high-status jobs. "Reverse discrimination" may have contributed to the situation referred to in the report of the National Advisory Commission on Civil Disorders, named by President Johnson to investigate the 1967 riots:

> the proportion of Negroes employed in high-skill, high-status, and well-paying jobs rose faster than the comparable proportion among whites from 1960 to 1966.

Justices Cardozo, Brandeis, and Frankfurter became justices of the Supreme Court in spite of being Jewish. Thurgood Marshall became Mr. Justice Marshall *because* he is Negro. He is a competent lawyer. No one ever accused him of being an outstanding jurist.

To be sure, politics has often played a role in nominations to the Supreme Court. More than one jurist was named for political reasons when many better-qualified lawyers were overlooked. One may argue that since there was for so long a time discrimination in favor of WASPs, some discrimination in favor of blacks can be justified. It is a dubious argument, appealing more to politicians, for whom two wrongs offset each other, than to the philosopher, for whom they do not make a right. In terms of equity, the argument runs as follows: well-connected whites in the past have often gained positions over more qualified competitors in corporations and elsewhere. Negroes have no such connections. Why not give them a similar opportunity by granting them preference over whites, even over more qualified ones.

Such an argument treats Negroes and whites as groups with competing claims to be balanced, and not as individuals whose individual qualifications ought to be considered paramount. Past practice may make the disregard for individual qualifications in favor of group discrimination seem equitable. But it reinforces rather than eliminates group discrimination and, despite apparent advantages, harms the members of all groups. Injustice—even when compensatory—is never in the social interest.

The actual, present, and future effects are more important than the intended equity of compensatory "reverse discrimination." To offset past deprivations, we now place Negroes in positions and ranks for which, as they are being placed, they are less qualified than competing whites. Could the effects of this "reverse discrimination" damage the Negroes who are to be favored? What specific effects can we expect on: (a) the self-image of Negroes; (b) the attitude of whites toward Negroes and of Negroes toward whites; and (c) the image of Negroes among whites?

(a) Negroes will not be able to overlook for long that they are being promoted in a discriminatory fashion. Even though the discrimination is in their favor, they are still not being treated in terms of individual merit, or qualifications, but as members of a group. Unlike Jews, they cannot have the feeling that their individual abilities have, in each particular case, overcome and defeated the prejudice against the group. On the contrary, they must be aware that they may be promoted not because of individual qualifications but, regardless of merit, because they are Negroes. They are reduced to members of a group. Thus, a Negro who is actually as well qualified as his white colleagues will never be sure whether he is promoted because of his individual qualifications, or to make up for the prejudice against his group by singling out members for especially favorable (discriminatory) treatment.

This doubt will not help the self-image even of those Negroes who are as well or better qualified than whites, while those who are not will come to believe that a job, and a status, is owed them as Negroes, regardless of qualifications—which will not strengthen their motivation to acquire qualifications.

(b) Some whites will resent favorable treatment given Negroes as such when it means disadvantages for whites of equal or superior merit. The need for qualified people in most occupations, however, is so great that few whites will actually suffer. Hence this effect may be regarded as materially negligible.

Psychologically, though, it is not negligible at all: it will help rationalize and intensify resentments against Negroes originating elsewhere. It will strengthen prejudice. Among Negroes, "reverse discrimination" will foster a "dependent attitude," which demands advantages and refuses to achieve them realistically by acquiring relevant qualifications.

(c) The effect of discrimination *in favor* of Negroes on the image of Negroes among whites will be disastrous—different, but ultimately not better than the effect of discrimination *against* Negroes. Preferential treatment of Negroes, placement in positions for which they are less qualified than white competitors, means that among students and faculties and in the professions, there will be more Negroes than before—and that on the average they will be less well qualified than the majority of their white colleagues. This disparity cannot remain hidden for long to either Negroes or whites. Ultimately, just as the Jewish image was largely created by the superiority of the most visible Jews so too the Negro image will be influenced strongly by the inferiority of the most visible Negroes to white colleagues.

The well-meant present policies of the friends of Negroes certainly yield advantages, in the short run, both to the individual Negroes who benefit and to the guilt-ridden consciences of their benefactors. But the long-range effects are likely to be calamitous for the Negro people. Groups of Negroes may profit: Negroes as a group will suffer. Their self-image of inferiority to whites and of inadequacy will be reinforced. And the white's image of Negroes as inferior, as less well qualified for most things than whites, will be confirmed.

It does not do justice to Negroes to discriminate against them. Neither does it do justice to them to discriminate in favor of Negroes. In promoting individuals, a just society must disregard anything other than the comparative qualifications of each individual for the rank to which he aspires. All irrelevant discrimination—discrimination based on group membership or other qualities not relevant to the task at hand—must be avoided, be it in favor of or against any particular group. If irrelevant discrimination has occurred in the past, the reverse irrelevant discrimination does not offset it; it adds to it.

Charity and benevolence, the attempt to make up for past suffering, have their place. A society without them will not be a good society. But nothing can take the place of justice. A society that neglects justice in favor of charity becomes unjust, and ultimately uncharitable as well. The first reaction of those who feel themselves unjustly treated will be vindictive harshness; they will ignore even the proper claims of charity.

Charity and love are virtues separate from (if related to) justice. A society must not only strive toward virtue; it must strive toward the right order of virtues. Nothing prevents the private citizen, and at times even his government, from helping Negroes to achieve qualifications and from helping them according to their need. If the need of Negroes is greater than that of others, so should the help be. Love discriminates in favor of needs. But in promotion for any one rank, the public virtue of justice must prevail. Only the qualifications actually attained should count. To ignore this simple rule, to slight justice in favor of charity, distorts the social order; and it will injure the recipients of favor above all others. Negroes once more will be made to suffer—this time from the guilt-ridden beneficence of their well-wishers.

32. Affirmative Racism

By CHARLES MURRAY

Focus
Like Ernest van den Haag (selection 31), Charles Murray believes that preferential treatment for black people, though well intentioned in purpose, perpetuates the belief in black inferiority. The system of racial preference, says Murray, "segments whites and blacks who come in contact with each other so as to maximize the likelihood that whites have the advantage in experience and ability." He presents the stories of Carol, John, and William, three constructs based upon the actual experiences of black people he has known, and tries to show how each has been hurt by what he describes as the "new racism" of affluent white liberals. On the job, Murray says, blacks who have been preferentially hired or promoted must face the constant humiliation of their exposure to white co-workers, who treat their inferior qualifications either with condescension or resentment. In universities, Murray explains, black students will often wind up in the bottom part of the class, and as a result, white students come to believe that black people are less capable than whites. The problem, Murray suggests, is only minor at the most prestigious universities and corporations (e.g., Harvard, IBM, Park Avenue law firms), which easily attract the top quality black talent. But a skimming process inevitably takes place, he says, which results in the less prestigious institutions—such as the large state universities—

being totally devoid of any blacks who are comparable to the better-qualified whites. Murray says the solution to the "new racism" and its harmful effects upon blacks is very simple—preferential treatment must be abandoned.

Charles Murray is a senior research fellow at the Manhattan Institute for Policy Research and author of *Losing Ground: American Social Policy 1950–1980*.

A FEW YEARS AGO I got into an argument with a lawyer friend who is a partner in a New York firm. I was being the conservative, arguing that preferential treatment of blacks was immoral; he was being the liberal, urging that it was the only way to bring blacks to full equality. In the middle of all this he abruptly said, "But you know, let's face it. We must have hired at least ten blacks in the last few years, and none of them has really worked out." He then returned to his case for still stronger affirmative action, while I wondered what it had been like for those ten blacks. And if he could make a remark like that so casually, what remarks would he be able to make some years down the road, if by that time it had been fifty blacks who had not "really worked out?"

My friend's comment was an outcropping of a new racism that is emerging to take its place alongside the old. It grows out of preferential treatment for blacks, and it is not just the much-publicized reactions, for example, of the white policemen or firemen who are passed over for promotion because of an affirmative action court order. The new racism potentially most damaging is located among the white elites—educated, affluent, and occupying the positions in education, business, and government from which this country is run. It currently focuses on blacks; whether it will eventually extend to include Hispanics and other minorities remains to be seen.

The new racists do not think blacks are inferior. They are typically longtime supporters of civil rights. But they exhibit the classic behavioral symptom of racism: they treat blacks differently from whites, because of their race. The results can be as concretely bad and unjust as any that the old racism produces. Sometimes the effect is that blacks are refused an education they otherwise could have gotten. Sometimes blacks are shunted into dead-end jobs. Always, blacks are denied the right to compete as equals.

The new racists also exhibit another characteristic of racism: they *think* about blacks differently than whites. Their global view of blacks and civil rights is impeccable. Blacks must be enabled to achieve full equality. They are still unequal, through no fault of their own (it is the fault of racism, it is the fault of inadequate opportunity, it is the legacy of history). But the new racists' local view is that the blacks they run across professionally are not, on the average, up to the white standard. Among the new racists, lawyers have gotten used to the idea that the brief a black colleague turns in will be a little less well rehearsed and argued than the one they would have done. Businessmen expect that a black colleague will not read a balance sheet as subtly as they do. Teachers expect black students to wind up toward the bottom of the class.

The new racists also tend to think of blacks as a commodity. The office must have a sufficient supply of blacks, who must be treated with special delicacy. The personnel problems this creates are more difficult than most because whites barely admit to themselves what is going on.

What follows is a foray into very poorly mapped territory. I will present a few numbers that explain much about how the process gets started. But the ways the numbers get translated into behavior are even more important. The cases I present are composites constructed from my own observations and taken from firsthand accounts. All are based on real events and real people, stripped of their particularities. But the individual cases are not intended as evidence, because I cannot tell you how often they happen. They have not been the kind of thing that social scientists or journalists have wanted to count. I am writing this because so many people, both white and black, to whom I tell such stories know immediately what I am talking about. It is apparent that a problem exists. How significant is it? What follows is as much an attempt to elicit evidence as to present it.

Preferential Treatment in Universities

As in so many of the crusades of the 1960s, the action began with a good idea. It was called "affirmative action," initiated by Lyndon Johnson through Executive Order 11246, in September

1965. It was an attractive label and a natural corrective to past racism: actively seek out black candidates for jobs, college, or promotions, without treating them differently in the actual decision to hire, admit, or promote. The term originally evoked both the letter and the spirit of the order.

Then, gradually, affirmative action came to mean something quite different. In 1970 a federal court established the legitimacy of quotas as a means of implementing Johnson's executive order. In 1971 the Supreme Court ruled that an employer could not use minimum credentials as a prerequisite for hiring if the credential acted as a "built-in headwind" for minority groups— even when there was no discriminatory intent and even when the hiring procedures were "fair in form." In 1972, the Equal Employment Opportunity Commission acquired broad, independent enforcement powers.

Thus by the early 1970s, it had become generally recognized that a good-faith effort to recruit qualified blacks was not enough—especially if one's school depended on federal grants or one's business depended on federal contracts. Even for businesses and schools not directly dependent on the government, the simplest way to withstand an accusation of violating Title VII of the Civil Rights Act of 1964 was to make sure not that they had not just interviewed enough minority candidates, but that they had actually hired or admitted enough of them. Employers and admissions committees arrived at a rule of thumb: if the blacks who are available happen to be the best candidates, fine; if not, the best available black candidates will be given some sort of edge in the selection process. Sometimes the edge will be small; sometimes it will be predetermined that a black candidate is essential, and the edge will be very large.

Perhaps the first crucial place where the edge applies is in admissions to college. Consider the cases of the following three students: John, William, and Carol, all seventeen and applying to college, are all equal on paper. Each has a score of 520 in the mathematics section of the Scholastic Aptitude Test (SAT), which puts them in the top third—at the sixty-seventh percentile—of all students who took the test. (Figures are based on 1983 data.)

John is white. A score of 520 gets him into the state university. Against the advice of his high school counselor, he applies to a prestigious school, Ivy U., where his application is rejected in the first cut—its average white applicant has math scores in the high 600s.

William is black, from a middle-class family who sent him to good schools. His score of 520 puts him at the ninety-fifth percentile of all blacks who took the test. William's high school counselor points out that he could probably get into Ivy U. Williams applies and is admitted—Ivy U. uses separate standards for admission of whites and blacks, and William is among the top blacks who applied.

Carol is black, educated at an inner-city school, and her score of 520 represents an extraordinary achievement in the face of terrible schooling. An alumnus of Ivy U. who regularly looks for promising inner-city candidates finds her, recruits her, and sends her off with a full scholarship to Ivy U.

When American universities embarked on policies of preferential admissions by race, they had the Carols of the world in mind. They had good reason to be optimistic that preferential treatment would work—for many years, the best universities had been weighting the test scores of applicants from small-town public schools when they were compared against those of applicants from the top private schools, and had been giving special breaks to students from distant states to ensure geographic distribution. The differences in preparation tended to even out after the first year or so. Blacks were being brought into a long-standing and successful tradition of preferential treatment.

In the case of blacks, however, preferential treatment ran up against a large black-white gap in academic performance combined with ambitious goals for proportional representation. This gap has been the hardest for whites to confront. But though it is not necessary or even plausible to believe that such differences are innate, it is necessary to recognize openly that the differences exist. By pretending they do not, we begin the process whereby both the real differences and the racial factor are exaggerated.

The black-white gap that applies most directly to this discussion is the one that separates blacks and whites who go to college. In 1983, for example, the mean SAT score for all blacks who took the examination was more than 100 points below the white score on both the verbal and the math sections. Statistically, it is an extremely wide gap. To convert the gap into more concrete terms, think of it this way: in 1983, the same SAT math score that put a black at the fiftieth percentile of all blacks who took the test put him at the sixteenth percentile of all whites who took the test.

These results clearly mean we ought to be making an all-out effort to improve elementary and secondary education for blacks. But that does not help much now, when an academic discrepancy of this magnitude is fed into a preferential admissions process. As universities scramble to make sure they are admitting enough blacks, the results feed the new racism. Here is how it works:

In 1983, only 66 black students nationwide scored above 700 in the verbal section of the SAT, and only 205 scored above 700 in the mathematics section. This handful of students cannot begin to meet the demand for blacks with such scores. For example, Harvard, Yale, and Princeton have in recent years been bringing an aggregate of about 270 blacks into entering class. If the black students entering these schools had the same distribution of scores as that of the freshman class as a whole, then every black student in the nation with a verbal score in the 700s, and roughly 70 per cent of those with a math score in the 700s, would be in their freshman classes.

The main problem is not that a few schools monopolize the very top black applicants, but that these same schools have much larger implicit quotas than they can fill with those applicants. They fill out the rest with the next students in line— students who would not have gotten into these schools if they were not black, who otherwise would have been showing up in the classrooms of the nation's less-glamorous colleges and universities. But the size of the black pool does not expand appreciably at the next levels. The number of blacks scoring in the 600s on the math section in 1983, for example, was 1,531. Meanwhile, 31,740 nonblack students in 1983 scored in the 700s on the math section, and 121,640 scored in the 600s. The prestige schools cannot begin to absorb these numbers of other highly qualified freshmen, and they are perforce spread widely throughout the system.

At schools that draw most broadly from the student population, such as the large state universities, the effects of this skimming produce a situation that confirms the old racists in everything they want most to believe. There are plenty of outstanding students in such student bodies (at the University of Colorado, for example, 6 per cent of the freshmen in 1981 had math scores in the 700s and 28 per cent had scores in the 600s), but the skimming process combined with the very small raw numbers means that almost none of them are black. What students and instructors see in their day-to-day experience in the classroom is a disproportionate number of blacks who are below the white average, and virtually none who are in the first rank. The image that the white student carries away is that blacks are less able than whites.

I am not exalting the SAT as an infallible measure of academic ability, or pointing to test scores to try to convince anyone that blacks are performing below the level of whites. I am simply using them to explain what instructors and students already notice and talk about among themselves.

One characteristic of the new racism is that whites deny in public but acknowledge in private that there are significant differences in black and white academic performance. Another is that they dismiss the importance of tests when black scores are at issue, blaming cultural bias and saying that test scores are not good predictors of college performance. At the same time, they watch anxiously over their own children's test scores.

The differences in academic performance do not disappear by the end of college. Far from narrowing, the gap separating black and white academic achievement appears to get larger. Various studies, most recently at Harvard, have found that during the 1970s blacks did worse in college (as measured by grade-point average) than their test scores would have predicted. Moreover, the black-white gap in the Graduate Record Examination (GRE) is larger than the gap in the SAT. The gap between black and white freshmen is a bit less than one standard deviation (the technical measure for comparing scores). Black and white seniors who take the GRE reveal a gap of about one-and-a-quarter standard deviations.

Why should the gap grow wider? Perhaps it is an illusion—for example, perhaps a disproportionate number of the best black students never take the examination. But there are also reasons for suspecting that in fact blacks get a worse education in college than whites do. Here are a few of the hypotheses that deserve full exploration.

Take the situation of William—a slightly above-average student who, because he is black, gets into a highly competitive school. William studies very hard during the first year. He nonetheless gets mediocre grades. He has a choice. He can continue to study hard and continue to get mediocre grades, and be seen by his classmates as a black who cannot do very well. Or he can explicitly refuse to engage in the academic game. He decides to opt out, and his performance gets worse as time goes on. He emerges from college with a poor education and is further behind the whites than when he was a freshman.

If large numbers of other black students at the institution are in the same situation as William, the result can be group pressure not to compete academically. (At Harvard the current term among black students for a black who studies like a white is "incognegro.") The response is not hard to understand. If one subpopulation of students is conspicuously behind another population and is visibly identifiable, then the population that is behind must come up with a good excuse for doing poorly. "Not wanting to do better" is as good as any.

But there is another crucial reason why blacks might not close the gap with whites during college: they are not taught as well as whites are. Racist teachers impeding the progress of students? Perhaps, but most college faculty members I know tend to bend over backward to be "fair" to black students—and that may be the problem. I suggest that inferior instruction is more likely to be a manifestation of the new racism than the old.

Consider the case of Carol, with oustanding abilities but deprived of decent prior schooling: she struggles the first year, but she gets by. Her academic skills still show the after effects of her inferior preparation. Her instructors diplomatically point out the more flagrant mistakes, but they ignore minor lapses, and never push her in the aggressive way they push white students who have her intellectual capacity. Some of them are being patronizing (she is doing quite well, considering). Others are being prudent: teachers who criticize black students can find themselves being called racists in the classroom, in the campus newspaper, or in complaints to the administration.

The same process continues in graduate school. Indeed, because there are even fewer blacks in graduate schools than in undergraduate schools, the pressures to get black students through to the degree, no matter what, can be still greater. But apart from differences in preparation and ability that have accumulated by the end of schooling, the process whereby we foster the appearance of black inferiority continues. Let's assume that William did not give up during college. He goes to business school, where he gets his master's degree. He signs up for interviews with the corporate recruiters. There are 100 persons in his class and William is ranked near the middle. But of the 5 blacks in his class, he ranks first (remember that he was at the ninety-fifth percentile of blacks taking the SAT). He is hired on his first interview by his first-choice company, which also attracted the very best of the white students. He is hired alongside 5 of the top-ranking white members of the class.

William's situation as one of 5 blacks in a class of 100 illustrates the proportions that prevail in business schools, and business schools are by no means one of the more extreme examples. The pool of black candidates for any given profession is a small fraction of the white pools. This works out to a 20-to-1 edge in business; it is even greater in most of the other professions. The result, when many hiring institutions are competing, is that a major gap between the abilities of new black and white employees in any given workplace is highly likely. Everyone needs to hire a few blacks, and the edge that "being black" confers in the hiring decision warps the sequence of hiring in such a way that a scarce resource (the blacks with a given set of qualifications) is exhausted at an artificially high rate, producing a widening gap in comparison with the remaining whites from which an employer can choose.

The more aggressively affirmative action is enforced, the greater the imbalance. In general, the first companies to hire can pursue strategies that minimize or even eliminate the difference in ability between the new black and white employees. IBM and Park Avenue law firms can do very well, just as Harvard does quite well in attracting the top black students. But the more effectively they pursue these strategies, the more quickly they strip the population of the best black candidates.

Preferential Treatment On the Job

People do differ in acquired abilities. Currently, acquired abilities in the white and black populations are distributed differently. Schools and firms do form a rough hierarchy when they draw from these distributions. The results follow ineluctably. The dangers they represent are not a matter of statistical probabilities, but of day-to-day human reactions we see around us.

The damage caused by these mechanistic forces should be much less in the world of work than in the schools, however. Schools deal in a relatively narrow domain of skills, and "talent" tends to be assigned specific meanings and specific measures. Workplaces deal in highly complex sets of skills, and "talent" consists of all sorts of combinations of qualities. A successful career depends in large part upon finding jobs that elicit and develop one's strengths.

At this point the young black professional must sidestep a new series of traps laid by whites who need to be ostentatiously nonracist. Let's say that William goes to work for the XYZ Corporation, where he is assigned with another management trainee (white) to a department where much of the time is spent preparing proposals for government contracts. The white trainee is assigned a variety of scut work—proofreading drafts, calculating the costs of minor items in the bid, making photocopies, taking notes at conferences. William gets more dignified work. He is assigned portions of the draft to write (which are later rewritten by more experienced staff), sits in on planning sessions, and even goes to Washington as a highly visible part of the team to present the bid. As time goes on, the white trainee learns a great deal about how the company operates, and is seen as a go-getting young member of the team. William is perceived to be a bright enough fellow, but not much of a detail man and not really much of a self-starter.

Even if a black is hired under terms that put him on a par with his white peers, the subtler forms of differential treatment work against him. Particularly for any corporation that does business with the government, the new employee has a specific, immediate value purely because he is black. There are a variety of requirements to be met and rituals to be observed for which a black face is helpful. These have very little to do with the long-term career interests of the new employee; on the contrary, they often lead to a dead end as head of the minority-relations section of the personnel department.

Added to this is another problem that has nothing to do with the government. When the old racism was at fault (as it often still is), the newly hired black employee was excluded from the socialization process because the whites did not want him to become part of the group. When the new racism is at fault, it is because many whites are embarrassed to treat black employees as badly as they are willing to treat whites. Hence another reason that whites get on-the-job-training that blacks do not: much of the early training of an employee is intertwined with menial assignments and mild hazing. Blacks who are put through these routines often see themselves as racially abused (and when a black is involved, old-racist responses may well have crept in). But even if the black is not unhappy about the process, the whites are afraid that he is, and so protect him from it. There are many variations, all having the same effect: the black is denied an apprenticeship that the white has no way of escaping. Without serving the apprenticeship, there is no way of becoming part of the team.

Carol suffers a slightly different fate. She and a white woman are hired as reporters by a major newspaper. They both work hard, but after a few months there is no denying it: neither one of them can write. The white woman is let go. Carol is kept on, because the paper cannot afford to have any fewer blacks than it already has. She is kept busy with reportorial work, even though they have to work around the writing problem. She is told not to worry—there is a lot more to being a journalist than writing.

It is the mascot syndrome. A white performing at a comparable level would be fired. The black is kept on, perhaps to avoid complications with the Equal Employment Opportunity Commission (it can be very expensive to fire a black), perhaps out of a more diffuse wish not to appear discriminatory. Everyone pretends that nothing is wrong—but the black's career is at a dead end. The irony, of course, is that the white who gets fired and has to try something else has been forced into accepting a chance of making a success in some other line of work whereas the black is seduced into *not* taking the same chance.

Sometimes differential treatment takes an even more pernicious form: the conspiracy to promote a problem out of existence. As part of keeping Carol busy, the newspaper gives her some administrative responsibilities. They do not amount to much. But she has an impressive title on a prominent newspaper and she is black—a potent combination. She gets an offer from a lesser paper in another part of the country to take a senior editorial post. Her current employer is happy to be rid of an awkward situation and sends along glowing refrences. She gets a job that she is unequipped to handle—only this time, she is in a highly visible position, and within a few weeks the deficiencies that were covered up at the old job have become the subject of jokes all over the office. Most of the jokes are openly racist.

It is important to pause and remember who Carol is: an extremely bright young woman, not (in other circumstances) a likely object of condescension. But being bright is no protection. Whites can usually count on the market to help us recognize egregious career mistakes and to prevent us from being promoted too far from a career line that fits our strengths, and too far above our level of readiness. One of the most prevalent characteristics of white differential treatment of blacks has been to exempt blacks from these market considerations, substituting for them a market premium attached to race.

The most obvious consequence of preferential treatment is

that every black professional, no matter how able, is tainted. Every black who is hired by a white-run organization that hires blacks preferentially has to put up with the knowledge that many of his co-workers believe he was hired because of his race; and he has to put up with the suspicion in his own mind that they might be right.

Whites are curiously reluctant to consider this a real problem—it is an abstraction, I am told, much less important than the problem that blacks face in getting a job in the first place. But black professionals talk about it, and they tell stories of mental breakdowns; of people who had to leave the job altogether; of long-term professional paralysis. What white person would want to be put in such a situation? Of course it would be a constant humiliation to be resented by some of your co-workers and condescended to by others. Of course it would affect your perceptions of yourself and your self-confidence. No system that produces such side effects—as preferential treatment *must* do—can be defended unless it is producing some extremely important benefits.

The Decisive Question

And that brings us to the decisive question. If the alternative were no job at all, as it was for so many blacks for so long, the resentment and condescension are part of the price of getting blacks into the positions they deserve. But is that the alternative today? If the institutions of this country were left to their own devices now, to what extent would they refuse to admit, hire, and promote people because they were black? To what extent are American institutions kept from being racist by the government's intervention?

It is another one of those questions that are seldom investigated aggressively, and I have no evidence. Let me suggest a hypothesis that bears looking into: that the signal event in the struggle for black equality during the last thirty years, the one with real impact, was not the Civil Rights Act of 1964 or Executive Order 11246 or any other governmental act. It was the civil rights movement itself. It raised to a pitch of acute and lasting discomfort the racial consciousness of the generations of white Americans who are now running the country. I will argue, however, that in the typical corporation or in the typical admissions office, there is an abiding desire to be not-racist. This need not be construed as brotherly love. Guilt will do as well. But the civil rights movement did its job. I suggest that the laws and the court decisions and the continuing intellectual respectability behind preferential treatment are rot holding many doors open to qualified blacks that would otherwise be closed.

Suppose for a moment that I am right. Suppose that, for practical purposes, racism would not get in the way of blacks if preferential treatment were abandoned. How, in my most optimistic view, would the world look different?

There would be fewer blacks at Harvard and Yale; but those attending would all be fully able to compete with the whites who were there. White students at the state university would encounter a cross section of blacks who span the full range of ability, including the top levels, just as whites do. College remedial courses would no longer be disproportionately black. Whites rejected by the school they wanted would quit assuming they were kept out because a less-qualified black was admitted in their place. Blacks in big corporations would no longer be shunted off to personnel-relations positions, but would be left on the main-line tracks toward becoming comptrollers and sales managers and chief executives. Whites would quit assuming that black colleagues had been hired because they were black. Blacks would quit worrying that they had been hired because they were black.

The Evil of Preferential Treatment

Would blacks still lag behind? As a population, yes, for a time, and the nation should be mounting a far more effective program to improve elementary and secondary education for blacks than it has mounted in the last few decades. But in years past virtually every ethnic group in America has at one time or another lagged behind as a population, and has eventually caught up. In the process, the ones who breached the barriers were evidence of the success of that group. Now blacks who breach the barriers tend to be seen as evidence of the inferiority of that group.

And that is the evil of preferential treatment. It perpetuates an impression of inferiority. The system segments whites and blacks who come in contact with each other so as to maximize the likelihood that whites have the advantage in experience and ability. The system then encourages both whites and blacks to behave in ways that create self-fulfilling prophecies even when no real differences exist.

It is here that the new racism links up with the old. The old racism has always openly held that blacks are permanently less competent than whites. The new racism tacitly accepts that, in the course of overcoming the legacy of the old racism, blacks are temporarily less competent than whites. It is an extremely fine distinction. As time goes on, fine distinctions tend to be lost. Preferential treatment is providing persuasive evidence for the old racists, and we can already hear it *sotto voce:* "We gave you your chance, we let you educate them and push them into jobs they could not have gotten on their own and coddle them every way you could. And see: they still aren't as good as whites, and you are beginning to admit it yourselves." Sooner or later this message is going to be heard by a white elite that needs to excuse its failure to achieve black equality.

The only happy aspect of the new racism is that the corrective—to get rid of the policies encouraging preferential treatment—is so natural. Deliberate preferential treatment by race has sat as uneasily with America's equal-opportunity ideal during the post-1965 period as it did during the days of legalized segregation. We had to construct tortuous rationalizations when we permitted blacks to be kept on the back of the bus—and the rationalizations to justify sending blacks to the head of the line have been just as tortuous. Both kinds of rationalization say that sometimes it is all right to treat people of different races in different ways. For years, we have instinctively sensed this was wrong in principle but intellectualized our support for it as an expedient. I submit that our instincts were right. There is no such thing as good racial discrimination.

33. Admitting Success

By DEREK BOK

Focus
Responding to the previous article by Charles Murray (selection 32), Derek Bok says that abandoning the current policies of racial preferences in higher education, as Murray recommends, would inevitably lead to a dramatic reduction in black enrollment in many of the nation's selective colleges and professional schools. This, Bok says, would have a devastating effect upon the morale and aspirations of black people and would only strengthen the negative racial stereotypes that white people have of blacks. He gives the results of a poll conducted among undergraduates at his own university, Harvard, which indicates that the vast majority of Harvard undergraduates, both black and white alike, have no reservations at all about the intellectual abilities of Harvard's black students. Preferential admissions policies are seen by Bok as part of a long-term national strategy that is intended to enable more black people to achieve the education, income, and occupational background that will enable them to instill higher educational aspirations in their children. The alternative suggested by Murray—i.e., racial neutrality in university admissions—was tried in the mid-1960s, Bok says, and simply did not work.

Derek Bok is the president of Harvard University.

FOR FIFTEEN YEARS, COLLEGES and universities have sought to increase educational opportunities for minority students by admitting blacks (as well as Hispanics and Native Americans) with SAT scores lower than those of white applicants. In the December 31, 1984, issue of the *New Republic,* Charles Murray criticizes this policy and accuses higher education of helping to foster a new racism. In his view, preferential admissions practices, and affirmative action programs by employers, only demoralize blacks by forcing them to compete beyond their abilities while fostering stereotypes among whites that blacks really are inferior.

Murray offers a simple solution to this problem. Treat all applicants equally in admissions (and hiring), and allow them to make their way without any discrimination or preference on grounds of race. The immediate consequence, he admits, will be a severe drop in the number of black students, especially at more selective colleges and universities. Eventually, however, blacks will participate fully and successfully in American life just as other initially disadvantaged ethnic groups have done.

Murray's arguments are not new. Even so, they may gain a wider following at a time when the nation seems to be reassessing many of its priorities and practices. University administrators need to take the criticisms seriously rather than ignore them in the hope that they will disappear.

Murray mentions only the disappointments and failures of preferential admissions without recognizing its many successes. Since his conclusions are subjective and not based on data, it is also hard to know what to make of his assertions about the effects of preferential admissions on white and black attitudes. For what it's worth, his impressions do not accord with the anonymous survey results at the one institution I know. In a Harvard poll of 1,200 undergraduates conducted in 1978, many students said they suspected that "others" might question the ability of blacks. But less than 5 per cent of black undergraduates felt they had moderate to severe doubts about their own academic ability, and over 75 per cent reported no doubts whatsoever. Almost 60 per cent of white undergraduates believed that they had no such doubts about blacks, and barely 10 per cent indicated moderate or severe doubts.

Historical evidence also cuts against Murray's proposals. In 1965 most colleges and universities outside the South were following the policy that Murray advocates now; they neither discriminated against black applicants nor gave them any preference. And what were the results? A full century after the Civil War, only 2 per cent of the nation's doctors and under 2 per cent of the lawyers were black. Although *Brown* v. *Board of Education* had been decided more than a decade earlier, the proportions of black students preparing for the major professions were still abysmally low. Only slightly more than 1 per cent of the nation's law students were black, and a mere handful of blacks attended the predominantly white graduate schools of medicine and business. Little or no progress had been made in raising these proportions over the preceding generation.

Murray professes a desire to help blacks by warding off a new racism hardly less vicious than the old. If so, he should explain in detail just how his policies would work and why they would fare any better now than they did prior to 1965. It is not enough merely to draw an analogy to the experience of other ethnic groups with backgrounds and problems that differ markedly from the legacy of slavery and discrimination that black people have had to overcome. Years of experience with this model yielded little or no progress for blacks and engendered prejudices and resentments just as severe as any that have accompanied affirmative action.

Murray may respond that 1985 is not 1965, and that blacks would now apply and be admitted to universities in much larger numbers than they were twenty years ago. If this is his argument, he should recognize that the very policies he deplores played a major role in encouraging more blacks to seek a college and professional education after 1965. Since he is ultimately concerned with the feelings, attitudes, and stereotypes that result from current admissions practices, he should also explain how universities could suddenly (by his own figures) reduce black enrollments to 1.5 per cent or less in scores of selective colleges and professional schools without a devastating effect on the morale and aspirations of blacks—not to mention a strengthening of racial stereotypes on the part of many whites.

I do not mean to overlook the resentments that can arise on the part of whites who feel unjustly excluded from the school of their choice. These disappointments are real, although I wonder why there are not similar resentments against other groups of favored applicants, such as athletes and alumni offspring. I also do not condone everything that has been done in the name of preferential admissions. Some schools have undoubtedly reached too far by admitting blacks with all but insurmountable academic handicaps. Some black students have failed to apply themselves sufficiently, and others have been too quick to reject efforts to help them academically as racist and insulting. Many universities have not been persistent or imaginative enough in developing special ways of assisting blacks and others needing help to overcome deficiencies in their academic backgrounds.

Notwithstanding these defects, most universities have had clear reasons for seeking to admit black students in significant numbers—better reasons, I believe, than those Murray advances to oppose preferential admissions. In the first place, admissions officers do not feel that high scores on the SAT and other standardized tests confer a moral entitlement to admission, since such tests are only modestly correlated with subsequent academic success and give no reliable indication of achievement in later life. Instead, they believe that it is educationally enriching for blacks and whites, and important for the country as a whole, for students of all races to live and study together. Academic officials also feel that blacks will have unusual opportunities to contribute to our society in the coming generation and that higher education can play a useful role by helping them to make the most of these possibilities. Finally, educators believe that the growing numbers of black doctors, lawyers, businessmen, and other professionals will serve as examples to encourage more black youths to set higher educational and career goals for themselves.

In adopting these policies, universities have taken the long view. Academic achievement and persistence depend in some significant part on the parents' education, income, and occupation. A promising long-term strategy for helping overcome the racial handicaps of the past is to do what we can to increase the number of blacks with an education, income, and occupational background that will not only serve their own interests, but also help to instill higher educational aspirations and achievement in their children. The hoped-for results may not be fully realized for several decades, and there will be plenty of disappointments along the way. But no one should ever have supposed that we could solve in a single generation problems that were the bitter fruit of so many years of oppression and discrimination.

In the end, the vital question is not whether preferential admission is a success after fifteen years, but whether it has made more progress toward overcoming the legacy of discrimination than other strategies that universities might have pursued. On that crucial point, Murray is not convincing. The policies he advances did not work in the past, and he offers no arguments and advances no data to suggest why they would work today. Instead, he gives us his pessimistic impressions of the current situation and compares them unfavorably with his hope of what might occur in some distant, unspecified future if we but followed his prescriptions. In the face of such arguments, universities should stick by their conviction that a judicious concern for race in admitting students will eventually help to lift the arbitrary burdens that have hampered blacks in striving to achieve their goals in our society.

34. Are Quotas Good for Blacks?

By THOMAS SOWELL

Focus   Thomas Sowell is one of the leading critics of affirmative action among black intellectuals. Sowell criticizes racial preference in hiring and in university admissions, as well as the policy of compulsory busing to achieve racial balance in the public schools. It is absurd, Sowell argues, to conclude from the aggregate statistics of an ethnic group's "underrepresentation" in a given job category that racial discrimination is the root cause of the matter. Ethnic groups, he says, vary enormously in average age, education, and other factors that will greatly affect each group's participation rate in various occupations and employment categories.

Like Charles Murray, Sowell charges that affirmative action policy in university admissions produces "a systematic mismatching of minority students and the institutions they attend." "Each academic level," he says, "ends up with minority students underqualified for that level, though usually perfectly qualified for some other level." Such a situation, he concludes, can have a disastrous and permanently scarring effect upon the young people involved.

The policy of compulsory busing to achieve racial balance is portrayed by Sowell as a monumental failure that has increased interracial hostility without improving the education of black people. Its supporters are seen by Sowell as fanatical social experimenters whose crusading zeal and ego have prevented a rational assessment of the policy's costs and benefits to the actual human beings who are affected by it. Sowell concludes that racial preference policies serve to undermine black pride in achievement and to convey the message that "minorities are losers who will never have anything unless someone gives it to them." Those who advocate result-oriented policies of racial preference, he says, fail to realize that "the ultimate results are in the minds and hearts of human beings."

Thomas Sowell is the author of *The Economics and Politics of Race, Ethnic America,* and more than half-a-dozen books on economics and social policy. He is currently a senior fellow of the Hoover Institution at Stanford.

R ACE HAS NEVER BEEN an area noted for rationality of thought or action. Almost every conceivable form of nonsense has been believed about racial or ethnic groups at one time or another. Theologians used to debate whether black people had souls (today's terminology might suggest that *only* black people have souls). As late as the 1920s a leading authority on mental tests claimed that test results disproved the popular belief that Jews are intelligent. Since then, Jewish IQs have risen above the national average and more than one-fourth of all American Nobel Prize winners have been Jewish.

Today's grand fallacy about race and ethnicity is that the statistical "representation" of a group—in jobs, schools, etc.—shows and measures *discrimination*. This notion is at the center of such controversial policies as affirmative action hiring, preferential admissions to college, and school busing. But despite the fact that far-reaching judicial rulings, political crusades, and bureaucratic empires owe their existence to that belief, it remains an unexamined assumption. Tons of statistics have been collected, but only to be interpreted in the light of that assumption, never to test the assumption itself. Glaring facts to the contrary are routinely ignored. Questioning the "representation" theory is stigmatized as not only inexpedient but immoral. It is the noble lie of our time.

Affirmative Action Hiring

"Representation" or "underrepresentation" is based on comparisons of a given group's percentage in the population with its percentage in some occupation, institution, or activity. This might make sense if the various ethnic groups were even approximately similar in age distribution, education, and other crucial variables. But they are not.

Some ethnic groups are a whole decade younger than others.

Reprinted with permission of the author. This article originally appeared in *Commentary*, June 1978.

Some are two decades younger. The average age of Mexican Americans and Puerto Ricans is under twenty, while the average age of Irish Americans or Italian Americans is over thirty—and the average age of Jewish Americans is over forty. This is because of large differences in the number of children per family from one group to another. Some ethnic groups have more than twice as many children per family as others. Over half of the Mexican American and Puerto Rican population consists of teenagers, children, and infants. These two groups are likely to be underrepresented in any adult activity, whether work or recreation, whether controlled by others or entirely by themselves, and whether there is discrimination or not.

Educational contrasts are also great. More than half of all Americans over thirty-five of German, Irish, Jewish, or Oriental ancestry have completed at least four years of high school. Less than 20 per cent of all Mexican Americans in the same bracket have done so. The disparities become even greater when you consider quality of school, field of specialization, postgraduate study, and other factors that are important in the kind of high-level jobs on which special attention is focused by those emphasizing representation. Those groups with the most education—Jews and Orientals—also have the highest quality education, as measured by the rankings of the institutions from which they receive their college degrees, and specialize in the more difficult and remunerative fields, such as science and medicine. Orientals in the United States are so heavily concentrated in the scientific area that there are more Oriental scientists than there are black scientists in absolute numbers, even though the black population of the United States is more than twenty times the size of the Oriental population.

Attention has been focused most on high-level positions—the kind of jobs people reach after years of experience or education or both. There is no way to get the experience or education without also growing older in the process, so when we are talking about top-level jobs, we are talking about the kind of positions people reach in their forties and fifties rather than in their teens and twenties. Representation in such jobs cannot be compared to representation in a population that includes many five-year olds—yet it is.

The general ethnic differences in age become extreme in some of the older age brackets. Half of the Jewish population of the United States is forty-five years old or older, but only 12 per cent of the Puerto Rican population is that old. Even if Jews and Puerto Ricans were identical in every other respect, and even if no employer ever had a speck of prejudice, there would still be huge disparities between the two groups in top-level positions, just from age differences alone.

Virtually every underrepresented racial or ethnic group in the United States has a lower than average age and consists disproportionately of children and inexperienced young adults. Almost invariably these groups also have less education, both quantitatively and qualitatively. The point here is not that we should "blame the victim" or "blame society." The point is that we should, first of all, talk sense. "Representation" talk is cheap, easy, and misleading: discrimination and opportunity are too serious to be discussed in gobbledygook.

The idea that preferential treatment is going to "compensate" people for past wrongs flies in the face of two hard facts:

1. Public-opinion polls have repeatedly shown that most blacks oppose preferential treatment either in jobs or college admissions. A Gallup Poll in March 1977, for example, found only 27 per cent of nonwhites favoring "preferential treatment" over "ability as determined by test scores," while 64 per cent preferred the latter and 9 per cent were undecided. (The Gallup breakdown of the U.S. population by race, sex, income, and education, found that "not a single population group supports affirmative action.")

How can you compensate people by giving them something they have explicitly rejected?

2. The income of blacks relative to whites reached its peak *before* affirmative action hiring and has *declined* since. The median income of blacks reached a peak of 60.9 per cent of the median income of whites in 1970—the year before "goals" and "timetables" became part of the affirmative action concept. "In

only one year of the last six years," writes Andrew Brimmer, "has the proportion been as high as 60 percent."[1]

Before something can be a "compensation," it must first be a benefit.

The repudiation of the numerical or preferential approach by the very people it is supposed to benefit points out the large gap between illusion and reality that is characteristic of affirmative action. So does the cold fact that there are few, if any, benefits to offset all the bitterness generated by this heavy-handed program. The bitterness is largely a result of a deeply resented principle, galling bureaucratic processes, and individual horror stories. Overall, the program has changed little for minorities or women. Supporters of the program try to cover up its ineffectiveness by comparing the position of minorities today with their position many years ago. This ignores all the progress that took place under straight equal-treatment laws in the 1960s—progress that has not continued anywhere near the same pace under affirmative action.

Among the reasons for such disappointing results is that hiring someone to fill a quota gets the government off the employer's back for the moment, but buys more trouble down the road whenever a disgruntled employee chooses to go to an administrative agency or a court with a complaint based on nothing but numbers. Regardless of the merits, or the end result, a very costly process for the employer must be endured, and the threat of this is an incentive *not* to hire from the groups designated as special by the government. The affirmative action program has meant mutually canceling incentives to hire and not to hire— and great bitterness and cost from the process, either way.

If blacks are opposed to preferential treatment and whites are opposed to it, who then is in favor of it, and how does it go on? The implications of these questions are even more far-reaching and more disturbing than the policy itself. They show how vulnerable our democratic and constitutional safeguards are to a relative handful of determined people. Some of those people promoting preferential treatment and numerical goals are so convinced of the rightness of what they are doing that they are prepared to sacrifice whatever needs to be sacrificed—whether it be other people, the law, or simple honesty in discussing what they are doing (note "goals," "desegregation," and similar euphemisms). Other supporters cf numerical policies have the powerful drive of self-interest as well as self-righteousness. Bureaucratic empires have grown up to administer these programs, reaching into virtually every business, school, hospital, or other organization. The rulers and agents of this empire can order employers around, make college presidents bow and scrape, assign schoolteachers by race, or otherwise gain power, publicity, and career advancement—regardless of whether minorities are benefited.

While self-righteousness and self-interest are powerful drives for those who have them, they can succeed only insofar as other people can be persuaded, swept along by feelings, or neutralized. Rhetoric has accomplished this with images of historic wrongs, visions of social atonement, and a horror of being classed with bigots. The tactics have worked best with those most affected by words and least required to pay a price personally: nonelected judges, the media, and the intellectual establishment.

The "color-blind" words of the Civil Rights Act of 1964, and even the protections of the Constitution, mean little when judges can creatively reinterpret them out of existence. It is hard to achieve the goal of an informed public when the mass media show only selective indignation about power grabs and a sense of pious virtue in covering up the failures of school integration. Even civil libertarians—who insist that the Fifth Amendment protection against self-incrimination is a sacred right that cannot be denied Nazis, Communists, or criminals—show no concern when the government routinely forces employers to confess "deficiencies" in their hiring processes, without a speck of evidence other than a numerical pattern different from the government's preconception.

Preferential Admissions

Preferential admissions to college and universities are "justified" by similar rhetoric and the similar assumption that statistical underrepresentation means institutional exclusion. Sometimes this assumption is buttressed by notions of "compensation" and a theory that (1) black communities need more black practitioners in various fields; and that (2) black students will ultimately supply that need. The idea that the black community's doctors, lawyers, etc., should be black is an idea held by white liberals, but no such demand has come from the black community, which has rejected preferential admissions in poll after poll. Moreover, the idea that an admissions committee can predict what a youth is going to do with his life years later is even more incredible—even if the youth is one's own son or daughter, much less someone from a wholly different background.

These moral or ideological reasons for special minority programs are by no means the whole story. The public image of a college or university is often its chief financial asset. Bending a few rules here and there to get the right body count of minority students seems a small price to pay for maintaining an image that will keep money coming in from the government and the foundations. When a few thousand dollars in financial aid to students can keep millions of tax dollars rolling in, it is clearly a profitable investment for the institution. For the young people brought in under false pretense, it can turn out to be a disastrous and permanently scarring experience.

The most urgent concern over image and over government subsidies, foundation grants, and other donations is at those institutions that have the most to maintain—that is, at prestigious colleges and universities at the top of the academic pecking order. The Ivy League schools and the leading state institutions have the scholarship money and the brand-name visibility to draw in enough minority youngsters to look good statistically. The extremely high admissions standards of these institutions usually cannot be met by the minority students—just as most students in general cannot meet them. But in order to have a certain minority body count, the schools bend (or disregard) their usual standards. The net result is that thousands of minority students who would normally qualify for good nonprestigious colleges where they could succeed, are instead enrolled in famous institutions where they fail. For example, at Cornell

University during the guns-on-campus crisis, fully half of the black students were on academic probation, despite easier grading standards for them in many courses. Yet these students were by no means unqualified. Their average test scores put them in the top quarter of all American college students—but the other Cornell students ranked in the top 1 per cent. In other words, minority students with every prospect of success in a normal college environment were artificially turned into failures by being mismatched with an institution with standards too severe for them.

When the top institutions reach further down to get minority students, then academic institutions at the next level are forced to reach still further down, so that they too will end up with a minority body count high enough to escape criticism and avoid trouble with the government and other donors. Each academic level, therefore, ends up with minority students underqualified for that level, though usually perfectly qualified for some other level. The end result is a systematic mismatching of minority students and the institutions they attend, even though the wide range of American colleges and universities is easily capable of accommodating those same students under their normal standards.

Proponents of "special" (lower) admissions standards argue that without such standards no increase in minority enrollment would have been possible. But this blithely disregards the fact that when more *money* is available to finance college, more low-income people go to college. The GI Bill after World War II caused an even more dramatic increase in the number of people going to college who could never have gone otherwise—and without lowering admissions standards. The growth of special minority programs in recent times has meant both a greater availability of money and lower admissions standards for black and other designated students. It is as ridiculous to ignore the role of money in increasing the numbers of minority students in the system as a whole as it is to ignore the effect of double standards on their maldistribution among institutions. It is the double standards that are the problem, and they can be ended without driving minority students out of the system. Of course, many academic hustlers who administer special programs might lose their jobs, but that would hardly be a loss to anyone else.

As long as admission to colleges and universities is not unlimited, someone's opportunity to attend has to be sacrificed as the price of preferential admission for others. No amount of verbal sleight of hand can get around this fact. None of those sacrificed is old enough to have had anything to do with historic injustices that are supposedly being compensated. Moreover, it is not the offspring of the privileged who are likely to pay the price. It is not a Rockefeller or a Kennedy who will be dropped to make room for quotas; it is a De Funis or a Bakke. Even aside from personal influence on admissions decisions, the rich can give their children the kind of private schooling that will virtually assure them test scores far above the cutoff level at which sacrifices are made.

Just as the students who are sacrificed are likely to come from the bottom of the white distribution, so the minority students chosen are likely to be from the top of the minority distribution. In short, it is a forced transfer of benefits from those least able to afford it to those least in need of it. In some cases, the loose term "minority" is used to include individuals who are personally from more fortunate backgrounds than the average American. Sometimes it includes whole groups, such as Chinese or Japanese Americans, who have higher incomes than whites. One-fourth of all employed Chinese in this country are in professional occupations—nearly double the national average. No amount of favoritism to the son or daughter of a Chinese doctor or mathematician today is going to compensate some Chinese of the past who was excluded from virtually every kind of work except washing clothes or washing dishes.

The past is a great unchangeable fact. Nothing is going to undo its sufferings and injustices, whatever their magnitude. Statistical categories and historic labels may seem real to those inspired by words, but only living people can feel joy or pain. Neither the sins nor the sufferings of those now dead are within our power to change. Being honest and honorable with the people living in our own time is more than enough moral challenge, without indulging in illusions about rewriting moral history with numbers and categories.

School Busing

It is chilling to hear parents say that the worst racists they know are their own children. Yet such statements have been made by black and white parents, liberals and conservatives, and without regard to geographical location. It is commonplace to hear of integrated schools where no child of either race would dare to enter a toilet alone. The fears and hatreds of these schoolchildren are going to be part of the American psyche long after the passing of an older generation of crusading social experimenters. It is quite a legacy to leave.

The ringing principles of equal rights announced in the 1954 Supreme Court decision in *Brown* v. *Board of Education* have been transformed by twenty years of political and judicial jockeying into a nightmarish pursuit of elusive statistical "balance." The original idea that the government should not classify children by race was turned around completely to mean that the government must classify children by race. The fact that the racial integration of youngsters from similar backgrounds has worked under voluntary conditions was seized upon as a reason for forcing statistical integration of schoolchildren, without regard to vast contrasts of income, way of life, or cultural values. Considerations of cost, time, feelings, or education all give way before the almighty numbers. As more and more evidence of negative consequences to the children has piled up, the original notion that this was going to benefit somebody has given way to the idea that "the law of the land" has to be carried out, even if the skies fall. Less grandly, it means that judges cannot back off from the can of worms they have opened, without admitting that they have made asses of themselves.

The civil rights establishment has a similar investment of ego and self-interest to protect. The NAACP Legal Defense Fund now insists that the issue is not "education" but "constitutional." This might be an understandable position for an academic association of legal theorists, but not for an organization claiming to speak in the name of black people—people who reject busing in nationwide polls and who reject it by large majorities in cities where it has been tried. The head of the NAACP Legal Defense Fund brushes this aside by saying that they cannot ask "each and every black person" his opinion before proceeding, but the real question is whether they can consistently go counter to the majority opinions of the very people in whose name they presume to speak.

The tragic Boston busing case shows all these institutional ego forces at work. Local black organizations urged Judge Garrity *not* to bus their children to South Boston, where educational standards were notoriously low and racial hostility notoriously high. Both the NAACP and the judge proceeded anyway. Black children were forced to run a gauntlet of violence and insults for the greater glory of institutional grand designs. In Detroit, Atlanta, and San Francisco the NAACP also opposed local blacks on busing—including local chapters of its own organization in the last two cities. The supreme irony is that Linda Brown, of *Brown* v. *Board of Education*, has now gone into court to try to keep her children from being bused.

That "a small band of willful men" could inflict this on two races opposed to it is a sobering commentary on the fragility of democracy. Moreover, what is involved is not merely mistaken zealotry. What is involved is an organization fueled by money from affluent liberals whose own children are safely tucked away in private schools, and a crusade begun by men like Thurgood Marshall and Kenneth B. Clark whose own children were also in private schools away from the storms they created for others. The very real educational problems of black children, and the early hopes that desegregation would solve them, provided the impetus and the support for a crusade that has now degenerated into a numerical fetish and a judicial unwillingness to lose face. What actually happens to black children, or white children, has been openly relegated to a secondary consideration in principle, and less than that in practice.

The 1954 *Brown* decision did not limit itself to ruling that it is unconstitutional for a state to segregate by race. It brought in sociological speculation that separate schools are inherently inferior. Yet within walking distance of the Supreme Court was an all-black high school whose eighty-year history would have refuted that assumption—if anyone had been interested in facts. As far back as 1939, the average IQ at Dunbar High School was 11 per cent above the national average—fifteen years before the Court declared this impossible. The counsel for the NAACP in that very case came from a similar quality all-black school in Baltimore. There are, and have been, other schools around the country where black children learned quite well without white children (or teachers) around, as well as other schools where each race failed to learn, with or without the presence of the other. The most cursory look at the history of all-Jewish or all-Oriental schools would have reduced the separate-is-inferior doctrine to a laughingstock instead of the revered "law of the land."

The Court's excursion into sociology came back to haunt it. When the end of state-enforced segregation did not produce any dramatic change in the racial makeup of neighborhood schools, or any of the educational benefits anticipated, the civil rights establishment pushed on for more desegregation—now stretched to mean statistical balance, opposition to ability grouping, and even the hiring and assignment of teachers by race. If the magic policy of integration had not worked, it could only be because there had not yet been enough of it! Meanwhile, the real problems of educating real children were lost in the shuffle.

However futile the various numerical approaches have been in their avowed goal of advancing minorities, their impact has been strongly felt in other ways. The message that comes through loud and clear is that minorities are losers who will never have anything unless someone gives it to them. The destructiveness of this message—on society in general and minority youth in particular—outweighs any trivial gains that may occur here and there. The falseness of the message is shown by the great economic achievements of minorities during the period of equal rights legislation before numerical goals and timetables muddied the waters. By and large, the numerical approach has achieved nothing, and has achieved it at great cost.

Compassion As Contempt

Underlying the attempt to move people around and treat them like chess pieces on a board is a profound contempt for other

human beings. To ignore or resent people's resistance—on behalf of their children or their livelihoods—is to deny our common
humanity. To persist dogmatically in pursuit of some abstract
goal, without regard to how it is reached, is to despise freedom
and reduce three-dimensional life to cardboard pictures of numerical results. The false practicality of results-oriented people
ignores the fact that the ultimate results are in the minds and
hearts of human beings. Once personal choice becomes a mere
inconvenience to be brushed aside by bureaucrats or judges,
something precious will have been lost by all people from all
backgrounds.

A multi-ethnic society like the United States can ill-afford
continually to build up stores of inter-group resentments about
such powerful concerns as one's livelihood and one's children.
It is a special madness when tensions are escalated between
groups who are basically in accord in their opposition to numbers games, but whose legal establishments and "spokesmen"
keep the fires fueled. We must never think that the disintegration
and disaster that has hit other multi-ethnic societies cannot
happen here. The mass internment of Japanese Americans just
a generation ago is a sobering reminder of the tragic idiocy that
stress can bring on. We are not made of different clay from the
Germans, who were historically more enlightened and humane
toward Jews than many other Europeans—until the generation
of Hitler and the Holocaust.

The situation in America today is, of course, not like that of
the Pearl Harbor period, nor of the Weimar Republic. History
does not literally repeat, but it can warn us of what people are
capable of, when the stage has been set for tragedy. We certainly
do not need to let emotionally combustible materials accumulate
from ill-conceived social experiments.

35. *Affirmative Action That Hurts Blacks*

By WILLIAM RASPBERRY

Focus Most of the major law schools in America publish scholarly legal journals known as "law reviews," which are staffed by a highly select group of people chosen from among each school's most outstanding third-year law students. To be appointed to the law review staff is generally considered a great honor, and the academic competition to become a law review member is often quite fierce. William Raspberry describes with considerable dismay the decision of the University of Virginia Law School to institute a special affirmative action path to law review membership. The university, as he describes, made the decision because of its embarassment over the fact that no black student had ever, in the history of the law school, made law review. But as Raspberry explains, one black student was already in the final stages of law review competition at the time the new policy was instituted, and together with two other black students, appears to have been on her way to making law review "in head-to-head competition with whites." Although Raspberry supports preferential treatment policies in certain other contexts, he sees the law school's affirmative action program as undermining the value of law review membership for black students and hurting most of all those black students who would have made law review on their own academic merit.

Raspberry does not offer any explanation for why no black student had ever made law review at Virginia, though there may be operating here the skimming process that Charles Murray (selection 32) and Thomas Sowell (selection 34) describe. The top quality black law students who otherwise would have made law review at Virginia—or at least had a good chance of doing so—have been siphoned off by the preferential admissions policies at Harvard, Yale, and Stanford law schools. Similarly Virginia, through its own preferential admissions policies, siphons off black law students who would have had a good chance of making law review at law schools less selective than Virginia. Law schools and many other professional schools, however, differ from undergraduate schools in that many of the black and Hispanic students in the lowest–ranking institutions would not have gotten into a professional school at all in the absence of preferential admissions policies. (See the articles by Derek Bok, Richard Sobol, and Ronald Dworkin, selections 33, 12, and 13.)

William Raspberry is a syndicated columnist for the *Washington Post*.

I FEEL SORRY FOR Dayna Bowen Matthew, the first black student to gain admission to the University of Virginia Law Review, and sorrier still for those blacks who will follow her in the next few years.

Matthew, a third-year law student from New York, apparently was on her way to winning a spot on the scholarly journal in head-to-head competition with whites. Two other black students appear to have been on their way to joining her. But the honor came a little late: the university, embarrassed by the fact that no black had made Law Review in the law school's history, has adopted a new affirmative action scheme designed specifically to bring in blacks.

Said Matthew: "Affirmative action was a way to dilute our personal victory. It took the victory out of our hands. I see this well-intentioned, liberal-white-student affirmative action plan as an intrusion."

Until the new plan, adopted 52-to-12 by Law Review members, there were two anonymous ways to make the Law Review. One was by grades. Students with the top scholastic averages received automatic invitations. The other was by writing. Any law student could enter a writing competition, with those whose work was deemed outstanding accepted on the Law Review.

The third method, the one that has left Matthew with such a bittersweet victory, evaluates students on the basis of "personal statements" on how their presence would increase the diversity of the Law Review on the basis of race, national origin, cultural background, experience, or physical handicap.

The review traditionally chooses about twenty-five members on the basis of grades and another fifteen on the basis of the writing competition. Under the affirmative action plan adopted this month, up to five more will be chosen.

Since Matthew and two other black students had passed the first phase of the two-phase writing competition before the new rule went into effect, they can console themselves that they would have made it without special concession. But the blacks who follow them, particularly those who write their way on, will always wonder how they might have fared in open competition. And more to the point, so will the firms to which they later apply for jobs.

The key advantage of making Law Review is that it sets law graduates apart as unusually bright. The more prestigious law firms regularly give extra consideration to applicants who made Law Review during their law school years, and many will not even consider non-Law Review applicants unless they have something special—family, for instance—to set them apart.

The glaring danger of the new plan is that it will cast doubt on the true qualifications of all blacks who make Law Review, no matter how qualified they may in fact be.

As a friend who has spent most of her life in academic circles noted: "All the awkwardness could have been avoided simply by voiding the requirement for anonymity in the original competition. Those who make the selection could then select top black students, at their discretion, without having to admit that they have been given a certain preferential treatment."

The reference is to the system, now used by almost all law schools (and bar review boards), that uses number rather than names to identify test papers. The idea is to guard against racists who, if they are able to identify a test-taker as black, will automatically downgrade the score.

Says my friend: "However true this may have been at some time and in some places (although in such places no black students would have been enrolled in the first place), nowadays preserving this anonymity works directly against black students. Efforts to give them every break, to make every allowance for them are stymied if nobody can identify them."

"I've lived in, or very close to, academe all my life, and I can remember the extra encouragement always offered to black students, and the teachers' pleasure when these students did well, and I know they were always given every break."

There are blacks who will roundly deny this special treatment, convinced that white faculty are not merely against them but are somehow able to crack the code and find out who they are.

But is it any solution to award extra merit on the basis of ethnicity or, for heaven's sake, physical handicap?

The likely results of the Virginia plan are 1) to reduce the value of Law Review, particularly for minorities, and 2) to penalize those minorities who would have made it on their own.

As Dayna Matthew put it: "I feel it's hurt us more than helped us."

36. Beyond Civil Rights

By GLENN C. LOURY

Focus
Glenn Loury contends that many of the problems besetting the black community are not amenable to antidiscrimination laws or civil rights strategies, and that thinking they are can have harmful effects. "The tendency to perceive every instance of differential performance between racial groups as remediable by some affirmative action-like treatment," he says, "may, if successfully continued, destroy the possibility of attaining 'real' equality of status for black Americans." Racial quotas, Loury contends, undermine black self-esteem and put even the best and highest achieving blacks "in the position of being the supplicants of benevolent whites." When employers institute policies of racial preference, a situation is created, Loury explains, in which it is a rational strategy for customers and co-workers to assume—in the absence of information to the contrary—that blacks are inferior in their level of performance. What black people ultimately seek, Loury says, is honor, self-respect, and the respect of their fellow Americans. The achievement of this goal is undermined, he believes, by any permanent policy of racial preference. Only the unaided accomplishments of individual black people, Loury holds, can produce the self-respect that black people desire.

Glenn C. Loury is a professor of political econ-

435

omy at the John F. Kennedy School of Government at Harvard University.

M Y THEME WILL BE the limitations of civil rights strategies for effectively promoting the economic and social progress of minorities. By a "civil rights strategy" I mean two things: first, that the cause of a particular socioeconomic disparity be identified as racial discrimination; and second, that the advocates seek such remedies for the disparity as the courts and administrative agencies provide under the law. It has by now become a common theme in commentary on racial inequality in American society to observe that not all problems of blacks are due to discrimination, nor can they be remedied via civil rights or, more broadly, through racial politics.

More than this, however, I want to suggest that the inappropriate specification of a particular obstacle to minority progress as a civil rights matter can have significant costs. Evoking civil rights remedies for circumstances to which they are not suited can obviate the pursuit of alternative, more direct, and effective approaches to the problem. Such activity uses scarce resources that might otherwise be applied—the time and attention of those engaged directly in the advocacy, but also the goodwill and tolerance of those expected to respond. Finally, I will argue that the broad application of the civil rights method to every instance of differential achievement by blacks can be positively harmful in attaining the long-sought goal of fully equal status in the society, and threatens, if continued successfully, to make it literally impossible for blacks to be genuinely equal in American society.

I continue to believe there is an important role for civil rights law enforcement, and for those organizations that have played such a crucial part in the historic struggle for civil rights in this country. I do not believe racism has disappeared from American

This article, which was presented as an address before the National Urban League, was originally published in *The State of Black America 1986* (National Urban League, January 23, 1986). A somewhat shorter version of it appeared in the *New Republic* (October 7, 1985). Reprinted with permission of the author.

life, nor that appeals to conscience, based upon the history of injustice to which blacks have been subject, no longer have a place in our public life. Yet, it is obvious, given the American political and philosophical tradition, that the reach of civil rights law is and will remain insufficient to eliminate all socially and economically relevant discriminatory behavior. In light of this fact (to be elaborated below), it is important for blacks to augment this historically important approach to the problem of racial inequality.

There are enormously important contractual relationships into which people enter, as a result of which their social and economic status is profoundly affected, but among which racial discrimination is routinely practiced. Choice of marital partner is the most obvious. People discriminate here by race with a vengeance. A black woman does not have an opportunity equal to that of a white woman to become the wife of a given white man. Indeed, though this inequality in opportunity cuts both ways, since white men are on the whole better off financially than black men, one could imagine calculating the monetary cost to black women as a class of the fact that white men engage in discrimination of this sort. A class action suit might be filed on their behalf, seeking redress for the "damages" that result. Yet, of course, this is absurd. In large part, its absurdity derives from our acceptance, *in principle* as well as in fact, of an individual's right to engage in discrimination of this sort.

The point is of much more general applicability. Voluntary associations among individuals of all sorts (residential communities, friendship networks, business partnerships) are the result of mutual choices often influenced by racial criteria, but that lie beyond the reach of civil rights laws. A fair-housing law cannot prevent a disgruntled resident from moving away if the racial composition of his neighborhood changes. Busing for school desegregation cannot prevent unhappy parents from sending their children to private schools. Withdrawal of university support for student clubs with discriminatory selection rules cannot prevent student cliques from forming along racial lines. Application of the nondiscrimination mandate has, in practice, been restricted to the domain of impersonal, public, and economic transactions (employment, credit, housing, voting rights), but has not been allowed to interfere much with personal, private, and intimately social intercourse.

Yet, the fact that such exclusive social "clubs" do form along group lines has important economic consequences. An extensive literature in economics and sociology documents the importance of family and community background as factors influencing a child's latter life success. Studies have shown that access to the right "networks" can beneficially affect the outcome of job search in the labor market. Indeed, it has been theoretically demonstrated that, under plausible assumptions, when social background influences offspring's opportunities to acquire human capital, and when two groups of equal innate capabilities start with unequal economic status, then elimination of racial discrimination in the economic sphere but not in patterns of social attachment is generally insufficient to bring about eventual equalization of economic outcomes. There are, thus, elemental limits on the degree of economic equality between the races that one can hope to achieve through the use of civil rights laws. These limits derive from the fact that the antidiscrimination principle has been, as a matter of historical fact, restricted in its application to a limited domain of personal interactions.

Moreover, it is possible to question the ability of civil rights strategies to reduce group disparities in those areas to which they have been freely applied—education and employment, for example. Elsewhere I have argued that some important part of group economic disparity is due to the nature of social life *within* poor black communities.

With upward of three-fourths of children born out-of-wedlock in some inner-city ghettos, with black high school drop-out rates of better than 40 per cent (measured as the fraction of entering freshmen who do not eventually graduate) in Chicago and Detroit, with 40 per cent of murder victims in the country being blacks killed by other blacks, with fewer black women graduating from college than giving birth while in high school, with black women ages fifteen to nineteen being the most fertile population of that age group in the industrialized world, with better than two in five black children dependent on public assistance, and with these phenomena continuing apace notwith-standing two decades of civil rights efforts—it is reasonably clear that civil rights strategies alone cannot hope to bring about full equality. This is not to deny that, in some basic sense, most of these difficulties are related to our history of racial oppression. I only suggest (as, for example, Eleanor Holmes Norton has argued that they have by now taken on a life of their own, and cannot be effectively reversed by civil rights policies.

Education

Further illustration of this point is provided by reference to the field of higher education. In the past (and not-too-distant past at that), there were severely limited opportunities for minorities to participate in higher education, as student or faculty, especially at the elite institutions. Nonetheless, many distinguished black scholars, scientists, inventors, jurists, writers and teachers had overcome the obstacles of racism to contribute to the common intellectual life of their country. Yet, in decades past, these men and women of genius learned and practiced their academic crafts under the most difficult conditions. Even after black scholars studied at the great institutions, their only possibilities for employment were at the historically black colleges, where they faced large teaching loads and burdensome administrative duties. Their accomplishments were often acknowledged by their white peers only grudgingly, if at all.

Today, opportunities for advanced education and academic careers for blacks abound. Major universities throughout the country are constantly searching for qualified black candidates to hire as professors, or admit to study. Most state colleges and universities near black population centers have made a concerted effort to reach those in the inner-city. Almost all institutions of higher learning admit blacks with lower grades or test scores than white students. There are special programs funded by private foundations to help blacks prepare for advanced study in medicine, economics, engineering, public policy, law, and other fields. Special scholarship and fellowship funds have been set up for black students throughout the country.

Yet, with all these opportunities, and despite some improvement, the number of blacks advancing in the academic world is distressingly low. The percentage of college students who are black, after rising throughout the 1970s, has actually begun to decline. And while the proportion of doctorate degrees granted to blacks has risen slightly over the last decade, it is still the case that the majority of doctorate degrees that blacks earn are in the field of education. Despite constant pressure to hire black professors and strenuous efforts to recruit them, the percentages of blacks on elite university faculties has remained constant or fallen in the past decade.

Meanwhile, other groups traditionally excluded are making impressive gains. Asian Americans though less than 2 per cent of the population, make up 6.6 per cent of U.S. scientists with doctorate degrees; they constitute 8 per cent of the student body at Harvard, 7.5 per cent at Yale, and 9 per cent at Stanford. Women have also made progress the fraction of doctorate degrees going to women has risen from less than one-seventh to nearly one-third in the last decade. At Harvard's graduate school less than 3 per cent of the students are black, but more than 30 per cent are women. Less than 2 per cent of Harvard professors at all ranks are black, but more than 25 per cent are women.

No doubt, blacks continue to experience some discrimination at these institutions. But it is not a credible assertion to anyone who has spent time in an elite university community that these institutions are racist in character, and deny opportunities to blacks whose qualifications are outstanding. A case could be made that just the opposite is true—that these institutions are so anxious to raise the numbers of blacks in their ranks that they overlook deficiencies when making admissions or appointment decisions involving blacks. But for my purpose it only need be accepted that this state of affairs, in which black representation languishes at what, for many campus communities are politically unacceptable levels, does not admit a viable civil-rights oriented solution. It would be very difficult to make the case that, upon finding and eliminating the racially discriminatory behavior of faculty and administrators, this circumstance would reverse itself.

One obvious reason for skepticism about the efficacy of a civil rights strategy here would seem to be the relatively poor academic performance of black high school and college students. Black performance on standardized college admissions tests, though improving, still lags far behind whites. In 1982, on the mathematics component of the Scholastic Aptitude Test (SAT), the median white score was 484, while the median black score was 369. There were only 205 blacks in the entire country who scored above 700, though 3,015 Asian Americans achieved this distinction. And, as Robert Klitgaard has shown convincingly, postadmission college performance by black students is less than that of whites, even when controlling for differences in high school grades and SAT scores.

These differences in academic performance are not just limited to poor blacks, or to high school students. On the SAT exam mentioned earlier, blacks from families with income in excess of $50,000 per year still scored 60 to 80 points below comparable whites. On the 1981 Graduate Record Exam, taken by virtually all college seniors seeking to pursue advanced studies in the humanities and sciences, the gap between black and white students median score on the quantitative mathematics component of this test was 171 points. At Harvard College there is a significant and disturbing difference in the grades earned by black and white students. According to professors at the Harvard Law School there have only been a few black students graduated in the top half of their class in the last five years. Klitgaard found that black law school admittees in the late 1970s had median scores on the Law School Admissions Test at the eighth percentile of the overall distribution of scores among law students.

It is clearly a matter of great concern that such substantial differences in educational results exist. One imagines that social background and limited past opportunities for blacks play an important role in accounting for these test score differences. It is also possible that the psychological effects on blacks of the "rumors of inferiority," which have circulated in American society about the intellectual capabilities of black people, partly explain this disparity. Arguably, the government should be actively engaged in seeking to attenuate them. But it seems equally clear that this is not a civil rights matter—that it cannot be reversed by seeking out and changing someone's discriminatory behavior. Moreover, it is possible that great harm will be done if the problem is defined and pursued in those terms. This is illustrated by the example of a recent controversy over racial quotas at the Boston Latin School.

The Boston Latin School is the pride and joy of the city's public school system. It was founded before Harvard, in 1635. It has been recognized for centuries as a center of academic excellence. Boston Latin maintains its very high standards through a grueling program of study, including Latin, Greek, calculus, history, science, and the arts. Three hours of homework per night is typical. College admissions personnel acknowledge the excellence of this program. Ninety-five percent of the class of 1985 will go to college: Harvard has accepted twenty-two Latin graduates for next year's freshman class.

The institution admits its students on the basis of their primary school marks, and performance on the Secondary School Admissions Test. In 1974, when Boston's public schools became subject to court-ordered desegregation, Judge Arthur Garrity considered closing Boston Latin, because at that time the student population had been more than 90 per cent white. Upon consideration though, it was ordered that a racial admissions quota be employed requiring 35 per cent of the entering classes to be black and Hispanic. Of the 2245 students [in 1984], over half were female, 57 per cent white, 23 per cent black, 14 per cent Asian, and 6 per cent Hispanic.

Historically the school has maintained standards through a policy of academic "survival of the fittest." Those who were unable to make it through the academic rigors simply transferred to another school. Thus, there has always been a high rate of attrition; it is now in the range of 30–40 per cent. But, unlike the pre-desegregation era, today most of those who do not succeed at Boston Latin are minority students. Indeed, though approximately 35 per cent of each entering class is black and Hispanic, only 16 per cent of last year's senior class was. That is, for each (non-Asian) minority student who graduates from Latin, there is one who did not. The failure rate for whites is about half as great. Some advocates of minority student interest have, in the face of this racial disparity, complained of discrimination, saying in effect that the school is not doing enough to assist those in academic difficulty. Yet there is reason to doubt the effectiveness of this "civil rights strategy." Surely one reason for the poor performance of the black and Hispanic students if the racial admissions quota ordered by Judge Garrity a decade ago. To be considered for admissions, whites must score at the seventieth percentile or higher on the admission exam, while blacks and Hispanics need only score above the fiftieth percentile. But the problems of minority students at Boston Latin have not prevented some from advocating that the minority admissions quota be increased.

Attorney Thomas Atkins, former general counsel of the NAACP, who has been representing the black plaintiffs in this law suit off and on for ten years, proposed to Judge Garrity in the spring of 1985 that the quota at Boston Latin be raised to roughly 50 per cent black, 20 per cent Hispanic and Asian, and 30 per cent white—a reflection of the racial composition of the rest of Boston's public schools. Absent a significant increase in the size of the school, this could only be accomplished by doubling the number of blacks admitted while cutting white enrollment in half. This in turn, under plausible statistical assumptions, would require an approximate doubling of the now twenty-point gap in threshold test scores of black and white admittees. Since the additional black students admitted would of necessity be less prepared than those admitted under the current quota, one would expect an even higher failure rate among minorities, were this plan to be accepted. The likely consequence would be that more than three-fourths of those leaving Boston Latin without a degree would be blacks and Hispanics. It is also plausible to infer that such an action would profoundly alter, if not destroy, the academic climate in the school.

This is not simply an inappropriate use of civil rights methods, though it is surely that. We have here an almost wanton surrender of the moral high ground by an advocate who would seek remedy from a federal judge for the failure of Boston's black students to excel. By what logic of pedagogy can these students' difficulty be attributed to racism in view of the fact that the school system has been run by court order for over a decade? By what calculus of fairness do those fighting for justice arrive at the position that outstanding white students, many from poor homes themselves (80 per cent of Latin graduates require financial aid in college) should be denied the opportunity for this special education so that minority students who are not prepared for it may nonetheless enroll? Responding to black student underrepresentation at Boston Latin as if this were a civil rights problem seems patently unwise. Is there so little faith in the aptitude of the minority young people that the highest standards should not be held out for them? Are their advocates so vindictive about the past that they would risk injuring their own children and inflict gross unfairness on the children of others all in the name of numerical racial balance?

Another example from the field of education illustrates how the use of civil rights methods, when not appropriate to the problem at hand, can have significant "opportunity costs." In 1977 the Ann Arbor public school system was sued by representatives of a class of black parents with children in the primary grades. The school system was accused of denying equal educational opportunity to these children. The problem was that the black students were not learning how to read at an acceptable rate, though the white youngsters were. The suit alleged that, by failing to take into account in the teaching of reading to these children the fact that they spoke an identifiable, distinct dialect of the English language—black English—the black students were denied equal educational opportunity. The lawsuit was successful.

As a result, in 1979 the court ordered that reading teachers in Ann Arbor be given special "sensitivity" training so that, while teaching standard English to these children, they might "accommodate" the youngsters' culturally distinct patterns of speech. Ann Arbor's public school system has dutifully complied. A recent discussion of this case with local educators revealed that, as of six years after the initial court order, the disparity in reading achievement between blacks and whites in Ann Arbor persists at a level comparable to that which obtained before the lawsuit was brought. It was their opinion that, though of enormous symbolic importance, the entire process had produced little in the way of positive educational impact on the students.

This is not intended as a condemnation of those who brought the suit, nor do I offer here any opinion on whether promotion of black English is a good idea. What is of interest is the process by which the problem was defined, and out of which a remedy was sought. In effect, the parents of these children were approached by public-interest lawyers and educators active in civil rights, and urged to help their children learn to read by bringing this action. Literally thousands of hours went into conceiving and trying this case. Yet, in the end only a hollow, symbolic victory was won. Apparently, the federal district judge did not have it within his power to eliminate the disparity between black and white children in rates at which reading competency was acquired.

But it is possible that, more than simply ineffective, this line of attack on the problem and the advocative instincts from which it sprang caused other viable strategies not to be pursued. One imagines for example that a direct effort to tutor the first and second graders might have made an impact, giving them special attention and extra hours of study through the voluntary participation of those in Ann Arbor possessed of the relevant skills. With roughly 35,000 students at the University of Michigan's Ann Arbor campus (a fair number of whom are black), it would have required that only a fraction of 1 per cent of them spare an afternoon or evening once a week for there to be sufficient numbers to provide the needed services. There were at most only a few hundred poor black students in the primary grades experiencing reading difficulties. And, more than providing this needed aid for specific kids, such an undertaking would have helped to cultivate a more healthy relationship between the university and its community. It could have contributed to building a tradition of direct service that would be of more general value. But none of this happened, in part because the "civil rights approach" was almost reflexively embraced by the parties concerned.

Affirmative Action

Indeed, there is a reason to be concerned that the tendency to perceive every instance of differential performance between racial groups as remediable by some affirmative action-like treatment may, if successfully continued, destroy the possibility of attaining "real" equality of status for black Americans.

The simplest version of this argument is by now very familiar—affirmative action creates uncertain perceptions about the qualifications of those minorities who benefit from it. If, in an employment situation say, it is known that differential selection criteria are used for different races, and if it is further known that the quality of performance on the job depends on how one did on the criteria of selection, then in the absence of other information it is a rational statistical inference to impute a lower perceived quality of performance to persons of the race that was preferentially favored in selection. Using race as a criterion of selection in employment, in other words, creates objective incentives for customers, co-workers, etc., to take race into account after the employment decision has been made.

More than this, however, the broad use of race preference to treat all instances of "underrepresentation" introduces uncertainty into the process by which individuals make inferences about their own abilities. A frequently encountered question today from a black man or woman promoted to a position of unusual responsibility in a "mainstream" institution is: "Would I have been offered this position if I had not been a black?" Most people in such situations want to be reassured that their achievement has been earned, and is not based simply on the organizational requirement of racial diversity. As a result, the use of racial preference tends to undermine the ability of people to confidently assert, if only to themselves, that they are as good as their achievements would seem to suggest.

It therefore undermines the extent to which the personal success of one black can become the basis of guiding the behavior of other blacks. Fewer individuals in a group subject to such preferences can confidently say to their fellows: "I made it on my own, through hard work, self-application, and native ability, and so can you!" And, disturbingly, the broad use of affirmative action as a vehicle for black achievement puts even the "best and brightest" of the favored group in the position of being the supplicants of benevolent whites.

But this is not the end of the story. Because in order to defend such programs in the political arena—especially at the elite institutions—it becomes necessary to argue that almost no blacks could reach these heights without special favors. This, when examined closely, entails the virtual admission that blacks are unable to perform up to the white standard. Thus, Harvard University president Derek Bok—arguing in defense of black interests, he thinks—has publicly declared that, without the use of quotas in undergraduate admissions, only 1 per cent of the entering class would be black (though roughly eight times as many would be Asian Americans). This practically forces the conclusion that blacks, on the whole, must make up through the use of quotas what they lack in intellectual capabilities.

In New York City, where the last examination for promotion to police sergeant was passed by 10.1 per cent of whites, 4.4 per cent of Hispanics, but only 1.7 per cent of blacks, the city has agreed to scrap the test and promote its quota of blacks. The test, they say, is illegally discriminatory since fewer blacks passed, and since the city's legal department does not think it could be defended as job-related. Yet, the test was explicitly prepared (at a cost of $500,000 and under a court-supervised consent decree), so as only to test job-relevant skills. No one really believes the *test* was unfair to nonwhite officers, only the *results* are questioned. But, after this episode, can anyone be made to believe that blacks are capable of the same results as whites?

The use of racial quotas, deriving from the civil rights approach to problems of racial differences in performance, can have subtle effects on the way in which black people think about themselves. When there is internal disagreement among black intellectuals, for example about the merits of affirmative action, critics of the policy are often attacked as being disingenuous, since they clearly owe their own prominence to the very policy they criticize. The specific circumstances of the individual do not matter in this, for it is presumed that *all* blacks, whether directly or indirectly, are indebted to civil rights activity for their achievements. The consequence of this is a kind of "socialization" of the individual black's accomplishments. The individual's effort to claim achievement for himself, and thus to secure the autonomy and legitimacy needed to lead and shape the groups' views of its condition, is perceived as a kind of betrayal.

This is, in a subtle but nontrivial way, destructive of black self-esteem. There is nothing wrong, of course, with acknowledging the debt all blacks owe to those who fought and beat the Jim Crow laws. There is everything wrong with a group's most accomplished persons feeling that the celebration of their personal attainments represents betrayal of their fellows.

Conclusion

In his recent, highly esteemed comparative history of slavery, *Slavery and Social Death,* Orlando Patterson defines slavery as the "permanent, violent domination of natally alienated and generally dishonored persons." Most discussion of the American slave experience in contemporary policy discourse focuses on the violent character of the institution, its brutalization of the Africans, and its destructive effects on social life among the slaves. There is much debate among historians and philosophers on the precise extent to which this history is related to current-day policy concerns. Less attention is paid nowadays to the *dishonored* condition of the slave, and by extension of the freedman. For Patterson this dishonoring was crucial. He sees as a common feature of slavery wherever it has occurred the parasitic phenomenon whereby masters derive honor and standing from their power over the slaves, and the slaves suffer an extreme marginality by virtue of having no social existence except that mediated by their masters. Patterson rejects the "property in people" definition of slavery, arguing that relations of respect and standing among persons are also crucial. But if this is so, it follows that emancipation—the ending of the master's property claim—is not of itself sufficient to convert a slave (or his descendant) into a genuinely equal citizen. There remains the intractable problem of overcoming the historically generated "lack of honor" of the freedmen.

This problem, in my judgment, remains with us. Its eventual resolution is made less likely by blacks' broad, permanent reliance on racial preferences as remedies for academic or occupational underperformance. A central theme in Afro-American political and intellectual history is the demand for respect—the struggle to gain inclusion within the civic community, to become coequal participants in the national enterprise. This is, of course, a problem that all immigrant groups also faced, and that most have overcome. But here, unlike some other areas of social life, it seems that the black population's slave origins, subsequent racist exclusion, and continued dependence on special favors from the majority uniquely exacerbates the problem.

Blacks continue to seek the respect of our fellow Americans. And yet it becomes increasingly clear that, to win the equal regard of our fellows, black Americans cannot substitute judicial and legislative decree for what is to be won through the outstanding achievements of individual black persons. That is, neither the pity, nor the guilt, nor the coerced acquiescence in one's demands—all of which have been over the last two decades amply available to blacks—is sufficient. For what ultimately is being sought is the freely conveyed respect of one's peers. Assigning prestigious positions so as to secure a proper racial balance—this as a permanent, broadly practiced policy—seems fundamentally inconsistent with the attainment of this goal.

It is a truth worth noting that not everything of value can be redistributed. With respect to personal traits like beauty or intelligence this is readily obvious. But it is no less true for other important nonpecuniary goods like dignity and respect. If, in the psychological calculus by which people determine their satisfaction such status considerations are important, then this observation places basic limits on the extent to which public policy can effect fully egalitarian outcomes. This is especially so with respect to the policy of racially preferential treatment, because its use to "equalize" can actually destroy the good that is being sought on behalf of those initially unequal. It would seem that, where the high regard of others is being sought, there is no substitute for what is to be won through the unaided accomplishments of individual persons.

PART FIVE

Asians at the Head of the Class

37. The Asian Difference

By JOHN H. BUNZEL AND JEFFREY K. D. AU

Focus　One of the great American success stories of recent times has been the history of the various Asian immigrants that have come to America since 1965, the year in which the older, pro-European immigration law was first abandoned. Asian immigrants have made enormous strides in a variety of fields, and in terms of both average education and per capita income, have often far exceeded the members of the various white-European ethnic groups. Their success has been particularly striking in the universities, where Asians can be found in proportions that far exceed the proportion in the general population. This success, however, has brought with it charges that universities, and particularly elite institutions, discriminate against Asians through unofficial ceiling quotas much in the way they once discriminated against the high-achieving Jews of an earlier generation. Ironically, in the past, organized Asian groups have often supported the idea of racial preference in university admissions (the Japanese American Citizens League, for instance, officially supported the University of California against Allan Bakke). By the 1980s, however, many Asian leaders began to have second thoughts about racial quotas.

John Bunzel and Jeffrey Au take up the issue of Asian admissions at four elite universities (Princeton, Harvard, Stanford, and Brown), and try to account for the significantly lower admission rates of Asians despite equal Scholastic Aptitude Test (SAT) scores, equal high school grades, and equal levels of participation in high school extracurricular activities. The authors conclude that much of the disparity is a result of a peculiar notion of "ethnic diversity," which in practice comes to be defined in terms of proportional representation of various ethnic groups based on the relative size of such groups within the total U.S. population. Asian applicants thus come to be viewed as members of an "overrepresented minority" and are admitted under a much stricter standard than that applied to others.

John H. Bunzel is a former president of San Jose State University, and recently served a three-year term as a member of the U.S. Commission on Civil Rights.

Jeffrey K. D. Au is a student at the Columbia University Law School.

CONTROVERSY HAS BEEN GROWING at many of our most selective universities regarding the admission of Asian Americans. Critics have leveled charges of bias, claiming that admissions policies have aimed specifically at slowing down the influx of Asian Americans into these colleges and have therefore discriminated against them. They point to Asian American admission rates (the number of Asian Americans offered admission divided by the number of Asian American applicants) that have been lower than those of Caucasians, despite Asian American performance as measured by test scores, high school grade-point averages (GPAs), and subsequent college GPAs that appears to be equal to and at times superior to that of Caucasians. A downward turn in Asian American admission rates at some institutions has raised the additional concern that admissions officers have put numerical limits on the number of Asian Americans they admit.

Most admissions officers deny any charges of discrimination. Referring to possible numerical ceilings on the number of Asian Americans admitted, Princeton's dean of the college has stated, "I can assure you that there is no such thing, and I believe it would be a serious disservice to suggest otherwise." Yet many university officials have taken such charges seriously. Largely in response to pressure from student and other groups, formal inquiries have been launched at several prominent institutions.

The focus here will be on various aspects of undergraduate admissions processes at four elite universities—Princeton, Harvard, Stanford, and Brown—where Asian Americans account for roughly 10 per cent of the applicant pool. At each of these institutions, Asian American admissions policies have been discussed at length by students, faculty, administrators, and, in some cases, alumni, with much of the debate centering on two different approaches that have been used to evaluate data. The

first, and the one often used in the public statements of university officials, compares the percentage "representation" of
Asian Americans in the admittance and/or enrollment pools of
their respective colleges and universities with the percentage of
the overall population in the country that is Asian American.
The second approach, which is most likely to be used by critics
of present admissions processes (as well as by many internal
university investigations), compares the number of Asian Americans offered admission with the number that actually applies.
This key statistic is the Asian American "admission rate."

Applicants and Admissions

Using the first approach, Asian Americans appear to be doing
well. They make up only 2.1 per cent of the American population, but constitute upwards of 8 per cent of the freshman classes
at the four universities under review. But this approach is flawed
for several reasons. It ignores the geographic concentration of
Asian Americans in a few states and in several key metropolitan
areas. In 1980, for example, they made up 6.7 per cent of
California's population and 22 per cent of those living in San
Francisco. One would therefore expect them to have at least a
slightly higher representation among the students attending a
school like Stanford, which is located in the San Francisco Bay
area. (At the University of California at Berkeley, Asian Americans made up one-quarter of the undergraduates in 1985.)

Aggregate national population figures alone also overlook the
fact that a much higher proportion of Asian Americans than
Caucasians is actually eligible for college admission. In 1983, for
example, 26 per cent of California's Asian American high school
graduates were academically qualified for freshman admission
to the University of California, compared to only 15.5 per cent
of their Caucasian counterparts. Not only do Asian Americans
have a high level of performance in terms of national standardized test scores and high school grade-point averages, but the
proportion that takes the SAT is much higher than that of
Caucasians.[1]

Furthermore, using simple ethnic representation in the national population as a guide fails to take into consideration the

reality that a much larger proportion of Asian Americans continues their education past the age of seventeen. Table 1 provides the percentages of Asian Americans and whites aged three to thirty-four enrolled in school or college. Finally, the use of Asian American national population figures of 2.1 per cent as a basis for evaluating a university's admission and enrollment figures can be misleading because such an analysis ignores the number of Asian Americans who actually apply to that institution. A 2.1 per cent representation in a freshman class would be absurdly low if more than 20 per cent of applicants were Asian American.

For these reasons, we believe a college's Asian American "admission rate" is the more appropriate statistical indicator for examining its treatment of Asian American applicants. We also believe that Caucasian admissions data are the most useful comparative basis for appraising Asian American admissions. But before comparing various ethnic admission rates, it is important to consider which factors might influence, for better or for worse, those rates. The statistical effect of affirmative action policies is to raise the admission rates of ethnic groups that receive preferences in admission. Such "targeted minorities," therefore, might have admission rates that are at least slightly higher than those of ethnic groups not so designated. One would expect, however, to find approximately equal admission rates for those not receiving preferential treatment, such as Cauca-

Table I.   Percentage of Asian Americans and Whites Enrolled in School and College in 1980[a]

Group	Age							
	3–4	5–6	7–15	16–17	18–19	20–21	22–24	25–34
Chinese	47.9	91.4	98.4	96 0	83.9	74.0	50.7	21.9
Filipino	27.6	89.1	98.8	92 8	62.7	38.3	20.2	9.6
Indian	51.4	92.3	98.2	92.2	72.0	54.3	39.2	14.8
Japanese	58.0	94.6	99.1	96.2	77.0	61.6	38.9	14.6
Korean	42.1	88.4	98.3	94.9	77.7	54.8	30.5	13.2
Vietnamese . .	29.4	83.6	96.5	90.2	66.6	47.5	37.8	22.4
White	32.0	86.1	98.8	89.0	52.8	33.3	17.4	8.5

[a]*Source:* Bureau of Census (1983b), reported in Sau-Lim Tsang and Linda C. Wing, *Beyond Angel Island: The Education of Asian Americans* ERIC/CUA Urban Diversity Series No. 90 (Oakland, ARC Associates, Inc., Winter 1985), p. 18.

sians and Asian Americans. If a "nontargeted" group has a significantly lower admission rate than another such group, two possible explanations must be considered: (1) that the applicant pool of the former group is on average less qualified for admissions than that of the latter, and/or (2) that the admissions process, or some aspect of it, either intentionally or unintentionally has been unfairly and perhaps discriminatorily treating applicants of the group with the lower admissions rates. Thus a key question: are the lower admission rates of Asian Americans the result of being less qualified than Caucasians, or have Asian Americans been the victims of barriers and inequities in the admissions process?

Historic Discrimination

Asian Americans, who have suffered a long history of racial discrimination in this country, were for the most part excluded from highly selective colleges and universities prior to the 1960s. By the early 1970s, most major universities were instituting affirmative action programs aimed at increasing ethnic minority enrollment, primarily through recruitment and by granting preferences in the selection process. Enrollment figures were used to show the progress of each minority group. There was little need to monitor the specific admission rates of these minorities inasmuch as they already tended to be higher than those of Caucasians (due, as mentioned above, to affirmative action policies).

Through the mid-1970s Asian Americans, like other minorities, remained underrepresented at many universities and received affirmative action preferences in the admissions process. In 1975, for example, Asian Americans constituted only 1.95 per cent of Brown's undergraduate applicant pool. By the end of the decade, however, rapidly increasing immigration and academic achievement resulted in growing numbers of qualified Asian Americans applying to selective universities. By 1983, they constituted more than 10 per cent of Brown's applicant pool. By this time, many universities decided that Asian Americans were sufficiently represented and qualified and therefore no longer needed special preferences. (Some critics, however, disagreed,

arguing that Asian Americans from lower socioeconomic backgrounds had still not reached parity with Caucasians.) It was
also at this time that the controversy of renewed discrimination
emerged between Asian Americans and college admissions officers. Citing Asian American admission rates that had dropped
below those of Caucasians—in some cases, quite suddenly—
critics began to suspect that upper limits were being placed on
Asian American admissions. While believing that university
officials might have been willing to promote minimal representation of Asian Americans and other ethnic minorities, critics
feared that like the immigration policymakers of the late 1800s,
they might have been adverse to admitting "too many" Asian
Americans.

The Question of Quotas

Despite emphatic denials of discrimination, university officials
over the last several years have examined their admissions
policies toward Asian Americans In February 1985, the issue
was discussed at a meeting of eight Ivy League admissions
directors. At Princeton, Brown, Harvard, and Stanford, various
faculty and student committees and subcommittees made detailed studies of the subject but reached considerably different
conclusions. In May 1985, Princeton's faculty-student Committee on Undergraduate Admission and Financial Aid (CAFA)
reported that it was "satisfied that Asian American applicants
are—and have been—treated fairly in the context of Princeton's
overall admissions policies." Brown's Corporation Committee
on Minority Affairs (COMA) said, however, "the subcommittee
is unanimous in finding that an extremely serious situation exists
and that immediate remedial measures are called for . . . [and]
we concur with the thrust of the statement that Asian American
applicants have been treated unfairly in the admission process."
Stanford's Faculty Senate Committee on Undergraduate Admissions and Financial Aids (C-UAFA) chose to keep its subcommittee's report confidential, although a summary was provided
to the faculty senate. C-UAFA reported that its subcommittee
found that no factor it analyzed could completely explain the
differential over the previous two years (1984 and 1985) in the

admission rates between Asian Americans and white. The sub-committee also concluded, however, that the "differential did not arise from an implicit quota," and that there was "no evidence of conscious bias." (We were unable to get similar official documents from Harvard.)

Because of numerous and, in our view, often questionable policies of confidentiality, it has been extremely difficult to collect official and comprehensive admissions data. Neverthe-less, the data we have obtained illustrate admission rates and trends. Through the late 1970s, admissions rates at Brown for Asian Americans were significantly higher than the overall ad-mission rate. Yet, while the number of Asian Americans admit-ted continued to increase, the rate of increase was slower than the rate of increasing Asian American applicants. Thus, by 1980, the Asian American admission rate dropped below that of the overall admission rate. By 1983, the Asian American admission rate (.14) was just 70 per cent of that of the overall rate (.20).

The data for Harvard, Princeton, and Stanford show similar trends. In 1982, Harvard's Asian American admission rate (.14) was just 74 per cent of the Caucasian admission rate (.19). In 1983, the admission rates were .14 and .20, respectively, with the rate of Asian Americans being admitted falling to 70 per cent

Table II.   Brown University—Comparison of Asian American and Overall
Admission Rates—Classes Entering 1975–1983[a]

	Class Entering in								
	1975	1976	1977	1978	1979	1980	1981	1982	1983
Asian American Admission Rate	0.44	0.40	0.48	0.47	0.26	0.22	0.18	0.19	0.14
Overall Admission Rate	0.33	0.33	0.34	0.28	0.25	0.23	0.22	0.22	0.20
Asian American Admission Rate as % of Overall Admission Rate	133	121	141	168	104	96	82	86	70

[a]*Source:* Brown University, Asian American Students Association (AASA), October 11, 1983, Table 5.

of that of Caucasians. At Princeton, the data indicate that in 1982 Asian American and Caucasian admission rates were .15 and .16, respectively, and .16 and .19 in 1983. Thus, in these two years, Asian Americans had admission rates that fell from approximately 94 per cent to 84 per cent, respectively, of those of Caucasians. For 1982, 1984, and 1985, the admission rate for Asian Americans applying to Stanford was only 70, 68, and 65 per cent, respectively, of that of Caucasians.[2]

Before looking to the characteristics of the university admissions process, both official and unofficial, to seek reasons for this imbalance, it is first necessary to consider whether Asian Americans might be academically less qualified than Caucasian applicants. After all, academic qualifications are the primary criteria for college admissions. Official data suggest, however, that Asian Americans are not less qualified.

For example, in 1982 Asian American appliants to Harvard had average SAT verbal and math scores of 594 and 657, respectively, for an average combined score of 1251. Caucasian students who applied in the same year had average scores of 618 and 640, for a combined score of 1258, just 7 points (out of 1600) higher. The slightly lower Asian American verbal score is understandable given the large number of Asian Americans who are recent immigrants, or who have parents who are immigrants, and/or speak English as a second language. Much more striking, however, are the SAT figures for both groups who were offered admission by Harvard: Asian Americans had average verbal and math scores of 742 and 725, respectively, for an average combined score of 1467, while the scores for Caucasians were 666 and 689, for a total of 1355, or 112 points lower. The figures suggest that in order to be offered admission, Asian Americans had to score on average 112 points higher on the SAT than the Caucasians who were admitted. The data reveal a similar pattern for Princeton in 1982 and 1983 and for classes entering Brown in 1979 through 1983, with Asian Americans having average combined SAT scores that were higher than those of nonminorities. It seems clear, then, that the academic qualifications of Asian Americans cannot explain their low admission rates.

Beyond Academic Qualifications

But what about "nonacademic" criteria? One study of thirty thousand Asian Americans and Caucasian high school students who were sophomores and twenty-eight thousand who were seniors shows that while Asian American participation rates in sports and artistic activities were slightly lower than those of Caucasians, the differences were not significant. For varsity athletics, the participation rates of the two groups were 30 per cent and 34 per cent, respectively, and for other athletic teams 37 per cent and 40 per cent. In debating or drama, the figures were 9 per cent and 13 per cent, respectively, 13 per cent and 14 per cent in band or orchestra, and in chorus or dance 15 per cent and 18 per cent. In "intellectual activities," such as honorary clubs, school newspapers, and subject-matter clubs, however, the figures show that Asian Americans tended to participate more than whites. With the exception of "junior achievement," the study found that Asian Americans tended to participate less in community activities. But another study found that among 1982–1983 SAT candidates, Asian Americans were more likely to participate in social, ethnic, or community organizations than other SAT candidates.

In summary, the data above do not support the common stereotype that Asian Americans have significantly lower rates of participation in extracurricular activities than do Caucasians. Furthermore, Stanford's C-UAFA reported that for 1984 and 1985 its sub-committee found that the lower admission rates of Asian Americans did not arise "from lesser academic/nonacademic ratings of Asian Americans." In other words, among Asian American and Caucasian applicants to Stanford who had the *same* academic and nonacademic ratings, Asian Americans still had significantly lower admission rates.

Another category of nonacademic qualifications that has importance at such highly selective institutions as Brown, Princeton, Harvard and Stanford are character and personality traits. Most people would probably agree that these qualities might be legitimate criteria for college admissions. After all, a university would have an interest in rejecting applicants who were dishon-

est, just as it might find desirable such traits as social conscience, creativity, compassion, intellectual curiosity, and personal integrity. But do Asian Americans as a group have
different personality characteristics from those of Caucasians?
And can such characteristics be accurately detected and measured without being influenced by cultural biases or racial stereotyping?

We know of no admissions officer who has produced conclu-
sive evidence of significant character and personality differences
between Asian American and Caucasian applicants. One study
does suggest some differences. Stanford sociology and education professor Stanford M. Dornbusch recently analyzed 7,836
high school students in the San Francisco Bay area. "My bottom
line is there's no question these Asians are working a heck of a
lot harder," he reported. Dornbusch found that Asian American
males spent an average of 11.7 hours a week doing homework,
while the white males in his study spent an average of 8.6 hours.

One would think industriousness would be regarded favorably
in the college admissions process. This might not be the case,
however, for Asian Americans. When asked what personality
traits might account for lower admission rates among Asian
Americans, one admissions officer responded that they tend to
be "driven." Such negative perceptions of otherwise positive
Asian American attributes could contribute to their low admission rates.

Another explanation often cited for the low admission rates of
Asian Americans is their tendency to major in the sciences and
technical fields. Harvard's former Dean of Admissions, L. Fred
Jewett, has stated that "a terribly high proportion of the Asian
students are heading toward the sciences. In the interests of
diversity, then, more of them must be left out." But national
data from the Department of Education's civil rights office
suggest that this presumed tendency might be exaggerated.
Some of these data are summarized in a report cited by the
Bureau of Census:

The greatest number of Asian Americans received bachelor's
degrees in business and management (3,177), followed in order

by engineering (1,838), social sciences (1,620), biological sciences (1,463), and health professions (1,087). In comparison, the top five majors among white bachelor's degree recipients were business management, education, social sciences, health professions, and engineering. For both Asian Americans and whites, business and management was by far the most popular major.

But the intended majors of Asian Americans actually applying are what admissions officers take into account. Brown's admission director, James Rogers, says that "the vast majority of Asian Americans applying here—70 to 75 per cent—are premedical students . . . The question is not one of race, it's academic balance." But the figures show only 39 per cent of Brown's Asian American applicants in 1982 were intended premedical majors. Mr. Roger's explanations of Asian American "premeds" and "academic balance" also raise a number of questions, for reasons best summarized by Brown's COMA report:

> We do not . . . agree that the number of Asian American premed applicants is sufficiently large to be deemed disproportionate, nor is it large enough to justify the disproportionality in the admit rates. This claim results from a reliance on inference and not necessarily on the declared concentration interests of the applicant. While the use of inferential factors may be valid for assessing nonminority applicants, any inferential conclusions are highly subject to cultural biases and stereotypes in the evaluation of minorities and in particular Asian American applicants . . . We also have concluded from our investigation that the admission process in reality looks at a number of admitted premed applicants when shaping the structure of the class. That is, instead of characterizing the total number of admitted premeds to be "over," it is the number of Asian American admits which is deemed to be "over." While we recognize the legitimate desire to seek a class with balanced academic interests, this must not be achieved at the cost of unfairness to any ethnic group.

Confidential data from another university in our study reveal that among every category of intended major in 1985, Asian

American applicants had a lower admission rate than Caucasians. While the intended major most popular with Asian Americans was engineering (20.6 per cent of all Asian American applicants), the same was true for Caucasians (17.2 per cent). The admission rate for Asian Americans intending to be engineers, however, was only .09, or nine per every hundred. This was half of the corresponding .21 admission rate for Caucasians planning to be engineers.

Procedural Problems

If the characteristics and qualities of Asian Americans cannot account for their low admission rates, the remaining possible explanations lie in the procedural characteristics of the college admissions process. For a variety of reasons, special consideration is given to several groups, which generally fall into four categories: (a) ethnic minorities "targeted" for affirmative action purposes; (b) athletes; (c) geographic preferences; and (d) legacies of alumni, faculty, and/or staff. Since college admission is a "zero-sum game," an increase in admissions for these groups will necessarily reduce the admission rates of other groups.

It is true that when compared to Caucasians, Asian Americans have lower rates of participation in certain major varsity sports such as football and basketball. But the effect of this difference is minimal. At Stanford, varsity athletes constitute only about 2 per cent of the Caucasian applicant pool.

The interest in admitting a geographically diverse student body might be especially significant for Stanford, which is located in an area that has a high concentration of Asian Americans, but C-UAFA's subcommittee found that the lower admission rates of Asian Americans did not arise from the "interaction of ethnicity" with other factors such as "geographic origin."

Preference for alumni children could explain some of the differences, since very few college-age minority students have parents who attended highly selective institutions. Data analysis done at Stanford found that alumni, faculty, and staff preferences had only a slightly negative effect on Asian American admission rates relative to those of Caucasians. At Princeton, however, alumni preferences might be a more significant factor. After making adjustments for athletes and alumni children, the admission rates for Asian Americans were actually, for the most part, higher than those of Caucasians. In addition, the *New York Times* reports that alumni children applying to Princeton in 1984 had an admissions rate of .48 compared to a rate of less than .20 for the entire applicant pool.

The procedural problem of measuring the characteristics that student applicants "should" have is an important component of the admissions process, made all the more problematic because it rests to a considerable degree on subjective judgments. The Brown COMA report, for example, concluded:

It was clearly stated by all admission staff to whom we spoke that Asian American applicants receive comparatively low nonacademic ratings. These unjustified low ratings are due to the cultural biases and stereotypes which prevail in the admission office. Such biases and stereotypes prevent admission officers from appreciating and accurately evaluating the backgrounds and nuances of the Asian American cultural experience. This subcommittee has found a clear need for sensitivity training of the admissions staff to the different experiences not only of Asian Americans but of all minority groups.

We also detect suggestions of racial stereotyping in the attitudes of some university officials with whom we spoke. One admissions director, for example, expressed the view that Asian Americans are "taught to be humble and obedient" at home. An official from another institution stated that the university was concerned about admitting students who had greater interests in "public service." He speculated that this might be inconsistent with Asian cultural values, implying that Asian Americans tend to be more selfishly career-oriented and less socially concerned than Caucasians. Another common stereotype is that because of cultural reasons, Asian Americans tend to be interested only in science and technical fields and lack an appreciation for a "well-rounded liberal education."

These views reflect a serious ignorance of Asian culture,

whose most significant distinguishing characteristic is perhaps the high priority it places on collective and societal interests. The cultural values that place primary importance on the individual are creations of the West. (Adam Smith was not Asian.) Preoccupation with modern science and technology is also the product of Western culture, not Asian. If Asian culture has made any significant contributions to human thought and civilization, it is in the areas of philosophy, literature, and the arts. According to Confucianism, the educational ideal was an enlightened scholar who was highly accomplished not only intellectually but also in calligraphy, poetry, painting, music, martial arts, government, and in family and other human relationships. The well-rounded Confucian scholar was a central figure in Asian society centuries before the discovery of the Renaissance man and the "liberal arts" university.

It is because none of the explanations reviewed here adequately accounts for the low admission rates of Asian Americans relative to Caucasians that critics continue to suspect that numerical limits have been placed on Asian Americans, a charge that is emphatically denied by admissions officers. Brown's COMA subcommittee on minority affairs concluded, however, that numerical limits were, in fact, in operation through the use of an "historical benchmark" mechanism:

By this we mean the process by which a set of enrollment goals is established using as a benchmark figure the enrollment figures of the previous year's freshman class. That is, in practice, the structure of an incoming class, i.e., the total size and the relative proportion of identifiable subgroups within it, such as athletes, various minority groups, alumni children, and the like, is mainly determined by numerical comparison with the structure of the preceeding year's entering class. . . . In the specific case of Asian Americans, this practice has resulted in a limit on the number of admitted applicants. In other words, when the Asian American admits closely approximates its historic benchmark number, the admission process is curtailed without regard to the total number of Asian American applicants for the current year or their academic qualifications.[3]

The Consequences of "Diversity"

It should be emphasized that we have not found any definitive evidence that numerical limits on Asian American admissions might be in effect at any other institutions. But it is equally important to note again that with the exception of Brown, we have not been given the kind of access to data and decision-making information that would permit us to support or refute conclusively such a finding. Because of the inadequacy of alternative explanations, the possibility of numerical limits on Asian Americans operating in the college admissions process (of at least some institutions) cannot be rejected out of hand. But we do not believe, in spite of its history in this country, that outright racism is a sufficient explanation. It seems to us that the answer is more complex. For example, our examination of the various reports of Asian American admissions, together with discussions with university officials, persuade us that a conceptual confusion over the meaning of "diversity" might in part account for the limiting of Asian American admissions.

Consider the questions posed in an internal document of one of the universities we studied:

> In order for us to make a recommendation on the specific questions of Asian American admissions, at least some of these policy issues must either be resolved or, failing that, given some boundary conditions.
>
> Is the goal to achieve an ethnic mix of . . . undergraduates that matches that of the applicant pool, the (state) population, the national population, or none of those?
>
> What is the underlying rationale for ethnic diversity? Are we trying to achieve ethnic diversity because it is good for [society] . . . or because it is fair and therefore good for the society at large, or because it is mandated, or popular, or what? How is the goal of ethnic diversity to be balanced against other factors?

When asked why Asian American admission rates tend to be so low, university officials most commonly respond that their goal is to achieve "ethnic diversity" in their student bodies and that Asian Americans are an "overrepresented minority." The apparent assumption is that because Asian American representation at these universities is higher than their approximately 2 per cent of the national population, admitting more Asian Americans would contradict the institution's goal of achieving "ethnic diversity." But increasing the number of students whose ethnicity is unlike that of the majority would, by definition, increase the ethnic "diversity" of the students. Furthermore, limiting Asian American admissions in the name of "diversity" inaccurately assumes the homogeneity of Asian Americans.[4]

Finally, the concept of "overrepresentation" is faulty to the extent that it is uniquely applied to Asian Americans. In the words of Brown's AASA report:

> One could only imagine the outcry from all sectors of the community if Brown decided to reduce its 25–30 per cent Jewish student population down to the 3 per cent that Jews represent in the national population. And if this isn't rediculous enough, try limiting the number of alumni sons and daughters in the university to their overall national representation. The point here is not that we wish to cut either the number of Jewish students or alumni children, but that this argument which Brown used to justify limiting acceptance of Asian Americans is invalid and inconsistent.
>
> Indeed, such an argument for limiting admissions to reflect the national population levels only reinforces the idea that there exists an unwritten quota for Asian Americans at Brown.

The controversy over Asian American admissions appears to have resulted in different policy outcomes at different institutions. After a three-year period in which Asian American applicants to Stanford were admitted at a rate only 65 to 70 per cent of the Caucasian admission rate, Stanford's 1986 Asian American rate rose to 89 per cent of its Caucasian admission rate. Combined with a higher proportion of Asian American admittees choosing to enroll at Stanford (50 per cent in 1985, and 63 per cent in 1986), this resulted in a more than 100 per cent increase of Asian Americans enrolled in Stanford's 1986 freshman class (119 in 1985 and 245 in 1986). Princeton's 1986 freshman class, however, witnessed a 25 percent decline of Asian Americans, which "dropped to 75 from 99 a year ago." These dramatic changes in a single year, shifting in opposite directions at institutions with similar admissions standards, lend further support to the hypothesis that Asian American admission rates have been determined more by the policies, preferences, and practices of college admissions officers than by the qualifications of Asian American applicants.

After concluding that there is no implicit quota or evidence of conscious discrimination on the part of the admissions staff, Stanford's C-UAFA addressed the problem of a negative bias in Asian Americans admissions:

> The remaining alternatives . . . are that real differences may exist between Asian Americans and whites in the subjective data on which admissions decisions are based, and/or that unconscious biases have influenced admissions decisions. For example, Asian Americans as a group might rate themselves, and be rated by others, as more narrowly focused in their interests than the white group . . . For instance, it is possible that descriptions of "focused interest," especially in science or engineering, might be interpreted positively when applied to whites ("the student delves deeply into one topic and learns it thoroughly") and negatively when applied to Asian Americans ("the student has narrow interests") . . . As a final complexity, (the subcommittee) stressed that even if real differences in the subjective data were found, such differences themselves could reflect unconscious bias in the minds of the providers of such data, such as high school teachers and the applicants themselves (even self-images can be biased) rather than real differences in populations.

Stanford has recently taken measures that are important and necessary steps designed to prevent a continuation of past problems. We also believe that an accurate historical record of what has actually caused consistently low college admission rates of Asian Americans is critical to public perceptions of Asian Americans. If Asian American admissions should suddenly rise at a university, it would be essential for all to understand that such an increase is not the result of "unfair advantages" being given to Asian Americans, but rather the effect of unfair disadvantages being removed.

Notes

Chapter 1:
Glazer, "Racial Quotas"

1. Richard B. Freeman, "Changes in the Labor Market for Black Americans: 1948–1972," *Brookings Papers on Economic Activity, 1973*, No. 1, pp. 67–120; Robert E. Hall and Richard A. Kasten, "Relative Occupational Success of Blacks and Whites," *Brookings Papers on Economic Activity, 1973*, No. 3, pp. 781–97.

Chapter 2:
Abram, "Fair Shakers and Social Engineers"

1. I first heard a black college administrator describe the movement in terms other than the principles of equal opportunity, as formulated by Roy Wilkins, Dr. Martin Luther King, Jr., and Hubert H. Humphrey, in the mid-1970s, during my tenure as chairman of the United Negro College Fund. As Professor Brest describes it, by this time some members of the civil rights coalition had adopted the "independent goal of assuring that no minority racial group [was]—for any reason—appreciably worse off than the rest of society" (*Harvard Law Review*, vol. 90, 1976, p. 2).

2. Social engineers ignore that it simply takes time for various groups to make their way fully into all sectors of society. For example, as recently as the mid-1960s, few Jews could be found in this country's executive suites. Discrimination is only part of the explanation. Beginning with different kinds of abilities and skills, all the major ethnic groups staked out areas of advancement for themselves (the Italians in construction, for example, the Irish on the police force and in local politics, Jews in law and medicine). Members of such groups may require several generations to position themselves for more diverse and powerful roles. Nor does discrimination fully explain the fact that certain groups continue to cluster in certain occupations; other factors, such as age, also influence group performance. The 1970 census revealed that the average age of the Jewish population was 46; the Puerto Rican, 18. Obviously, there will be proportionally more Jewish than Puerto Rican representatives among professionals. By insisting on even rough proportional representation, we may well be working against our own best interests as a society.

3. For example, if test results show minority candidates passing at less than 80 percent of the nonminority passing rate, then the test is presumed discriminatory. See *Uniform Guidelines on Employee Selection Procedures* (1978) ("procedure having adverse impact constitutes discrimination unless justified". . . . "A selection ratio for any race . . . which is less than four-fifths of the rate for the group with the highest rate will generally be regarded . . . as evidence of adverse impact . . ."). These provisions apply to persons subject

to Title VII of the Civil Rights Act of 1964, Executive Order 11246, or other equal employment opportunity requirements of federal law.

4. Many individual civil rights advocates and civil rights groups, including the Leadership Conference on Civil Rights and the NAACP, have abandoned fair-shake objectives in areas other than voting.

5. This order, issued in 1965, required government agencies and private contractors to undertake "affirmative action" and "insure that applicants are employed, and that employees are treated during employment, without regard to their race, creed, color, or national origin."

6. As Professor William W. Van Alstyne has written: "This [plan implemented under Executive Order 11246] is affirmative action (i.e., action of a positive character, discriminating against none, dispreferring no one, involving neither quotas nor queues nor targets nor presumptions of what is the 'right' mix or 'proper' share of each according to race). It has nothing to do with such a philosophy. . . . It seeks the better protection of *each* person from racial discrimination that might otherwise occur, whether in a white-owned enterprise against blacks, in a black-owned enterprise against whites, or whatever. It takes a strong national policy seriously. It is action undertaken consciously (and sometimes at considerable expense) to vindicate more effectively a commitment opposed to racial discrimination in *all* its forms."

7. See Laurence Silberman, "The Road to Racial Quotas," *Wall Street Journal*, August 11, 1977, p. 14. Of course, many employers will thus adopt proportional representation as a norm in hiring to avoid litigation. . . . One small company in Kansas, upon failing to meet the Executive Order 11246 requirement that 12.7 per cent of its truck drivers be minorities and 6.9 per cent of its employees in five job categories be female, was told: "United Bridge Company, Inc. will recruit and hire qualified minorities and females until such time as the required utilization goals have been met. Should no qualified minorities and females be available, the company will document its efforts to meet its goals for the trades." Government directives to employers subject to Executive Order 11246 thus effectively treat statistical goals as presumptive quotas.

8. *Harpers*, December 1980, pp. 31–32.

9. New York City has chosen not to base its hiring solely on the test, but to accept quotas, promoting some 200 candidates who failed the examination.

10. New York City Police Commissioner Benjamin Ward has asserted that New York City's legally mandated quota system for promotions to police sergeant is "bad for morale," more for black and Hispanic officers than for whites, because "it does make minorities appear to be second-class citizens."

11. Justice Potter Stewart wrote in refutation of this claim that "no race . . . has a monopoly on social, educational, or economic disadvantage." (*Fullilove v. Klutznick*, 1980). He also noted that "in 1978, 83.4 per cent of persons over the age of 25 who had not completed high school were 'white', . . . and in 1977, 79.0 per cent of households with annual incomes of less than $5,000 were 'white.' "

12. If the purpose of civil rights enforcement litigation is to stop discrimination, it is remarkable to me that civil rights attorneys do not press for jailing and firing discriminators; rather, they demand goals, timetables, and quotas.

13. This declaration asserts that "everyone has the right to work, to free

choice of employment," and "to just and favourable remuneration ensuring for himself and his family an existence worthy of human dignity."

Chapter 3:
Kennedy, "Persuasion and Distrust"

1. "Affirmative action," "preferential treatment," and "affirmative discrimination" are used as synonyms. At the level of semantics, "affirmative action" avoids the problem of preference that is inescapable if one uses the term "preferential treatment." It also avoids the problem of discrimination made salient by the term "affirmative discrimination." On all too many occasions, however, proponents of affirmative action have hurt their own cause by evading the difficulties posed and costs incurred by the policy they advance. These difficulties and costs will not disappear behind euphemistic terminology. To properly convince the public that these costs are worth shouldering, proponents of affirmative action will have to grapple straightforwardly with them—a process that involves, at the least, conceding their existence.

[This article] is concerned solely with the debate over affirmative action for American blacks. I recognize that affirmative action programs often include other groups and exclude still others that arguably should be included. And I acknowledge that questions of fairness regarding the criteria by which preference is conferred constitute important issues in the controversy. While practical limitations prevent exploration of this issue, my basic position with respect to it is that the nation should use affirmative action policies to eradicate the oppression and isolation of *any* "specially disadvantaged group."

2. To take one famous example, under the "regular" admissions program of the University of California at Davis Medical School, only one black applicant would have qualified for admission between 1970 and 1974; twenty-six were admitted due to affirmative action. In the employment context, affirmative action has played a major role in upgrading the relative position of black workers.

3. Affirmative action in medical school admissions was begun, among other reasons, to ensure the training of persons likely to enter primary care specialties, to practice in underserved areas of the country, and to serve black patient populations. According to a recent study of the career paths of black physicians, these goals are being met.

4. The stigma problem, moreover, is mainly an affliction besetting elite occupations. There are a great many jobs, generally those requiring relatively little specialized training, to which the problem of stigma is largely irrelevant. After all, when an occupation requires no more than on-the-job training, there is little reason to suspect that blacks who have undergone such training are any less qualified than their white counterparts.

5. The advancement registered by members of the black middle class is not necessarily evidence that old-fashioned discrimination has been eradicated. Often, this advancement proceeds despite the presence of continuing prejudice and is made possible precisely because of the lift provided by affirmative action.

6. There remains the apprehension that affirmative action will elevate

blacks to positions for which they are unqualified and in which they fail, further entrenching the very assumptions that preferential treatment seeks to combat. For example, the lower rates with which black physicians obtain specialty board certification and black attorneys pass state bar examinations lends support to the view that, by and large, even after training, black beneficiaries of affirmative action constitute a class of professionals decidedly less competent to supply vital services than their white counterparts. On the other hand, this fear is probably out of proportion to any real basis in fact. The most comprehensive survey of affirmative action in employment (by Jonathan Leonard) concludes that no significant evidence exists indicating that affirmative action leads to marked efficiency costs. Moreover, there is little support for the frequent allegation that affirmative action necessitates the wholesale abrogation of relevant standards. Any sensible affirmative action program will require the satisfaction of certain minimal requirements appropriate to a given context. Once these minimum standards are met, the minority status of an applicant can then play a legitimate role in hiring or admissions decisions.

7. Some commentators have stated that beneficiaries of affirmative action feel guilty about their "tainted" achievements. Blacks seem to be the primary targets of such ruminations. Justice Sandra Day O'Connor, the first woman to be appointed to the Supreme Court, was certainly not nominated because of her demonstrated mastery of federal law. Among the principle reasons for her elevation was her status as a competent *woman* jurist. She appears, however, to have escaped the suggestion that she is silently suffering a crisis of conscience or confidence because her sex played an essential role in her appointment.

8. Members of the organized black community, Republicans and Democrats alike, are virtually united in calling for the continuation of affirmative action programs. Black Republican organizations for example have urged President Reagan not to rescind Executive Order 11246, which mandates affirmative hiring goals in all contracts with the government.

9. It is quite true that some of the civil rights movement's most illustrious leaders have posited the idea that the constitution mandates strict color blindness in government policy. (See William Bradford Reynolds, "Individualism vs. Group Rights: The Legacy of Brown," *Yale Law Journal*, volume 93, pp. 995, 998–1001 (1984), citing Justice Thurgood Marshall, Jack Greenberg, Roy Wilkins, and Dr. Martin Luther King, Jr.) It is a mistake, however, to view these leaders as a new set of founding fathers whose original intent regarding the post-segregation Constitution must now control contemporary interpretations. First, the meaning of all statements must be derived from the surrounding context. Therefore, little is advanced by merely citing language used by civil rights activists during the initial, crucial victories over the Jim Crow system. After all, insofar as widespread trauma accompanied the demand that blacks simply be treated the same as whites, it made perfect tactical sense not to raise additional issues that could result only in increased resistance. Second, it is clear that initially neither civil rights leaders nor the Supreme Court really knew what racial equality would entail; it was a goal that gained clarity only in the process of actual realization. Racial equality is not a static concept; it is a living idealization that gathers meaning only in the context of changing historical conditions.

10. Benjamin Hooks, the executive director of the NAACP, recently described Assistant Attorney General Reynolds, who heads the Justice Department's civil rights division, and other leading Reagan administration opponents of affirmative action, as "latter day Bilbos."

11. Representative of the view of many civil rights activists is Vernon Jordan's statement that "the attack on affirmative action is conducted under the cover of concern for individual rights simply because in our enlightened times you need a fig leaf as a cover for a naked defense of racial privilege."

12. The blinders imposed by the conflict-within-consensus perspective may account for Dean Ely's statement that he had "trouble understanding the place of righteous indignation on either side" of the affirmative action debate. If one recognizes, however, that opposition to affirmative action—at least on the part of some—may quite plausibly be viewed as an act of racial aggression, it becomes quite clear why many proponents of preferential treatment wage their struggle with righteous indignation.

13. Explaining the administration's opposition to affirmative discrimination, President Reagan observed that "we want what I think Martin Luther King asked for. We want a color-blind society."

Chapter 4:
Nieli, "Ethnic Tribalism and Human Personhood"

1. The two exceptions were for American Indians living on or near Indian reservations who could be granted "preferential treatment" in employment by a business on or near a reservation (Section 703(i)); and for special instances where national origin was a "bona fide occupational qualification reasonably necessary to the normal operation" of a business or enterprise (Section 703(e)).

2. Senator Clark also had read into the *Congressional Record* a letter rebutting Senator Hill's arguments by Walter Reuther, the president of the United Auto Workers Union, who was one of labor's most outspoken supporters of the Civil Rights Bill. "Under the pending law," Reuther wrote, "every Negro worker will have a fair opportunity for a job if he is qualified, and every white worker will know that he cannot be laid off or refused employment for a racial reason because discrimination against a white worker is just as forbidden as discrimination against the Negro" (110 *Cong. Rec.*, p. 7206).

3. Personalistic ideas of the type described formed a major component of New England transcendentalism, and can be seen, for instance, in the mystically grounded personalism of Walt Whitman. In his *Democratic Vistas,* for instance, he writes:

Only in the perfect uncontamination and solitariness of individuality may the spirituality of religion positively come forth at all. Only here, and on such terms, the mediation, the devout ecstasy, the soaring flight. Only here, communion with the mysteries, the eternal problems, whence? whither? Alone, and identity, and the mood—and the soul emerges, and all statements, churches, sermons, melt away like vapours. Alone and silent thought and awe, and aspiration—and then the interior consciousness, like a hitherto unseen inscription, in magic ink, beams out its wondrous lines to the sense. Bibles may convey and priests expound, but it is exclusively for the noiseless operation of one's isolated Self, to enter the pure veneration, reach the divine levels, and commune with the unutterable (E. P. Dutton, N.Y., 1930, p. 333).

I have written elsewhere on this passage: "The intimately private nature of (the depth experience Whitman describes here) was the basis of Whitman's personalism—i.e., of his belief that the ultimate unit of human reality was the individual person in his immediacy before God. This immediacy before God, Whitman believed, conferred upon every man, regardless of membership in any race, religion, state, class, or family, an untouchable dignity. It was, in fact, the transgression of this dignity by the social institution of slavery that inspired Whitman and many of his contemporaries in their support of the abolitionist cause" (*Wittgenstein: From Mysticism to Ordinary Language*, State University of New York Press, 1987, p. 123).

4. The view of human persons presented here is similar to that of Ernest Barker as outlined in his introduction to Otto Gierke's *Natural Law and the Theory of Society* (Cambridge, 1934):

Now we may admire the nation moving and heaving: we may admire the surge of its thought: we may admire the philosophy of super-personal Group-persons—the Folk; the Fellowship; the *Verband* in all its forms. It is, indeed, a philosophy which can ennoble the individual, and lift him above self-centered concern in his own immediate life. But it may also be a philosophy which engulfs his life, and absorbs his individuality; and it may end, in practice, in little more than the brute and instinctive automatism of the hive. We have to admit, after all, the justice of Troeltsch's saying, that the end of the idealization of Groups may be 'to brutalize romance, and to romanticize cynicism'. We have to confess that the cult of super-personal Beings has had some tragic results. . . . While it has grandeur and flame, it has also a cloud of smoke. Individualism is often used as a word of reproach; but it is good to see simple shapes of 'men as trees, walking' and to think in simple terms of human persons. Persons—individual persons—have a finitude or limit which can satisfy our intelligence, and an infinity or extension which can satisfy our faith. They have finitude or limit in the sense that, in any and every scheme of social order, each of them occupies a definite position, with its definite sphere of rights and duties, under the system of law which necessarily regulates their external relations with one another. They have infinity or extension in the sense that, *sub specie aeternitatis*, each of them is 'a living soul' (as nothing but the individual person is or can be) with an inner spring of spiritual life which rises beyond our knowledge and ends beyond our ken. If we look at Groups from this angle, we shall not call them persons. We shall call them organizations of persons, or schemes of personal relations, in all their successive phases, from the village or club to the State or the League of Nations. And because they are organizations or schemes, made by the mind of man, we shall regard them as constructed by the thought of persons, consisting in the thought of persons, sustained by the thought of persons, and revised or even destroyed by the thought of persons—but never as persons themselves, in the sense in which individuals are persons.

5. In a commencement address at Lincoln University, for instance, he said of the American dream:

It is a dream of a land where men of all races, of all nationalities, and of all creeds can live together as brothers. The substance of the dream is expressed in these sublime words, words lifted to cosmic proportions: We hold these truths to be self-evident—that all men are created equal; that they are endowed by their Creator with certain inalienable rights; that among these are life, liberty, and the pursuit of happiness" (quoted in Kenneth L. Smith and Ira G. Zepp Jr., *Search for the Beloved Community,* University Press of America, 1986, p. 127).

Similar thoughts and images were used in the 1963 "I Have a Dream" speech:

I say to you today, my friends, so even though we face the difficulties of today and tomorrow, I still have a dream. It is a dream deeply rooted in the American dream. I have a dream that one day this nation will rise up and live out the true meaning of its creed—we hold these truths to be self-evident, that all men are created equal

And in *Stride Toward Freedom,* his book on the Montgomery bus boycott, he wrote:

Ever since the signing of the Declaration of Independence, America has manifested a schizophrenic personality on the question of race. She has been torn between selves—a self in which she has proudly professed democracy and a self in which she has sadly practiced the antithesis of democracy. The reality of segregation, like slavery, has always had to confront the ideals of democracy and Christianity. Indeed, segregation and discrimination are strange paradoxes in a nation founded on the principle that all men are created equal (op. cit., pp. 190–191).

6. Similar themes are addressed in a sermon Dr. King delivered "On Being a Good Neighbor," where he comments on the story of the good Samaritan:

Too seldom do we see people in their true *humanness.* A spiritual myopia limits our vision to external accidents. We see men as Jews or Gentiles, Catholics or Protestants, Chinese or American, Negroes or whites. We fail to think of them as fellow human beings made from the same basic stuff as we, molded in the same divine image. The priest and the Levite saw only a bleeding body, not a human being like themselves. But the good Samaritan will always remind us to remove the cataracts of provincialism from our spiritual eyes and see men as men. If the Samaritan had considered the wounded man as a Jew first, he would not have stopped, for the Jews and the Samaritans had no dealings. He saw him as a human being first, who was a Jew only by accident. The good neighbor looks beyond the external accidents and discerns those inner qualities that make all men human, and therefore, brothers (*Strength to Love* Simon and Schuster, N.Y., 1964, p. 23).

Within the domain of specifically Christian symbols, Dr. King frequently made use of the Pauline image of a mankind one in Christ. Thus, for instance, in *Stride Toward Freedom* he wrote:

In the final analysis the problem of race is not a political but a moral issue. . . . The broad universalism standing at the center of the gospel makes segregation morally unjustifiable. Racial segregation is a blatant denial of the unity which we have in Christ; for in Christ there is neither Jew nor Gentile, bond nor free, Negro nor white (ibid., p. 205).

7. Biblical religious themes were interspersed throughout the "I Have a Dream" speech, perhaps nowhere more magnificently than in its climactic

crescendo: "When we allow freedom to ring, when we let it ring from every village and every hamlet, from every state and every city, we will be able to speed up that day when all of God's children —black men and white men, Jews and Gentiles, Protestants and Catholics—will be able to join hands and sing in the words of the old Negro spiritual, 'Free at last, free at last; thank God Almighty, we are free at last.' "

8. Quoted in *Racial Thought in America,* Volume 1, edited by Louis Ruchames (University of Massachusetts Press, 1969), pp. 47 and 51. Even where the doctrine that all men are equally the children of God did not lead to abolitionist feelings, it had, it would seem, at least some effect in mitigating the severity of the institution of slavery. Frank Tannenbaum, for instance, in his comparative study of slavery in the Americas, makes the following observation: "If one thing stands out clearly from the study of slavery, it is that the definition of man as a moral being proved the most important influence both in the treatment of the slave and in the final abolition of slavery. Once it was believed that all men are free by nature and equal in the sight of God, once the doctrine of the spiritual identity of all men, slave or free, came to rule men's minds and condition their legal systems, then the very nature of slavery came to reflect the accepted doctrine. The idea of the moral value of the individual outlasted slavery and became the chief source of its undoing" (*Slave and Citizen,* Alfred A. Knopf, N.Y., 1947, pp. vii–viii).

9. *The Liberator,* May 7, 1831 (quoted in Ruchames, ibid., pp. 308–9).

10. Ibid., pp. 312–13.

11. One can get a good sense of the high moral tone of the movement from the following "Commitment Blank," which Martin Luther King, Jr., and his aides asked demonstrators to read before participating in the marches in Birmingham, Alabama:

COMMANDMENTS FOR THE VOLUNTEERS

I hereby pledge myself—my person and body—to the nonviolent movement. Therefore I will keep the following ten commandments:

1) Meditate daily on the teachings and life of Jesus.
2) Remember always that the nonviolent movement in Birmingham seeks justice and reconciliation—not victory.
3) Walk and talk in the manner of love, for God is love.
4) Pray daily to be used by God in order that all men might be free.
5) Sacrifice personal wishes in order that all men might be free.
6) Observe with both friend and foe the ordinary rules of courtesy.
7) Seek to perform regular service for others and for the world.
8) Refrain from the violence of fist, tongue, or heart.
9) Strive to be in good spiritual and bodily health.
10) Follow the directions of the movement and of the captain on a demonstration.

I sign this pledge, having seriously considered what I do and with the determination and will to persevere.

12. George S. Schuyler, the *Pittsburgh Courier,* June 13, 1942 (quoted in Gunnar Myrdal, *An American Dilemma,* Harper and Row, N.Y., 1944, 1962, p. 1184). A related comment is made by Frank Tannenbaum in his *Slave and Citizen* (op. cit., pp. 113–14): "It is not enough to say, as we often do, that

there are so many Negro doctors, lawyers, politicians, business men, and scholars. It is requisite that there should not be Negro doctors, Negro lawyers, or Negro scholars. Their professional standing must overshadow their racial origin. It is only when we can say he is a great actor, a great scholar, a great lawyer, a great citizen, that the step has been taken which endows the Negro with the moral worth as a man which ob iterates the invidious distinction and sweeps away the condescending fawning of the better-than-thou attitude. When the time does come that a Negro judge on the bench is a judge and not a Negro judge, when a Negro scholar is a scholar and not a Negro scholar . . . the gap between legal equality and moral acceptance will be obliterated.''

13. It probably still is. According to a study conducted by *Public Opinion* magazine, the vast majority of black Americans oppose racial and ethnic favoritism in hiring and in college admissions, and believe that merit, as determined by test scores, should govern decisions in these areas. The question asked was taken from an earlier Gallup survey: ''Some people say that to make up for past discrimination, members of minority groups should be given preferential treatment in getting jobs and places in colleges. Others say that ability, as determined by test scores, should be the main consideration. Which point of view comes closer to how you feel on this matter?'' The *Public Opinion* survey showed, however, that while the black population as a whole opposes affirmative action by a ratio of greater than three to one (77 per cent v. 23 per cent), black leaders support the policy by the exact same ratio. (See *Public Opinion* magazine, August/September 1985, p. 41).

14. This is not the case, however, in the area of government contracting. The ''minority business enterprise'' provision of the Public Works Employment Act of 1977, for instance, specifically required at least 10 per cent of federal funds going to state and local public works projects to be spent on businesses owned by citizens who are ''Negroes, Spanish-speaking, Orientals, Indians, Eskimos, and Aleuts.'' This ''slap-dash'' measure, as Justice Stevens termed it in his dissenting opinion in *Fullilove* v. *Klutznik* (1980), was passed during the first year of the Carter administration with little debate and virtually no public hearings. Its set-aside provisions have expired, but a number of other federal set-aside programs, including specifically ones established by the Small Business Administration and by the Department of Transportation (under the Surface Transportation Assistance Act of 1982), have been so administered as in effect to give special preference to contractors solely on the basis of race and ethnicity.

15. The cynicism, dishonesty, and blatant disregard for public law that federal bureaucrats have displayed in their efforts to transform the meaning of the 1964 Civil Rights Act, is well captured in the following remark by a staff member of the Equal Employment Opportunity Commission. Speaking in 1970 to representatives of the *Harvard Law Review,* the staffer boasted: ''The anti-preferential hiring provisions [of Title VII of the 1964 Civil Rights Act] are a big zero, a nothing, a nullity. They don't mean anything at all to us.'' (quoted in Elliott Abrams, ''The Quota Commission,'' *Commentary,* October 1972, p. 54). When one considers that the EEOC was explicitly set up by the Civil Rights Act to enforce the provisions of Title VII, one gets a sense of the truly frightening lengths to which affirmative action supporters have gone in the pursuit of their policies.

16. Even this characterization does not capture fully the arbitrariness and absurdity of the policy. According to the guidelines of the EEOC—America's official race classification board—an Arab American with the complexion of, say, an Anwar Sadat, would be considered "white," as would the very darkest skinned Turk, Sicilian, or Sephardic Jew.

Steven Plaut, an economics professor at Oberlin, has well captured the arbitrariness and injustice of the current system when he writes:

> I have always been disturbed by the fact that many ethnic groups who have been the victims of discrimination in the past because they were minorities (e.g. Jews, Italians, etc.) are now the victims of discrimination because they have been designated by some bureaucrat as belonging to the "majority."

Plaut, however, has successfully outfoxed the affirmative action bureaucrats, for although he himself is of Jewish origins, he has been able to turn their Nuremberg-like laws to his own advantage. As he explains:

> For years, I have been listing myself as an Asian American or Oriental American on "affirmative action" questionnaires. I am a Jew, whose ancestors, culture, and "roots" originated in the Middle East, i.e., Asia. The fact that I and my immediate ancestors were not born in Asia should be irrelevant; the same holds true for many Japanese and Chinese Americans. And I defy anyone to prove that Asia ends at the Himalayas. Ethnic identity, as pointed out above, is subjective, and only the worst racist would deny me my self-definition because of the pigmentation of my skin (a rather pale, insipid shade). I urge all other potential Asian Americans to follow my example.
>
> If I should ever be pressed about this, I am prepared to alter my self-definition. It seems that my ancestors on my father's side (hence my surname) lived in Spain until they were forcibly expelled in the fifteenth century, migrating to central Europe. So, you see, I am also a "Spanish surnamed" American, an Ibero American, or—if you will—an Hispanic (*Midstream*, February, 1980, p. 49).

17. See footnote 13. A June 1977 *Gallup Opinion Index* survey revealed that 64 per cent of the "nonwhites" and 82 per cent of the females questioned believed that "ability as determined by test scores" should be the main consideration in hiring and university admissions decisions rather than preferential treatment based on ethnicity or gender. More recently, a poll conducted by *USA Today* (March 31, 1987) found that women, by a 2-to-1 majority, disagreed with the decision of the U.S. Supreme Court upholding a preferential hiring scheme for blacks and women on the part of Santa Clara County, California.

18. This is probably most common in the area of preferential admissions to prestige universities. Joseph Adelson, for instance, describes the following case of preferential treatment in graduate school admissions in his own department of psychology at the University of Michigan: "One afternoon several years ago, while serving on our admissions committee, I came across the applications of two young women. One was an ambassador's daughter who had been educated in private secondary schools, and was attending a most prestigious Ivy League university. The other might have stepped out of a Harriet Arnow novel. She had been born in Appalachia, the daughter of a poor farmer. The farm failed, the family moved north, her father died, the family

survived on welfare and odd jobs, she married young, bore a child, was divorced, began attending a municipal university and ultimately was graduated with an excellent record. With respect to objective measurements—test scores and the like—these two young women were more or less evenly matched. It was the ambassador's daughter who, being black, was offered an invitation . . . The welfare child, being white, was not admitted, did not come close."

Adelson goes on to describe what the admissions committee found when it began to take a closer look at the individual economic backgrounds of the so-called minority applicants: "This past year our admissions committee decided to give some attention to the socioeconomic status of all plausible candidates. What we found was startling: of the five minority 'finalists', three were attending elite private colleges, and two were at selective state universities. Only one had received scholarship help. Three of the five came from affluent—not merely comfortable—families, and one of these gave every evidence of being rich. The committee member who interviewed most of them reported back to our faculty, somewhat ruefully, that their average family income was considerably higher than that enjoyed by the faculty itself" (*Commentary*, May 1978, p. 27).

19. That members of the disfavored groups are subject to an injustice (and hence, can be properly described as victims) when they are passed over in hiring and promotion situations for less-qualified people belonging to the officially favored groups is by no means universally acknowledged by affirmative action supporters. Indeed, it would seem to be a position held by only a very tiny minority of those who support racial and ethnic preference in employment. The argument here, nevertheless, is worth considering, at least as a hypothetical defense of current policy.

20. The term is also used in the 1964 Civil Rights Act in Section 706(g), where it refers to forms of redress for acts of discrimination against individuals—redress such as hiring or reinstatement, the granting of back pay, or similar acts of affirmative action. The usage of the term here was apparently taken over from the 1935 National Labor Relations Act (Wagner Act), where employers could similarly be required to reinstate employees, grant back pay, and take other such affirmative action to compensate union members who had been fired or otherwise adversely treated because of union activities. Needless to say, the racial and ethnic quota hiring often mandated by courts under this section is inconsistent with the explicit letter, spirit, and legislative history of the Civil Rights Act.

21. A number of federal court decisions were effectively to rewrite Title VII of the Civil Rights Act of 1964, the most important being *United Steelworkers of America* v. *Weber* (decided June 27, 1979). The majority opinion in this case, written by Justice William Brennan, must surely rank as one of the most blatantly dishonest judicial decisions ever handed down by an American court. It has been the subject of numerous commentaries and of two elaborate and devastating refutations, one by Justice Rehnquist in his impassioned thirty-seven-page dissent, the other by Carl Cohen in *Commentary* ("Justice Debased: The Weber Decision," September 1979, pp. 43–53). These latter critiques contain valuable information on the legislative history of the 1964 Civil Rights Act, as well as on the personalistic mode of thought embodied in

that act. See also Bernard D. Meltzer, "The *Weber* Case: The Judicial Abrogation of the Antidiscrimination Standard in Employment," *The University of Chicago Law Review,* Spring 1980, pp. 423–66.

22. Revised Order No. 4 was issued in December 1971. It summarized and clarified a policy that the OFCC had been gradually developing, though without clarification as to its true intentions, since May 1968. The ultimate intentions of the OFCC's affirmative action policy first became clear only in early 1970 with the issuance of its Order No. 4, which stated that federal contractors must devise affirmative action plans that included

> an analysis of areas within which the contractor is deficient in the utilization of minority groups and further, goals and timetables to which the contractor's good faith efforts must be directed to correct the deficiencies and thus to achieve prompt and full utilization of minorities at all levels and in all segments of his work force where deficiencies exist.

Regarding Order No. 4 (1970) and its 1971 elaboration and revision, Kenneth C. McGuiness and his colleagues write: "These revisions significantly altered both the direction and the purpose of the compliance program. What was at first an effort to provide equal employment opportunity for all groups had become a program to provide minorities and women with a share of the existing jobs, commensurate with their representation in the work force and/ or the population. Success was to be measured in the number of jobs won for minorities and women, and not by the establishment of nondiscriminatory employment practices. . . . The purpose of the program had become, not equal employment opportunity, but simply equal employment. Equal opportunity was considered a distant, although worthy goal. For the present, the program had become the vehicle for establishing and monitoring preferential treatment" (See *Preferential Treatment in Employment,* Kenneth C. McGuiness, editor, Equal Employment Advisory Council, Washington, D.C., 1977, p. 21).

23. Actually less than one person in six lists himself on Census Bureau forms as of English, Welsh, or Scottish ancestry. Since many people refuse to categorize themselves ethnically at all, and since many are of mixed ancestry, this figure is no doubt too low as an estimate of the percentage of the American people who are of predominant WASP ancestry, but it does show that America is clearly *not* a nation where the members of any one ethnic group are in the majority.

24. The term "liberal" is set in quotation marks to stress the fact that affirmative action is anything but a liberal policy, and that those who support it have ceased to be liberals in any meaningful sense of the term. From the British Levellers of the seventeenth century, to the American welfarists of the New Deal, Fair Deal, and Great Society, liberals have always endeavored to view human beings as individual persons with individual human rights, rather than as members of classes, castes, or ethnic groups whose rights and privileges are contingent upon their membership in such groups.

25. *Report of the National Advisory Commission on Civil Disorders* (Bantam Books, N.Y., 1968), p. 419. Among the things the report recommends to increase equal opportunity in employment is the following:

> d) Undertaking, through the Equal Employment Opportunity Commission, an industry and area-wide enforcement effort based not only upon individual

complaints but upon employer and union reports showing broad patterns of discrimination in employment and promotion.

e) Linking enforcement efforts with training and other aids to employers and unions, so that affirmative action to hire and promote may be encouraged in connection with investigations of both individual complaints and charges of broad patterns of discrimination.

The term "affirmative action" here is very vague and might arguably mean only "affirmative nondiscrimination" or "active color blindness." It appears, however, to be assuming its later role as a code word for preferential treatment based on showings of racial and ethnic imbalance ("underutilization") in a given work force.

26. The understanding of this term has been so corrupted by recent history that it may be worthwhile to introduce here a simple dictionary definition. The term "civil" in "civil rights" comes from the Latin *civilis* and the French *civil* and means "of or belonging to citizens"; "of or pertaining to the whole body or community of citizens"; "of or pertaining to the individual citizen"; "becoming or befitting a citizen" (OED). A civil right is a right that each citizen has solely by virtue of his citizenship, whether in a republic, commonwealth, or other political body. It is not a right conferred on the basis of ethnic, tribal, or genealogical relationships. The Fourteenth Amendment to the U.S. Constitution laid the foundation for the modern American understanding of civil rights by granting to "all persons born or naturalized in the United States and subject to the jurisdiction thereof" equal status as citizens and the full and equal political rights that citizenship confers.

27. The tendency to romanticize the poor, however, predates Western modernity and the Left/Right political cleavage, and can be traced back to the Gospel of Luke. It is not to be found in Greek thought, however, nor, as far as the present writer is aware, in Buddhist, Hindu, or Chinese philosophy.

28. For complicated historical reasons, a comparable intensity is not felt in the case of American Indians.

29. Consider in this context the following account of a recent gathering of Left-liberal and Socialist students at Rutgers University:

Encouraged by the rebirth of campus activism, students from a score of institutions began in January 1987 at Hampshire College, to lay the foundation for a national student organization designed to radically transform American society. Eventually the National Student Convention '88 (NSC) was planned and held at Rutgers University, February 5–7, 1988.

The organizers had expected about 200 activists at Rutgers. . . . Contrary to these expectations, Rutgers was swamped by almost 700 registrants representing approximately 130 institutions. . . . Overall, the assembled multitude was over 95 per cent white, geographically diverse, a mixture of the modish and those expressing reverence for the sixties through dress and hairstyle. . . . In addition to students, a host of New Left elder statesmen attended.

On the convention's last day, when the campus delegates were supposed to debate and vote on a constitution and various workshop-generated proposals, a twenty-five member Students of Color Caucus declared that insufficient care and skill had been devoted to assuring the presence of greater numbers of nonwhite students. The caucus . . . demanded that the convention postpone any vote on a proposed constitution until new outreach efforts were undertaken. If this were not acceptable to the delegates, Students of Color would disassociate itself from the organization. Pandemonium ensued. Privately, the conveners said their considerable outreach efforts had aroused little enthusiasm among black and Hispanic student groups about the prospect of joining a multiracial, multi-issue organization in which their interests might frequently be subordinated to other pressing concerns. Publicly, they remained mute on the issue. Some students spoke against the caucus's proposal.

Nevertheless, with widespread white guilt clearly evident, a voice vote of those assembled . . . easily carried the day for the caucus's demands. Regional delegates were chosen to conduct the outreach. . . . But there was no adequate attempt to create a temporary national organizing committee to whom outreach efforts should be reported and which in turn would plan the demonstrations or the next convention. . . . Finally, since the assembly just voted itself insufficiently representative of student radicalism, there was no logical rationale to vote on the myriad positions and proposed actions that had been discussed at workshops earlier. Students drifted aimlessly about the gym and eventually began to leave for home (from "Rutgers, DSA, and the Revival of the New Left," by Milton Mankoff, *Tikkun,* May/June 1988, pp. 85–86).

"Pandemonium" is the precise term to describe the phenomenon under observation here. Pandemonium (literally: "place of all [evil] demons") is the capital of Hell in Milton's great epic literary myth (*Paradise Lost,* I. 756; X. 424), and symbolizes the moral depravity and social chaos that result when men are cut off from the redeeming power of Divine Grace.

30. Other names for the self-representation-only principle might include the no-proxy principle, or the flesh-and-blood-only principle.

31. Cf. "Man's sinfulness sinks to such devastating depths in his collective life that Reinhold Niebuhr could write a book titled *Moral Man and Immoral Society.* Man collectivized in the group, the tribe, the race, and the nation often sinks to levels of barbarity unthinkable even among lower animals. We see the tragic expression of Immoral Society in the doctrine of white supremacy that plunges millions of black men into the abyss of exploitation, and in the horrors of two world wars that have left battlefields drenched with blood, national debts higher than mountains of gold, men psychologically deranged and physically handicapped, and nations of widows and orphans" (Martin Luther King, Jr., *Strength to Love,* op. cit., p. 111).

32. Cf. "A multi-ethnic society like the United States can ill-afford continually to build up stores of inter-group resentments about such powerful concerns as one's livelihood and one's children [i.e., employment quotas and busing]. . . . We must never think that the disintegration and disaster that has hit other multi-ethnic societies 'can't happen here'. The mass internment of Japanese Americans just a generation ago is a sobering reminder of the tragic idiocy that stress can bring on. We are not made of different clay from the Germans, who were historically more enlightened and humane toward Jews than many other Europeans—until the generation of Hitler and the Holocaust. The situation in America today is, of course, not like that of the Weimar Republic. History does not literally repeat, but it can warn us of what people are capable of, when the stage has been set for tragedy. We certainly do not need to let emotionally combustible materials accumulate from ill-conceived social experiments" (Thomas Sowell, *Commentary,* June 1978, p. 43).

Chapter 11:
Mosk, "For Bakke"

1. A convincing refutation of the university's argument is made by a commentator as follows: "The argument that a racial classification that discriminates against white people is not inherently suspect implies that the white majority is monolithic and so politically powerful as not to require the constitutional safeguards afforded minority racial groups. But the white majority is pluralistic, containing within itself a multitude of religious and ethnic minorities—Catholics, Jews, Italians, Irish, Poles—and many others who are vulnerable to prejudice and who to this day suffer from the effects of past discrimination. Such groups have only recently begun to enjoy the benefits of a free society and should not be exposed to new discriminatory bars, even if they are raised in the cause of compensation to certain racial minorities for past inequalities."

Chapter 15:
Powell, "Race as a 'Plus' Factor"

1. In the view of [Justices Brennan, White, Marshall, and Blackmun] the pliable notion of "stigma" is the crucial element in analyzing racial classifications. The Equal Protection Clause is not framed in terms of "stigma." Certainly the word has no clearly defined constitutional meaning. It reflects a subjective judgment that is standardless. *All* state-imposed classifications that rearrange burdens and benefits on the basis of race are likely to be viewed with deep resentment by the individuals burdened. The denial to innocent persons of equal rights and opportunities may outrage those so deprived and therefore may be perceived as invidious. These individuals are likely to find little comfort in the notion that the deprivation they are asked to endure is merely the price of membership in the dominant majority and that its imposition is inspired by the supposedly benign purpose of aiding others. One should not lightly dismiss the inherent unfairness of, and the perception of mistreatment that accompanies, a system of allocating benefits and privileges on the basis of skin color and ethnic origin.

Chapter 21:
Powell, "Race-Based Preference"

1. Of course, when a state implements a race-based plan that requires such a sharing of the burden, it cannot justify the discriminatory effect on some individuals because other individuals had approved the plan. Any "waiver" of the right not to be dealt with by the government on the basis of one's race must be made by those affected. Yet Justice Marshall repeatedly contends that the fact that Article XII was approved by a majority vote of the Union somehow validates this plan. He sees this case not in terms of individual constitutional rights, but as an allocation of burdens "between two racial groups." Thus, Article XII becomes a political compromise that "avoided placing the entire burden of layoffs on either the white teachers as a group or the minority teachers as a group." But the petitioners before us today are not "the white teachers as a group." They are Wendy Wygant and other individ-

uals who claim that they were fired from their jobs because of their race. That claim cannot be waived by petitioners' more senior colleagues. . . . The Constitution does not allocate constitutional rights to be distributed like bloc grants within discrete racial groups; and until it does, petitioners' more senior union colleagues cannot vote away petitioners' rights.

2. The board's definition of minority to include blacks, Orientals, American Indians, and persons of Spanish descent, further illustrates the undifferentiated nature of the plan. There is no explanation of why the board chose to favor these particular minorities or how in fact members of some of the categories can be identified. Moreover, respondents have never suggested—much less formally found—that they have engaged in prior, purposeful discrimination against members of each of these minority groups.

Chapter 22:
Stevens, "Minority Teachers"

1. The fact that the issue arises in a layoff context, rather than a hiring context, has no bearing on the equal-protection question. For if the board's interest in employing the more minority teachers is sufficient to justify providing them with an extra incentive to accept jobs in Jackson, Michigan, it is also sufficient to justify their retention when the number of available jobs is reduced. Justice Powell's suggestion, that there is a distinction of constitutional significance under the Equal Protection Clause between a racial preference at the time of hiring and an identical preference at the time of discharge is thus wholly unpersuasive. He seems to assume that a teacher who has been working for a few years suffers a greater harm when he is laid off than the harm suffered by an unemployed teacher who is refused a job for which he is qualified. In either event, the adverse decision forecloses "only one of several opportunities" that may be available to the disppointed teacher.

Chapter 27:
Cohen, "Justice Debased"

1. The argument called a "negative pregnant" is technically described as one having the form *modus tollens:* if *p* entails *q,* and *q* is false, then *p* must be false. The form is valid, of course—but in this application of it the argument (in either of two possible reconstructions of it) is built upon a false premise.

Version A: "If Congress had intended to forbid all racial preference they would have said that explicitly. They did not say that explicitly. Hence they did not intend that." In this version the second premise is plainly false; the congressional ban against racial preference in Section 703(a) is perfectly explicit.

Version B; "If Congress had intended to forbid all racial preference they would have expressed that intention explicitly in Section 703(j). They did not express that intention there. Hence they did not have that intention." In this version the second premise is true but the first is false. There was no need for Congress to repeat, in Section 703(j), the ban it had already made explicit earlier, and there was good reason not to do so.

Arguments relying upon false premises, even when valid in form, are not sound.

Chapter 34:
Sowell, "Are Quotas Good for Blacks?"

1. *Black Enterprise,* April 1978, p. 62. A newly released corporation study similarly concludes that very little credit should be given to government affirmative action programs for any narrowing of the income gap between white and black workers. The RAND researchers write, "our results suggest that the effect of government on the aggregate black–white wage ratio is quite small and that the popular notion that . . recent changes are being driven by government pressure has little empirical support" (*New York Times,* May 8, 1978).

Chapter 37:
Bunzel and Au, "The Asian Difference"

1. In 1983, for example, Asian Americans constituted only 6.2 per cent of public high school graduates in California, but 13.2 per cent of the students who took the SAT in California. On the other hand, Caucasians made up 64.7 per cent of the state's public high school graduates, but only 56.6 per cent of the SAT candidates.

2. Unlike the practice at most colleges, prior to 1986, applicants to Stanford were never asked to identify their ethnicity on an application form. (A policy of voluntary self-identification has been recommended for the future by C-UAFA.) As Jean Fetter, dean of undergraduate admissions, told us: "In the past we have chosen to rely on our 'best estimates' based on applicant's surname, the mother's maiden name, and the birthplaces of the parents. When the applicant chooses to submit a photograph, that occasionally proves helpful also."

3. Princeton Professor Uwe Reinhardt reports that he found similar mechanisms operating when he was on a committee for graduate school admissions in 1983: "We were going over the applicant list and we came to a clearly qualified Asian American student. And one committee member said, 'We have enough of them.' And someone else turned to me and said, 'You have to admit, there are a lot.' "

4. Aside from the fact that Asian Americans tend to have black hair and yellowish skin, heterogeneity is perhaps their most distinctive characteristic. They come from many countries, including China, Japan, Korea, Singapore, Hong Kong, Vietnam, Laos, Thailand, Cambodia, India, Indonesia, Malaysia, the Philippines, Guam, Samoa. They differ widely in their linguistic, cultural, historical, and socioeconomic backgrounds.

APPENDIX A

The Impact of Affirmati
on Employment

By Jonathan Leonard

Affirmative action, mandated by Executive Order 11246 in 1965, is one of the most controversial government interventions in the labor market since abolition. While much has been said concerning the propriety of affirmative action in theory, little is known about the impact of affirmative action in practice. If affirmative action has not changed the employment patterns of nonwhites and females, then much of the discussion since 1965 of its philosophical merits amounts to shadowboxing. The goal of affirmative action is to increase employment opportunities for females and minorities. Has affirmative action been successful in achieving this goal? This paper will use a new set of rich establishment-level data to examine how being a federal contractor subject to the affirmative action obligation and to undergoing compliance review affects a firm's employment of minorities and females.

The evidence to be presented in this paper indicates that affirmative action under the contract compliance program has led to improved employment opportunities for females and minorities. This result is based on a statistical comparison of the change in demographics at more than 68,000 establishments with more than 16 million employees between 1974 and 1980. I shall argue that minorities' and females' share of employment has increased more at establishments that are federal contractors, and so subject to affirmative action, than at noncontractors. Compliance reviews, while questionably targeted, will be shown to have been an effective regulatory tool in increasing black and female employment. I shall also draw implications for the relative wages of members of protected groups.

The Impact on Minorities and Females

I model affirmative action as a tax on the employment of white males in the contractor sector. If these workers are immobile, they bear the tax burden and

---

This article is a condensed version of a study that appeared in the *Journal of Labor Economics* (vol. 3, no. 4, October 1984). Copyright, University of Chicago Press. Reprinted with permission of the publisher.

relative white male wages fall. Intuitively, an increase in the affirmative action "tax" shifts the demand curve for white male labor downward. I assume that the wage elasticity of labor demand is the same in the contractor and noncontractor sectors.

I will compare shifts in the proportional employment of members of protected groups across contractor and noncontractor establishments across time. The hypothesis is that if affirmative action has been ineffective, these employment shifts will be the same for contractors and noncontractors. An effective affirmative action program is expected to shift the demand curve for blacks in the contractor sector to the right, driving black wages up, increasing black employment in the contractor sector, and decreasing it in the noncontractor sector. In reality, there are other policies, such as Title VII, promoting the employment of blacks in the noncontractor sector, so I will measure only the differential impact of affirmative action over and above the effects of general policies or changes in tastes.

Employment of males has fallen steadily since 1960 as females have flooded into the labor force. At the same time, both females' and nonwhite males' share of unemployment has been growing, along with their employment shares. The period between 1974 and 1980 witnessed growth in females' share of employment, and in nonwhite males share of male employment. What part has affirmative action played in these increases?

We have seen that affirmative action may usefully be thought of as a tax on the employment of white males in the contractor sector, a tax that shifts the demand for white male labor downward. If affirmative action is effective, then the rate of change of protected groups will be higher in contractor establishments than in noncontractor establishments, *ceteris paribus*. [Comparison of the mean changes in employment shares in the contractor and noncontractor sectors] shows that between 1974 and 1980 black and female employment shares increased significantly faster in contractor establishments than in noncontractor establishments.

The interpretation of tests of affirmative action would be less straightforward were scale effects to differ greatly across sectors. There is only a small difference, however, in the growth rates of contractor and noncontractor establishments; both are growing at between 2 per cent and 3 per cent per year, so differences across sectors are likely to be negligible. On net, in these establishments members of protected groups are in part being substituted for white males over time. This also suggests that contractor firms are not growing fat on government largess that allows them to expand total employment to take on relatively unproductive minorities and females. This is consistent with evidence presented in other work that the productivity of members of protected groups relative to that of white males did not fall as their relative employment share increased.

Reviewed Versus Nonreviewed

Given that contractor establishments have increased their employment of nonwhites and females more than noncontractor firms have, what administrative tools have been useful? Do compliance reviews matter? One alternative is that the threat of a compliance review is sufficient to obtain the desired behavior, so that reviewed establishments do not differ significantly from nonreviewed contractor establishments. This would be plausible if the threatened penalty were severe enough to outweigh the small probability of being caught. In fact, both the probability of review and the penalties imposed are not great. The OFCCP has records of at least 27,000 reviews completed between 1973 and 1981 at 11,000 different identifiable establishments. In 1980, roughly 115,000 establishments were government contractors, so at least 10 per cent of all contractor establishments had been reviewed between 1973 and 1981. Twenty-six of these reviews resulted in the ultimate penalty of debarment. Between 1969 and 1976, compliance reviews produced 331 conciliation agreements, according to a Department of Labor memorandum. The agreements awarded $61,279,000 in back pay, or $185,133 per company in a heavily skewed distribution. Short of debarment or backpay awards, affirmative action extracts only promises, although, as we have seen, these promises are not empty.

Do compliance reviews and contractor status have the same impact if other variables are controlled for? For example, the size of the establishment could be a crucial variable. Large plants may tend to be good corporate citizens, or they may be more likely to have formalized and rationalized personnel systems. Or simply by being large they may escape the familial or tribal tendencies of small work forces. For any of these reasons, one might expect larger firms to have better affirmative action records.

[The results of multiple regression analysis show] a consistent pattern across demographic groups of effective affirmative action. Over a six-year period [1974–1980] the employment of members of protected groups grew significantly faster in contractor than in noncontractor establishments. The growth rate is 3.8 per cent faster for black males, 7.9 per cent for other minority males, 2.8 per cent for white females, and 12.3 per cent for black females. A summary measure, white male employment, grew 1 2 per cent slower in the contractor sector. All of these effects are highly significant at the 99 per cent confidence level or better, and the effects for blacks and for white males are robust across a number of specifications.

The growth rate of black male employment over six years in the contractor sector is 3.8 per cent greater than among noncontractors. Taking the sixth root yields an annual growth rate that is 0.62 per cent greater in the contractor sector. For white males, the annual growth rate is 0.2 per cent slower among contractors, so contract status appears to shift the demand for black males relative to white males by 0.82 per cent per year.

Compliance reviews have played a significant role over and above that of contractor status, advancing black males by 7.9 per cent, other minority males by 15.2 per cent, and black females by 6.1 per cent among reviewed establishments. Compliance reviews have retarded the employment growth of whites.

With the exception of white females, compliance reviews have an additional positive impact on protected-group employment beyond the contractor effect. Direct pressure does make a difference.

The growth rate of black male employment increased 3.8 per cent more in contractor establishments, not counting the direct effect of reviews: 6.8 per cent of all contractor establishments, accounting for 17.4 per cent of all contractors employment, were reviewed in subsequent years. In these establishments the black male growth rate was an additional 7.9 per cent faster than in nonreviewed contractors, so 12 per cent faster than noncontractors. The total impact of affirmative action among contractors is then the weighted average of the annual 0.62 per cent shift among nonreviewed contractors and the 1.91 per cent shift among reviewed contractors, or 0.84 per cent per year. The demand shifts for other minority males, white females, and black females are 1.69 per cent, 0.37 per cent, and 2.13 per cent, respectively. These are not small demand shifts. The shift is largest for black females, although the ranking of these effects is sensitive to specification. It has been commonly assumed that employers can kill two birds with one stone by hiring black females. The evidence here is that black females not only have gained relatively more under affirmative action than white females, but have also gained more than black males, as one might have expected if they were relatively favored.

Employment opportunities depend critically on growth. Minorities and females experienced significantly greater increases in representation in establishments that were growing and so had many job openings. The elasticity of white male employment growth with respect to total employment growth is .976, significantly less than one. This indicates that members of protected groups dominate the net incoming flows in both contractor and noncontractor establishments. The respective elasticities for black males, other males, white females, and black females are 1.22, 1.09, 1.02, and 1.19, all significantly greater than one. Particularly in the case of blacks, of whom the quantity supplied has not greatly increased, this suggests the importance of Title VII, which applies to all establishments in the sample, in expanding employment opportunities. Establishments that are not part of multiplant corporations have significantly lower growth rates of employment of members of protected groups. Corporate size is probably of greater consequences than establishment size, with large corporations showing greater increases in minority and female employment. Establishment size itself has insignificant effects on white and black males, but other males and black females grow significantly faster at larger establishments, while white females grow significantly slower. It is also important to note that the tests here also control for the skill requirements of each establishment. Establishments that are nonclerical, white-collar intensive exhibit faster employment growth for both male and female blacks and significantly slower growth for white males.

The efficacy of affirmative action depends critically on employment growth. In every case, being a contractor or undergoing a compliance review have significantly greater effects if the establishment is growing. The evidence with respect to interactions of affirmative action with establishment size is mixed. While black male employment grows 5.6 per cent faster at contractor establishments than at noncontractor establishments with stable employment, it grows 6.7 per cent faster at the mean total employment growth rate of 5.1 per cent and 7.4 per cent faster if total employment grows by 15 per cent. Affirmative action has been far more successful at establishments that are growing and have room to accommodate federal pressure.

Members of protected groups have enjoyed improved employment opportunities at contractor establishments, and compliance reviews appear to have been an effective tool in changing employment patterns. The evidence here is that a process that has been frequently criticized as largely an exercise in paper pushing has actually been of material importance in prompting companies to increase their employment of minorities and females.

Changes in Contractor Status

One would expect protected groups to experience the fastest employment growth at establishments that remained contractors, followed in order by establishments that left contractor status those that became contractors, and finally, those that never were contractors. This assumes no cohort effect and a lagged adjustment to affirmative action over time because of inertia in employment stocks and personnel policies. For all protected groups, employment gains were significantly greater at establishments that were contractors in both 1974 and 1980 than in other establishments. As one might expect, the impact of affirmative action is greater at establishments that remain under the affirmative action obligation for longer periods of time. For most protected groups, establishments that pass through contractor status are insignificantly different from those that remain noncontractors. On the other hand, the growth rate of white males is significantly slower at establishments that were contractors at any time than at noncontractors. In relation to white males, then, members of protected groups have experienced employment gains at establishments that were contractors at some time.

The statistical tests shown in this section give evidence of a contract compliance program that works. Executive Order 11246 has led to significant employment gains for females and for blacks in contractor establishments, and compliance reviews have played an important role in this process.

The Impact on Racial-Earnings Inequality

Those who have argued about the propriety of affirmative action have not been quibbling over a fine point. The federal contract compliance program has substantially improved employment opportunities for members of protected groups. The growth rates of females' and minorities' shares of employment are greater in contractor establishments obligated to undertake affirmative action than in noncontractor establishments with no such obligation. Compliance reviews, the major enforcement tool of the affirmative action program, while poorly targeted against discrimination, have contributed significantly to improving the employment of members of protected groups.

The scale of the demand shifts due to affirmative action found in this paper is not small, but this can best be appreciated by comparing them to relative wage changes during the same period. Between 1974 and 1980, the ratio of black males to white males with respect to mean earnings of full-time, full-year workers increased by 2.3 per cent, from .684 to .700. I estimated that the relative demand for black male to white male workers increased by 6.5 per cent in the contractor sector between 1974 and 1980.

Conclusion

The tests pesented here suggest that while generating tremendous public criticism and resistance and while undergoing frequent regulatory reorganization, affirmative action has actually been successful in promoting the employment of minorities and females, though less so in the case of white females. In the contractor sector affirmative action has increased the demand relative to white males for black males by 6.5 per cent, for nonblack minority males by 11.9 per cent, and for white females by 3.5 per cent. Among females, it has increased the demand for blacks relative to whites by 11.0 per cent. For a program lacking public consensus and vigorous enforcement, this is a surprisingly strong showing. While the gains of white females are smaller than those of blacks, it is important to keep in mind that the employment of females and minorities has been increasing in both sectors. Indeed, if the OFCCP pressured establishments to hire more females and minorities relative to their own past records rather than to industry and region averages, the observed pattern is just what we would expect to see during a period when female labor supply has been growing.

This paper has presented significant evidence with detailed controls at the establishment level that minority and female employment has increased faster at contractor establishments that bear the affirmative action obligation. It has also shown that compliance reviews have not been well targeted against discrimination but have been an effective enforcement tool. In sum, despite vigorous contention and weak enforcement, affirmative action appears to have played a major role in improving the economic position of minorities and females.

APPENDIX B

Closing the Gap: Forty Years of Economic Progress for Blacks

By James P. Smith and Finis R. Welch

Forty years ago, Gunnar Myrdal published his masterwork on race relations in America, *An American Dilemma*. He began his chapter on the economic situation of blacks with the following summary:

> The economic situation of the Negroes in America is pathological. Except for a small minority enjoying upper- or middle-class status, the masses of American Negroes, in the rural South and in the segregated slum quarters in southern cities, are destitute. They own little property; even their household goods are mostly inadequate and dilapidated. Their incomes are not only low but irregular. They thus live from day to day and have scant security for the future. Their entire culture and their individual interests and strivings are narrow.

In the forty years since Myrdal's bleak assessment, this country has gone through a series of dramatic and far-reaching changes. The economy shifted from its traditional agricultural and manufacturing base to one that is service and technology oriented. As part of this shift, a major technological advance during the 1950s eliminated the system of black sharecropping in cotton, the primary economic activity of southern blacks since the Civil War. As a result, large numbers of southern rural blacks accelerated the movement to the inner cities of the North, eventually transforming the black population from predominately rural to largely urban. During the 1970s, the American economic structure suffered additional shocks. Because of increased international competition, the older industrialized sectors of the Northeast and North Central states, where blacks had made hard-won advances, were particularly hard hit.

Racial tensions have persisted throughout this forty-year period. The civil rights movement achieved stunning judicial and legislative successes in the 1950s and 1960s, partly by appealing to the moral conscience of the nation. The Civil Rights Act of 1964 and subsequent executive orders prohibited

Reprinted from *Closing the Gap: Forty Years of Economic Progress for Blacks*, February, 1986. The Rand Corporation, 1700 Main Street, P.O. Box 2138, Santa Monica, CA 90406-2138.

soon improve. The black middle class in 1940 was correspondingly small, counting among its members only one in five black men. At the other extreme, the black economic elite resembled an exclusive white club.

The changes over the last forty years were dramatic. Fully 20 per cent of working black men in 1980 were still part of the poor black underclass, a reminder that many blacks remained left out and left behind. But placed in historical perspective, such figures still represent enormous progress toward eradicating black poverty. Political rhetoric on the race issue must eventually balance two compelling truths. America has made considerable strides in reducing black poverty; but by the standards of a just society, black poverty remains at unacceptably high levels.

The real story of the last forty years, however, has been the emergence of the black middle class, whose income gains have been real and substantial. The growth in the size of the black middle class was so spectacular that as a group it outnumbers the black poor. Finally, for the first time in American history, a sizable number of black men are economically better off than white middle-class America. During the last twenty years alone, the odds of a black man penetrating the ranks of the economic elite increased tenfold.

Causes of the Narrowing Wage Gap

In this report, we tried to quantify how much of the closing of the racial gap was due to black gains in education and its quality, and how much should be attributed to migration and the resurgence of the southern economy. First, we explored schooling's role in promoting black economic mobility and in explaining the closing of the racial wage gap. Many observers have disputed the historical importance of schools as a vehicle for achieving pay equity. Their claim is based largely on two beliefs. First, they point to a series of historical studies showing that black income benefits from schooling were negligible. They also argue that long-term advances in black education did not produce any closing of the racial income gap, at least until the mid-1960s. In this report, we demonstrate that black schools have played a far more fundamental role in shaping the economic history of blacks than these claims would suggest.

Our evidence began with a description of some prominent patterns associated with racial wage ratios across schooling classes. Racial wage disparities within education levels have historically been quite large. Evaluated at the same amount of schooling, black male wages averaged 50 to 55 per cent of those of white men. By 1980, comparably educated black men earned 75 to 82 per cent as much as white men. These wage ratios were ten percentage points higher than the aggregate ratio across all schooling groups in those years. That contrast informs us that education does play a significant role in explaining part of the racial wage gap. It also warns, however, that simply equalizing the number of years of schooling alone would leave a sizable racial wage gap left unexplained.

Across the full forty-year period, the two dimensions of education that closed the racial wage gap, in a quantitatively significant way, were the narrowing of education disparities between the races and the improving economic return to black schooling.

Our first step in assessing the overall impact of schooling towards explaining the closing of the racial wage gap was to examine the extent to which black educational accomplishments have been catching up to those of whites. Not surprisingly, the education levels of each new generation of workers increased over the last forty years. While this trend exists for both races, it has been much sharper for black men. Educational differences still persist between the races, but they are far less today than at any time in our history. In 1980, a typical black man had a year-and-a-half less schooling than the average white male worker. A majority of black men in 1980 were high school graduates. Forty years earlier, white men had 3.7 years more schooling than did the black male workers with whom they competed in the labor market. The typical 1940 black worker had completed only 4.7 years of schooling. During the last forty years, 60 per cent of the education gap between the races has been eliminated.

Based on our study, approximately one-third of the forty-year narrowing of the racial wage gap can be assigned to the smaller racial differences in schooling completed in 1980 than in 1940.

School Quality

The second part of our story was concerned with what schooling was able to buy in terms of increased labor-market earnings. In our research, we obtained estimates for each race of the monetary economic payoff associated with an additional year of schooling. The income benefits that blacks received from schooling were, indeed, historically quite low. In 1940, attending school for another year raised black male wages by less than 4 per cent—half the amount for whites; this improved little by 1950. Among older black workers, each year of schooling increased wages by less than 3 per cent.

Over the last forty years, however, a persistent narrowing of racial differences in income benefits from schooling took place. The end result of this forty-year persistence is that the magnitude of change became quite large. For example, among those in their first five years of work in 1940, white men's income increased 5 per cent more than did black men's for each additional year of school attended. In that year, for example, white men's income would increase 20 per cent more than black men's as a result of attending and completing college. This white advantage declined, however, as each new cohort of workers entered the labor market. In fact, among men who first entered the labor market during the 1970s, the income benefits that blacks received from schooling now exceed those of white men.

Alternative explanations can be offered for this racial convergence in the economic payoff from schooling. The civil rights movement and its associated antidiscrimination legislation during the 1950s is one obvious candidate. Affirmative action attempts to increase black employment in those high-skill jobs where they previously had been scarce. Consistent with this argument, the increase in the income benefits to black education was more rapid in the 1970s and 1960s than it was earlier.

Affirmative action cannot be the whole story, however, nor, for that matter, a very large part of it. The principal reason is that the increase in the economic benefits of black schooling began long before the affirmative action pressures of the last two decades. More than half of the narrowing of the gap in income benefits from schooling between the races took place before 1960. As a result, the narrowing of racial differences in the benefits from education was as large during the twenty years from 1940 to 1960 as it was in the twenty years after 1960.

Because of this, we must search for causes that lie far deeper in black American history than contemporary political movements. The root cause of the improvements in black economic payoffs to schooling lies within long-term improvements across birth cohorts that enabled blacks to translate an incremental year of schooling into more income. The evidence we have accumulated clearly points to improving quality of black schools as the most plausible explanation for this improvement. This consistent picture of simultaneous convergence in all dimensions of schooling quality makes the overwhelming case that improving relative quality of black schools is the underlying cause of the increase in black economic benefits from education relative to those of whites.

Our research indicates that the long-term historical impact of investments in black schools—both in additional years of schooling and in the quality of that schooling—was enormous. Improvements in the quality of black schools increased black wages relative to those of whites from 11 to 38 per cent, with younger blacks at the higher end of that range. Adding these quality effects to the gains achieved for quantity of schooling, black education is identified as the key factor elevating the long-run economic status of black men.

Migration

Americans have always tried to improve their economic lot by moving to places where prospects for their economic advancement were better. Since the end of slavery, large numbers of black men have exercised their freedom to choose the place where they lived and worked. For many decades, most of this migration took place within the South. Beginning in 1910, the great black migration northward started, a movement which accelerated after 1940.

We first measured migration's direct effect—the percentage increase in black-white wages that results from the movement of blacks from low-wage to higher-wage areas. Two dimensions of migration were highlighted: the movement to the North and urban places.

The years from 1940 to 1970 witnessed a massive movement of blacks from the South to the cities of the North. As a result, the percentage of black men living in the South declined from 75 per cent to about 50 per cent. After 1970, however, the flow reversed and the net movement of blacks turned to the South. Meanwhile, the distribution of the white population between the South and North remained remarkably stable. Slightly less than 30 per cent of white men lived in the South, a figure that has stayed roughly the same for decades.

While the great northern migration had profound effects, it is also easy to exaggerate them. Even today, a slight majority of blacks remain citizens of the South where, more so than whites, their economic well-being is closely tied to the robustness of the southern economy.

This century has also witnessed the transition of the black citizenry from largely rural to predominantly urban. Although it began in the early decades of the century, this transition was completed during the forty-year period that we study in this report. Relative to whites, the largest changes in black urbanization occurred in the twenty years between 1940 and 1960. Today, the principal locational difference between the races is where they live within urban areas. The majority of whites live in the suburban fringes, most blacks in the central cities. Fully 75 per cent of all black SMSA residents live in the central cities, compared with only 38 percent of whites.

Migration was an important source of the long-run closing of the racial wage gap. Southern black migration to the northern cities increased black-white male wage ratios by 11 to 19 per cent between 1940 and 1980. These gains were a reflection of the movement both from the South to the North and from rural to urban places. The direct wage-benefits from migration rival convergence in education as a factor closing the racial income gap.

The income gains from migration, however, have diminished steadily over time and, by 1970, were exhausted. The black people were essentially transformed from their rural southern base to a predominantly urban group during the twenty years after 1940. As a consequence, the positive black benefits from going to urban places were largely completed by 1960. The wage gains achieved from moving North lasted another decade.

Regional Racial Wage Gap

Our main interest centered on the racial wage gap in the South. Until 1960, that gap was about 20 per cent greater than in the North. Between 1960 and 1970, the gap narrowed for younger workers but remained at historical levels among mature male workers. The truly dramatic story occurred between 1970 and 1980: The black-white male wage gap declined very sharply in the South. These racial wage differentials fell by half to two-thirds of their 1970 levels. As a result, the southern racial wage gap has moved toward the national norm. Today, the racial wage gap is only 6 per cent higher in the South, compared with the 20 per cent differentials that prevailed before 1970.

The narrowing of the racial wage gap in the South was an important reason why blacks were catching up. The improving black situation in the South raised black-white male wages, at a nationwide level, by 4 to 10 per cent between 1940 and 1980. Virtually all this improvement took place during the

1970s. To summarize our two major findings on geographical location: Migration raised black wages 11 to 19 per cent between 1940 and 1980; the closing of the southern wage gap added another 4 to 10 per cent.

Agriculture

Forty years ago, the traditional southern system of sharecropping cotton still dominated the economic activities of blacks. By 1940, one-third of all black men were still employed in agriculture. But the changes after 1940, and particularly between 1940 and 1960, were swift. As a percentage of the total work force, black agricultural employment fell by 70 per cent between 1940 and 1960. By 1960, only one in ten black workers worked on the farm, with rates even lower among young black workers. And ten years later, in 1970, black farm employment, particularly among younger workers, was a thing of the past. We can now safely describe, for the first time in American history, the economic role of blacks with no mention of agriculture.

There were long-term trends already in place in 1940 that were shifting the black labor force out of agriculture, but this process accelerated markedly during the 1950s. Since the Civil War, cotton cultivation had remained a labor-intensive process.

The technological change that would revolutionize black agriculture was the introduction of the mechanical cotton picker. In 1950, over 90 per cent of all cotton produced in the United States was picked by hand. Twelve years later, in 1962, over 70 per cent was picked by machine.

These changes in the methods of cultivation reduced the demand for black labor in southern agriculture and also ended the system of tenant sharecropping. One of the consequences of ending the system of tenant farming is that there was a switch from tenants to hired wage labor. As a result of the use of the cotton picker, output per man rose by 238 per cent between 1950 and 1970 in a period during which total farm output rose by 36 per cent.

As a consequence, during the 1950s, there was a sharp decline in the demand for a largely southern black labor force in cotton. This gave additional impetus to the migration of young southern blacks to the north. There were negative short-run consequences, but positive long-run effects. In the short run, this reduction in demand for black workers temporarily reduced black incomes. In our view, this is the primary reason why the 1950s were a temporary departure from the long-run trend towards improving economic status of blacks. The long-run effects, however, were quite different. Blacks were able to end their dependence on low-wage southern agriculture and become more integrated into a wider scope of American economic activity.

Affirmative Action

Affirmative action still dominates the political debate concerning government labor-market policy regarding race. This debate began with the passage of the Civil Rights Act of 1964, which was aimed at eliminating employment discrimination against protected minority groups. American blacks, who had endured centuries of blatant and intense discrimination, were the principal group that this legislation was meant to protect. Since the Civil Rights Act prohibited discrimination on the basis of race and sex on all major terms of employment—pay, promotion, hiring, training, and termination—the protection was quite broad.

Two governmental agencies have been given the primary responsibility to enforce affirmative action. The Equal Employment Opportunity Commission (EEOC) was set up to monitor compliance with the provisions of the Civil Rights Act of 1964. All private-sector firms with 100 or more employees were required to report to EEOC on the numbers of minorities employed and the types of jobs they held. The second major federal enforcement agency was the Office of Federal Contract Compliance Program (OFCCP). This agency was established by Executive Order 11246 and was given the primary responsibility of monitoring discrimination and enforcing penalties among government contractors.

Our research highlighted two possible labor market effects of affirmative action. The first question we asked was whether affirmative action significantly altered the firms where black men worked and the jobs they were able to obtain. The second question dealt with the wage side of work. Put simply, how has affirmative action affected the incomes of black men?

Because only establishments with 100 or more employees must report to EEOC, affirmative action reporting coverage varies widely across industries. For example, coverage is almost universal in the large-scale durable manufacturing goods sector. On the other hand, less than 10 per cent of workers are covered in the retail trade, personnel services, and construction industries, where small establishments are common. As a result, firms can be divided into three sectors: (1) federal contractors; (2) other EEOC reporting firms; and (3) those firms not covered by EEOC or OFCCP.

It may be surprising to learn that only about half of the nongovernment, noneducation workforce is directly covered by affirmative action. In the same vein, federal contractors employed 35 per cent of all nongovernment, noneducation institution workers in 1980 and 70 per cent of all EEOC-covered workers.

Employment Effects

We tested for employment effects by measuring whether affirmative action has altered the location of black employment among these three sectors. If affirmative action is effective and is adequately enforced, minority representation should expand more among firms that are required to report to EEOC than among firms that are not. In addition, since federal contractors have more to lose, the greatest relative gains in employment and wages should occur among those EEOC-reporting firms that are federal contractors.

While such relocation of black workers should occur in total employment, the largest minority gains should be detected within professional and managerial jobs for firms that are reporting to EEOC. Once again, these changes should be even larger among those firms that are federal contractors.

While such relocation of black workers should occur in total employment, the largest minority gains should be detected within professional and managerial jobs for firms that are reporting to EEOC. Once again, these changes should be even larger among those firms that are federal contractors.

Our statistical evidence strongly supports these hypotheses. Black men were 10 per cent less likely to work in reporting firms in 1966. By 1980, however, black men were 25 per cent more likely to work in EEOC-reporting firms. To put these changes in another way, less than half (48 per cent) of black male workers were employed in EEOC-reporting firms in 1966; the figure rose to 60 per cent by 1980.

The largest employment changes occurred between 1966 and 1970 (the first four years of reporting). Between those years, there was a 20 per cent increase in the number of blacks working in reporting firms. The trend continued at a diminished pace until 1974, and then apparently stabilized. After 1974, there was little further change in the location of black employment by EEOC coverage. Within the reporting sector, black jobs shifted towards firms with contracts from the federal government. Between 1970 and 1980, black employment in nonfederal contractor firms that report to EEOC grew by 5 per cent. Among federal contractors, total black employment expanded by more than 15 per cent.

As large as those increases in total employment seem, they pale next to changes within the managerial and professional jobs. Black managers and professionals were half as likely as white managers and professionals to work in EEOC-reporting firms in 1966. By 1980, black managers and professionals were equally likely to be found in reporting firms. Some of this improvement is exaggerated. In our research, we found evidence that firms have been reclassifying jobs held by blacks into the professional and managerial categories, in order to inflate overall minority representation. But many of the gains in the reporting sector were real. The number of black managers and professionals who work in covered employment is far larger as a result of affirmative action. Once again, this growth in black representation in managerial and professional jobs was concentrated in firms with federal contracts, and most of the change was completed by 1974.

In summary, affirmative action resulted in a radical reshuffling of black jobs in the labor force. It shifted black male employment towards EEOC-covered firms and industries, and particularly into firms with federal contracts. Reshuffling is the right term, because the mirror image is that black employment in the noncovered sector plummeted. Affirmative action also increased the representation of black male workers in the managerial and professional jobs in covered firms.

APPENDIX G

KAISER/UNITED STEELWORKERS COLLECTIVE BARGAINING
AGREEMENT
(1974)

It is . . . agreed that the joint committee will specifically review the minority representation in the existing trade, craft, and assigned maintenance classifications, in the plants set forth below, and, where necessary, establish certain goals and timetables in order to achieve a desired minority ratio.

As apprentice and craft jobs are to be filed, the contractual selection criteria shall be applied in reaching such goals; at a minimum, not less than one minority employee will enter for every nonminority employee entering until the goal is reached unless at a particular time there are insufficient available qualified minority candidates.

Index of Names

ACLU, *see* American Civil Liberties Union
Acts, Book of, 76
Adam, 76, 135
Affirmative Discrimination (Nathan Glazer), 7
AFL-CIO, 124
Africa, 92, 103, 140
Africans, 76, 78, 449
Albemarle v. *Moody* (1975), 319
Aleutians, 223, 229–31, 234, 238, 243, 272
Alexander v. *Gardner-Denver Co.* (1974), 303
American Association of University Professors, 120
American Bar Association, 212
American Civil Liberties Union (ACLU), 281, 289–90, 306
American Indians, 20, 93–94, 96, 154, 170, 182, 223, 229–31, 234, 238, 243, 257, 272, 411
American Jewish Committee, 26
American Jewish Congress, 26, 84
American Telephone and Telegraph Co. (AT&T), 17, 26
Amherst University, 108
An American Dilemma (Gunnar Myrdal), 499
Animal Farm (Sinclair Lewis), 214
Ann Arbor, Michigan, 445–46
Anti-Defamation League of B'nai B'rith, 26, 281
AP (Associated Press), 24
Apache Indians, 216
Arab Americans, 88
Armenia, 103
Armenian Americans, 88
Aryans, 217
Asia, 103, 107
Asian Americans, 20, 107, 371, 441–42, 448, 457–73
Asians, 105, 107, 208, 223, 229–31, 234, 238, 243, 257, 272, 275, 367, 418, 443–56

Associated General Contractors of Massachusetts Inc. v. *Altshuler* (1973), 298
Atlanta, Georgia, 32, 426
Atkins, Thomas, 444
AT&T, *see* American Telephone and Telegraph Co.

Bakke, Allan, x, 26, 122–24, 129, 133, 159, 161, 175–78, 180–89, 191, 195, 199, 209, 211–12, 219, 228, 241, 257, 281–82, 286, 298–99, 304–5, 309–11, 455
Balkans, 103
Baltimore, Maryland, 427
Baudhuin, Gretchen, xi
Belgium, 103
Berry, Mary Frances, 43, 63
Bible, 76, 93, 98, 107
Bickel, Alexander, 37, 52–53
Birmingham, Alabama, 274, 354–55, 363
Birmingham Fire Fighters Association, 355, 360
Black Defense League, 85
Blackmun, Harry A., 298
Blue Bell, Inc., 13
Bob Jones University, 58
Bok, Derek, 368, 430, 448
Boston Latin School, 443–45
Boston, Massachusetts, 426
Boston University, 74
Brandeis, Luis D., 389
Brennan, William, 46, 323, 332, 334
Brightman, Edgar S., 74
Brimmer, Andrew, 15, 420
Brooklyn, New York, 59
Brown, Anne, 80
Brown University, 455, 457, 460–64, 466, 468–69, 471
Brown v. *Board of Education of Topeka* (1954), 53–55, 179, 192, 196, 260, 370, 412, 425–26
Buber, Martin, 69

527

Buffalo, New York, 155
Bunker Hill, 78
Burger, Warren E., 229, 323, 332, 335, 346
Burundi, 103

California, 40, 170–71, 458
California Supreme Court, 155, 159, 167–68, 172, 174, 177, 180
California, University of, at Berkeley, 458; at Davis, 26, 107, 122, 159, 161, 167, 169–73, 175–77, 180, 184–86, 189, 191, 195, 197–98, 200, 209–10, 212, 219, 241, 282, 298, 306, 455; *see also Regents of the University of California* v. *Allan Bakke*
Canada, 103
Canarsie, Brooklyn, New York, 59
Cardozo, Benjamin N., 389
Carnegie Council on Policy Studies in Higher Education, 181
Carter, Jimmy, administration, 121, 144
Carver, George Washington, 80
Case, Clifford, 65–66, 341, 343, 349
Catholics, 80, 99
Caucasians, 154, 457–61, 463–65, 467, 469
Celler, Emmanuel, 339, 349
Census, Bureau of, 86, 465
Change magazine, 113
Chicago, Illinois, 108, 439
Chicanos, 154–55, 170–71, 182, 195, 208
China, 107
Chinese, 34, 154–56, 424
Civil Rights Act of 1964, x, 3, 5, 8–9, 11, 13–14, 29, 47, 57–59, 64, 119, 127, 134, 184, 191, 274, 279, 281, 283, 285–86, 295–96, 313–14, 317–18, 329–32, 337, 341, 350–52, 355, 397, 406, 421, 499, 507
Civil Rights Commission, 25, 41, 43, 143
Civil War (American), 33, 78, 99, 202, 412, 499, 506
Clark, Joseph, 65–66, 71–73, 313, 317, 333, 341, 343, 347–49
Clark, Kenneth B., 426
Cleveland, Ohio, 155
Coalition of Black Trade Unionists, 281
Colorado, University of, 400
Colvin, Reynold H., 183–84, 186
Commerce Clause, 232
Communist party, 518
Communists, 421
Confucianism, 469
Congressional Record, 337, 349

Congress, U.S., 8–9, 13, 23–24, 33, 58, 91, 121, 123–24, 138, 148, 223–28, 232, 239, 246, 248, 251, 253, 270, 272–74, 284, 313, 316–19, 323, 325, 329, 330, 333–34, 337, 344–47, 349–53, 515–16
Constitution, U.S., 22, 33, 36–37, 53–54, 119, 121, 124, 151–52, 172, 183, 193, 197, 204, 211–12, 224, 227–33, 235, 247–48, 253, 292, 316, 341, 353, 355, 421
Contractors Association of Eastern Pennsylvania v. *Secretary of Labor* (1971), 12
Cooper, John, 348
Cornell University, 220, 422
Cox, Archibald, 180–83
Croson Co., x, 237, 251, 269, 271–72
Cubans, 20
Czech Americans, 88

Darwinism, 172
Daughters of the American Revolution, 79
Declaration of Independence, 70–71, 78
DeFunis v. *Odegaard* (1974), 151, 154, 159, 163, 282, 299
DeFunis, Marco, 63, 151, 299
Democratic party, 129, 337
Department of Defense, 13
Department of Education, 465
Department of Health, Education, and Welfare, 111, 113, 120, 512
Department of Justice, 18, 26, 66–67, 107, 117, 119, 121–22, 144–46, 284, 341, 344
Department of Labor, 12, 119, 213, 495, 512; Revised Order No. 4, 37–38, 91, 522
Detroit, Michigan, 119, 121, 426, 439
De Wolf, L. Harold, 74
Dirksen, Everett M., 320, 345
Dirksen-Mansfield amendment, 345, 347
Dornbusch, Stanford M., 465
Douglas, William O., 37, 63, 160, 163, 192
Douglass, Frederick, 33–34
Due Process Clause, 202, 226, 231
Dunbar High School (Washington, D.C.), 427
Dworkin, Ronald, 46, 54, 368, 430

Eastern Europe, 103, 218
Echols County (Georgia), 32
England, 42

English, 22, 217, 342
English, Raymond, xi
Ensley, Alabama, 355
Equal Protection Clause, x, 36–37, 46,
    153, 156–57, 162–63, 193, 202, 204,
    223, 231–32, 237, 239, 244, 247, 253–
    55, 259, 262, 264–65, 272, 316, 362
Equal Employment Opportunity Bill of
    1964, 36
Equal Employment Opportunity Commis-
    sion (EEOC), 5, 8–11, 16–19, 24, 84,
    119, 338–39, 349, 397, 405, 507–9,
    512
Ervin, Sam, 348
Eskimos, 223, 229–31, 234, 238, 243, 272
Ethiopians, 76
Europe, 92, 385
Europeans, 428
Executive Order: *11246*, 12, 36, 84, 90,
    120, 145, 148, 295–96, 396, 406, 493,
    497, 507, 521, 511; *11375*, 84, 522

Fair Housing Act of 1968 (Open Housing
    Act), 5, 57
Fallon, Richard, 55
Falwell, Jerry, 148
Farley, Reynolds, 17
Federal Rules of Civil Procedure, 274, 356
Fifth Amendment, 151, 229, 231
Filipinos, 154–55
First Amendment, 157, 200, 205–7, 286,
    305
Florida, 372
Ford, Gerald, administration, 4, 25–26
Ford, Henry, II, 51
Ford Motor Co., 19, 51
Foreign Service Officers Examination
    Board, 37
Fourteenth Amendment, x, 53, 65, 151,
    160, 162, 169, 172, 199–203, 208–9,
    223, 226, 229, 231–33, 238, 245, 247,
    257, 265, 272, 281, 292
Frankfurter, Felix, 389
Franks v. *Bowman Transportation Co.*
    (1976), 287
Freeman, Richard, 14, 17
Fullilove v. *Klutznick* (1980), x, 237, 245,
    247–48, 252–53
Fulton County (Georgia), 32
Furnco Construction Corp. v. *Waters*
    (1976), 336

Galatians, 77
Gallup Poll, 23, 419

Garrison, William Lloyd, 76–78
Garrity, Arthur, 426, 443–44
General Electric Co., 19
General Motors Corp., 19
Genesis, Book of, 76
Gentiles, 342, 383–88
George, Robby, xii
Georgia, 32–33
German National Socialism, 103
Germans, 22, 34, 80, 155, 217, 418, 428
Germany, 386–87
GI Bill, 423
Gittell, Marilyn, 13
Glatt, Erma, 213
Glazer, Nathan, 7, 41, 92, 132, 143
Grade-point average (GPA), 197, 457
Graduate Record Exam (GRE), 400–1,
    442
Graham, Ray J., 19
Gramercy, Louisiana, 283, 287, 290, 306–
    7, 314–15, 321, 325, 331
Greeks, 77, 103
Griggs v. *Duke Power Co.*, 9–10, 14, 273,
    336
Gypsy Americans, 88

Hammond, Ray, 148
Harlan, John M., 231
Harvard University, 107, 122, 133, 136–
    37, 153, 180, 200, 207, 393, 399–401,
    403, 407, 409, 411, 430, 441–43, 448,
    455, 457, 461–65
Hill, Lister, 66
Hispanic Americans, 20, 238
Hispanics, 93, 105, 107, 275, 395, 411,
    443–44, 448
Hochschild, Jennifer, xi
Holocaust, 428
Hooks, Benjamin, 56
Hook, Sidney, 14
House of Representatives, U.S., 339,
    350–51
Howard, Jeff, 148
Howard University, 120
Hudnut, William H., 146
Hughes, Langston, 80
Humanist, The, 113
Humphrey, Hubert H., 36, 40, 65, 134,
    313, 317–20, 333, 340–42, 345, 349
Humphrey v. *Moore* (1964), 309
Hungarian Americans, 88, 155–56

IBM Corp., 393, 403
Idaho, 200

Immigration Act of 1965, 5
India, 22, 77, 103
Indians, *see* American Indians
Internal Revenue Service (IRS), 58
IQ (intelligence quotient), 376, 417
Irish, 22, 34, 157, 164, 210, 216–17
Irish Americans, 88, 418
Iroquois Indians, 216
Italian Americans, 418
Italians, 22, 80, 156, 182, 210, 216, 342

Jackson (Michigan) Board of Education,
   257, 263, 265, 267–68
Japan, 107
Japanese, 34, 155–56, 424, 428
Japanese American Citizens League, 455
Jefferson County (Alabama) Personnel
   Board, 355
Jefferson, Thomas, 135
Jencks, Christopher, 20
Jewett, L. Fred, 465
Jewish Americans, 418
Jews, 22, 26, 77, 80, 93, 103, 129, 157,
   164, 187, 210, 216, 342, 383–88, 390–
   91, 417, 419, 428, 471
Jim Crow laws, 94, 99, 379, 449
Johnson, Lyndon B., 12, 71–72, 84, 90,
   108, 120, 135, 389, 396–97
Judeo-Christian religious tradition, 70–71,
   74–75, 83
Justice Department, *see* Department of
   Justice

Kaiser Aluminum and Chemical Corp.,
   123, 215, 279–81, 283–90, 295–96,
   298, 306, 310–11, 313, 315, 325–27,
   331, 335, 343
*Kaiser Aluminum and Chemical Corpora-
   tion and United Steelworkers of
   America, AFL-CIO v. Brian F.
   Weber, see United Steelworkers of
   America v. Weber*
Kaiser/United Steelworkers Collective
   Bargaining Agreement (1974), 283,
   285, 287, 290, 303, 310–11, 313, 315–
   16, 320, 331, 335, 343, 525
Keith, Damon J., 35, 123
Kennedy, Anthony, xi, 237, 272, 359
Kennedy, Edward, 145
Kennedy, John F., 318
Kennedy, Randall, 30, 368
Kerner Commission, ix, 94, 124, 500
King, Martin Luther, Jr., 58, 61, 63, 71,
   74–75, 78

Klitgaard, Robert, 442
Kuchel, Thomas, 341, 345
Ku Klux Klan, 79, 85, 99

Labor Department, *see* Department of
   Labor
Latin, 443
Law School Admission Test (LSAT), 152–
   54, 156, 442
Lebanese, 22
Lebanon, 103
Lehman, Herbert H., 80
Lewis, Sinclair, 214
Lindsay, John, 94, 339
Lone Ranger, 215–16
Louisiana, 306, 327
LSAT, *see* Law School Admission Test
Lubin, Isador, 80

"Mandatory Achievement of Goals"
   (MAG), 18–19
Mansfield, Mike, 345
Marshall, Thurgood, 62, 129, 217, 240,
   246, 263, 267, 349–50, 389, 426
Marsh, Stuart, 98
Martin v. Wilks, xi, 269, 274, 353–56, 359
Marxism, 98, 135
Matthew, Dayna Bowen, 431, 433
McAleer v. AT&T (1976), 26
MCAT, *see* Medical College Admission
   Test
*McDonald v. Santa Fe Trail Transporta-
   tion Co.* (1976), 316, 336, 350
Medical College Admission Test (MCAT),
   159, 185
Meese, Edwin, 107
Memphis, Tennessee, 98, 119, 123, 143
Mexican Americans, 20, 86, 93, 96, 116,
   155, 170, 418
Michigan, University of, 446
Miller, Jack, 320
Mill, John Stuart, 68
Milwaukee, Wisconsin, 155
Minority Business Enterprise (MBE),
   223, 225–28, 232–34, 242
Minority Report, 338
Modesto, California, 108
Mohawk Indians, 215
Montgomery, Alabama, 74
Morgenthau, Hans J., 80
Moss, Frank, 352
Moynihan, Daniel Patrick, 20, 39
Murphy, Walter, xii
Murray, Charles, 368, 409, 412–15, 430

Muskie, Edmund, 351
Myrdal, Gunnar, 499–500

NAACP (National Association for the Advancement of Colored People), 25, 146, 425–27, 444
National Advisory Commission on Civil Disorders, 389
National Council of Churches of Christ, 167
National Education Association, 281, 300
National Labor Relations Board, 8
Native Americans, *see* American Indians
Nazi Germany, 83, 217, 421
NCAA (National Collegiate Athletic Association), 371
New Bedford, Massachusetts, 155
New Republic, The, 271, 274
Newsweek, 24
New York City, 39–40, 155, 372, 448
New York Times, 24, 113, 271, 292, 468
Nieli, Bruce, C.P., xi
Nieli, Russell, 111
Nigeria, 103
Nisbet, Lee, 105, 113–14
Nixon, Richard, administration, 4, 25, 512
North Carolina Board of Education v. *Swann* (1971), 227
North Carolina, University of, 111, 113
Norton, Eleanor Holmes, 440
Norwegians, 156

O'Connor, Sandra Day, 107, 272, 359
Office of Federal Contract Compliance Programs (OFCCP), 12, 24, 84, 91, 291, 295–96, 495, 498, 507, 523
Open Housing Act, *see* Fair Housing Act
Orientals, *see* Asians
Oshkosh, Wisconsin, 212

Patterson, Orlando, 449
Pearl Harbor, 428
Pendleton, Clarence, 143
"Philadelphia Plan," 12, 296
Pittsburgh, Pennsylvania, 241
Plessy v. *Ferguson* (1896), 57, 231
Poles, 155–57, 164, 216
Polish Americans, 22, 88, 182
Portuguese Americans, 88, 155
Powell, Lewis F., Jr., 133, 191, 209–10, 212, 215, 263–64, 299, 305–6
Price, Leontyne, 213
Princeton University, 399, 455, 457, 461–64, 467–68, 472

Public Works Employment Act of 1977, 223, 225, 228, 232
Puerto Ricans, 20, 24, 86, 93, 96, 156, 418–19

Ramirez, Blandina Cardenas, 43, 63
Reagan, Ronald, administration, 4, 46, 48, 57–9, 117, 119, 122, 129, 148
Regents of the University of California v. *Allan Bakke*, x, 26, 122–24, 129, 133, 159, 177–78, 184, 191, 199, 209, 211–12, 219, 228, 257, 282, 286, 298, 304–5, 511
Rehnquist, William, xi, 271, 323–24, 326, 332, 337–49, 359
Republican party, 58, 337
"Reverse Discrimination—A Personal Encounter," (Lee Nisbet), 113 Revolution, American, 78
Reynolds, William Bradford, 56, 117, 119, 121–23, 144–46
Richmond City v. *J. A. Croson Co.* (1989), x, 237, 269, 271
Richmond Plan, 239, 243, 245–47, 252, 255, 272
Richmond, Virginia, 237–43, 245–46 248–54, 353, 359
Robeson, Paul, 80
Robinson, Jackie, 81, 219
Rogers, J. A., 80
Royal, Robert, xi
Rustin, Bayard, 39, 41, 85

Saltonstall, Leverett, 347
San Antonio, Texas, 155
San Francisco, California, 80, 154, 183, 426, 458
SAT, *see* Scholastic Aptitude Test
Savage, Augusta, 80
Scalia, Antonin, xii, 237, 359
Scholastic Aptitude Test (SAT), 371, 397, 399–400, 402, 411, 413, 442, 456, 458, 463–64
Scottish Americans, 22
Sears Roebuck and Co., 18, 19
Secondary School Admissions Test, 443
"Selling of Joseph, The" (Samuel Sewall), 76
Senate, U.S., 72, 340, 343–46, 350
Sewall, Samuel, 76, 78
Shelley v. *Kraemer* (1948), 201, 232, 239, 292
Silberman, Laurence, 38, 39